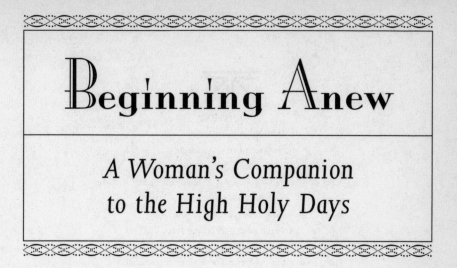

Beginning Anew

A Woman's Companion to the High Holy Days

EDITED BY

Gail Twersky Reimer and Judith A. Kates

A TOUCHSTONE BOOK   *Published by Simon & Schuster*

TOUCHSTONE
Rockefeller Center
1230 Avenue of the Americas
New York, NY 10020

Copyright © 1997 by Gail Twersky Reimer and Judith A. Kates

TOUCHSTONE and colophon are registered trademarks
of Simon & Schuster Inc.

Designed by Jenny Dossin

Manufactured in the United States of America

3   5   7   9   10   8   6   4   2

Library of Congress Cataloging-in-Publication Data
Beginning anew : a woman's companion to the High Holy Days / edited by
Gail Twersky Reimer and Judith A. Kates.
p.   cm.
"A Touchstone Book."
Includes bibliographical references.
1. High Holidays—Meditations.   2. Bible. O.T. Pentateuch—
Meditations.   3. Haftarot—Meditations.   4. Jewish religious
literature—Women authors.   I. Reimer, Gail Twersky.   II. Kates,
Judith A., date.
BM693.H5B44   1997
296.4'31'082–dc21   97-24410   CIP
ISBN 0–684–82687–9

Selections from *The Holy Scriptures According to the Masoretic Text,*
copyright © 1955 by Jewish Publication Society of America, are reproduced
by permission of Jewish Publication Society of America.

For my husband, William W. Kates

זְמִרוֹת הָיוּ לִי חֻקֶּיךָ בְּבֵית מְגוּרָי

For my daughters, Tamara and Ziva

וְאַהֲבַת עוֹלָם אֲהַבְתִּיךְ

In memory of my teacher, Judith Hurwich

מִלֶּמֶד דַּעַת מְבִינִים אֶפְתְּחָה פִי

G.T.R.

Contents

Yom Kippur—The Day of Atonement

Introduction

GAIL TWERSKY REIMER AND JUDITH A. KATES

EVERY YEAR on Rosh Hashana and Yom Kippur, we and our families sit together in a temporarily large but informal congregation. Located in a university, the congregation fosters active intellectual engagement with the holiday services and prides itself particularly on lively discussion of the Torah and *Haftara* portions, the prescribed Biblical readings for each day. This setting has reinforced our own inclination to involve ourselves with traditional texts as a central part of our experience of, and participation in, the Days of Awe. Our shared commitment to feminist questions and to the search for women's voices within the Biblical text and Jewish tradition led us to the compelling realization that women are central to the Rosh Hashana readings: women as characters, and through them, concerns that have traditionally been felt to be of particular importance to women. Each year we have noticed and begun anew to try to find meaning in this phenomenon. Reflections on Rosh Hashana from women-centered perspectives have led inevitably to our wondering about the possibility of women's modes of response to Yom Kippur.

Clearly we are not alone. We have read and learned from scattered essays, poems and midrashic meditations that contemporary women have written on these texts. But it is also clear that few of these new and exciting interpretations reach the majority of those who find themselves in synagogue on the High Holy Days. Even in our highly participatory, egalitarian congregation, the centrality of women in these readings is only rarely discussed.

Most anthologies devoted to explanation and interpretation of these holidays treat the Biblical readings only by way of summary, indicating the general thematic connections. But when the reading for the first day of Rosh Hashana is referred to as "the birth of Isaac," we easily lose sight of how much it revolves around Sarah and her handmaiden Hagar. When the reading for the second day is discussed as a test of Abraham's faith and/or of Isaac's trust, we easily forget that

Sarah's absence from this story is as potent as her presence in the earlier one. This book thus arises from frustration, but also from imagination—imagination of how our experience of the High Holy Days might be transformed by an intensive exploration of the centrality of women both as characters in the texts intended to shape our experience of the day and as readers of them.

Such exploration responds to the needs of Jews who regularly engage in Torah study and of those who choose for two or three days to engage intensively with their tradition. Rosh Hashana and Yom Kippur draw in the full spectrum, from those highly involved in Judaism to the marginally affiliated. These holidays, unlike the home-based celebrations of Passover or Chanukah, are observed primarily in synagogue. Synagogues overflow with women and men seeking to connect with their tradition, hoping to find personal meaning in the communal assertion that these autumnal days are Days of Awe. Jewish tradition emphasizes private, individual self-scrutiny and acts of repentance in the weeks before these holidays and during the "ten days of repentance" between them. Yet the holidays themselves fully engage us in the community, both the living people gathered in synagogue sanctuaries, large public halls, hotel ballrooms, and even borrowed church buildings and the community of the past, represented in inherited rituals and the voices of traditional prayers and Biblical texts.

Major themes of Rosh Hashana and Yom Kippur demand communal enactment. Jews understand new year not only as one specific group's marker in time, transforming undifferentiated flow into significant distinction between past and future, but also as commemoration of the most significant moment in all human time, the creation of the entire world. "Today the world was conceived," the traditional liturgy declares as we blow the *shofar*. We can envision ourselves enjoying with all of creation the benefits of divine energy and care. Traditional language expresses the theme through the metaphor of proclaiming God as "king," associating the powerful sound of the *shofar* with "blasts" and "calls" that accompanied the crowning of a king in ancient times. The tradition declares this to be a time of internal and external judgment of our pasts so as to strengthen the future. Not only individuals, but the community, even the entire world, pass in judgment before divine scrutiny. Similarly on Yom Kippur, the process of self-evaluation, attempts at repair of wrongs done to other people and efforts at self-improvement culminate in a collective gathering, speaking a liturgy of confession and repentance couched wholly in the plural. Even in what might seem the most individualistic of internal processes, the repair of our relationship with God, the Jewish understanding of individuals as profoundly embedded in community has led to a way of enacting that process that draws us toward the group, into the synagogue.

Certain synagogue observances convey the taste and sound, the palpable experience, of these holidays, to Jews of all sorts. On Rosh Hashana the strange calls of the *shofar,* looking "ancient" as only an instrument made from animal horn can, represent the essence of the day. The haunting melody of *kol nidre,* the legal statement with which Yom Kippur begins in the evening, seems to draw more Jews into the synagogue than at any other moment of the year. On Yom Kippur day, the recitation of the *Yizkor* prayer, allowing for commemoration of family members who have died in the midst of a community of mourners is a similarly compelling ritual. But the synagogue services of these days also bring people into extended contact with prayers and Biblical readings that speak a language from which many feel distant, which in fundamental ways they don't really understand, even when the *machzor* (the special prayer book for the High Holy Days) is mostly in English. Contemporary Jews often experience alienation in the very place they turn to in search of connection and meaning.

While several of the essays in this book either explicitly or implicitly address various parts of the liturgy, the book's primary focus is the Torah and *Haftara* readings, the portions of the Bible read on Rosh Hashana and Yom Kippur. It is true that much of our time in synagogue is spent in prayer. Sometimes we recite the words ourselves, and at other times the *chazan,* or cantor, chants them for us. Sometimes the words spoken are in a contemporary idiom, and at other times they are the words of centuries past. But as in all synagogue services, in the High Holy Day services there is a time to speak and a time to hear, a time to pray and a time to listen.

In modern congregations it is often assumed that the time to listen is when the rabbi rises to give his/her sermon. But the traditional structure of the service designates the time for listening as the Torah service—the moment when the scrolls are removed from the ark and specific sections of the Bible are read aloud before the congregation.

Today's rabbi has the distinct advantage of addressing the congregation in words they understand. The Torah, on the other hand, ad-
dresses us in a tongue and an idiom that many contemporary Jews
cannot comprehend. So often we don't listen very carefully, and if we
hear the readings at all, it is mostly through their summary and ex-
position in the rabbi's sermon. In this collection we bring together a
range of women who have listened carefully and who we expect will
stimulate others to listen more carefully to the readings and thus also
enable them to speak more meaningfully and knowledgeably about
them.

The Biblical readings, *Parashot* (sections from the Torah, the five
books of Moses) and *Haftarot* (selections from the prophetic books of
the Hebrew Bible), form an essential part of the experience of each
day. Chosen by the rabbis of the Talmudic age, they speak to the
themes of birth and renewal, judgment, repentance, and atonement
that have marked these holidays for thousands of years. Through
compelling narrative and poetry, they also pull us into encounters
with issues of central interest to modern people in general and especially to modern women. They deal with family relationships, conflicts between husband and wife and between women, issues of
justice, spirituality, connections between God and human beings, the
struggle to change oneself and one's world, efforts toward purity and
holiness within a flawed and complex world. By focusing on these
Biblical texts, the contributors to *Beginning Anew* address the relationship between women's concerns and the central themes of the
holidays. They open up the spirituality as well as the psychological
and emotional import of the texts that people encounter in synagogue
and reflect on the effect of reading these texts in the context of this
sacred time.

In doing so, they address the problems some women encounter
during the synagogue service. The observance of these holidays in
public space rather than domestic space, in the synagogue rather than
in the home, contributes to the feeling many women share with Letty
Cottin Pogrebin that Rosh Hashana and Yom Kippur are their "father's
holidays." For some, the motif of God as king that dominates the
liturgy further reinforces their sense of the holiday's masculine character. As we bring to the fore the stories of our foremothers, the ex-

plicit and implicit women's voices within the Biblical readings, the ground shifts to reveal the female experiences at their very foundation. And as we allow our female experiences to guide our reading, even the rituals of Yom Kippur, which in ancient times were the exclusive domain of male priests, assume a distinctly female complexion.

The present collection moves forward the project we began with our last collection, *Reading Ruth,* bringing women's points of view to bear on Biblical texts connected with Jewish holidays and thereby illuminating new dimensions of both the texts and the holidays. The book is designed to foster understanding of a special set of Biblical texts within the particular context in which we encounter them on the High Holy Days. In the synagogue service, each reading from the Torah is paired with a section from a prophetic book. Texts stand in particular relationships to each other and to liturgical texts. When we read of Rachel weeping over her children directly after reading of Abraham's near sacrifice of his son Isaac, themes that might otherwise go unnoticed forcefully emerge. When it is not just the near sacrifice of Isaac that is read in relation to the sounding of the *shofar,* but also the text describing Rachel's tears, the sounds we hear take on new meanings, as does the ritual itself. The reading of both texts in the context of the larger liturgical concern of these days with *zikhronot*— remembrance—leads to additional considerations of who is remembered—by God, by the Biblical writer, by the Biblical hero, by us.

Contributors also try to understand the role of the Biblical readings in our efforts at repentance and renewal. We therefore follow the traditional sequence of readings found in the *machzor.* Each holiday is introduced with an overview of the full compass of readings and the traditional explanations for the choice of these readings. The brief introductions to each reading are intended to orient readers to the discussions that follow.

Variations in how the holidays are observed among different Jewish groups, as well as more fundamental theological or ethical considerations, have led to one or another of the texts traditionally read on these holidays being eliminated from the liturgy. In designing this collection, we tried to be sensitive to these variations in practice while also attempting to make sense, from women's perspectives, of why Jewish tradition chose the particular texts it did for the High Holy Days.

The contributors to *Beginning Anew* are all students of the Bible, though not necessarily traditional students. Some are scholars, rabbis, and Jewish educators trained in study of the Bible in universities or in Jewish religious institutions. Others study and write about Jewish texts from their perspective as writers, psychologists, activists, teachers of law, anthropology, philosophy, women's studies, or literature. All are Jewishly involved women, whose individual expressions of that commitment span the full range of Jewish affiliation. Yet all have written and spoken in ways that demonstrate their interest in women's perspectives on Jewish texts. As editors we have been particularly excited to discover how many contemporary Jewish women are potential contributors to this enterprise and have tried again to widen the circle of Jewish women able and willing to offer their insights into traditional texts. This volume happily includes several Israeli women, speaking from perspectives influenced by their immersion in the Jewish national experience.

Although most contributors have shaped their commentaries as essays, some speak in traditional genres of Jewish discourse, such as the *shiur* (oral presentation that weaves together traditional Jewish texts) given by Avivah Zornberg; *chevruta* (partnership) study, represented in a piece by Rebecca Goldstein and her daughter, Yael Goldstein; the *techine* (women's prayer of supplication) with which Alice Shalvi concludes her commentary; or the sermon (by Rabbis Laura Geller and Rachel Cowan). Others have created their own forms, such as Rosellen Brown's "rewritten Bible," which draws on models from both modern feminism and Jewish literature of the second Temple period or the fictional meditation through which Carolivia Herron imagines her way into the characters of Abraham, Sarah, Hagar, and Ishmael. Women as Biblical commentators transform not only the content of Torah study, but its very forms.

Because of the extraordinarily concentrated focus on women in the Rosh Hashana readings, the majority of the pieces in this book comment on those texts. That weighting of the book's balance also reflects the way the narratives we confront and try to absorb on Rosh Hashana resonate with contemporary events and conflicts, in particular the story of the *Akeda* (the binding of Isaac) and the equally problematic account of the relationship of Sarah and Hagar and the expulsion of Ishmael. That sense of contemporary connection is the most obvious way in which this book participates in the age-old Jewish enterprise of midrash, through which Jews have interpreted the words of the Bible, so as simultaneously to affirm our connection to tradition and to hear the words in new ways that speak to our own lives.

In fact, all the pieces in this book participate in that midrashic enterprise, bringing women's voices, women's perspectives, into the quintessential mode of Jewish spirituality, the study of Torah. Although for centuries Torah study has been the province of men, contemporary women are increasingly claiming a place for themselves in that territory. The writers in this book, some for many years and some only recently, have been exploring new terrain, asking their own questions of our foundational texts, emphasizing aspects of our sacred texts that had been neglected or marginalized.

Interest in the marginalized, the oppressed, the silenced and silences, is everywhere evident in *Beginning Anew*. Women readers of the powerful drama of father and son enacted in the *Akeda,* like the writers of classical midrash, insist on reinserting Sarah into the story. But unlike the Rabbis, as Tikva Frymer-Kensky points out in her essay on the *Akeda,* "we no longer view things from the perspectives of male heads of household, and are just as apt to identify with the dependent members of [the] family." Reading the story through the eyes of Sarah, for instance, radically reenvisions its meaning. Similarly, in their discussion of the readings for the first day of Rosh Hashana several writers move Hagar to the foreground of our attention. For them the expulsion of Ishmael is first and foremost what Ruth Behar calls a "story about women wronging women." It is also a story with a background, so they insist that Genesis 21 be read as part of a larger story of relationship between two women, Sarah and Hagar. The relationships between women, usually described simply as rivalrous, are given depth and complexity by writers on the first day's *Haftara* as well. The *Haftara* portions for both days of Rosh Hashana cease to be mere supplements to the Torah readings as writers develop the heroines into paradigms of Jewish spirituality. Hannah is not just a woman who knows how to pray, she is a woman who, like Moses, dares to challenge God. Rachel is not simply weeping over the sufferings of the Jewish people; she is, in Tamar Frankiel's resonant phrase "Our Mother of Sorrows," uniquely sensitive to the sorrow and suffering of life.

The maleness of the Yom Kippur texts and the rituals described draws the attention of a number of writers. But in addition to registering that fact, they challenge us to reinterpret the rituals and the texts in light of our own female experience. Bonna Haberman, for instance, in a provocative and bold interpretation of the service of the high priest on Yom Kippur suggests that we think about the Tabernacle, Temple, and synagogue as "analogous to the female body." Judith Plaskow sees in the subject matter of Leviticus 18, the traditional reading for Yom Kippur afternoon, an opportunity "to connect the notion of atonement to the quest for holiness in intimate relations."

The ethos of these holidays, with their emphasis on personal and communal transformation, pervades many of the essays in this book in one form or another. For some, such transformation begins with reflection on our traditional texts but leads to the creation of new texts. These new texts, like the *techina* with which Alice Shalvi concludes her comments on Isaiah 58 or the notes toward a sexual ethic at the end of Judith Plaskow's essay, reflect women's intimate knowledge of "the social issues that form the web of our daily lives" and themselves represent the move into activism to which they urge us.

This collection was designed to deepen the experience of those who celebrate the High Holy Days. Whether the essays are read outside or inside the walls of the synagogue, before, during, or after the service, they will enable participants to discover new meanings in Biblical texts and thereby transform their understanding of the Days of Awe. Some readers may wish to read through the book from beginning to end in the weeks preceding Rosh Hashana, traditionally a period of reflection and preparation. Others may choose to take the book with them to synagogue and use appropriate parts of it as a guide to the day's readings. Still others may choose to read various pieces in response to questions or thoughts generated by the readings themselves, the rabbi's sermons, or discussions with fellow congregants.

This collection was also designed to embody our tradition's pleasure in multiple interpretations, dialogue, and argument. Insight, within Judaism, emerges from the interplay of minds and voices. With but one exception, we have included at least two essays on each Biblical reading so as to counter any suggestion that there can be a single, authoritative interpretation, even among women readers. Although each piece stands on its own and opens up new interpretive possibilities, reading all the pieces on a single text will enable readers to hear an interplay of voices. We hope that the excitement generated by this "conversation" among women will stimulate others who until now have been passive listeners to engage more actively with the texts of their tradition. But that engagement needn't be limited to the High Holy Days, or to Jews. Anyone interested in women-centered interpretations of Biblical texts will find stimulating and provocative material here that opens up exciting directions for study throughout the year.

Exploration of the Torah and *Haftara* readings for the Days of Awe from women-centered perspectives allows us to discern in the Rosh Hashana readings a range of women's voices, both heard and not heard, and in the Yom Kippur readings a series of texts that address some of our most urgent questions—as mothers and wives, as actors and those acted upon, and as questers for more meaningful religious lives, more satisfying familial lives, and more ethical social and political lives.

Rosh Hashana

The Day(s)
of Remembrance

First Day
Introduction

CONGREGATIONS that celebrate Rosh Hashana for two days read the two chapters from Genesis (21 and 22) prescribed by the Rabbis of the Talmud. Although some Reform congregations (where Rosh Hashana is usually celebrated for one day) focus on the theme of creation by reading the first chapter of Genesis, most read Genesis 22 along with the traditional *Haftara* for the first day. Both the traditional Torah reading (Genesis 21) and the *Haftara* (I Samuel 1–2) for the first day of Rosh Hashana tell stories of miraculous births. Sarah and Hannah, childless women who had endured years of suffering from their "barrenness," are granted the gift of pregnancy through the direct intervention of God. In both stories the children born are sons destined to play essential roles in the continuing life of the Jewish people. When read in the context of a holiday understood to commemorate God's creation of the world and to celebrate God's continued sovereignty in it, these stories of the "birth of Isaac" and the "birth of Samuel" articulate essential themes of creation and renewal through the power of God. Within the created world, humanity, figured as a particular family, receives God's special concern. This commonly heard explanation for the Rabbis' choice of these readings for Rosh Hashana focuses our attention on the birth of sons, narrowing both stories into versions of what psychologist Otto Rank called "the myth of the birth of the hero."

Another commonly heard explanation connects the readings to the essential idea of "remembrance" *(zikaron)* in the Days of Awe. The Torah reading for the first day of Rosh Hashana begins at the moment in the Genesis narrative when God "remembers" Sarah and she gives birth to Isaac. In the *Haftara* Hannah's prayers are answered when "God remembered her" and she bears a son. As we stand before God in prayer, we too yearn for our prayers to be answered and find comfort or solace in the story of our foremothers whose desire for children of their own is finally answered.

But unlike Hannah's, Sarah's pain and yearning for the child she is granted remain in the background, located in earlier chapters of Genesis that are not part of the day's reading. On Rosh Hashana our attention is drawn to the moment of "delivery." For women readers, however, the moment of delivery is a complicated one. It recalls, rather than erases, the pain from which Sarah is delivered. We are acutely aware that the reading for Rosh Hashana begins in medias res, that all new beginnings are rooted in a past. We understand that on this day of remembrance it is not God's task alone to remember, but ours as well.

The Torah reading assists us in our efforts to remember through a range of linguistic and narrative allusions to earlier moments in Sarah's story. With the naming of Isaac, as well as in the early parts of the narrative of Ishmael's banishment, we recall Sarah's ambiguous laughter when the angel of God first informs her that she will soon be with child. Rather than seeing Sarah as a mere vessel for the child who will carry on the covenant, we perceive her in the fullness of her personal history.

The banishment of Hagar and Ishmael in the day's reading repeats and recalls Sarah's earlier banishment of Hagar, which was clearly not motivated by either maternal protectiveness or matriarchal vision. And as we recall that earlier story, we are led to an understanding of Sarah and Hagar as part of a complex family unit, which is in turn part of a patriarchal culture whose ethos affects the relationship between husband and wife, between wife and wife, between father and son, and between mother and son.

The birth of Isaac is but the first of several deliveries that punctuate the day's reading. Jewish tradition sees the banishment of Ishmael as the delivery of Isaac from the evil influence of his half brother. Though midrash abounds with fantasies about what precise evil Ishmael was involved in, the text itself is unusually enigmatic. Perhaps here too the intent is to keep us focused on the moment of delivery.

Hagar and Ishmael are also ultimately delivered when the angel of God appears to the despairing Hagar, enabling her to find the water she and her son crave. Interestingly, in this episode in the story the suffering that precedes the delivery is poignantly evoked. The *Haftara* portion elaborates even further on the woman's pain and supplication, as well as on the prayer that such moments occasion.

Delivery is also the theme of the second day's reading—the binding of Isaac. But in contrast with the narrative of Sarah's maternal fulfillment read on the first day, the narrative of the near sacrifice of Isaac, terse and concentrated though it is, invites us to see quite clearly the tragedy that is ultimately aborted. While the reading allows us to live through the terror of Abraham and Isaac as they climb Mt. Moriah, just as on the previous day we lived through the terror of Hagar and Ishmael in the desert of Beersheba, it again keeps Sarah's pain at bay, leaves out of the story altogether her terror at the sacrifice of the child she had finally been granted.

A child's weaning (a significant event in both the Torah reading and the *Haftara* reading) is a complicated moment for mothers. Women sense that what for Abraham is an occasion of pure celebration, is for Sarah a confusing and unsettling time. They see in this moment the laying of the groundwork for the chapter that follows, in which the child of Sarah and Abraham seems to become the child of the father only. But even as we understand Sarah better, we remain profoundly troubled by Sarah's behavior following Isaac's weaning.

Writers responding to Genesis 21 draw on women's experiences to lead us toward insights into Sarah's turmoil and troubling questions about our origins as a people and our understanding of ourselves as individuals. In many of the pieces Hagar and Ishmael emerge from the background to engage us fully as complex subjects of action and feeling and as sources of moral and spiritual concern. Women readers in this collection understand the mothering of sons as only one, though a crucial, element in Sarah's and Hagar's relationship with each other, with Abraham, and with God. They probe what was, but also ask what might have been and what might yet be. Rosellen Brown has created her own genre of writing for *Beginning Anew*. Drawing on the model of "rewritten Bible" to be found in Jewish texts from the Second Temple period, as well as on Elizabeth Cady Stanton's feminist *Women's Bible,* she reenvisions what had been a tale of conflict and separation into one of reconciliation and "extended" family.

Ruth Behar requires us to name this chapter "a story of women wronging women," a failure of compassion that we must recognize before we can "imagine our own liberation." Like Rosellen Brown and the other contributors to this section, she sets Sarah's and Hagar's actions against the background of their earlier history (recounted in Genesis 16) and asks how this painful history of oppression by our foremother can speak to our longing to connect with other Jews during the Days of Awe. Does it not, she wonders, push us away in disgust? Instead Behar shows how the story of Sarah and Hagar can awaken in the Jewish listener "both the humility and the courage to stand before the cold winds of self-scrutiny" and enable us to return from "the sanctuary of Jewish penitence" to the wider world with a renewed commitment to social justice.

Judith Kates places Sarah's motherhood in the context of the "complex history" of the relationship between God and Sarah. Although the opening verses of the Rosh Hashana chapter sound a note of reassurance and fulfillment, they represent only one aspect of Sarah's "difficult" and often ambiguous connection with the Divine. Kates interrogates the texts in Genesis in which Sarah appears and traditional commentaries on them to discover the intense but troubling history of Sarah's individual relationship with God and God's with Sarah. She suggests we can find in Sarah a different and perhaps more accessible teacher as we struggle toward our own dialogue with God.

In her effort to see Sarah as a full human being, Ruth Behar calls on the compelling figure of the Egyptian slave woman created by "African American midrash," Hagar as imagined in the writing of black women. Novelist Carolivia Herron weaves together her own African American heritage and her chosen Jewish identity in a haunting fictional meditation on the story. Biblical language and imagery pervade her narrative of "the house of Abraham," but we also enter the consciousness of Hagar in a prose reminiscent of both ancient Hebrew and African American cadences. Herron deploys her own image of a tangled, desert plant, the "chamisa bush," in increasingly resonant movements to make vivid for us the tangled connections of our original family.

Marsha Mirkin brings her experience as a feminist family therapist to bear on the troubled relationships in this foundational family. Locating the core of the story in God's command to Abraham to "listen to [Sarah's] voice," Mirkin offers a striking reinterpretation that urges us to understand that phrase as a directive to "empathic listening," not to oppressive or exploitive action. According to Mirkin, it is not only Abraham who tragically misunderstands that directive. Failures of empathy underlie the human faults so evident in the entire set of narratives from Genesis read on Rosh Hashana. These stories call our attention to the consequences of such failures, suggesting to Mirkin the nature of the *teshuva* (repentance) to which we are called.

For Tamara Cohen, Sarah's story is also a problematic yet compelling means for understanding the meanings of *teshuva*. Through lyrical meditation and textual analysis, she confronts her own unhappiness with the idea of Sarah as the mother of the Jewish people, when her primary response to Sarah until now has focused on Sarah's ugly treatment of Hagar. In this reading, she finds ways to "return" to a Sarah whose story can teach us about *teshuva* (return or repentance) within oneself, between self and others (especially women), and between the individual and the Divine.

Contemporary Israelis are painfully aware of themselves and their neighbors as the descendants of the protagonists in this story and heirs to its ambiguities and conflicts. In the final essay on Genesis 21 Sidra Ezrahi powerfully draws the connection between this foundational story and the painfully tangled interactions of Israelis and Palestinians. The story enacts "our greatest conundrum, then as now." Is Ishmael part of the family or an "other"?

Francine Klagsbrun deepens our understanding of both the Torah and the *Haftara* readings by reading them in relationship to one another. Far from simple repetitions of a pattern, the stories, in her reading, create two distinctive women who embody two different versions of women's desire. Basing herself on the Biblical text and Rabbinic commentaries, Klagsbrun traces a full life history for each woman that makes sense of their sons' personalities and pushes us to recognize the adult Isaac and Samuel as truly their mothers' children. Strong women both, they most resemble each other in their "clear-cut insights into divine goals" and "steadfast determination to achieve those goals."

The final essay in this section develops the intriguing suggestion that the Rabbis only partially understood their choice of a woman to both illustrate the efficacy of prayer and to "chart out the model of all prayers to come." Nehama Aschkenasy draws a portrait of Hannah as a woman entering into a "daring dialogue" with God and reconfigures the story of the barren woman as a celebration of a "countercultural" heroine. This interpretation of Hannah as the representation of every human being in need of connection to God prepares readers for a return to prayer, encouraging us to initiate our own discourse with God.

"And God Remembered Sarah" (Genesis 21)

Torah Reading—First Day Rosh Hashana

21 And the LORD remembered Sarah as He had said, and the LORD did unto Sarah as He had spoken. ²And Sarah conceived, and bore Abraham a son in his old age, at the set time of which God had spoken to him. ³And Abraham called the name of his son that was born unto him, whom Sarah bore to him, Isaac. ⁴And Abraham circumcised his son Isaac when he was eight days old, as God had commanded him. ⁵And Abraham was a hundred years old, when his son Isaac was born unto him. ⁶And Sarah said: 'God hath made laughter for me; every one that heareth will laugh on account of me.' ⁷And she said: 'Who would have said unto Abraham, that Sarah should give children suck? for I have borne him a son in his old age.'

⁸And the child grew, and was weaned. And Abraham made a great feast on the day that Isaac was weaned. ⁹And Sarah saw the son of Hagar the Egyptian, whom she had borne unto Abraham, making sport. ¹⁰Wherefore she said unto Abraham: 'Cast out this bondwoman and her son; for the son of this bondwoman shall not be heir with my son, even with Isaac.' ¹¹And the thing was very grievous in Abraham's sight on account of his son. ¹²And God said unto Abraham: 'Let it not be grievous in thy sight because of the lad, and because of thy bondwoman; in all that Sarah saith unto thee, hearken unto her voice; for in Isaac shall seed be called to thee. ¹³And also of the son of the bondwoman will I make a nation, because he is thy seed.' ¹⁴And Abraham arose up early in the morning, and took bread and a bottle of water, and gave

א וַיהֹוָה פָּקַד אֶת־שָׂרָה כַּאֲשֶׁר אָמָר
ב וַיַּעַשׂ יְהֹוָה לְשָׂרָה כַּאֲשֶׁר דִּבֵּר: וַתַּהַר וַתֵּלֶד שָׂרָה לְאַבְרָהָם בֵּן לִזְקֻנָיו לַמּוֹעֵד
ג אֲשֶׁר־דִּבֶּר אֹתוֹ אֱלֹהִים: וַיִּקְרָא אַבְרָהָם אֶת־שֶׁם־בְּנוֹ הַנּוֹלַד־לוֹ
ד אֲשֶׁר־יָלְדָה־לּוֹ שָׂרָה יִצְחָק: וַיָּמָל אַבְרָהָם אֶת־יִצְחָק בְּנוֹ בֶּן־שְׁמֹנַת יָמִים
ה כַּאֲשֶׁר צִוָּה אֹתוֹ אֱלֹהִים: וְאַבְרָהָם בֶּן־מְאַת שָׁנָה בְּהִוָּלֶד לוֹ אֵת יִצְחָק
ו בְּנוֹ: וַתֹּאמֶר שָׂרָה צְחֹק עָשָׂה לִי
ז אֱלֹהִים כָּל־הַשֹּׁמֵעַ יִצְחַק־לִי: וַתֹּאמֶר מִי מִלֵּל לְאַבְרָהָם הֵינִיקָה בָנִים שָׂרָה
ח כִּי־יָלַדְתִּי בֵן לִזְקֻנָיו: וַיִּגְדַּל הַיֶּלֶד וַיִּגָּמַל וַיַּעַשׂ אַבְרָהָם מִשְׁתֶּה גָדוֹל
ט בְּיוֹם הִגָּמֵל אֶת־יִצְחָק: וַתֵּרֶא שָׂרָה אֶת־בֶּן־הָגָר הַמִּצְרִית אֲשֶׁר־יָלְדָה
י לְאַבְרָהָם מְצַחֵק: וַתֹּאמֶר לְאַבְרָהָם גָּרֵשׁ הָאָמָה הַזֹּאת וְאֶת־בְּנָהּ כִּי לֹא יִירַשׁ בֶּן־הָאָמָה הַזֹּאת עִם־בְּנִי עִם־
יא יִצְחָק: וַיֵּרַע הַדָּבָר מְאֹד בְּעֵינֵי
יב אַבְרָהָם עַל אוֹדֹת בְּנוֹ: וַיֹּאמֶר אֱלֹהִים אֶל־אַבְרָהָם אַל־יֵרַע בְּעֵינֶיךָ עַל־הַנַּעַר וְעַל־אֲמָתֶךָ כֹּל אֲשֶׁר תֹּאמַר אֵלֶיךָ שָׂרָה שְׁמַע בְּקֹלָהּ כִּי בְיִצְחָק
יג יִקָּרֵא לְךָ זָרַע: וְגַם אֶת־בֶּן־הָאָמָה
יד לְגוֹי אֲשִׂימֶנּוּ כִּי זַרְעֲךָ הוּא: וַיַּשְׁכֵּם אַבְרָהָם | בַּבֹּקֶר וַיִּקַּח־לֶחֶם וְחֵמַת

29

it unto Hagar, putting it on her shoulder, and the child, and sent her away; and she departed, and strayed in the wilderness of Beer-sheba. ¹⁵And the water in the bottle was spent, and she cast the child under one of the shrubs. ¹⁶And she went, and sat her down over against him a good way off, as it were a bowshot; for she said: 'Let me not look upon the death of the child.' And she sat over against him, and lifted up her voice, and wept. ¹⁷And God heard the voice of the lad; and the angel of God called to Hagar out of heaven, and said unto her: 'What aileth thee, Hagar? fear not; for God hath heard the voice of the lad where he is. ¹⁸Arise, lift up the lad, and hold him fast by thy hand; for I will make him a great nation.' ¹⁹And God opened her eyes, and she saw a well of water; and she went, and filled the bottle with water, and gave the lad drink. ²⁰And God was with the lad, and he grew; and he dwelt in the wilderness, and became an archer. ²¹And he dwelt in the wilderness of Paran; and his mother took him a wife out of the land of Egypt.

²²And it came to pass at that time, that Abimelech and Phicol the captain of his host spoke unto Abraham, saying: 'God is with thee in all that thou doest. ²³Now therefore swear unto me here by God that thou wilt not deal falsely with me, nor with my son, nor with my son's son; but according to the kindness that I have done unto thee, thou shalt do unto me, and to the land wherein thou hast sojourned.' ²⁴And Abraham said: 'I will swear.' ²⁵And Abraham reproved Abimelech because of the well of water, which Abimelech's servants had violently taken away. ²⁶And Abimelech said: 'I know not who hath done this thing; neither didst thou tell me, neither yet heard I of it, but to-day.' ²⁷And Abraham took sheep and oxen, and gave them unto Abimelech; and they two made

מַיִם וַיִּתֵּן אֶל־הָגָר שָׂם עַל־שִׁכְמָהּ וְאֶת־הַיֶּלֶד וַיְשַׁלְּחֶהָ וַתֵּלֶךְ וַתֵּתַע בְּמִדְבַּר בְּאֵר שָׁבַע: וַיִּכְלוּ הַמַּיִם מִן־ 15 הַחֵמֶת וַתַּשְׁלֵךְ אֶת־הַיֶּלֶד תַּחַת אַחַד הַשִּׂיחִם: וַתֵּלֶךְ וַתֵּשֶׁב לָהּ מִנֶּגֶד הַרְחֵק 16 כִּמְטַחֲוֵי קֶשֶׁת כִּי אָמְרָה אַל־אֶרְאֶה בְּמוֹת הַיָּלֶד וַתֵּשֶׁב מִנֶּגֶד וַתִּשָּׂא אֶת־ קֹלָהּ וַתֵּבְךְּ: וַיִּשְׁמַע אֱלֹהִים אֶת־קוֹל 17 הַנַּעַר וַיִּקְרָא מַלְאַךְ אֱלֹהִים | אֶל־הָגָר מִן־הַשָּׁמַיִם וַיֹּאמֶר לָהּ מַה־לָּךְ הָגָר אַל־תִּירְאִי כִּי־שָׁמַע אֱלֹהִים אֶל־קוֹל הַנַּעַר בַּאֲשֶׁר הוּא־שָׁם: קוּמִי שְׂאִי 18 אֶת־הַנַּעַר וְהַחֲזִיקִי אֶת־יָדֵךְ בּוֹ כִּי־ לְגוֹי גָּדוֹל אֲשִׂימֶנּוּ: וַיִּפְקַח אֱלֹהִים 19 אֶת־עֵינֶיהָ וַתֵּרֶא בְּאֵר מָיִם וַתֵּלֶךְ וַתְּמַלֵּא אֶת־הַחֵמֶת מַיִם וַתַּשְׁקְ אֶת־ הַנָּעַר: וַיְהִי אֱלֹהִים אֶת־הַנַּעַר וַיִּגְדָּל 20 וַיֵּשֶׁב בַּמִּדְבָּר וַיְהִי רֹבֶה קַשָּׁת: וַיֵּשֶׁב 21 בְּמִדְבַּר פָּארָן וַתִּקַּח־לוֹ אִמּוֹ אִשָּׁה מֵאֶרֶץ מִצְרָיִם: פ

וַיְהִי בָּעֵת הַהִוא וַיֹּאמֶר אֲבִימֶלֶךְ וּפִיכֹל 22 שַׂר־צְבָאוֹ אֶל־אַבְרָהָם לֵאמֹר אֱלֹהִים עִמְּךָ בְּכֹל אֲשֶׁר־אַתָּה עֹשֶׂה: וְעַתָּה הִשָּׁבְעָה לִּי בֵאלֹהִים הֵנָּה אִם־ 23 תִּשְׁקֹר לִי וּלְנִינִי וּלְנֶכְדִּי כַּחֶסֶד אֲשֶׁר־ עָשִׂיתִי עִמְּךָ תַּעֲשֶׂה עִמָּדִי וְעִם־הָאָרֶץ אֲשֶׁר־גַּרְתָּה בָּהּ: וַיֹּאמֶר אַבְרָהָם אָנֹכִי 24 אִשָּׁבֵעַ: וְהוֹכִחַ אַבְרָהָם אֶת־אֲבִימֶלֶךְ 25 עַל־אֹדוֹת בְּאֵר הַמַּיִם אֲשֶׁר גָּזְלוּ עַבְדֵי אֲבִימֶלֶךְ: וַיֹּאמֶר אֲבִימֶלֶךְ לֹא יָדַעְתִּי 26 מִי עָשָׂה אֶת־הַדָּבָר הַזֶּה וְגַם־אַתָּה לֹא־הִגַּדְתָּ לִּי וְגַם אָנֹכִי לֹא שָׁמַעְתִּי בִּלְתִּי הַיּוֹם: וַיִּקַּח אַבְרָהָם צֹאן וּבָקָר 27

a covenant. ²⁸And Abraham set seven ewe-lambs of the flock by themselves. ²⁹And Abimelech said unto Abraham: 'What mean these seven ewe-lambs which thou hast set by themselves?' ³⁰And he said: 'Verily, these seven ewe-lambs shalt thou take of my hand, that it may be a witness unto me, that I have digged this well.' ³¹Wherefore that place was called Beer-sheba; because there they swore both of them. ³²So they made a covenant at Beer-sheba; and Abimelech rose up, and Phicol the captain of his host, and they returned into the land of the Philistines. ³³And Abraham planted a tamarisk-tree in Beer-sheba, and called there on the name of the LORD, the Everlasting God. ³⁴And Abraham sojourned in the land of the Philistines many days.

וַיִּתֵּן לַאֲבִימֶלֶךְ וַיִּכְרְתוּ שְׁנֵיהֶם בְּרִית:

כח וַיַּצֵּב אַבְרָהָם אֶת־שֶׁבַע כִּבְשֹׂת הַצֹּאן

כט לְבַדְּהֶן: וַיֹּאמֶר אֲבִימֶלֶךְ אֶל־אַבְרָהָם מָה הֵנָּה שֶׁבַע כְּבָשֹׂת הָאֵלֶּה אֲשֶׁר

ל הִצַּבְתָּ לְבַדָּנָה: וַיֹּאמֶר כִּי אֶת־שֶׁבַע כְּבָשֹׂת תִּקַּח מִיָּדִי בַּעֲבוּר תִּהְיֶה־לִּי לְעֵדָה כִּי חָפַרְתִּי אֶת־הַבְּאֵר הַזֹּאת:

לא עַל־כֵּן קָרָא לַמָּקוֹם הַהוּא בְּאֵר שָׁבַע

לב כִּי שָׁם נִשְׁבְּעוּ שְׁנֵיהֶם: וַיִּכְרְתוּ בְרִית בִּבְאֵר שָׁבַע וַיָּקָם אֲבִימֶלֶךְ וּפִיכֹל שַׂר־צְבָאוֹ וַיָּשֻׁבוּ אֶל־אֶרֶץ פְּלִשְׁתִּים:

לג וַיִּטַּע אֶשֶׁל בִּבְאֵר שָׁבַע וַיִּקְרָא־שָׁם

לד בְּשֵׁם יְהוָה אֵל עוֹלָם: וַיָּגָר אַבְרָהָם בְּאֶרֶץ פְּלִשְׁתִּים יָמִים רַבִּים: פ

31

Hagar and Sarah, Sarah and Hagar

ROSELLEN BROWN

Everyone, real or imagined, deserves the open destiny of life.

GRACE PALEY,
A Conversation with My Father

Now Sarai, Abram's wife, bore him no children; and she had a hand-maid, an Egyptian, whose name was Hagar. And Sarai said unto Abram: "Behold now, the Lord hath restrained me from bearing; go in, I pray thee, unto my handmaid; it may be that I shall be built up through her." And Abram hearkened to the voice of Sarai. And Sarai, Abram's wife, took Hagar the Egyptian, her handmaid, after Abram had dwelt ten years in the land of Canaan, and gave her to Abram her husband to be his wife. And he went in unto Hagar, and she conceived; and when she saw that she had conceived, her mistress was overcome with sorrow admixed with joy, for her husband's house was thereby strengthened without her.

Now Sarai would not make free with her pain, but Hagar came before her and said "How is it with you? Was it not your wish that your house and your husband's house wax with my waxing?" And Sarai wept that her handmaid should supplant her in the eyes of her husband and become the mother of generations by the hand of the Lord. But Hagar embraced her mistress and swore loyalty to her house, saying, "You also shall be as a mother to this child."

And the angel of the Lord, seeing that Hagar dealt kindly with her mistress, said unto her, "I will greatly multiply thy seed that it shall not be numbered for multitude." And the angel of the Lord said unto her: "Behold, thou art with child, and shalt bear a son; and thou shalt call his name Ishmael. And he shall be a gentle deer of a man; his hand shall be joined in friendship with every man, and every man's with his; and he shall dwell in the heart of all his brethren." And Hagar invited the empty hand of her mistress to lie upon the round of her flesh as she labored to bring forth the son of Abram.

And Abram, now Abraham by the grace of the Lord, was ninety years old and nine, when he was circumcised in the flesh of his foreskin. And Ishmael his son was thirteen years old, when he was circumcised in the flesh of his foreskin. And all the men of his house, those born in the house, and those bought with money of a foreigner, were circumcised with him.

And the Lord remembered Sarai, now Sarah, and she conceived, and bore Abraham a son in his old age. And Abraham was a hundred years old, when his son Isaac was born unto him. And Sarah said: "God hath made laughter for me; every one that heareth will laugh on account of me." And she said: "Who would have said unto Abraham, that Sarah should give children suck? for I have borne him a son in his old age." And the child grew, and was weaned. And Abraham made a great feast on the day that Isaac was weaned. And Sarah saw the son of Hagar the Egyptian, whom she had borne unto Abraham with Sarah's blessing, making sport. Wherefore she upbraided Hagar that she did naught to make him heed. And Hagar said once more, as she had said at the time of his birth, "Let him do no thing that is grievous in thy sight. Thou also shall be as a mother to this child. Go thou and reprove him and he shall pay heed to thee as to a mother." So Sarah spoke words to Ishmael as if he were of her own making, now speaking hard words, now gentle. And in his trust Ishmael became as the Lord had promised, a man who loved goodness and hated injustice.

And they were supple as he-goats running and sporting together, Isaac and Ishmael. And if one called for help, the other heeded his cry. When this one pulled on his bow, the other held the arrows. Whosoever found favor in the sight of one was loved by both. And it came to pass that a stranger, seeing Isaac, asked after Ishmael, for he was tall and strong, well-favored of face. The stranger said: "Is this Egyptian not a slave for sale to another man's house? Behold, here is a sack of shekels for his purchase." And Isaac refused him, saying: "Go thou and buy some other soul. This is my brother."

Now Hagar and Sarah had seen the love of Isaac and Ishmael and together they rejoiced, but Abraham favored Isaac, who was the seed of Sarah's fathers and her fathers' fathers. But Sarah rebuked him, saying: "There shall be no peace in our house if thou dividest thy love as a loaf of bread, in unequal portions. Forasmuch as God hath opened our wombs together to thee, neither son shalt thou put above the other. Flesh is flesh and blood blood and the sinew that binds us one to one is nothing but the breath of life."

And all their days their sons were not divided, but as if under covenant they shared their portion and lived as brothers who stood before but a single mother. And each in time was father to a multitude which lived in harmony according to their wishes, Ishmael and Isaac, the sons of Abraham borne by two stars in the firmament who, in this prayer to what might have been, held them close and loved them equally.

Sarah and Hagar:
The Heelprints upon Their Faces

RUTH BEHAR

*What woman here is so enamored of her own oppression that she cannot
see her heelprint upon another woman's face? What woman's terms of
oppression have become precious and necessary to her as a ticket into the
fold of the righteous, away from the cold winds of self-scrutiny?*

AUDRE LORDE
"The Uses of Anger: Women Responding to Racism"
from *Sister Outsider: Essays and Speeches* (1984)

If feminism is about the search for sisterhood, then the story of Sarah
and Hagar is a foundational story about the impossibility of feminism.
The story of Sarah and Hagar is a story about women wronging
women. It is a story so sad, so shameful, so sorrowful, that to own up
to it is to admit that feminism has its origins in terrible violence and
terrible lack of compassion between women. The story of Sarah and
Hagar is a key source for the painful lesson Audre Lorde, an African
American feminist, taught us: that women, who have the potential to
bring each other into the world, also have the potential to oppress
one another, to leave their heelprints upon each other's faces. Feminism begins, not with assumptions about the automatic sisterhood of
women, but with seeing those heelprints women have left on one another's faces. Neither Sarah nor Hagar was capable of seeing the heelprint each left on the other's face. Yet the failure of their mutual
recognition has buried utopian dimensions that feminists must attempt to rescue if we are to break the impasse of our foremothers and
imagine our own liberation.

But you may ask: What does all this feminist stuff have to do with
the Jewish people? And the Jewish New Year? Why is the story of

Sarah and Hagar retold and remembered by Jews, year after year, during the holiest days of the Jewish religious calendar? Is the plight of feminism really so central to Jewish concerns? How can the impasse of Sarah and Hagar nourish the strong desire Jews have to connect with other Jews during the Days of Awe? Are we not more likely, after hearing their story again, to turn away in disgust from our Jewish identity? And since we also care about how non-Jews see us, what face do we present to the world by acknowledging the sorry story of Sarah and Hagar?

In the following reflections I want to show that feminist concerns are always central to Jewish concerns. Further, I want to show that the purpose of the story of Sarah and Hagar is to awaken in the Jewish listener both the humility and the courage to stand before the cold winds of self-scrutiny, an act essential to the spirit of the Days of Awe. Last, I want to show that the story of Sarah and Hagar gives both women and men a fundamental basis for returning from the sanctuary of Jewish penitence to the wider world with an altered empathy for those we have wronged, a renewed sense of commitment to social justice.

Sarah and Hagar are drawn into a relationship because of Sarah's barrenness. God has promised Abraham as many offspring as there are stars. So how is it, Sarah wonders, that her womb is closed? God seems to have forgotten that her biological clock is ticking; soon her years of birthing will be over. If the only way a woman's life gains meaning is if she bears sons for her husband, why has God chosen to degrade her by keeping her barren? Sarah decides she must take matters into her own hands: she names Hagar, her handmaid, as a surrogate and has Abraham consort with Hagar so that Sarah can have a son through her.

In the language of the Biblical narrator, I hear a judgment on Sarah's faithlessness, fickleness, and impatience, but no recognition of her rage, desperation, and fierce independence of spirit. Let us try to imagine in its fullness the emotional depth of Sarah's pain and sense of loss in the only way we can do so passionately, from our own contemporary perspective. We know that one aim of the feminist movement was to persuade women that they have an inherent value as persons. Women have wombs, yes, but they must not derive their whole sense of self from biology. Motherhood should be a choice, not an obligation. Liberated from the tyranny of their wombs, women would become free to reframe their lives in terms of their careers, their relationships, their communities, their ambitions. And what happened? Women pursued their careers, relationships, communities, and ambitions, but the desire to bear children did not disappear. Instead, mothering made a dramatic comeback in the form of surrogate motherhood, in elaborate technologies to promote fertility among women in their late-bearing years, and, most unexpectedly, in the advent of lesbian motherhood, which drove a wedge into the new communities of women whose hope was to undo the ideology that the female body was good only for procreation.[1]

I have a close friend, a talented scholar and writer, a Jewish Cuban like me, who is forty-four and has been through several miscarriages as well as a uterine operation in her efforts to bear a child. She tells me about the sense of grief she feels, knowing she probably won't have children of her body. Her sense of loss is especially acute because she is the child of a double Jewish diaspora, from Europe to Cuba and from Cuba to the United States, and as a family psychologist she recognizes that it was the strong bonds of her family that maintained coherence and unity during all the years of exodus. Yet she asks herself why she needs children of her own. Is it not enough that her two sisters have children? Why can't she be content to be the much beloved aunt she already is? But the fact is she is not content; she and her husband will adopt, she says, as soon as she finishes making peace with her grief. I understand her; I have a son, and I feel blessed, yet I mourn for the daughter I will never have. Nor do I forget how during the years when I lived in rural Mexico, before I had my son, before I knew I could have a son, I would be accused of giving other women's children the evil eye if I played with them too long and thus too longingly.

The simple fact is that enormous pressure is placed on women to bear children. Even women who choose not to have children are tormented by feelings of grief. For Jewish women this grief is laced with guilt because we are expected not only to bring forth new life, but to resurrect the dead.[2] No one has expressed this view more movingly than Irena Klepfisz, a Holocaust survivor, who feels she is viewed as "perverse, stubborn, ungiving, selfish" for not producing the children who will insure the continuity of her family and of the Jewish people after the staggering loss of the six million whose bones stayed in Europe.[3]

I bring the full burden of the procreative weight that rests on the shoulders of Jewish women to bear upon the story of Sarah and Hagar because it is not at all easy to feel compassion for Sarah, yet we must feel compassion for her if we are to inherit something better from this foremother than self-loathing for ourselves as women and as Jews. Sarah appears unredeemable and unlovable. She is totally unlike Hannah, another foremother whose story we read on Rosh Hashana. Hannah converts her heartbreak about being barren into a prayer so poetic that God cannot help but hear her and open her womb. But Sarah refuses to turn her suffering inward by humbling herself before God. No, she turns her suffering outward, creating yet worse suffering for Hagar, her Egyptian servant, the woman whose womb she thinks she controls.

Hagar gives the ultimate gift—she bears a child for Sarah. But this gift is not given with a full heart. And perhaps it cannot be, for Sarah has demanded it, and gifts must always be exchanged freely. What is certain is that from the time she conceives, Hagar develops a newfound sense of self-esteem; she no longer sees herself in servile terms. She can conceive a child and her mistress cannot. Why then is Sarah to rule over her? Are they not equals now? Or is Hagar perhaps more favored in the eyes of God? Why else has her womb opened so quickly while Sarah's has stayed shut so long? Sarah, her mistress, "is lowered in her esteem."

Hagar's loss of respect for her mistress devastates Sarah. If we view Sarah solely in terms of power dynamics, then we are likely to see her core emotion as being fury, fury that Hagar, a human being who existed only to serve the needs of her mistress, should dare to look down upon her. But say we view Sarah as less enraged and more despondent. Might it not be possible that Sarah hoped Hagar would feel for her as a woman? That Hagar, even though downtrodden, would summon compassion out of the depths of her being for the pain Sarah felt at being barren? That Hagar, in the service of her mistress rather than herself, would not grow disdainful but take delight in conceiving a child for Sarah? That Hagar, even though used by Sarah, would express not a lesser but a fuller humanity, a fuller sense of grace, a fuller overcoming? If we view the relation between Sarah and Hagar this way, we redeem Sarah a little, and just as important, we are able to see Hagar not only as being at the mercy of Sarah, and therefore abject and powerless, but as a person who also has agency.

In any case, Sarah is angry or disappointed—however you wish—by Hagar's slighting of her, and she complains to Abraham. Perhaps Sarah fears she has fallen in his eyes, too. But Abraham won't take responsibility. "Your maid is in your hands. Deal with her as you think right," he says to Sarah. And Sarah, unforgivably, treats Hagar harshly. More than harshly. The original Biblical language reads, "Sarah afflicted her," the same expression used to characterize the subsequent affliction of the Hebrew slaves in Egypt, except here it ironically depicts the suffering of a lone Egyptian slave woman at the hands of a Hebrew woman in Canaan.[4]

Hagar uses the limited agency she has to flee from Sarah. She wanders into the wilderness but soon returns to serve Sarah again after she is ordered to do so by an angel of God, who promises her, as the patriarchs are promised, many offspring. As for the child in her womb, Ishmael, he will be a wild son, the angel tells her. We are not told of Hagar's return, but the years seem to pass quietly. Ishmael grows and is circumcised by Abraham. Then, in her ripe old age, Sarah conceives. Long ago she stopped thinking about her barrenness and laughs at the idea that she, so withered, will bear a child. God, who catches her laughing and scares her, is reminding Sarah just who's in charge.

Can we assume that after so many years Sarah had made peace with the fact that Ishmael would be Abraham's heir? For it seems clear that he would never be hers; Hagar had firmly asserted that she, and not Sarah, had been raised up by the birth of Ishmael. But now, by the sheer will of God, Sarah gives birth to Isaac. Once she weans the son of her own womb, put there by God, the mere sight of Ishmael playing troubles Sarah. When she had no choice but to accept Ishmael as Abraham's heir, Sarah tolerated his presence. Tolerated, perhaps, the way he too, like his mother, looked askance at her. But having given birth to Isaac, she need no longer feel ashamed. Now it is Isaac's inheritance that concerns her. Will it be lost to Ishmael, the firstborn, the son who belittled her? She demands of Abraham that he cast out "that slave-woman and her son," displaying by not naming them how, in her turn, Hagar and Ishmael have fallen in her regard. Abraham hesitates, for he hates to lose a precious son, but God, who seems to welcome Sarah's reaction, tells him not to worry, that since Ishmael is "his seed," he too, like Isaac, will be made into a great nation. Abraham is traumatized, but not being one to doubt God, he provides Hagar and Ishmael with bread and a flask of water. And off they go into the wilderness of Beersheba, where they nearly die of hunger and thirst. Desperate, Hagar leaves Ishmael by a bush—sacrificing him to God, as Abraham will later be willing to sacrifice Isaac. And as she weeps, an angel of God again calls to her, opening her eyes so she can see a well of water with which to relieve Ishmael's thirst and thereby save him, insuring that his progeny, the nation of Islam, will survive.

Without further ado, Hagar and Ishmael are dismissed from the Jewish story. Only in Arabic legends will they reappear in a much happier incarnation, accompanied by Abraham on their journey to Arabia and eventual settlement in Mecca.[5]

From the Jewish perspective, Hagar seems to be a "throw-away" character. After all, "she is not part of Israel's salvation history. On the contrary, Hagar and Ishmael are depicted as a *threat* to the fulfillment of God's promise to Abraham and Sarah." Yet the fact that Hagar has not been erased from the Jewish canon suggests that we are not to forget her: "Hagar must not be thrown away. We must affirm what Abraham and Sarah do not: Hagar is more than a possession; she is a human being. . . . Hagar's story reminds us that one person's salvation history can be another person's history of oppression."[6]

If we are not to forget Hagar, how then should we remember her? In searching for an answer, I found myself turning to the African American response to Hagar's call from the wilderness. For African American readers have lovingly claimed Hagar as their own, made her a foremother, taken pride in her struggle, formed spiritual churches in her name, and led the way in creative appropriations of her story. In the last century African American artists, scholars, and preachers, as well as ordinary black people, have continually invoked the Biblical figure of Hagar.[7] Richard Wright referred to the African American family as Hagar's children. Anthropologist John Gwaltney described Aunt Hagar as "a mythical apical figure of the core black American nation."[8]

From an African American perspective, Hagar's story is the story of "a female slave of African descent who was forced to be a surrogate mother, reproducing a child by her slave master because the slave master's wife was barren. . . . Like Hagar and her child, Ishmael, African American female slaves and their children, after slavery, were expelled from the homes of many slaveholders and given no resources for survival. Hagar, like many women through African American women's history, was a single parent. But she had serious personal and salvific encounters with God—encounters that aided Hagar in the survival struggle of herself and her son."[9] The bitter connection between motherhood and slavery has long been recognized by black feminists, who have examined the way black women were valued for their capacity to breed, to "produce" more black workers, while always being expected to care for and protect the children of their white masters.[10] But what has always saved black women in the face of their suffering is the depth of the religious quests they have undertaken in the wilderness of their solitude. There, "in the midst of trouble and what appears to be impending death and destruction," they have met God, their own God, not the God of their oppressors, but the God to whom they have given their own name. As black theologian Delores Williams notes, Hagar is the only person in the Bible who names God, and it is through this communion with God that she makes "a way out of what she thought was no way." Hagar has come to embody, for black women, the possibility of triumph in impossible struggles, showing how an ex-slave mother withstood desolation by being utterly alone with God.[11]

This Hagar of the African American *midrash* is quite compelling. It allows us to return to Hagar as a figure of strength, as the proud single mother she was, as the brave woman who could fend for herself in the wilderness, as the Egyptian who knew the grief of expulsion and homelessness and diaspora long before her Hebrew masters. It allows us to better imagine the humiliation Hagar underwent in her position as servant and surrogate and, indeed, slave to Sarah and to understand just how terribly alone she was, how terribly bereft of sympathy and support. Sarah could at least complain to Abraham, but to whom could Hagar complain? Hagar may have lacked compassion for Sarah's barrenness, but Sarah was unwilling even to begin to fathom the terror of Hagar's vulnerability, Hagar's voicelessness, Hagar's lack of freedom, Hagar's exile. That is why Sarah left so large a heelprint on Hagar's face and why we must search hard to find the fainter hint of one that Hagar left on Sarah's.

"We are not only descendants of slaves, but we are also the descendants of slave *owners*," writes Alice Walker. And she adds, "Just as we have had to struggle to rid ourselves of slavish behaviors, we must as ruthlessly eradicate any desire to be mistress or 'master.'"[12] This, I believe, is the valuable lesson of the story of Sarah and Hagar. We were slaves in Egypt, yes, but let us not forget that we also enslaved. Let us not forget that slavery was carried out by human beings, by the very human beings whose names we invoke in our Jewish prayers, but it was inhumane. And let us not forget that women, too, sadly, mournfully, must hold themselves as accountable as men. It is a story that makes you want to weep precisely because it unfolds between two women, both of whom are ultimately insignificant under patriarchy, both of whom are unable to recognize their mutual insignificance and thereby become truly significant to one another.

As Jews we read the story of Sarah and Hagar as we begin the new year, brimming with hope, desperately seeking that state of grace where we are ready "to risk loving again those who have wounded us," and ready for "others to trust us to try again despite the fact that we have broken their hearts."[13] Reading the story of Sarah and Hagar, we can begin to risk compassion for ourselves and for others. The failure of their feminism develops our sympathy, educates our sentiments, encourages us to cross the borders of our differences with more respect.

We emerge caring "profoundly about the bad things that happen to others, what reasons to get involved, to take risks, for the sake of social justice and beneficence."[14] We emerge with a renewed Whitmanesque sensibility: "Whoever degrades another degrades me." We emerge painfully aware that we have cast out others whom we did not know how to include, and that those we cast out do not forget. We emerge, beating our hearts, for now we know that only at the truly terrible expense of others have we become "a people."

Or, at the very least, we emerge ready to lay Sarah and Hagar to rest, side by side, in the same blood-ravaged land.

The Trials of Sarah

JUDITH A. KATES

"Now YHWH took account of Sara as he had said, YHWH dealt with Sara as he had spoken" (Genesis 21:1). These are the first words we read from the Torah on Rosh Hashana. God, we are told, fulfills promises. And the result of God's "taking account of," "dealing with" Sarah, is that a passionately desired, unbearably long-deferred wish is granted—"Sara became pregnant and bore Abraham a son in his old age" (21:2). What greater reassurance could we ask for on the day of judgment? What more poignant reminder of the ever-present possibility of renewal on the day of celebrating creation? The Hebrew verb *pakad,* here rendered as "took account of," can also be translated "remembered." When we then hear the verse as "God remembered Sarah," we recognize an inspiring example for Rosh Hashana, the day of remembering. In this narrative, however, remembering takes on a special character. God pays attention not to a generic human being, but to a woman, using as the medium of communication a specifically female life event. This mode of interaction between God and a woman involves more than the apparently simple fulfillment of a promise. The relationship between God and Sarah has a complex history that we may find more troubling than reassuring.

Part of that complication arises from the fragmented and ambiguous nature of the interaction between Sarah and God as we perceive it in the Biblical text. We first encounter Sarah (initially called Sarai) at the end of the ten-generation genealogy that leads from Noah to Abraham. The text mentions the names of all the members of Abram/Abraham's family but offers a characterizing phrase about only one. Sarah is not only named but identified by her condition of childlessness. "The name of Avram's wife was Sarai. . . . Now Sarai was barren, she had no child" (11:29, 30). Sarah later interprets what the genealogy states as fact. The first time we hear her speak she explains her barrenness as God's doing—"Now here, YHWH has obstructed me from bearing" (16:2). In contrast with Abraham, whom

44

the text constantly presents as recipient of divine attention, object of divine initiatives, Sarah constructs for herself a sense of God's role in her life—at this time, as author of her suffering.

Her initiative doesn't stop there. Sarah also "gives" her Egyptian maidservant, Hagar, to Abraham to serve as a surrogate mother for their long-delayed child (16:3). Although Sarah has not been explicitly included in the covenantal promises of offspring as numerous as the stars (15:5), she acts to close the apparently unbridgeable gap between divine promise and reality. Her speech embodies an implied theology. God, whose covenant with this family can take on reality only if there is a continuation of their line into the next generation, has nevertheless "obstructed," stopped up, the only body that can bring that next generation into being. Sarah seems to see that paradox as a call to human action. Instead of silently accepting her condition or interrogating its author (as Abraham does in 15:2–4), she takes the initiative, producing the plan to "build a son" through her maidservant (the Hebrew of 16:2 plays on the root to suggest both "having a son"—*ben*— and being "built up"—*ibane*).

The plan, in its lived reality, goes painfully wrong. When Hagar becomes pregnant, she finds ways to belittle her mistress ("her mistress became of light-worth in her eyes" 16:4). Sarah calls on God to activate Abraham on her behalf ("May YHWH see-justice-done between me and you!" 16:5). God does not intervene, however, and Abraham leaves the entangled consequences of Sarah's initiative entirely to her. Her response is to "afflict" (16:6) her servant/co-wife. We can explain, though not excuse, her acts of oppression on psychological grounds. She resents Hagar for "making light" of her and for ingratitude toward her generosity in sharing such a husband (the midrashic explanation), or she acts out of the frustration of her hope for personal fulfillment. But we can also postulate an unspoken yet deep anger at the limitation imposed on human initiative within the divine scheme. The text reinforces such a reading when, after Hagar gives birth, the child is clearly considered Abraham's son, but not Sarah's. His father names him (16:15) in accordance with instructions given by God's messenger to Hagar (16:11) with a name that reflects Hagar's particular experience ("call his name: Yishmael/God Hearkens, for God has hearkened to your being afflicted"). Sarah has apparently been cut off from any covenantal role.

Notice to the contrary comes not to Sarah, but to Abraham, again at God's initiative. In Genesis 17 God changes both their names to names associated with the reiterated covenantal promises of multiple offspring and national greatness. Sarah is the only woman in the Bible whose name is changed by God, suggesting, as Everett Fox notes, that "she shares the blessing of God and . . . is not merely the biological means for its fulfillment."[1] But that blessing and, even more crucially, the explicit promise of a son that she will bear is spoken to Abraham alone (17:6–18). Abraham's reaction: "But Avraham fell on his face and laughed [*vayitzchak*], he said in his heart: To a hundred-year-old man shall there be [children] born? Or shall ninety-year-old Sara give birth?" (17:17). He is not only amused (or incredulous) at the idea that Sarah would give birth, but he begs God to choose his firstborn, Ishmael, as the designated "seed"—"Avraham said to God: If only Yishmael might live in your presence!" (17:18). Let Ishmael be the one to find favor with You, to be granted blessing and the singular relationship of covenant ("live in Your presence"). His prayer stems not only from an understandably human clinging to reality (Ishmael after all already exists), but from the patriarch's culturally reinforced sense of "rightness" in choosing *his* firstborn for primacy, for the role of special, chosen one. But God insists that God's choice of a covenantal partner among the father's sons is related to the mother. "God said: Nevertheless, Sara your wife is to bear you a son, you shall call his name: Yitzchak/He Laughs. I will establish my covenant with him as a covenant for the ages, for his seed after him" (17:19). Ishmael, God promises, will also be "a great nation," ancestor of twelve tribes (17:21); "But my covenant I will establish with Yitzchak, whom Sara will bear to you at this set-time another year hence" (17:21). What distinguishes this promised child from the son already born to Abraham at this point is simply the identity of his mother. Although his God-given name, Yitzchak (from the root *TzChK*, meaning "laugh") links him to his father ("Avraham . . . laughed . . . in his heart"), he is insistently declared his mother's son by the usually economical text's repetition that he will be borne by Sarah.

The name, too, that constant reminder of the joy and surprise inherent in his conception, becomes a link with Sarah when the "annunciation" of her incipient pregnancy is, finally, made to her as well. But that apparently direct speech also encapsulates the ambiguities of

God's dealings with Sarah. God "appears" to Abraham (18:1), who then "sees" three "men," recipients of his eager hospitality. In the subsequent talk, however, the text slides between a plural "they said" (18:9) and a singular voice, subsequently identified as YHWH, making the astounding promise that Sarah hears—"Now he said: I will return, yes, return to you when time revives, and Sara your wife will have a son! Now Sara was listening at the entrance to the tent, which was behind him" (18:10). Sarah, in fact, overhears an announcement made not directly to her, but to her husband. Yet the text becomes preoccupied with her response. As though justifying her astonishment, the narrator reminds us that Abraham and Sarah were not only old, but Sarah had stopped menstruating ("the way of women had ceased for Sara" 18:11). Then "Sara laughed within herself, saying: After I have become worn, is there to be pleasure for me? And my lord is old!" (18:12). Sarah's laughter sounds remarkably similar to Abraham's, a laughter of surprise, even incredulity, based on clear-sighted awareness of reality. She too owns a share in the laughter-boy's name, the text seems to indicate. But her laughter generates not just the reiterated assurance of renewed possibility given to Abraham, but a theological lesson, a lesson meant for her yet not addressed to her directly. "But YHWH said to Abraham: Now why does Sara laugh and say: Shall I really give birth, now that I am old? Is anything beyond YHWH? At that set-time I will return to you, when time revives, and Sara will have a son" (18:13–14). God is responding to Sarah's inward probing and astonished questioning yet still speaks directly only to Abraham, misquoting her in the process. The medieval commentator Rashi, basing himself on midrash, praises this revisionary tactic: "Scripture changed [her words] for the sake of peace." God, in this view, is protecting their marriage from the shock of Sarah's candor. But in the history of Sarah's engagement with God, this misquotation delivers a shock to an equally important relationship—that between Sarah and the God of covenantal promises.

Traditional and modern commentators hear the overt statement of the theological principle—"Is anything beyond YHWH"—as a rebuke to Sarah. Why does her laughter deserve rebuke, when Abraham's had evoked reassurance? Rashi directs us to the ancient Aramaic translation, Onkelos, which translates the same Hebrew root with two different verbs. In Abraham's case, *vayitzchak* means "he rejoiced"; for Sarah, *vatitzchak* is translated "she laughed at, she jested." From this we learn, according to Rashi, that Abraham trusted and rejoiced, but Sarah did not trust and mocked. Therefore God responded with anger only to her doubt (Rashi on 17:17). The shift of one consonant, indicating the same verb with a feminine subject, signals, to such commentators, a move into a radically different spiritual world.

Sarah also seems to hear God's words as a rebuke to her, because we are told that she responds with anxiety, even though the speech was ostensibly directed to Abraham—"Sara pretended [otherwise], saying: No, I did not laugh, For she was afraid." And this finally pushes God into speaking directly to her: "But he said: No, indeed you laughed" (18:15). We can hear this final assertion from God in a tone that transforms the unspoken as well as spoken dialogue. Up to this point Sarah has been listening from the margins ("at the entrance to the tent") and hears her own reaction revised into what she thinks is taken as unacceptable doubt. Her fear (or awe; both are implied in the verb *yareia*) at being recognized and included, albeit indirectly, in the interaction, yet perhaps misunderstood, leads her to disclaim her own inner life ("Sara laughed within herself"). To this God responds by acknowledging, even validating, what she has felt "within herself." This first, and only, moment of direct dialogue between Sarah and God confirms that God has heard the silent voice of her inner reality, in all its complexity.

Reading God's response, not as rebuke but as affirmation, we can also hear the theological statement as reassurance instead of anger. Sarah, the one who earlier had seen most clearly the gap between divine promise and reality, acknowledges more fully than Abraham the physical impossibility of conception, reflecting as she does on the waning not only of her menstrual cycle, but of their sexual life ("After I have become worn, is there to be pleasure for me? And my lord is old!" 18:12). Her doubt and astonishment are therefore more deeply rooted.

She has lived her whole life in a mode of what Avivah Zornberg calls "staunch realism." In Sarah's experience, "God [has been] more effectively hidden," and her faith, therefore, has been "a more difficult faith than Abraham's, which is based on promises, transcendent intimations."[2] We can vividly perceive the pressure of reality on

Sarah's faith in the two episodes in which Abraham and Sarah leave the promised land. Each time Abraham feels it necessary to protect his life among possibly lascivious foreigners by claiming that Sarah is not his wife, but his sister. Sarah is the one who bears the brunt of this ploy, ending up in the harem of the foreign king, in danger of being raped. In both Biblical accounts (12:10–20; 20:1–18), she is utterly silent. The voice of the narrator asserts God's concern with her plight and intervention on her behalf ("But YHWH plagued Pharaoh with great plagues . . . because of Sarai, Avram's wife," 12:17; "For YHWH had obstructed . . . every womb in Avimelekh's household on account of Sara, wife of Avraham," 20:18). But we are not told how Sarah herself understands what happens to her. A poignant midrash (Genesis Rabba 41:2) responds to this gap, dramatizing her experience of entrapment and danger and her awareness of the harsh reality pressing on her. "All that night [while she was in Pharaoh's household], Sarah lay on her face, saying, 'Master of the universe, Abraham went out [from his birthplace] because of a promise, but I went out because of faith; Abraham has gone out from this prison, but I am inside this prison.' The Holy One said to her, 'Everything I am about to do, I do for your sake. Everyone will say it is "because of [al devar] Sarai, Avram's wife"' [quoting 12:17]." Another midrash, with a play on words quoted by Rashi, understands the phrase al devar as "at the word of," construing the narrator's statement (12:17) as "YHWH plagued Pharaoh . . . at the word of Sarai. . . ." This reading transforms her silent abandonment to the forces surrounding her into a powerful alliance with God, who is ready to respond to her need (literally, to her word). Yet even these rabbinic responses to the text, which invest Sarah with power and control through her connection to God, also give voice to a sense of the difficulties in that connection. She cannot ignore the dangerous "prison" in which she finds herself. Her cry of protest recalls the absence of direct "promise" to her at the beginning of the journey, creating her need to actively construct her emuna (faith or trust). The midrash, even as it expands the narrator's assurances of God's concern for her into a direct dialogue between Sarah and God, still conveys the ambiguity that characterizes her experience of God.

But in the dialogue found in the Biblical text (18:15), God responds to Sarah with the strongest possible assertion of divine capacity for the miraculous. What she, from the margins, heard as rebuke was meant as response to the intense conflict between doubt and hope expressed in that internal laughter. Far from requiring that she disclaim her laughter, God claims her as one whom God knows and, finally, speaks to directly. In the intensity of her spiritual struggle, Sarah has pushed God into establishing an unmediated relationship with her. From this perspective, the child's God-chosen name, Yitzchak/He Laughs, reflects his mother's, as much as his father's, connection to the God who promises him into being.

In the opening verse of the Rosh Hashana reading, we enter into the fullest, most unqualified moment in the complex relationship between Sarah and God—"Now YHWH took account of Sara as he had said, YHWH dealt with [or "did for"] Sara as he had spoken" (21:1). God here pays attention to Sarah in direct, unambiguous fulfillment of promises to her. And although Abraham gives the child his name, Sarah declares its meaning—"Now Sara said: God has made laughter [tzchok] for me, all who hear of it will laugh for me" (21:6).[3] Just as she constructed meaning for her childlessness, declaring it the active intervention of God in her life ("YHWH has obstructed me from bearing"), she now sees the transformation of her sorrow into laughter as God's gift specifically to her. With a shift in emphasis, we can also hear her joy in the realization that it is indeed God who has acted on her behalf, "making" laughter for her—both the child whose name is laughter and the joyous surprise she shares with "all who hear of it."

A midrash (Genesis Rabba 53:8) reports the realistic, if rather mean-spirited, question of a group of rabbis who ask why Sarah would imagine that anyone else cared about her happiness, however wondrous its origin—"If Reuben has a reason to rejoice, how does it concern Simon? Similarly, if Sarah was remembered, what did it matter to others?" Their explanation for such widespread good feeling is that others, too, must have had personal reasons for joy. And, they assert, not only Sarah was "remembered" at this time, but many other barren women "were remembered," many sick people were healed, many prayers were answered, so that there was much joy (schok) in the world (Rashi paraphrasing the midrash). Similarly, midrashim pick up on an apparent puzzle in Sarah's little poem of triumph (21:7)—"Who would have declared to Avraham: Sara will nurse sons? Well, I have borne him a son in his old age!" How can she claim to nurse sons, in the plural? But according to one midrashic comment (in the Talmudic tractate Baba Metzia 87a), she did literally nurse many sons. When Abraham made his celebratory feast at the time of Isaac's weaning (21:8), inviting people from all over to the party, his guests assumed that this elderly couple had brought home a foundling from the marketplace. "This is our son," they declared, and Abraham's invitation to them confirmed it. "What did Abraham our father do? He invited all the most eminent men of the time and Sarah our mother invited their wives. Each woman brought her child with her but no wetnurse. A miracle was performed for Sarah our mother. Her breasts overflowed like two springs and she nursed them all," clearly demonstrating to all those skeptics that she had indeed given birth. In another, more generous version (Genesis Rabba 53:9), Abraham, when Isaac is born, tells Sarah, who is extremely modest, "This is no time for modesty. Uncover your breasts so that everyone will know that the Holy One has begun to make miracles." When Sarah's breasts gush forth milk, the noblewomen whose children she nurses are overwhelmed—"We are not worthy of having our children suckled by the milk of that righteous woman." Those children, in fact, drank righteousness from that mother's milk and became "God-fearing."

These *midrashim* give a "hyperliteral" reading to Sarah's words, words we could hear simply as an outpouring of enthusiasm. But that literalism paradoxically opens the door for imaginative constructions that embody perennial religious struggles—in this case, the realist's inevitable doubt about miracle stories.[4] When the Rabbis hear Sarah's poem as a response to doubt, however, they also, perhaps unconsciously, register the trajectory of Sarah's own spiritual struggles. Although the midrashic narratives project onto others skepticism about a ninety-year-old woman's capacity to give birth and nurse a child, Sarah herself has come through precisely that state of mind. We can hear her words as doubly enthusiastic because God has not only fulfilled the promise, but "spoken" to her, "done for" her, responded to her doubt with presence in her life.

The image of "mother Sarah" created by midrash takes on an almost goddesslike power here. With her breasts pouring forth milk "like two springs *(mayanot)*," she is depicted as a force of nature, nurturing uncounted numbers of children through her alliance with the source of the miracle of life. In addition, the Rabbis transform Sarah's milk, metaphorically, into "soul" food, through which her spiritual descendants imbibe knowledge of the one God.

But in the Biblical text, this state of fulfillment and power lasts only until Isaac's weaning. As we experience narrative time, Abraham's celebration of his son's growth is immediately followed by Sarah's perception of trouble. "Once Sara saw the son of Hagar the Egyptian-woman, whom she had borne to Avraham *metzachek* [laughing, playing . . .]." Ironically and tragically, the complication in the family configuration that Sarah herself had brought into being, in her effort to close the gap between divine promise and empty reality, now challenges the satisfactory conclusion of her long quest. Sarah now "sees" Hagar not as "Sarah's servant," but as an unnamed Egyptian woman who had borne a son to Avraham. The child is son of that woman *and Abraham*. Sarah, that is, perceives the genuine relationship between Abraham and his older son. And the boy himself *metzachek*. Commentators call on the full range of associations with this verb from other Biblical contexts to fill the open-ended ambiguities of his "laughing" or "playing" with sinister connotations that they think will justify Sarah's alarm, vilifying Ishmael in the process. Some medieval commentators, however, take Sarah's words to Abraham seriously—"The son of this slave-woman shall not share-inheritance with my son, with Yitzchak (21:10)." Ibn Ezra and Rashbam, both known for their attention to the "plain sense" of Biblical language, explain *metzachek* as literally "playing," because that is what boys do. But Ishmael's play reveals that he is very much the older brother (Ibn Ezra), clearly the firstborn to Abraham, and Sarah worries that he will soon want to make a claim to inheritance from his father (Rashbam).

What traditional commentaries do not articulate is the textual hint that Sarah "sees" the complex nature of Abraham's connection to this first son of his. He is the son borne to Abraham by Hagar, yet he is acting in ways described by the verb *metzachek,* the word repeatedly connected to the name of the special, chosen one, the one through whom God has promised the covenant will continue, explicitly designated as the son of Sarah. When Sarah sees Ishmael *metzachek,* she sees him "Isaac-ing,"[5] taking on the identity of an Isaac for his father. When she demands that the boundary be reestablished, "The matter was exceedingly bad in Avraham's eyes because of his son" (21:11).

This is his response, even though, as the medieval commentator Radak points out, Sarah has reminded him by her doubled reference to "my son, Isaac," that God had said, "I will establish my covenant with Isaac whom Sarah will bear to you" (17:21). Even though Isaac is no longer a promise but actually exists, Abraham remains bound to the "rightness" of his firstborn's claims to primacy. Sarah's harsh and uncompromising insistence on total separation may respond to the strength of that continuing bond, the patriarchal commitment to primogeniture, which threatens to undermine the divinely articulated choice.

Sarah continues her activism on behalf of covenantal continuity. And her initiative receives powerful validation—"But God said to Avraham: Do not let it be bad in your eyes concerning the lad and concerning your slave-woman; in all that Sara says to you, hearken to her voice, for it is through Yitzchak that seed will be called by your [name]" (21:12). The voice of God echoes the voice of Sarah, confirming her perception that Abraham needed to be reminded of the unconventional path demanded by the God he has chosen to follow. The necessity for direct intervention from God indicates the intensity of Abraham's resistance to what seems an essential separation. (Both the necessity and the pain of the separation are suggested by the linguistic link between Sarah's demand that Abraham "drive out"—*garesh*—Ishmael and Hagar and God's "driving out"—*vayegaresh*—Adam and Eve from the Garden, 3:24). We may even explain, though not excuse, Abraham's apparent harshness and inadequate provision for Hagar and Ishmael, as a sign of his need to banish them immediately and completely, lest he be unable to separate at all.

Sarah's fulfillment as mother and as covenantal partner with God is immediately qualified by a return to the complexities of human relationships and emotions. Her connection to God is both deepened and strained by the difficult language of family relationships through which it is created. That connection may enable her to see clearly and to act, but both her vision and her activism exact an enormous price in suffering for others and for her. Greatest of the many ironies in this history, God becomes an open ally of Sarah, telling Abraham to "listen to Sarah's voice" at the moment when she falls silent. We never hear her voice again, nor is she visible in the Biblical text until the notice of her death (23:2).

But the difficulty and complication of the relationship between Sarah and God, God and Sarah, make her our teacher and our inspiration on Rosh Hashana. Refusing to abandon her clear-eyed perception of reality and its distance from the promises made by the divine voice (or the sacred text), she holds on to hope and stays loyal. It is precisely through her struggle with doubt and skepticism that she pushes God into manifesting presence, into direct speech. The Rabbis notice, with some condescension (Genesis Rabba 48:20), how rarely the Bible records speech between God and a woman and "how many circles [God] encircled" *(kirkurim kirker)* in speaking even to Sarah. But we may find that mode of "roundabout" communication, which the Rabbis see as fit only for a woman, to be the most plausible source of hope for us. Unlike Abraham, to whom God calls and with whom God is persistently the initiator of connection and mission, Sarah actively constructs her awareness of God's workings in her life. She tries to push a flawed, incomplete reality into the shape she knows, through faith, that God has designed. Her activism also entails floundering and wrongdoing, yet we can derive reassurance from God's continuing presence to her precisely in her flawed striving. God fulfills promises, "does for" Sarah as God had spoken. But fulfillment is only a moment, giving way to anxiety, struggle, complicity in morally problematic action. Sarah, from this perspective, is truly our ancestor. By entering her story, we can find a language to construct our own dialogue with God.

Chamisa

CAROLIVIA HERRON

It was growing there upon the desert in Canaan when Hagar and Sarai strove together before the face of Abram and God, and then Ishmael was cast out from the tents of his father Abram, along with Hagar, his mother; but the son of Sarai, Abram's favored son, Isaac, remained in the tents with his father and his mother.

It was growing there tangled and dry near the empty watercourses, the chamisa bush, spreading along sandy gullies with its half-green color. And twice a year it crested in gold seeds that drifted as bright yellow dust on the gray brown desert floor.

So many years Abram and Sarai had been childless, and the day came in which Abram came before God in anguish and spoke, saying, "Shall all my inheritance, the goods you have given to me, pass to Eliezar, a slave born in my house? Will you not give me a child? What can your goods do for me, if you will not give me a child?" And terror seized Abram for his boldness before God. Yet still he spoke out. "Shall I die leaving no one, leaving only strangers and slaves?" He walked in the desert near the tents, praying, there where the dry chamisa rattled its branches.

And the word of God came to Abram, saying, "Look at the stars, are you able to number the stars? I brought you away to this land. Look up and count your descendants by counting the stars. Your own son shall be your inheritor."

And God said further, "Bring a sacrifice to me, a heifer, a female goat, a ram, a turtledove, a pigeon, a young bird." Abram brought them and cut all save the young bird in two and laid one against another upon an altar of stone. And when great birds of prey came down to feast on the sacrifice Abram scattered them away and would not let them approach. But dread, great dread, came upon him as he waited by the sacrifice and as darkness descended upon him and he fell into a deep sleep of fear.

In his dream God spoke to Abram, saying, "It is true that your descendants shall be slaves and strangers in a land that is not their own for four hundred years. But I shall bring them out to this land as I brought you out. After long life you will go to your fathers in peace, and I shall bring them out in the fourth generation."

Abram awoke from his dream as the sun set, and he saw upon the altar a smoking fire pot. From the fire pot there came a flaming torch that passed between the pieces of the sacrifice. The flame passed between and split even the stones of the altar, dividing as if it were a sundering of great lands and nations: Kenites, Kenazites, Kadmonites, Hittites, Rephaim, Amorites, Canaanites, Girgashites, Jebusites. The burning and dividing torch was a fire of terror, splitting land from land for the sake of the descendants of Abram. But in grief and dread Abram whispered, "Take back your gift, take it back." But the empty, echoing land answered, "Which gift? Take what back?" For the voice of God had already departed from that place and only the rattling brush, clashing of tangled chamisa, was there for answer.

Lurid stems of the chamisa almost green as if they need more water, but with more water they die. The clustered seeds dip gold when the sun goes down, as numerous as the stars. "O my people, I shall live to a ripe old age, then go to my fathers. I shall have years of peace, but you, my unborn children? Oh, where are you, Sarai, my sister-wife?" Abram spoke, returning to the tents.

And when Abram returned from the burning of that sacrifice there was a new look upon him such that his smiles and his laughter and his speech were thin cloths beyond which ever before his eyes he saw the awe of the fire. Only with Sarai, his sister-wife, sometimes when he looked upon her, thinking of their childhood together and the fears and travels they had known, did he forget his great awe, and his eyes looked warm and clear upon the wife of his youth, his sister and his love.

Now it was the custom in that place for the first handmaid of the wife to wash a ceremonial jar each morning for her mistress, and to fill the jar with cool water set aside for the delight of the mistress. And the first handmaiden of Sarai, the wife of Abram, was Hagar, a slave out of Egypt. Each morning Hagar washed and filled the ceremonial jar of water for Sarai. Each morning Sarai woke to the clack of the jar and the sound, the dip of cool water. And each morning when Sarai heard these sounds she knew that all was well in the tents.

But all was not well with Sarai, the wife of Abram, because she had not borne any children to Abram. So Sarai came to Hagar, her handmaid, the same who waited upon her, bringing to her each dawn the jar of cool water. Sarai spoke to Hagar, and bathed her in sweet oils, and placed a new cloth upon her, and wept upon her shoulder, saying, "Will you be a wife unto my husband, Abram, that we be not childless?" And Hagar, the Egyptian handmaiden said, "I will."

So Sarai came to her husband, Abram, and said to him, "Go in to my slave-girl, Hagar, and take her to your bosom. I give her to you as a wife—perhaps we shall gain a child through her." And Abram went in unto Hagar.

And Abram looked with kindness upon Hagar, yes, even the kindness unto love when they lay together. And Sarai bade her handmaiden not to rise in the morning to bring the jar of cool water, but rather to lie with Abram while Sarai herself washed a jar and brought the ceremonial water to Hagar. For it was in the heart of Sarai to do this thing for Hagar, her handmaiden, that Hagar, in her pleasure, might bring forth a child for Abram and Sarai.

But Hagar said, "She is his sister. He looks at her with brother eyes, she looks at him with sister eyes. I cannot come close to him. I was not there when he was a boy and she was a girl and they laughed together or played or when the storms came they clung together, children. I was not there. What is it to me that Sarai washes the jars for me and brings the cool water in sign that we are both his wife? I am not what her jars of cool water make me. Her cool water is nothing to me. Yet she thinks she is caring for me." Thus Hagar said in her heart.

And when Hagar thought about Abram as he lay with her she said, "I cannot sleep. His eyes are vacant and kind and loving. He is a good man and comely, but his eyes do not see me. We are too crowded, too close, Sarai, Abram, and I. We are tangled together. But when she thinks we are lying together he is walking among the chamisa, counting the stars. My only peace from the tangle is in sleep. But she comes at dawn breaking that sleep with the washing of jars and the dip of cool water.

"He loves, or at least remembers when he was young with Sarai, and there is the slightest adjustment of his eyes, an adjustment that says I know her and am known by her."

And Hagar kept her grief in her heart, and Abram lay with her the early part of each night, and she conceived, and she thought then she would see the warming of his eyes toward her. But when she came heavy with child to Abram and Sarai, though they both smiled upon her, the eyes of Abram never warmed toward her. Still all was well until Hagar saw how Abram looked upon Sarai, and his eyes changed into warm color.

And Hagar was grieved in her heart, saying, "Why is there no room to love two women, and me, the mother of his child? Is it because she is his sister?"

On the next day Hagar lay asleep by dawn, for Abram no longer lay in Hagar's tent, seeing she was with child, and he walked as before among the chamisa. On that morning, when Sarai came before the tent of Hagar, and stood before the tent, clacking the jars and dipping the cool water, Hagar came forth from the tent and strove in words with Sarai in great anger.

"Bring no more water to me in the morning. I hate the dip of the cool water that you bring. You wake me with the clacking of the jars. Am I his wife or your wife? Are you his wife or his sister? Is he married to us or to God that he walks so long in the brush and shrubs and leaves us in the night! Go away, Sarai, do not serve me."

And Sarai, in surprise and anguish, said to Hagar, "But I love you and I care for you."

And Hagar answered, "I don't want cool water, I want to sleep." And she cursed Sarai to her face, cursed her away from her jars and her tents.

Sarai in anger broke the jar upon the grinding stone and went away to her own tent in great bitterness, for she loved Hagar with a love that knew nothing of what Hagar thought. And when Abram came Sarai said to him, "It's your fault that Hagar despises me now, it's because I gave her into your affection, and through you she has conceived a child." And she came again to Hagar, speaking harshly, and Hagar ran into the desert and sat under the chamisa.

Yet Hagar's heart yearned for her child, and how could she feed and keep her child alone in the desert, and perhaps Sarai would not keep her anger forever. Perhaps Abram would look upon his firstborn with love. The heart of Hagar was entangled with the heart of Sarai and the heart of Abram, and she could not leave them. So Hagar returned and gave birth to a son. And Abram named the son that Hagar bore Ishmael; which is to say, God heeds.

It is a desert plant. The green of the stem seems to be mixed with an iridescent yellow so that it glows in the dark. A dry bush with the clustered seeds dipping when the sun goes down as numerous as the stars. As Abram walked in the chamisa he thought about the words of God and at times he talked with God. "O my son Ishmael, I shall live to a ripe old age and be gathered to my fathers, but you my son, you, son of my sister's slave. The Lord God has told me that Sarai herself shall bear my son, but O my Lord, O that Ishmael might live in your eyes." The Lord answered Abram, "As for Ishmael, I have heard you, and he shall become a great nation. But my covenant is with you and Sarai, and the son you shall have, and his descendants, and henceforth you shall add a portion of my name to your names, you shall be Abraham and Sarai shall be Sarah." And Sarah conceived and bore a son, and Abraham named this son Isaac; which is to say, laughter, for Sarah laughed to have a son in her old age.

And it came to pass, after a time, that Ishmael and Isaac both played in the sand before the tents. And Ishmael had a great vision. And Ishmael said, "This is the mountain, this is the sea, this is the floor of the sea, this is a cloud of foam. Ishmael looked down from a high place, yes, a mountain from which he looked down upon the plain of the world, or a great ocean which opened to show the scalloped floor of the sea. In awe but in firmness he saw it. And he looked carefully upon the floor of that sea, And looking upon it, he saw that it was more than a cloud of foam, for beneath the foam were further mountains of seas, downward and downward, roiling, opening farther and farther beneath him.

And while Ishmael was gazing in his vision, sitting still upon the sand, Isaac played with stones and pebbles and sticks and mud and the sap of brush and trees. Isaac said, "I put the sticks and stones and earth together to build a house, but the house falls down and I must try again. It is a puzzle. I try again. I want to build a house, a little house, and I shall build a great house later. I try and I try and I call them to look, I have built a house. See, here is the house. But if it falls down, it is not a house after all. But I do it again and again. And I can do it. This the puzzle, I can solve the puzzles of the dust of the ground. I can move the objects upon the earth until I know what they do and make them into something, and then I laugh."

Ishmael saw light upon water where there was no water. Isaac made patterns in the sand, spirals and cubes. He moved the objects before him until they were something else that he had made. And when Ishmael became aware of Isaac again, having returned from his vision, and knew that Isaac had not seen the vision, he looked upon Isaac and laughed at him.

Sarah saw how the two boys played in the sand, how Ishmael sat in a trance while Isaac built toys with his hands. And it seemed to her that the ways of the boys were overmuch for one family to bear, a son who sees visions of heaven, and a son who solves problems of earth. So Sarah went to Abraham and asked him to cast out Hagar and her son. Sarah said to him, "Let Hagar go, my husband, let her go with Ishmael and may they find their own true path. This path is ours."

It is a crowded house, tangled like the chamisa.

And though Abraham grieved for his son Ishmael, yet he cast out Hagar and Ishmael, giving them bread and a skin of water.

And Hagar spoke to Abraham, saying, "And will you truly cast me out? Me and the child? Is your love so far removed from me? You say that God has spoken to you, and that I shall be cared for, but you blame God because you hate me and cast me out. You would not do this to your other son, the son you love, Isaac. You would not threaten him with death as you threaten my child with death. Is it so much that a child should mock at a child? Ishmael did but laugh at the toys of Isaac. Though Ishmael be the elder by many years, yet he is but a child, and for this you cast him off to die."

And Hagar walked off into the desert with Ishmael, and when they had drunk all the water she cast her child under a chamisa bush. Ishmael, dying of thirst, looked up through the chamisa, seeing a hand drawing a cloth from water into fire, a great burning, a tangle of brush, chamisa twisting entangles hot prickling. And Ishmael lay there softly crying.

But Hagar sat a good way off from her son, turning her back to him that she might not see the boy's death. There she lifted up her voice, and cried aloud in the midst of the silent desert, for her son was to die a pitiable death, and she also must die there of thirst.

And God heard the soft whimpering of the lad Ishmael, lying under the chamisa, and the angel of God called out to Hagar, showing her a well of water. Hagar filled the water bottle, lifted up the head of her boy, and gave him cool water. Then she looked back along the way toward the tents of Abraham. "Yet we are one family," she said, "We are one. This is the well of the Living One Who Sees Me, and we are one."

And when his thirst was quenched Ishmael played with the yellow seeds of the chamisa, and his body was caressed by the fluffy gold of the seeds, and he lifted up his head to drink the water again and again.

The house of Abraham is a chamisa bush, life that flourishes from a desert, bringing forth seeds.

Soon after that the lad Ishmael became an archer and learned to feed himself by his bow. Then Hagar said to him, "I must go back to Egypt, my son, there to find a wife for you and then return. Abide my coming."

When Hagar returned from Egypt she said to Ishmael, "And you should know, my son, dear Ishmael, that even as you were cast out, God was preparing some great gift for Isaac. For even as I was turning away, grieving, the voice of God opened to me and I heard God saying to Abraham. 'Take your son, your favored one, Isaac, whom you love, and bring him . . .' I did not hear what followed, for Abraham turned away and the voice was no longer open to me. But surely it was some great gift that God had reserved for Isaac."

Footsteps crossed vacantly on the desert, from another home to another exile. Is it not the step of a child of Abraham?

This house of Abraham is a chamisa bush, tangled and connecting and yet keeping its own place. It is a bush that burns without being consumed.

Hearken to Her Voice: Empathy as Teshuva[1]

Marsha Pravder Mirkin

On Rosh Hashana we read the tragic and transforming family story of Sarah, Hagar, Abraham, Ishmael, and Isaac. We read it on a holiday, that emphasizes *teshuva,* turning around, becoming a better person, living a life closer to what God wants from us. How can we experience *teshuva?* The clues, I believe, are in the story. The clues, when pulled from the story, teach us that *teshuva* needs to include empathy, empathic listening, paying attention, hearing beyond words to the soul and meaning of what is uttered. With this idea in mind, let us revisit the story of our foreparents.

Retelling the Story

The background to the Rosh Hashana reading begins with Abraham and Sarah unable to fulfill the covenant because of their childlessness (Genesis 16). As was accepted at the time, Sarah suggested that her Egyptian handmaid, Hagar, bear a child with Abraham. This arrangement could elevate Sarah's status in a society where a woman's worth was determined by her fertility.[2] Hagar had no choice in the matter. She became pregnant, and the infertile Sarah felt despised by Hagar. Sarah felt wronged, yet she did not question the system that connected women's worth to reproductive capacity. Instead she became abusive toward Hagar. Neither God nor Abraham intervened.

Finally, the abuse became intolerable and a pregnant Hagar ran away to become the first woman in the Torah to be approached by a messenger of God. The messenger sent her back to Sarah, with the promise that she too would be a mother of a great nation. Hagar, spunk intact, becomes the first woman in the Torah to come up with a name for God, whom she called "El Ro'i," "Thou God Seest Me" (Genesis 16:13). Although Hagar might have felt invisible in the presence of Sarah and Abraham, she knew that she was not invisible to God. The well was named after the One Who Saw Her, the God for whom race, class, and gender do not render people invisible. Hagar then returned to give birth to Ishmael.

Sarah and Abraham, both aged, were then told by a messenger of God that Sarah would have a son (Genesis 18). The Rosh Hashana reading (Genesis 21) brings us to the time when Sarah feared that Ishmael would compete for Isaac's birthright and status. She dealt with her fear by asking Abraham to send Hagar and Ishmael away, which he did, giving them pitifully little water and food. In the desert God intervened after Hagar, desperately thirsty and fearing that her son would die, sat apart from her son and cried. A messenger of God told Hagar to hold her son. God then opened Hagar's eyes, at which point she discovered a fountain of water. God again promised to make Ishmael a great nation. The last we hear of Hagar is when she became the only woman in the Bible to choose a wife for her son, reasserting her ethnicity by choosing for him an Egyptian woman.

The Backdrop: Failures of Empathy[3]

The story unfolds as a powerful example of both the joys of empathy and the devastation caused by its absence. The failures of empathy in the story are most repeatedly demonstrated by Abraham. There is no indication that Abraham responded empathically to Sarah's childlessness. Unlike our Rosh Hashana *Haftara* story, in which Hannah was reassured by her husband that their relationship is important even if she bears no children (I Samuel 1), here Abraham never expresses such reassurance to Sarah. Unlike Isaac, who prayed to God to allow his wife to conceive (Genesis 25), Abraham never prayed on his wife's behalf. When Sarah turned to Abraham in anguish and said, "I have given my maid into thy bosom; and when she saw that she had conceived, I was despised in her eyes" (Genesis 16:5), Abraham did not address the feelings that brought Sarah to this level of hopelessness and frustration. Instead Abraham told Sarah to do whatever she desired with Hagar. Rather than appreciating and responding to Sarah's distress, rather than listening empathically to her feelings, Abraham seemed to wash his hands of the situation. Frustrated, misunderstood, and alone, Sarah took out her anger on the hapless servant.

Sarah should have known better than to turn to Abraham for support. Abraham more than once demonstrated that he was incapable of
mutuality in their relationship. Earlier, when Abraham and Sarah
went to Egypt, Abraham wanted to guarantee himself a safe journey.
So he told Pharaoh that Sarah was his sister, allowing Pharaoh to take
Sarah as his wife and sleep with her, and Pharaoh rewarded Abraham
with wealth. Abraham demonstrated no empathy with Sarah's
plight—it was Pharaoh who, after finding out about the deception,
was guilt ridden. And Abraham, allowed to keep Pharaoh's gifts,
never learned that what he did was wrong. In spite of Abraham's un-
conscionable behavior, it didn't dawn on Sarah to be angry at the
powerful Abraham or to find support and friendship from Hagar.
(Years later, Abraham repeated this injustice. This time, when Sarah
was about to become pregnant with Isaac, Abraham tried to convince
Abimelech that Sarah was his sister and again received much wealth
when Abimelech took her for a wife. God intervened before Abimelech could touch Sarah, and although Abimelech angrily berated
Abraham for his scheme, Abraham showed no remorse.)

In her own bereft state, Sarah tried and failed to get Abraham to
listen to her despair about Hagar despising her. Sarah thought Hagar
mocked her because of her childlessness. This self-involved focus on
her own childlessness made her incapable of appreciating Hagar's
feelings and led to another failure of empathy. Perhaps Hagar was despising Sarah not for her childlessness, but rather for her nonem-
pathic way of dealing with her childlessness. Hagar was about to bear
a baby not just for Abraham, but for Sarah. He was to be brought up
in the ways of the Hebrews, not the Egyptians. Once this baby was
born, Hagar would lose her maternity and her opportunity to pass on
her ethnicity. Hagar's defiance—her struggle to keep her integrity intact and her wish to maintain her maternal presence even after the
birth of her son—was misunderstood by Sarah to be another slight,
another reprimand saying that Sarah was worthless because she
could not conceive a child.

At first, Sarah turned to Abraham, saying, "My wrong be upon
thee" (Genesis 16:5). Sarah recognized how wrong she had been to assume that she could obtain a child through Hagar. Initially she
blamed Abraham for that error. Perhaps she recognized that if Abraham had been able to support, value, and comfort her, she might not

have needed to resort to this way of getting a son. Perhaps she now understood that Hagar would not simply turn the child she had borne over to Sarah and that Hagar's influence over this child would not disappear. (In fact, the text clearly suggests this outcome by stating that Hagar bore a son to Abraham, not to Abraham and Sarah.) For a fleeting moment, Sarah confronted Abraham's lack of empathy toward her by blaming the present situation on him. But the moment passed and Sarah lashed out at Hagar instead of Abraham. So Sarah became the oppressor as well as the oppressed, too caught up in her own sorrow to reach out to her servant with that woman-to-woman empathy that could transcend their ethnic and class differences.

Hearken to Her Words

With this as a backdrop, we get to the heart of the Rosh Hashana lesson about empathy: the casting out of Ishmael and Hagar. By the time Isaac was born, Abraham already had thirteen years to develop a relationship with Ishmael. Sarah, seeing this strong bond, worried that Ishmael would be Abraham's heir along with Isaac. Driven by her fear and insecurity and unable to express her fears directly to a man who previously had been unable to listen to her, Sarah demanded of Abraham that he turn out Hagar and Ishmael.

God intervened and told Abraham to listen or hearken to Sarah's voice, *shema bekola* (Genesis 21:12), and then promised to make nations of both his sons. Traditional interpretation takes these verses to imply that God meant Abraham to obey Sarah and expel Ishmael. Such traditional interpretations often hear language through a patriarchal sensibility. However, a feminist understanding of this language creates a world of difference between "listening to her voice" and "obeying." Sarah was distraught, she was lonely, she was frightened. She needed Abraham to empathize with her feelings, to listen to her feelings. As I often tell the couples I see in psychotherapy, there is a maxim that men say, "Don't just sit there, do something!" while women say, "Don't just do something, sit there." Sarah needed Abraham to sit there in empathy. She did not need him to take action, nor do we need to hear God's words as a request that Abraham take action.

Many parents who have more than one child can relate to a conversation that parallels the one between Sarah and Abraham. How many older siblings have told their parents, "I don't want this baby brother anymore! Bring him back to the hospital!" I hope that we could listen to that child, even though we are not planning to obey her words. In listening, we try to hear empathically the jealousy and pain that are behind the words of the older child. We try to make that child feel truly loved and appreciated within the expanded family. I don't think it would have dawned on many of us to wrap the newborn baby in a blanket and return him to the hospital! Is that really what God wanted from Abraham?

I believe God was saying, "Listen to Sarah, hear her feelings, be empathic with Sarah. Then, let her know there's no reason to compete, there's room enough for both boys to grow up with my blessings." Abraham, instead, acted. He didn't listen or question, but simply turned his son into the wilderness, where he could die.

In the wilderness for the second time, Hagar suffered feelings of desperation and helplessness that led to her own loss of empathy. She sat away from Ishmael and cried about his impending death rather than holding him and comforting him in his pain. Perhaps the Torah registers this lack of empathy when it tells us that "God heard the cry of the lad" (Genesis 21:17), not of Hagar. God teaches Hagar how to regain empathy: "Arise, lift up the lad, and hold him in thy hand" (Genesis 21:18). God instructed Hagar to reach out to her son, to transcend her self-absorption. By holding Ishmael, by being able to sit there with him, Hagar regained her attentiveness and was able to see the lifesaving water: "And God opened her eyes and she saw a well of water" (Genesis 21:19). When Hagar filled the bottle of water and gave it first to Ishmael, rather than taking it for herself, we see a true example of *teshuva*.

The themes of empathy and *teshuva* reemerge in the other story we read on Rosh Hashana, the *Akeda* (Genesis 22). In the story above, Abraham interpreted God to mean that he should sacrifice Ishmael, and he does so, in spite of Hagar's grief. In the story of the *Akeda,* Abraham interpreted God to mean that he should sacrifice Isaac, leaving Sarah bereft. Although there is nothing in the text indicating Sarah was present on the morning of the *Akeda,* I imagine that when she saw her son walking into the wilderness, already too far for her to call to him and in her mind never to return, she might have finally understood Hagar. At the moment of the *Akeda,* Sarah could emotionally connect with Hagar in their common horror that Abraham was willing to sacrifice his sons for an ideal.

Moments of Empathy

If the people we read about on Rosh Hashana were perfect, there would be no need for our foreparents to do *teshuva* and we would be taught no lessons about empathy. The beauty of our tradition is that its stories are about good but imperfect people, people who at times can be much wiser than ourselves but at times can make mistakes that are even more devastating than our own. Their failures are all the more tragic because they have also experienced brilliant moments of empathy.

After Hagar gives birth to Ishmael, we read "And Avram called *his son's* name, *whom Hagar bore,* Ishmael" (Genesis 16:15). At that moment, Abraham is able to claim Ishmael as his son, not solely as a maid's son or as an offspring who serves the purpose of fulfilling the covenant, but as a son in his own right with whom there is a meaningful connection. Also, at that moment, Hagar is acknowledged in her personhood, not as a maid or as a surrogate for Sarah, but as a full person who bore a son.

Later, when God foreshadows the birth of Isaac, Abraham responds to God from the depths of his heart: "O that Ishmael might live before thee!" (Genesis 17:18). His love for Ishmael, his known son, exceeds his excitement about the son to be born. He sadly recognizes the implications for Ishmael of this new son, his son with Sarah, fulfilling the covenant. Abraham is comforted by God, and God promises that although the covenant is with Isaac, Ishmael will be blessed and become a great nation. The consequence of Abraham's love for Ishmael is that two great nations will call him their father.

Abraham's empathy is evident again when he hears about the impending destruction of Sodom and Gomorra (Genesis 18). There, he argues and negotiates persistently with God, and God supports Abraham by agreeing not to destroy the city if even ten good people are found in Sodom.

Yet even after these powerful empathic experiences, Abraham

again passed Sarah off as his sister, later expelled Hagar and Ishmael, and finally, as I understand it, did not listen to God carefully enough and thus brought Isaac to be sacrificed.

Toward Teshuva

This sequence of the Sarah-Hagar story followed by the *Akeda* teaches an important lesson about the obstacles one faces in developing empathy. It culminates when Abraham is able to do *teshuva*—to hear, listen, and respond to God's voice telling him not to kill Isaac. The ability to hear attentively the voice of God, the voice that says "listen to Sarah" and does not mean obey, the voice that says "do not kill Isaac," is the essence of *teshuva*.

We see that the primary obstacle to *teshuva* is the failure to pay attention to our own experience and to the experience of others. During Hagar's pregnancy, Sarah could not resonate with Hagar's experience of wanting a child and yet fearing his loss. When Sarah told Abraham to get rid of Hagar and Ishmael, he could not hear the pain, loneliness, and fear behind her words. Similarly, had Abraham paid attention and truly listened for the voice of God, he could not have bound his son. Perhaps the test of the *Akeda* was whether Abraham was sufficiently attentive to hear the critical contradiction in God's instructions: God said, "Take now thy son, *thy only son Isaac*" (Genesis 22:2). Yet God had already recognized both Isaac and Ishmael as Abraham's sons. Had he listened, Abraham could have responded to the contradiction by saying that he had two sons whom he loved. Initially Abraham did not listen carefully enough[4] and therefore failed to respond in the way I believe God wanted. Yet just as Hagar experienced *teshuva* when she heard God's voice in the wilderness, held her son, and then saw water, Abraham experienced *teshuva* when he listened to the true voice of God telling him not to kill Isaac, stopped the action, and then saw the ram-offering. When Abraham was at last able to listen attentively and respond empathically, he experienced *teshuva* and thus finally passed God's test.

But what about Sarah? What was her experience of *teshuva*? After Sarah tells Abraham to cast out Hagar and Ishmael, we never hear another word from her. I imagine a lonely, jealous, loving, wise, and sometimes shortsighted woman waking up the next morning and discovering that Hagar and Ishmael are gone, that Abraham took literally the words she meant figuratively. I imagine her horror when she realized that her words led to the abandonment and possible death of the boy she had wanted for a son and the woman who served her for so many years. I imagine that she felt so guilty that her words wronged others so severely, she vowed never again to hurt another with her words. Then she silenced herself. Tragically, her silence precluded a final movement toward *teshuva,* toward speaking words that by authentically reflecting our inner experience allow us to move closer to each other and to God.

While Sarah was very much responsible for the wrongs done to Hagar, she was not solely responsible. Inflammatory words announced publicly certainly can be dangerous, as we witnessed so tragically in the assassination of Yitzhak Rabin. Yet in our private realm we hope that our partners can not only hear our words, but also help us understand them at a deeper level so that we can find new words that more meaningfully reflect our experience. What a betrayal if, even in our private lives, inflammatory words become dangerous because somebody chooses to act on them! Sarah's words to Abraham arose from and only partly expressed her complicated feelings but in themselves did not harm Hagar or Ishmael. It was Abraham's response to the words that caused pain. While we never hear either Abraham or Sarah explicitly acknowledge the wrong done Hagar and Ishmael, I hear Sarah's silence as an acceptance of her responsibility. Instead of using the power of her words to right the wrong, she became frightened of her words and was silent.

In my reading, Sarah took her lapses of empathy to heart and could not forgive herself for them. As a result, her experience of *teshuva* was only partial, because while she "turned" and was remorseful, she never completed the turn to a more full and meaningful life. This reading is supported by the report of Sarah's death: "Sarah was one hundred and twenty-seven years old: these were the years of Sarah's life" (Genesis 23:1). This statement contrasts with the report of Abraham's death, where he is described as dying "full of years" (Genesis 25:8). The implication is that Abraham lived his life fully—that the experience of *teshuva* led him to a life full of meaning. Sarah, on the other hand, simply had years, many years, but not full years. By Sarah's example, guilt and remorse are not enough for *teshuva:* reparation and living a full life of attentiveness and empathy complete the turn. Perhaps we can allow ourselves to feel the sorrow that Sarah lived and died with, learn from her, and move toward our own *teshuva*.

This family story is a cautionary tale of how lack of empathy comes back to haunt us. Through it we come to appreciate that many of the disconnections we feel and are called upon to repair during the Days of Awe result from lack of attention and lack of empathy. Empathy is, in some ways, a halt to the action. It is valuing another person enough to listen and hear her voice, not her voice as a mirror of our own. It is a halting that then allows us to take action, action that brings us closer to becoming the best we can be rather than action that could be exploitative. Empathy is the active ingredient of *teshuva,* propelling us to turn in a direction that is closer to ourselves, our loved ones, and God.

On Rosh Hashana we ask God to be empathic toward us, even though empathy was often so lacking in ourselves and in our foreparents. We realize that we address God without an intermediary because our foreparents were simply human beings, just like us, with all their human strengths and weaknesses. These stories leave us with the hope that *teshuva* is possible, if only we can commit ourselves to being more fully empathic human beings.

Returning to Sarah

Tamara R. Cohen

As the High Holy Days approach, I find myself involved in three levels of *teshuva* (repentance, return). First, there is the internal process of returning to myself. I ask myself for forgiveness for the ways in which I have not been a good enough friend and caretaker of my body and soul. I also need to forgive myself, and this is just as difficult as the acknowledgment of the need for *teshuva*.

The next level of *teshuva* is that which the rabbis call *bein adam lechavero,* between an individual and his or *her* friends and fellow human beings. There are many relationships to consider—loved ones, relatives, friends, and co-workers. I currently work in a Jewish feminist organization and find myself particularly interested in the stumbling blocks that impede relationships between women, some of which are very particular. So I want to call a subset of this category of *teshuva* the process of *teshuva bein isha le'isha,* women turning toward each other.

When I was younger I learned that one had to ask forgiveness of others three times, and then, no matter the answer, the duty of *teshuva* was complete. Now my life demands a model that goes far beyond "I am sorry, I am sorry, I am sorry." I want to be able to acknowledge the way that differences between individuals can be painful but also strengthening. I am especially interested in finding ways out of the destructive envy that can cripple relationships between women. I want to find a model of *teshuva* that moves toward realization of how much we have to gain from being a collective as opposed to exceptional individual women who have made it in a man's world precisely by rejecting alliances with other women.

Then, of course, there's God, the Divine, or in the words of the wonderful traditional phrase *teshuva bein adam lamakom* (between a person and God). Because my reckoning with God is not confined to repentance for "sins" committed against God, I see this level of *teshuva* as an opportunity to continue working through the very complex relationship I have with God, as a Jewish feminist. Thus, for me, *teshuva* between women and God implies not just God holding me responsible for the ways I have failed to be a human being, but also me holding God responsible for failing me as a Jewish woman by giving me a world and a people and a text that continue to betray women, often making it difficult for us to uphold our side of the covenant.

❖

It is with these three levels of *teshuva* in mind that I want to approach the text of the Torah reading for the first day of Rosh Hashana.

The *Parasha* (Torah reading) of the first day of Rosh Hashana begins with the story of Sarah giving birth to Isaac. I have always understood this reading as primarily a preparation for the more important reading of the second day, the *Akeda*. More recently I have been drawn back to this first day reading by a nagging discomfort with my feelings about the main character, our foremother Sarah.

How is it that I am supposed to embrace Sarah as the mother of the Jewish people when the primary image in my mind is that of her ugly treatment and banishment of her maidservant Hagar? And why is it that I am forced to confront the story of this mistreatment of an Egyptian slavewoman by my foremother not once a year but twice, on its Shabbat cycle and on the first day of Rosh Hashana? Who is Sarah? And what does she have to teach me about these processes of *teshuva*—within myself, between me and others (particularly women), and between me and the Divine?

Sarah and the Return to the Self

I begin with Sarah. She is one hundred and twenty-seven years old and her husband and son are far away on a mountaintop. But she is not alone. I do not want to imagine our mother Sarah dying alone. So I strain my ears and pick up my *machzor* (High Holy Day prayer book) and listen. I close my eyes and peer far back into my wilderness memory and wait. "Sarah, I need you to speak to me," I whisper.

I begin with *teshuva*. Not repentance in its stiff, starched whites, but return like a spiral of purple silks. Not a beating of my chest, but a soothing hand on my heart. I want to be involved in a process of *teshuva* that lets me see where I have failed without drowning me in the self-doubt I am finally learning my way out of. I want a *teshuva* that is about integrating different parts of myself and understanding that the more whole I allow myself to be, the closer I will come to righteousness.

The character of Sarai (Sarah before her name change) is introduced into the Torah text with three descriptions. Sarai is the wife of Abram; she has no children; and she has a maidservant named Hagar (Genesis 16:1). The first two identifications for Sarai are common ones for women of the Bible. Women are most often identified by to whom they are married and to whom they give birth (as well as whose daughters they are). But why immediately identify Sarai also through her relationship with her slave?

Within the answer to this question lies my first reading of the *Parasha* of Rosh Hashana's first day. I want to suggest a reading of the *Parasha* that imagines Hagar and Sarah as two parts of one woman. Who would this Sarahagar woman be? She would be a woman who could build herself up on her own, not needing to manipulate and take advantage of others to do so (see Genesis 16:2). She would be a woman who would not have to exile any part of herself in order to maintain a sense of power and importance. She would be a woman whose laughter *and* crying would be heard by God.

As long as there is conflict between Hagar and Sarah, neither can be fully at peace with the range of her own womanhood—barren and fertile, slave and master, sexually desirable to men and reproductively linked only to God. The truth is Sarah is all of these things, as is Hagar. But in banishing Hagar, Sarah allows herself to be permanently split off from parts of her own experience of womanhood.

Each of us has, at one time or another, felt the need to send a piece of ourselves out into the wilderness to die. Perhaps that piece of ourselves reminded us too much of what we were like before being "remembered by God" or noticed by someone who made us feel creative long after we thought our creativity had "dried up." Each of us who wants to dwell (*gar*) like a princess (*sar*) in her own safe tent fears the stranger (*ger*) within her who keeps being drawn back to the desert. We don't want our quiet chosen miraculous selves playing games with that within us that is wild and untamed like Ishmael.

But listen. Listen beyond the text. Pick up your *machzor* and put it to your ear like a seashell. Listen to the faint crackling sound more like fire than ocean. Hear in Sarah's laughter the giggling tears. Hear her bitterness, hysteria, sarcasm, and cynicism. Hear the joyous, care-free, all-knowing, childlike laughter of a pregnant barren woman of ninety; a woman who will die, according to Rashi, with the inno-cence, beauty, and wisdom of a girl of seven, a woman of twenty, and a crone of one hundred.

Teshuva is an opportunity to return to oneself. Refusing to be frag-mented by systems or people who cannot withstand our power, we honor the memories of Sarah and Hagar, the laughing woman remem-bered and the crying woman provided for by God. In undertaking the process of *teshuva,* we open ourselves up to the connection be-tween the waters that finally broke between Sarah's legs and the deep well Hagar saw when she finally opened her eyes.

Another Look at the Conflict Between Sarah and Hagar

The relationship between Sarah and Hagar is one of the most trou-bling relationships for me in the entire Torah. As the very first exam-ple of a relationship between women in the Torah, it sets out a model of interaction that will not be redressed even by the unique relation-ship between Ruth and Naomi in the Book of Ruth at the very end of the Bible.

When I pick up my *machzor* and listen to this story, it is most of-ten Hagar's cries in the desert that I hear. What I find is far from a model of *teshuva*. Instead of returning, Sarah casts out. Instead of asking Hagar for forgiveness for the way she treated her in the previ-ous chapter, Sarah here does the opposite. She expels Hagar and her son for the second time.

Instead of teaching her son reconciliation, she casts out his play-mate, Ishmael, choosing to read their play together as dangerous. In taking this action, Sarah perpetuates the conflict between herself and Hagar to the next generation. The perpetuation of the conflict, of course, does not stop there.

When the Torah text first introduces Sarai she is an active, vocal woman who basically controls the show. She is the one who begins a conversation about children in the first place. She offers her own explanation for her childlessness (blaming it on God), and she proposes her own solution. It is only after Abram carries out the deed that the problems that chapter 21 (the Rosh Hashana text) inherits are born.

> And he came unto Hagar and she conceived and she saw that she had conceived and her mistress became lesser in her eyes. And Sarai said to her husband, "I am angry with you. I gave my servant into your arms and then she found out she conceived and I became lesser in her eyes. May God judge between you and me." And Abram said to Sarai, "Here, your servant is in your hands, do whatever you want with her." And Sarai treated her harshly and she escaped from her.

Why doesn't the Torah offer us a model of *teshuva* through Sarah's actions? On one level, the answer is very clear to me. The primary objective of this text is to ensure that the covenant between God and Abraham is passed on successfully to Isaac, Sarah's son. Since Ishmael is a threat to this inheritance, he must be gotten rid of. Sarah is simply clearing the way for God's plan.

Even though I understand that this is the motivation of the text, I am also much more suspicious of it. I believe that the Bible text does not want to imagine a bond between these two women. Virginia Woolf has pointed out how profoundly the absence of such a bond pervades secular literature. The absence is all the more painful in a text that is not only literature, but history and identity. I believe that this absence is not incidental.

The text depends on structures of class and ethnicity to keep Sarah and Hagar from relating to each other. Since the text needs to establish one chosen son, it cannot withstand a bond between these two women. Such a bond would threaten the design of Biblical patriarchy.

What happens in the foregoing critical verses is that Sarai goes from seeing herself as a woman with creative power to seeing herself as a woman so weak that her only power derives from hurting another woman. There is no reason to believe that Sarah's not having children was a major factor of her life before her move to Canaan. But once she has entered the land and, more important, the covenant, her procreative status becomes tantamount.

In the universe of Genesis, where what ultimately counts is being the chosen one who will pass on the covenant to the next generation,

there is room only for one woman and one man. As soon as Sarai real-
izes that she may not be God's choice for the position of "woman," because Hagar has been chosen, her sense of power is diminished. Sarai
then tries one last formulation that would allow her to maintain her
power. When she challenges Abram with the words "May God judge
between you and me," she is operating out of a self-image where she
is not on the level of Hagar at all, she is on par with Abram. It is almost as if Sarai is here saying, "Okay, if you won't consider me for the
position of procreator [the woman's position in this covenant], then,
God, choose me over Abram for the position of primary holder of
the covenant." It is only when Abram totally undercuts this self-
perception of Sarai's by offering his chattel back to Sarai that she
gives in totally. Sarai accepts that her only power is over Hagar, and
as a woman bitter over this defeat, she takes out her anger at Abram
and God on the only person lower in status than she, Hagar.

The Sarah we meet in the reading for Rosh Hashana is this defeated
Sarah, only now pregnant. While this late pregnancy might serve to
help Sarah regain her self-image, I think it does not. She remains a
bitter woman who feels that God is laughing at her in his fulfillment
of a promise she didn't even ask for. I read Sarah's continued aggression toward Hagar in this portion as further indication of her distance
from herself. A woman whose last words in the Torah are words of
casting out is not a woman at peace with herself. She might be a
woman who has "made it" in a world where only one mother can be
the chosen one, but she is not a model of integration or *teshuva*
within oneself.

Even as I well up with anger against this image of Sarah, I fear giving up on her. As much as I don't want to forgive her or listen to anything she has to say, I know that she is in this *Parasha* for a reason.
Also, Sarah is the mother of the Jewish people. Adding her name to
Abraham's at the end of my *Amida* (silent prayer) has made prayer
more meaningful for me. Can I really afford to banish Sarah as she
banished Hagar?

So I listen to the text again. Not for the Sarah recorded in the text,
but for the Sarah who is not recorded. I listen and listen and then I
hear. Sarah is calling out for Hagar's companionship as she nears her
death and finds herself alone.

I do not believe Sarah was bad. She acted in a way that any "good Jewish mother" would probably act. She was willing to do anything to protect her son from harm. She was willing to do anything to protect her primary relationship from being threatened. She also wanted desperately to maintain whatever role she could get in a covenantal process that was excluding her almost completely. Each of us makes similar choices every day. We are able to work in high-powered jobs because we leave our children in the care of other women whose children are less well off than our own. We ask our secretaries to do the kind of work we always resented doing in the days before we got higher degrees. We agree to be token women on boards and panels, letting go of a vision that would insist on more women than just one.

Part of *teshuva* is about moving from a place of judgment against Sarah to a place of recognizing our identification with her. Are we being competitive with one another because we, too, operate in an academy or an institution or a family that revolves around men's power and can share only a limited amount of power with a limited number of women? When we are granted access to power in these kinds of structures, how do we use it? Do we use it to liberate other women or to hurt them as Sarah did?

Unless we first allow ourselves to identify with Sarah, unless we realize how much she is us, we will not be able to move beyond the dualistic thinking of Isaac or Ishmael, me or Hagar. I believe that each of us who allows differences between women to keep us apart is playing into the hand of a structure that will ultimately rob us of all our power. Hagar might be the obvious victim of the story, but Sarah loses too.

Imagine Sarah nearing her death and calling out for a woman friend to hold her hand. Imagine Hagar hearing the voice, across desert miles and many years of silence. Does Hagar come? Does Sarah embrace her? What do these two tired mothers say to each other? Do they learn to see each other with eyes that look not for differences that will keep them apart (Genesis 16:4), but for the ties that will help them see their own beauty in each other's gaze?

Let us not wait until our one hundred and twenty-seventh year to return to women whose differences we fear or with whom we feel competitive. *Teshuva* is an opportunity to open new, unimagined dialogues between women, focusing on what's really keeping us apart and how we might move beyond it.

Helping God Remember Sarah

The Torah reading for the first day of Rosh Hashana begins with the sentence "And God remembered Sarah" (Genesis 21:1). The most common and simple way to understand this sentence is to read it as directly connected to the one that follows it: "And Sarah conceived and gave birth to a son for Abraham in his old age" (Genesis 21:2). Thus, God's remembering of Sarah is a remembering of the promise to give Sarah a child. Yet the text does not say, as it could have, "And God remembered God's promise to Sarah." The text says, "God remembered Sarah." Furthermore, since the text never actually describes Sarah asking God for a child, I do not feel bound to understand God's remembrance of Sarah as simply related to conception.

Instead I'd like to suggest that the sentence "And God remembered Sarah" can be read as a sort of chapter heading for the entire story. What does it mean that God remembered Sarah? First of all, it means that God had forgotten her.

For me, this sentence represents a profound moment in Torah. Sarah was indeed forgotten. Sarah was not directly addressed by God with the words *Lekhi lakh* (go forth, in feminine) when her husband was personally told to go to Canaan. Sarah was not spoken to by the messengers of God that visited her family tent. Sarah was always assumed to be present but never directly remembered.

It is true that God defends Sarah's voice to Abraham. But this does not constitute a remembering. The voice that God defends is the voice that serves as a vessel of God's will. Sarah's voice is right because it is the one that confirms and strengthens Isaac's position as Abraham's heir. What is forgotten in this text is a voice of Sarah's that is listened to not just by Abraham, but by God. A voice with enough authority to truly change the story.

This "forgetting" will happen again and again, throughout the Bible and throughout history. Sarah's daughters won't be remembered. Her granddaughters and great-granddaughters will be totally forgotten.

Thus I want to suggest a reading of this first sentence that sees in it a promise not to be fulfilled in the text, but to be fulfilled in the studying and interpreting of the text by women in the future, women today. In this sentence God is taking responsibility for having forgotten Sarah and is promising to remember her. This promise will take centuries to complete. God has done a lot of forgetting of women. But if we can hear in these words God's intention to do *teshuva* with women, then we can be freed to see our struggles with the text and our reinterpretation of it as holy work. By daring to imagine God's *teshuva*, we elevate the importance of our work in recovering the untold stories of Jewish women.

If we use what we've learned in our lives to complete the unfinished stories of our foremothers in the Torah, then we are accepting our role as partners to God in a *teshuva* of Jewish history and memory. When we strain to hear the silenced voices of Sarah and Hagar and other women in the text who say even less than they do, we are helping them complete their stories. By writing our own *midrashim* and by living our own integrated lives, we are aiding God in the fulfillment of the Torah's words by truly and fully remembering Sarah.

Brothers and Others

SIDRA DEKOVEN EZRAHI

And the Lord singled out Sarah as He had said, and the Lord did for Sarah as He had spoken. And Sarah conceived and bore a son to Abraham in his old age at the set time that God had spoken to him. . . . And Abraham made a great feast on the day Isaac was weaned. And Sarah saw the son of Hagar the Egyptian, whom she had born to Abraham, laughing [metzachek]. And she said to Abraham, "Drive out this slavegirl and her son, for the slavegirl's son shall not inherit with my son, with Isaac."
(GENESIS 21:1–2, 8–10)

Genesis 21 is a story of births. The miraculous birth of Isaac is recounted and the birth of Ishmael is recalled. Begats establish lineage; births establish origins. But the second son "born to Abraham" creates a need for hierarchy, and the characters regroup for a family portrait that reflects the new order. Without the high drama of Genesis 22, this chapter foreshadows all of its themes, most specifically the *Akeda* (Binding of Isaac). Except that it all happens to the "other one," to the one who is not quite brother and not quite other. If he were fully fraternal, he (and his mother) would stay and fight for the birthright; if he were completely exogamous, he would have nothing to stay for—or to laugh about—in the first place.

That may be the site of our greatest conundrum, then as now. Who is this Ishmael, son of Abraham, and who are all his sons and daughters? Do the rules of family lineage, rivalry, and honor prevail among the progeny of Abraham or the rules of tribal and ethnic competition?

Chapter 21 outlines all the social and religious landscapes on which our stories of origin and destination will be foregrounded: when Isaac is born, ol' Abe makes a big party in Gerar (urbanity, social status, and stasis); when Hagar and Ishmael are sent away, they go to the wilderness of Beersheba (desert solitude, revelation, and possibility). The passage itself is a shadow play of both the *Akeda* and the Exodus from Egypt.[1] But from where I sit, it appears more than anything as the first instance of violent disgorgement stemming from the inability to separate. The struggle in the ancient, as in the modern, Middle East is between engorgement and separation, between proximity and invisibility.

So the task I set before myself on the first day of Rosh Hashana, when the Torah reading opens with, and all attention focuses on, the divine memory of the promise to Sarah and of the covenant with Abraham, is to summon the effaced memory of the other woman and the other son—effaced not because they are strangers, but precisely because they are too familiar.

Abraham casts Ishmael into the wilderness, which is the place of potentiality, of becoming. The casting-off could be seen as a gesture that divides property and grants autonomy, especially since Abraham was assured by God that the boy would somehow be saved and would engender a great nation: "And God said to Abraham: . . . 'But the slavegirl's son, too, I will make a nation, for he is your seed'" (Genesis 21:13). But this act is complicated because Ishmael is not *granted* the territory to which he is sent, as part of a division of the land, as was his cousin Lot before him:

> And Abram said to Lot: "Pray, let there be no contention between you and me, between your herdsmen and mine; for we are kinsmen. Is not all the land before you? Pray, let us part company; if you take the left hand, then I shall go right; and if you take the right hand, I shall go left." (Genesis 13:8–9)

Ishmael is not separated, he does not "part company," from Isaac; he is, rather, cast off, blending into the landscape—neither separate nor autonomous, but a repressed, invisible, presence:

> And Abraham rose early in the morning and took bread and a skin of water and gave them to Hagar, placing them on her shoulder, and he gave her the child, and sent her away, and she went wandering through the wilderness of Beer-sheba. And when the water in the skin was gone, she flung the child under one of the bushes and went off and sat down at a distance, a bowshot away, for she thought, "Let me not see when the child dies." And she sat at a distance and raised her voice and wept. (Genesis 21:14–16)

So she set him down where she could not see him, and of course where Sarah and Abraham and baby Isaac could not see him. Only God and the angels saw Ishmael, as he was dehydrating under the blazing desert sun.

In a way, Hagar and Ishmael are still there: just beyond eyesight, under the bushes, not quite visible because they are so well camouflaged.

In *Children of the Earth,* Marc Shell argues that there is an inherent tolerance built into particularist as opposed to universalist schemes of collective definition. Christianity, according to this reading, posits universalism based on brotherly love—implying, necessarily, that anyone who is not a brother is not human, not part of the "family of man," and that if all humans are defined as siblings, then the only possible relations are either celibate or incestuous. What Shell defines as "the particularism of Judaism," on the other hand, encourages "tolerant coexistence insofar as its ancient Hebrew Commonwealth had rules recognizing that there are not only Jewish siblings but also other human beings" and that "those 'others' have specific legal and political rights as human beings."[2] That is, the religion based on brotherly love proves to be (by the evidence of history as of logic) exclusive because of its inclusivity, and the avowedly particularist religions promise to be more tolerant because they can conceive of other particularities. (Shell argues that Islam is fundamentally a particularistic and therefore a tolerant religion as well.)

This argument is highly problematic at best, but the Jewish recognition of discrete particularities would not in any case apply to the children of Ishmael, who are not fully brothers—but who, being brothers of a sort, cannot be fully others. . . .

The brotherhood of Isaac and Ishmael is complicated by the role of Hagar, who does not have the status of wife in her own right but is rather a stand-in for Sarai—at least until the latter conceives her own child: *"ulai ibane mimena"* ("perhaps I shall be built up through her"—Genesis 16:2), Sarai says as she proposes her handmaiden to Abram.[3] Hagar's surrogate status, against the background of Abraham's repeated strategy of passing off Sarah as his sister, may have prompted the medieval commentators to reshuffle the kinship so that Isaac and Ishmael would appear not as brothers, but as *cousins*. But in effect they are both—as, by Abraham's account to Abimelech, Sarah is indeed " 'my sister, my father's daughter, though not my mother's daughter' " (Genesis 20:12). Sarah's issue, then, would be both Abraham's son *and* his nephew, making Isaac and Ishmael both brothers and cousins. . . . The rules of kinship are still applicable, but the danger of incest is obscured. As is the prospect of fratricide when the relationship becomes coded in Jewish memory as inimical.

> And God heard the voice of the lad and God's messenger called out from the heavens and said to her, "What troubles you, Hagar? Fear not, for God has heard the lad's voice where he is." (Genesis 21:17)

Ishmael's vulnerability signals for many commentators his future aggression. Rashi glosses the previous passage by conflating it with Isaiah 21; he explains that "where he is" refers to the primordial state of kinship between Isaac and Ishmael: when the children of Israel were being led into Babylonian captivity by Nebuchadnezzar and spied *orchot dedanim* (a convoy of Dedanites), they said to their captors, *"Holikheinu etzel benei dodeinu Yishma'el"* ("lead us to our cousin Ishmael"), "misreading" *dedanim* (Dedanites) as *dodim* (cousins) (whereupon, Rashi adds in vivid detail, their Arabian "cousins" greeted them with the treachery worthy of their contemptuous reputation). To this day Israeli Jews refer to the Arabs, with a mixture of familiarity and scorn, as *benei dodeinu*.

And that is what makes the Zionist enterprise, some millennia down the line, just a bit more than a colonial venture of the conventional sort, or even of the "Orientalist" sort: it is the total embracing of the Arab as brother or doppelgänger or cousin—the model of cooptation through incorporation rather than either coexistence or conversion. It is the definition of the Arab as primordial Jewish *self* that colors the portraits of Arab-Jewish encounters in the Hebrew culture

of the *Yishuv* (period before statehood) and the early years of the Israeli state. The narrator of Y. H. Brenner's story "Azabim" (Nerves,
1910) recounts his voyage to Palestine:

> Perhaps what kept . . . impelling me . . . to come here was simply a
> yearning for natural beauty . . . and also perhaps for a place to call
> my own, which as a Jew was something I had never had. . . . I may
> have been living all that time with the hope . . . of finding a
> foothold . . . in our picturesque ancestral corner of Asia, in which
> Bedouin, the great-grandchildren of Abraham the Hebrew, pitch
> their tents to this day and bring to the well real camels as once
> did his bondsman Eliezer . . . and in which . . . third- and fourth-
> generation children of Polish Jewish money-lenders are learning to
> follow the plow. . . .[4]

Such scenarios, which recur almost formulaically in Hebrew literature and landscape painting, reflect with a kind of geological preci-
sion the different semantic layers of attachment of the Jewish
immigrant to this land: the yearning for nature as a signal of a normal
relationship ("foothold") in space; the Biblical text as both a code of
memory and a travel guide; and the ubiquitous Bedouin, who is ro-
mantic embodiment of the self in a double sense. He (or she) is at once
the "autochthon," noble savage in an organic, preindustrialized connection to the land, *and* aboriginal Semite, ancestral Jew moving naturally in these surroundings next to the clumsy, plow- (later tractor-)
wielding children of Polish Jewish money lenders. The Bedouin, like
the Dead Sea Scrolls, becomes a relic of an authentic past, of the lost
self. But the Bedouin or the Arab who is claimed as ancestral self then
becomes altogether invisible as other, *not because he is overlooked, but
because he is so totally incorporated and superseded.*

The denial of otherness may be one of the unspoken motives that
brought Jews "back" to Palestine from all four corners of the earth,
but especially from Eastern and central Europe.[5] The implications of
embracing the Arabs as manifestations of sameness become clearer
once we see how the language of "sameness" and of "homecoming"
overlap: coming "home" to a place that these Jews had never seen
may have been like owning as "cousins" people whom they never
knew . . . as if the place were waiting, bereft and frozen in time, to be
reunited with its wayward people. Edward Said laments the myth

that posits "the arrested development of the Semites": "The Semitic myth bifurcated in the Zionist movement; one Semite [the Jew] went the way of Orientalism, the other, the Arab, was forced to go the way of the Oriental. Each time tent and tribe are solicited, the myth is being employed."[6] But this association of the Arab with the past is a form of arrest that predates even the colonialist, Orientalist, and Zionist projects: the Holy Land, and by extension its inhabitants, are, in the Jewish vision of exile and redemption, in a state of suspension, awaiting the Return.

Jerusalem or Zion is the Center, and when the Jews begin to reconnect with the Center, everything within it becomes centrified. Ishmael is reengorged, and separation becomes, once again, all but impossible: the Center itself knows no bounds—it expands with the appetite of its people. (I am making a deliberate distinction here between the "inhabitants" of the land—perceived as so much shrubbery—and the "people" of the land, with whom the covenant was made.) Ishmael as distant cousin and aboriginal self can be a picturesque—or even useful—element in the landscape, but he is invisible as a separable other. It turns out that his task, all these years, was to guard the family territory until his brother would return to reclaim it—sort of like lizards awaiting the return of the dinosaurs.

For the self-styled nationalists in contemporary Israel, especially the religious nationalists, the claim to that primary "Semitic" kinship with the Palestinians is connected to the denial of their separate political identity and draws rhetorically and conceptually on an ancient tradition of effacement by engorgement. As long as Ishmael remained passive, he represented our lost self; when he began to reclaim his birthright, we had to follow the script and cast him out. Every time we would impose a *seger* (closure) on the West Bank and Gaza, we would cast Ishmael out, sealing him off hermetically from our sight and sending him to the wilderness to die of hunger and thirst.

If the center can expand almost infinitely in trying to approach the largely mythical boundaries of the ancient Biblical Holy Land, it can, by the very same logic, contract. When Israeli Jews are finally prepared to acknowledge in the Palestinians a significantly different set of cultural and religious codes and competing claims to Abraham's inheritance, they will also be prepared to give up the idea of the whole that swallows all of its parts. It is precisely the growing respect for, as well as the fear of, difference that makes the argument for separation a viable way to unlock the chains of myth that have bound Isaac and Ishmael, Sarah and Hagar, in a dance of engorgement and effacement. It is what may save the youngest of Abraham's progeny, that fragile child of Isaac and Ishmael called the Peace Process (temporary name), from being sacrificed, yet again, in our lifetime.

"And Hannah Prayed to the Lord" (I Samuel 1—2:10)

Haftara Reading—First Day Rosh Hashana

1 Now there was a certain man of Ramathaim-zophim, of the hill-country of Ephraim, and his name was Elkanah, the son of Jeroham, the son of Elihu, the son of Tohu, the son of Zuph, an Ephraimite. ²And he had two wives: the name of the one was Hannah, and the name of the other Peninnah; and Peninnah had children, but Hannah had no children. ³And this man went up out of his city from year to year to worship and to sacrifice unto the LORD of hosts in Shiloh. And the two sons of Eli, Hophni and Phinehas, were there priests unto the LORD. ⁴And it came to pass upon a day, when Elkanah sacrificed, that he gave to Peninnah his wife, and to all her sons and her daughters, portions; ⁵but unto Hannah he gave a double portion; for he loved Hannah, but the LORD had shut up her womb. ⁶And her rival vexed her sore, to make her fret, because the LORD had shut up her womb. ⁷And as he did so year by year, when she went up to the house of the LORD, so she vexed her; therefore she wept, and would not eat. ⁸And Elkanah her husband said unto her: 'Hannah, why weepest thou? and why eatest thou not? and why is thy heart grieved? am not I better to thee than ten sons?' ⁹So Hannah rose up after they had eaten in Shiloh, and after they had drunk—now Eli the priest sat upon his seat by the door-post of the temple of the LORD; ¹⁰and she was in bitterness of soul—and prayed unto the LORD, and wept sore ¹¹And she vowed a vow, and said: 'O LORD of hosts, if Thou wilt indeed look on the affliction of Thy handmaid, and

א וַיְהִי

אִישׁ אֶחָד מִן־הָרָמָתַיִם צוֹפִים מֵהַר
אֶפְרָיִם וּשְׁמוֹ אֶלְקָנָה בֶּן־יְרֹחָם בֶּן־
אֱלִיהוּא בֶּן־תֹּחוּ בֶן־צוּף אֶפְרָתִי׃
² וְלוֹ שְׁתֵּי נָשִׁים שֵׁם אַחַת חַנָּה
וְשֵׁם הַשֵּׁנִית פְּנִנָּה וַיְהִי לִפְנִנָּה
יְלָדִים וּלְחַנָּה אֵין יְלָדִים׃
³ וְעָלָה הָאִישׁ הַהוּא מֵעִירוֹ מִיָּמִים
יָמִימָה לְהִשְׁתַּחֲוֹת וְלִזְבֹּחַ לַיהֹוָה
צְבָאוֹת בְּשִׁלֹה וְשָׁם שְׁנֵי בְנֵי־עֵלִי
⁴ חָפְנִי וּפִנְחָס כֹּהֲנִים לַיהֹוָה׃ וַיְהִי
הַיּוֹם וַיִּזְבַּח אֶלְקָנָה וְנָתַן לִפְנִנָּה
אִשְׁתּוֹ וּלְכָל־בָּנֶיהָ וּבְנוֹתֶיהָ מָנוֹת׃
⁵ וּלְחַנָּה יִתֵּן מָנָה אַחַת אַפָּיִם כִּי אֶת־
חַנָּה אָהֵב וַיהֹוָה סָגַר רַחְמָהּ׃
⁶ וְכִעֲסַתָּה צָרָתָהּ גַּם־כַּעַס בַּעֲבוּר
הַרְּעִמָהּ כִּי־סָגַר יְהֹוָה בְּעַד רַחְמָהּ׃
⁷ וְכֵן יַעֲשֶׂה שָׁנָה בְשָׁנָה מִדֵּי עֲלֹתָהּ
בְּבֵית יְהֹוָה כֵּן תַּכְעִסֶנָּה וַתִּבְכֶּה וְלֹא
⁸ תֹאכַל׃ וַיֹּאמֶר לָהּ אֶלְקָנָה אִישָׁהּ
חַנָּה לָמֶה תִבְכִּי וְלָמֶה לֹא תֹאכְלִי
וְלָמֶה יֵרַע לְבָבֵךְ הֲלוֹא אָנֹכִי טוֹב לָךְ
⁹ מֵעֲשָׂרָה בָּנִים׃ וַתָּקָם חַנָּה אַחֲרֵי
אָכְלָה בְשִׁלֹה וְאַחֲרֵי שָׁתֹה וְעֵלִי
הַכֹּהֵן יֹשֵׁב עַל־הַכִּסֵּא עַל־מְזוּזַת
¹⁰ הֵיכַל יְהֹוָה׃ וְהִיא מָרַת נָפֶשׁ
וַתִּתְפַּלֵּל עַל־יְהֹוָה וּבָכֹה תִבְכֶּה׃
א וַתִּדֹּר נֶדֶר וַתֹּאמַר יְהֹוָה צְבָאוֹת אִם־
רָאֹה תִרְאֶה ׀ בָּעֳנִי אֲמָתֶךָ וּזְכַרְתַּנִי

87

remember me, and not forget Thy
handmaid, but wilt give unto Thy
handmaid a man-child, then I will
give him unto the LORD all the days
of his life, and there shall no razor
come upon his head.' ¹²And it came
to pass, as she prayed long before the
LORD, that Eli watched her mouth.
¹³Now Hannah, she spoke in her
heart; only her lips moved, but her
voice could not be heard; therefore
Eli thought she had been drunken.
¹⁴And Eli said unto her: 'How long
wilt thou be drunken? put away thy
wine from thee.' ¹⁵And Hannah answered and said: 'No, my lord, I am
a woman of a sorrowful spirit; I have
drunk neither wine nor strong drink,
but I poured out my soul before the
LORD. ¹⁶Count not thy handmaid
for a wicked woman: for out of
the abundance of my complaint and
my vexation have I spoken hitherto.'
¹⁷Then Eli answered and said: 'Go
in peace, and the God of Israel grant
thy petition that thou hast asked
of Him.' ¹⁸And she said: 'Let thy
servant find favour in thy sight.' So
the woman went her way, and did
eat, and her countenance was no more
sad. ¹⁹And they rose up in the morning early, and worshipped before the
LORD, and returned, and came to their
house to Ramah; and Elkanah knew
Hannah his wife; and the LORD re-

membered her. ²⁰And it came to pass,
when the time was come about, that
Hannah conceived, and bore a son;
and she called his name Samuel:
'because I have asked him of the
LORD.'

²¹And the man Elkanah, and all his
house, went up to offer unto the LORD
the yearly sacrifice, and his vow.
²²But Hannah went not up; for she
said unto her husband: 'Until the
child be weaned, when I will bring
him, that he may appear before the
LORD, and there abide for ever.' ²³And
Elkanah her husband said unto her:
'Do what seemeth thee good; tarry

וְלֹא־תִשְׁכַּח אֶת־אֲמָתֶךָ וְנָתַתָּה
לַאֲמָתְךָ זֶרַע אֲנָשִׁים וּנְתַתִּיו לַיהוָה
כָּל־יְמֵי חַיָּיו וּמוֹרָה לֹא־יַעֲלֶה עַל־
רֹאשׁוֹ: 12 וְהָיָה כִּי הִרְבְּתָה לְהִתְפַּלֵּל
לִפְנֵי יְהוָה וְעֵלִי שֹׁמֵר אֶת־פִּיהָ:
13 וְחַנָּה הִיא מְדַבֶּרֶת עַל־לִבָּהּ רַק
שְׂפָתֶיהָ נָּעוֹת וְקוֹלָהּ לֹא יִשָּׁמֵעַ
14 וַיַּחְשְׁבֶהָ עֵלִי לְשִׁכֹּרָה: וַיֹּאמֶר
אֵלֶיהָ עֵלִי עַד־מָתַי תִּשְׁתַּכָּרִין הָסִירִי
15 אֶת־יֵינֵךְ מֵעָלָיִךְ: וַתַּעַן חַנָּה
וַתֹּאמֶר לֹא אֲדֹנִי אִשָּׁה קְשַׁת־רוּחַ
אָנֹכִי וְיַיִן וְשֵׁכָר לֹא שָׁתִיתִי וָאֶשְׁפֹּךְ
16 אֶת־נַפְשִׁי לִפְנֵי יְהוָה: אַל־תִּתֵּן
אֶת־אֲמָתְךָ לִפְנֵי בַּת־בְּלִיָּעַל
כִּי־מֵרֹב שִׂיחִי וְכַעְסִי דִּבַּרְתִּי עַד־הֵנָּה:
17 וַיַּעַן עֵלִי וַיֹּאמֶר לְכִי לְשָׁלוֹם וֵאלֹהֵי
יִשְׂרָאֵל יִתֵּן אֶת־שֵׁלָתֵךְ אֲשֶׁר שָׁאַלְתְּ
18 מֵעִמּוֹ: וַתֹּאמֶר תִּמְצָא שִׁפְחָתְךָ חֵן
בְּעֵינֶיךָ וַתֵּלֶךְ הָאִשָּׁה לְדַרְכָּהּ וַתֹּאכַל
19 וּפָנֶיהָ לֹא־הָיוּ־לָהּ עוֹד: וַיַּשְׁכִּמוּ
בַבֹּקֶר וַיִּשְׁתַּחֲווּ לִפְנֵי יְהוָה וַיָּשֻׁבוּ
וַיָּבֹאוּ אֶל־בֵּיתָם הָרָמָתָה וַיֵּדַע
אֶלְקָנָה אֶת־חַנָּה אִשְׁתּוֹ וַיִּזְכְּרֶהָ יְהוָה:
20 וַיְהִי לִתְקֻפוֹת הַיָּמִים וַתַּהַר חַנָּה
וַתֵּלֶד בֵּן וַתִּקְרָא אֶת־שְׁמוֹ שְׁמוּאֵל
כִּי מֵיְהוָה שְׁאִלְתִּיו:
21 וַיַּעַל הָאִישׁ אֶלְקָנָה וְכָל־בֵּיתוֹ לִזְבֹּחַ
לַיהוָה אֶת־זֶבַח הַיָּמִים וְאֶת־נִדְרוֹ:
22 וְחַנָּה לֹא עָלָתָה כִּי־אָמְרָה לְאִישָׁהּ
עַד יִגָּמֵל הַנַּעַר וַהֲבִאֹתִיו וְנִרְאָה אֶת־
פְּנֵי יְהוָה וְיָשַׁב שָׁם עַד־עוֹלָם:
23 וַיֹּאמֶר לָהּ אֶלְקָנָה אִישָׁהּ עֲשִׂי

88

until thou have weaned him; only the LORD establish His word.' So the woman tarried and gave her son suck, until she weaned him. [24]And when she had weaned him, she took him up with her, with three bullocks, and one ephah of meal, and a bottle of wine, and brought him unto the house of the LORD in Shiloh; and the child was young. [25]And when the bullock was slain, the child was brought to Eli. [26]And she said: 'Oh, my lord, as thy soul liveth, my lord, I am the woman that stood by thee here, praying unto the LORD. [27]For this child I prayed; and the LORD hath granted me my petition which I asked of Him; [28]therefore I also have lent him to the LORD; as long as he liveth he is lent to the LORD.' And he worshipped the LORD there.

2 And Hannah prayed, and said:
My heart exulteth in the LORD,
My horn is exalted in the LORD;
My mouth is enlarged over mine
   enemies;
Because I rejoice in Thy salvation.
[2]There is none holy as the LORD;
For there is none beside Thee;
Neither is there any rock like our
   God.

[3]Multiply not exceeding proud talk;
Let not arrogancy come out of
   your mouth;
For the LORD is a God of knowledge,
And by Him actions are weighed.
[4]The bows of the mighty men are
   broken,
And they that stumbled are girded
   with strength.
[5]They that were full have hired out
   themselves for bread;
And they that were hungry have
   ceased;
While the barren hath borne seven,
She that had many children hath
   languished.

[6]The LORD killeth, and maketh
   alive;

הַטּוֹב בְּעֵינַיִךְ שְׁבִי עַד־גָּמְלֵךְ אֹתוֹ
אַךְ־יָקֵם יְהוָה אֶת־דְּבָרוֹ וַתֵּשֶׁב הָאִשָּׁה
וַתֵּינֶק אֶת־בְּנָהּ עַד־גָּמְלָהּ אֹתוֹ :

24 וַתַּעֲלֵהוּ עִמָּהּ כַּאֲשֶׁר גְּמָלַתּוּ בְּפָרִים
שְׁלֹשָׁה וְאֵיפָה אַחַת קֶמַח וְנֵבֶל יַיִן
וַתְּבִאֵהוּ בֵית־יְהוָה שִׁלוֹ וְהַנַּעַר נָעַר :

25 וַיִּשְׁחֲטוּ אֶת־הַפָּר וַיָּבִיאוּ אֶת־הַנַּעַר

26 אֶל־עֵלִי : וַתֹּאמֶר בִּי אֲדֹנִי חֵי נַפְשְׁךָ
אֲדֹנִי אֲנִי הָאִשָּׁה הַנִּצֶּבֶת עִמְּכָה בָּזֶה

27 לְהִתְפַּלֵּל אֶל־יְהוָה : אֶל־הַנַּעַר הַזֶּה
הִתְפַּלָּלְתִּי וַיִּתֵּן יְהוָה לִי אֶת־שְׁאֵלָתִי

28 אֲשֶׁר שָׁאַלְתִּי מֵעִמּוֹ : וְגַם אָנֹכִי
הִשְׁאִלְתִּהוּ לַיהוָה כָּל־הַיָּמִים אֲשֶׁר
הָיָה הוּא שָׁאוּל לַיהוָה וַיִּשְׁתַּחוּ שָׁם
לַיהוָה :

ב וַתִּתְפַּלֵּל

1 חַנָּה וַתֹּאמַר עָלַץ לִבִּי בַּיהוָה
רָמָה קַרְנִי בַּיהוָה רָחַב פִּי עַל־
אוֹיְבַי כִּי שָׂמַחְתִּי בִּישׁוּעָתֶךָ :

2 אֵין־קָדוֹשׁ כַּיהוָה כִּי־אֵין בִּלְתֶּךָ וְאֵין

3 צוּר כֵּאלֹהֵינוּ : אַל־תַּרְבּוּ תְדַבְּרוּ
גְּבֹהָה גְבֹהָה יֵצֵא עָתָק מִפִּיכֶם כִּי אֵל
דֵּעוֹת יְהוָה וְלוֹ נִתְכְּנוּ עֲלִלוֹת :

4 קֶשֶׁת גִּבֹּרִים חַתִּים וְנִכְשָׁלִים אָזְרוּ
5 חָיִל : שְׂבֵעִים בַּלֶּחֶם נִשְׂכָּרוּ וּרְעֵבִים
חָדֵלּוּ עַד־עֲקָרָה יָלְדָה שִׁבְעָה וְרַבַּת
בָּנִים אֻמְלָלָה :

He bringeth down to the grave,
and bringeth up.
7The LORD maketh poor, and maketh rich;
He bringeth low, He also lifteth
up.
8He raiseth up the poor out of the
dust,
He lifteth up the needy from the
dung-hill,
To make them sit with princes,
And inherit the throne of glory;
For the pillars of the earth are the
LORD's,
And He hath set the world upon
them.

9He will keep the feet of His holy
ones,
But the wicked shall be put to
silence in darkness;
For not by strength shall man
prevail.
10They that strive with the LORD
shall be broken to pieces;
Against them will He thunder in
heaven;

The LORD will judge the ends of the
earth;
And He will give strength unto His
king,
And exalt the horn of His anointed.

יְהֹוָה מֵמִית 6
וּמְחַיֶּה מוֹרִיד שְׁאוֹל וַיָּעַל :
יְהֹוָה מוֹרִישׁ וּמַעֲשִׁיר מַשְׁפִּיל אַף־ 7
מְרוֹמֵם :

מֵקִים מֵעָפָר דָּל מֵאַשְׁפֹּת 8
יָרִים אֶבְיוֹן לְהוֹשִׁיב עִם־נְדִיבִים
וְכִסֵּא כָבוֹד יַנְחִלֵם כִּי לַיהֹוָה מְצֻקֵי
אֶרֶץ וַיָּשֶׁת עֲלֵיהֶם תֵּבֵל :

רַגְלֵי 9
חֲסִידָו יִשְׁמֹר וּרְשָׁעִים בַּחֹשֶׁךְ יִדָּמּוּ
כִּי־לֹא בְכֹחַ יִגְבַּר־אִישׁ : יְהֹוָה יֵחַתּוּ 10
מְרִיבָו עָלָו בַּשָּׁמַיִם יַרְעֵם יְהֹוָה
יָדִין אַפְסֵי־אָרֶץ וְיִתֶּן־עֹז לְמַלְכּוֹ וְיָרֵם
קֶרֶן מְשִׁיחוֹ :

90

Sarah and Hannah:
The Laughter and the Prayer

FRANCINE KLAGSBRUN

Childless women give birth to heroes in the Bible, and according to tradition, they conceive them on Rosh Hashana. On Rosh Hashana, the Talmudic sages said, God "remembered" Sarah, Rachel, and Hannah, all of them infertile for many years of marriage, and gave them the gift of conception (Rosh Hashana 11a).

On the first day of Rosh Hashana we read about two of those women: Sarah in the Torah portion and Hannah in the prophetic reading. Their stories are juxtaposed in part because God's remembrance is one of the themes of this holiday. We recite the *zikhronot* (remembrance) prayers, in which we call on God to remember us favorably and apply the deeds of our ancestors to our credit.

But the narratives of Sarah and Hannah are juxtaposed also because they parallel each other. Each woman longs for a child, and each eventually bears a son who will be an imposing figure in Israel—Sarah the patriarch Isaac, and Hannah the prophet Samuel.

The suffering of both these women because of their childlessness has the feel of immediacy. Anyone who has ever monitored her temperature and timed her sexual intercourse to the best moment of ovulation will know the Biblical women's sense of urgency in wanting to conceive. Anyone who has taken fertility drugs, attempted in vitro fertilization, or contemplated engaging a surrogate mother will understand their desperation.

The Biblical word for barren is *akara,* which also means "uprooted." At a time when a married woman's worth was measured almost entirely by the number of children she had, a woman without a child was like a plant torn from the ground, its roots dried and useless. After Israel was exiled from its land, it was called by its prophets an *akara,* a desolate, uprooted nation. To be without a child in the modern world does not have such dire connotations, but the unful-filled yearning for offspring can be heartbreaking to a contemporary woman as well.

In many ways, of course, the ancient, mythic stories of childless women are larger than life, designed for a profound religious pur-pose: to show the origins of Israel's heroes and demonstrate the all-encompassing power of Israel's God. It is God who closes women's wombs and God who opens them in the Biblical accounts. No fertility rites, goddesses, or powers of nature can turn barren women fertile. That is God's domain alone, the texts want us to know.

The texts also make clear that the longed-for children are sons, not daughters. Hannah, for example, prays not just for a child, but for a "male child" (I Samuel 1:11). In ancient Israel sons carry the family line and fulfill God's promises to the nation, and sons become the he-roes through whom God's presence in history unfolds.

Yet the son's stories are intertwined with their mother's stories, and the mythic women are also real women whose sorrows and successes seem close to home. Sarah and Hannah are not simply types: barren women who miraculously become mothers. They are also individuals who respond in individual ways to their life situations. Though their stories crisscross at various points, they diverge sharply at others. In her own manner each woman suffers, each finds fulfillment, and each shapes her son into the hero he becomes.

Longings

Before we ever meet Sarah, we know that her childlessness has mo-mentous implications for the fate of her people. Several chapters be-fore our Rosh Hashana readings, a long genealogy recounts the ten generations descending from Noah's son Shem. Suddenly, at the end of this conventional listing of "begats," we are brought up short by the information that Abram, son of Terah, took a wife named Sarai, and "Sarai was barren, she had no child" (Genesis 11:30). This Abram and Sarai will later be known as Abraham and Sarah, but for now, the stark statement of Sarai's barrenness is followed almost immediately by God's promise to Abram that he will become a "great nation." The disparity between that promise and Sarai's infertility is not lost on us, and it is made obvious when, after God's repeated pledges about future offspring, Abram finally bursts out, "O Lord God, what can You give me, seeing that I shall die childless" (15:2).

Sarai's barrenness seems a barrier to the birth of a nation, and the pressures on her to produce a child who will fulfill the divine prophecy are enormous. At the same time, Sarai's personal longing for children is palpable. The measure of that longing is her desperate decision to give Abram her maidservant Hagar as a concubine. Sarai's words are poignant: "Perhaps I shall have a son through her" (16:2). "I," she says, not "we" or "you." She may wish to help Abram fulfill his destiny as the progenitor of a great people, but she wants this child as much for herself as for him. In Hebrew the word "son" has the same root as the word "build," and the text plays on that connection. Sarai is ready to build a family, build her life around a surrogate's son, so eager is she for a child.

Sarai's plan backfires. After the maidservant becomes pregnant, she denigrates her mistress, and Sarai treats her harshly. But Sarai also lashes out at Abram. "The wrong done me is your fault!" she accuses him (16:5). The medieval commentator Rashi explains, with some empathy, that Sarai blames Abram for her domestic troubles because when he cried out to God about his childlessness, he did not include her in his words. Rashi imagines Sarai saying, "You prayed only for yourself, but you should have prayed for the two of us and I would have been remembered along with you."[1]

Indeed, Abram has shown little concern for his wife. He expressed no sympathy for Sarai's desperation in giving him a concubine and makes no attempt to ease the tension between her and Hagar. "Your maid is in your hands," he tells Sarai. "Deal with her as you think right" (16:6). This husband does not wish to be involved in family matters or feel his wife's—or concubine's—pain.

Abram's lack of involvement in Sarai's emotions reveals itself most forcefully in a pivotal moment in the couple's life. Hagar has given birth to a son, Ishmael, who is thirteen years old now, and Abram and Sarai are advanced in years. God establishes a covenant with Abram, then changes the couple's names to Abraham and Sarah. His new name means "father of a multitude of nations," hers, "princess"— both names indicating that their bearers are on the edge of portentous events. In more specific language than ever before, God promises that Sarah herself will have a son.

And what is Abraham's reaction? First he laughs and wonders to himself how he and Sarah could possibly conceive a child in their old age. Then he says to God, "Oh that Ishmael might live by Your favor!" (17:18). Abraham is satisfied with Ishmael, his concubine's son, as his heir. This man of faith does not have faith enough in God's promise for Sarah or concern enough about Sarah's desires to inquire further about his promised child.

Sarah also laughs to herself, some time later, when she overhears God's messengers tell Abraham that by the next year she will bear a son. "Now that I am withered, am I to have enjoyment—with my husband so old?" she says (18:12). The medieval commentator Nachmanides speaks of joyous laughter as originating in the mouth, but "laughter originating in the heart is not spoken of as joyous" (Nachmanides on Genesis 18:15). Sarah's internal laughter is not joyous, but bitter, laced with irony and, one suspects, some anger at God. She has lived almost an entire lifetime longing for a child, and now, worn down by the waiting and wanting, is she to become a mother? And are she and her aged, remote husband to find sexual pleasure again? The messengers' words sound like a cruel joke to Sarah.

Nachmanides also suggests that Abraham had not told Sarah of God's earlier announcement to him that she would have a child. In neglecting to tell her, he put her in the awkward position of disbelieving the messengers' tidings. Once again, Abraham had closed himself off to his wife's concerns.

Hannah's husband, Elkanah, does not close himself off. "Am I not better to you than ten sons?" he asks sympathetically (I Samuel 1:8). In that question he demonstrates his love and respect for his wife in a way Abraham seems incapable of doing. Nevertheless he, too, misses the boat. For, in fact, he is not better than ten sons or even than one. A husband is not a substitute for a child, and he cannot make up for the agony Hannah suffers because of her lack of children. Moreover, content with heirs through his other wife, Peninnah, Elkanah is able to dismiss Hannah's longings without truly understanding them. "Why are you crying?" he asks her. "Why are you so sad?" (1:8). Her sorrow touches him, but he is no more capable than Abraham of penetrating it.

Hannah's story begins at what might be regarded as the midpoint of Sarah's. When we meet Hannah she is miserable because Peninnah is taunting her for her childlessness, much as Sarah was miserable because of Hagar's taunts. Peninnah, however, is not Hannah's servant. She is an equal wife over whom Hannah has no power. Aware that Elkanah favors Hannah, Peninnah uses her children as a means to denigrate Hannah. (It should be noted that women in the Bible are more often portrayed as competing than cooperating, which may be an expression of the male narrators' perspectives on women or a reflection of the rivalry that probably existed in homes in which men took more than one wife.)

The Rabbis elaborated on Peninnah's techniques by picturing her needling Hannah to wash her children's faces or greet them after school, knowing full well there were no children to wash or greet (Pesikta Rabbati, 43). In the Biblical narrative, Hannah responds to Peninnah's barbs by weeping and refusing to eat. She seems a helpless victim of Peninnah's nastiness.

Every year Hannah accompanies Elkanah, Peninnah, and Peninnah's children to a shrine at Shiloh where they bring sacrifices to God. One year, with Peninnah's taunts crashing about her head, Hannah stands at the door of the temple and offers a prayer to God.

It is an extraordinary moment in the history of religion. Hannah prays silently, the first person in the Bible to do so in a public place of worship. Later rabbis pointed to her as a model of how to pray: That she moved her lips teaches us that we must form our words distinctly with our lips. That her voice could not be heard shows that we must not raise our voices unduly during prayer (Berakhot 31a). Standing in the doorway, seeming to mumble to herself so that the priest Eli mistakes her for a drunken woman, Hannah originates silent prayer, the prayer of the heart.

But the content of that prayer is shocking.

Hannah makes a bargain with God and takes a vow. "If You will look upon the suffering of Your maidservant and will remember me . . . and if You will grant Your maidservant a male child, I will dedicate him to the Lord for all the days of his life" (I Samuel 1:11). If God answers her prayers and gives her a son, she, in turn, will give up the child to live in the temple at Shiloh and to serve God for his entire life.

Hannah wants a son more than anything in the world, yet she willingly bargains him away. With originality and grace (the meaning of her name) she pleads from the depths of her heart for a child—whom she then offers not to raise, rarely to see, and never, perhaps, to play with by day or comfort at night.

No childless woman in the Bible before Hannah—neither Sarah, Rebecca, nor Rachel—made such a promise in return for a child. The nearest precedent to her is Samson's unnamed mother in the Book of Judges (13). She dedicates her unborn son to be a Nazirite, forbidden to cut his hair or drink wine. At the end of Hannah's prayer she also promises to make her son a Nazirite. But whereas Samson grows up within his family, Hannah's son will be given away to religious service.

Some people would regard Hannah's vow as that of a woman desperate for a child under any circumstances. Tradition has accepted it as the ultimate in self-sacrifice, the commitment of a woman so devout that she is willing to relinquish what she most treasures. Though the sages generally disapproved of vows—because such promises were hard to keep—they approved of Hannah's (Genesis Rabbah 70:3).

Some people might wonder, however, whether in a hidden corner of Hannah's praying heart there resided a degree of ambivalence about the child she pleaded for so eloquently. Shamed in her society for being an *akara* and beaten down by Peninnah's harassments, Hannah fervently desired to bear a son. What seems less fervent was her desire for motherhood.

Despite her victimization by Peninnah, Hannah conducts herself with strength and determination. She has the courage to pray in a temple as no person before her did and to defend herself vigorously against Eli's charges of drunkenness. "Oh, no, my lord!" she cries when he accuses her. "I have drunk no wine or other strong drink, but I have been pouring out my heart to the Lord" (I Samuel 1:15). From Hannah we learn, Rabbi Eleazar said, that one must vindicate oneself against false charges (Berakhot 31a).

Can we not imagine, then, that this creative and innovative woman had some inner reluctance—a reluctance she may not even have recognized—about submerging herself in maternal life? Or, isn't it imaginable that overwhelmed by Peninnah's aggressive maternity, Hannah could not picture herself—or did not wish to be—in the same role?

To be sure, we cannot with any certainty read Hannah's motivation into her vow to give up her son. We can only imagine causes. We can also note that in the Biblical text, her wish for a son is connected to Peninnah's bullying and not to expressions of motherly feelings.

Rabbinic commentators seemed to note this as well. In describing the purpose of Peninnah's taunts toward Hannah, the text uses the Hebrew word *hare'ima,* meaning "to make her miserable" (I Samuel 1:6). Peninnah ridiculed Hannah to make her miserable. However, the same letters form the root for the word "thunder," leading some rabbis to argue that Peninnah intended not to make Hannah miserable, but to make her thunder toward God in prayer (Pesikta Rabbati, 43). In this interpretation, Peninnah is not a villain, but the catalyst for Hannah's prayer for a child—perhaps forcing her to overcome her inner reservations.

Sarah, as we have seen, places a rival in her husband's bed to assure herself a child. Hannah seeks a child in response to her rival's attacks. The behavior of both women will have consequences for them and for the sons they bear.

Mothers

Sarah's son is born when she is ninety years old and Abraham a hundred—and this is where our holiday reading begins. Pregnancy and childbirth have agreed with her. In the midrash, even before she conceives, her body is rejuvenated and her wrinkles smoothed out, so that in carrying her child, she is restored to her youthful beauty (Baba Metzia 87a). In the midrash also, when gossipers question whether the son Abraham had in his old age is really Sarah's, her breasts swell with milk and overflow like two fountains, enticing children from many nations to suckle from them (Genesis Rabbah 53:9). That, said the Rabbis, explains why Sarah speaks of suckling children, in the plural, after her baby is born: "Who would have said to Abraham that Sarah would suckle children!" (Genesis 21:7).

These words introduce a little song Sarah recites after she gives birth: "Who would have said to Abraham / That Sarah would suckle children! / Yet I have borne a son in his old age." Sarah is almost giddy with amazement at the existence of this late-in-life child. As a sly rebuke, perhaps, she makes Abraham the subject of her song. It was God who had said to Abraham that Sarah would suckle children, but Abraham had not believed it.

Before her song, Sarah laughs aloud, her earlier bitter laughter turned to joy. "God has brought me laughter," she exults, "everyone who hears will laugh with me" (21:6), to which the Rabbis added that all the infertile women in the world laughed with Sarah, because when she became pregnant, they too became pregnant, and when she gave birth, they too gave birth (Pesikta Rabbati, 42).

Laughter has become the trademark of this family, washing over it like ripples of water that cleanse it of past sorrow. The new baby is called Yitzchak, Isaac, meaning "he laughs," a name given to him before birth by God when the couple had laughed at the idea of his conception. He is circumcised after eight days, and when he is weaned two years later, his parents hold a great feast. So honored are these parents and child that, in rabbinic imagination, leaders of the world come to celebrate with them (Genesis Rabbah 53:10).

Sarah's life is complete. In speaking to Abraham before she conceived, God had promised to bless her "so that she shall give rise to nations" (Genesis 17:16). Much later, the prophet Isaiah will remind the people of Israel to look back "to Sarah who brought you forth" (Isaiah 51:2). She has become the quintessential mother, parent of a son and through him matriarch of a nation.

Then, suddenly, everything changes.

Sarah notices Ishmael playing with Isaac. The Hebrew word used for playing is *metzachek,* from the same root as Yitzchak, the root of laughter. Ishmael seems to be laughing with Isaac, or at Isaac. The text does not say what Sarah observes in this play/laughter, leaving the door open to a range of rabbinic speculation. Maybe Ishmael is building altars to idols. Or maybe the playing is of a sexual nature, and Ishmael is corrupting the young Isaac (Genesis Rabbah 53:11).

Or maybe, as the text seems to indicate, in her fierce motherhood Sarah fears that with Ishmael in the picture her son will not receive his full inheritance. Whatever the immediate cause, Sarah's insistence on casting Ishmael and Hagar out of the family home has enveloped her in criticism throughout the ages.

Earlier, where the text referred to Sarah's harsh treatment of Hagar, Nachmanides commented, "Our mother did transgress"[2] (Nachmanides on Genesis 16:6). Now, when Sarah drives Hagar and Ishmael out, the text itself sympathizes with their suffering, obliquely criticizing Sarah through Abraham's reluctance to send them away. "The matter distressed Abraham greatly" (Genesis 21:11), we read, and we are particularly moved by the distress of this man who had previously shown so little emotion toward his family.

Sarah appears coldhearted and cruel, so obsessed with her own child that she is able to shut off all human feeling for another woman and her child.

Nevertheless, Sarah's obsession is in harmony with divine will. "Whatever Sarah tells you, do as she says," God commands Abraham (Genesis 21:12), and we are left with two impressions. First, Sarah, like Rebecca who comes after her, plays the role of "heavy" in our male-oriented Scriptures. It is Rebecca who convinces her son Jacob to steal his brother Esau's blessing, as if such a thought would not have occurred to Jacob. Here it is Sarah who carries the moral burden of sending Ishmael and Hagar away against Abraham's wishes, leaving his character unblemished.

More significant, the impression we get from the text is that Sarah, like other strong women of the Bible, has a clear image of her son's destiny. "Sarah saw," Scripture says when she observes Ishmael playing with Isaac (21:9). Ultimately, what she saw was the future of Abraham's line, which had been promised to her son through her. Abraham had lost sight of the promise, had actually shrugged it off when it was given, concerned only about Ishmael. But Sarah saw and, in seeing, knew she had to act. Motherhood focused her vision.

Motherhood was more of a conflict for Hannah. In tradition, her son, like Sarah's, was born prematurely, in the seventh month (Rosh Hashana 11a), a foreshadowing of his specialness in years to come. And he too receives a name packed with meaning: "Samuel," Hannah says, "because I asked the Lord for him" (I Samuel 1:20). A little later she elaborates on the name's definition by adding, "I . . . hereby lend him to the Lord" (1:28).

The only difficulty with those name explanations is that the Hebrew for Samuel, Shemuel, does not mean either to ask or lend. It is more closely tied to *shem El,* "God's name," indicating a name—and a person—given by God. Asking and lending define the name Shaul, or Saul, the first king of Israel, who will figure prominently in Samuel's life. Hannah connects those meanings to Samuel, however, because her whispered asking brought him into being and her vow lends him back to God for life.

Like Sarah, Hannah utters a jubilant song after her boy is born. Hers takes the form of a stately victory prayer of thanksgiving to God. So stately and similar to later psalms is it that some Bible critics regard it as a later work put into Hannah's mouth. According to this theory, Hannah eventually came to represent Israel oppressed by foreign nations, and her prayer served as a promise of redemption for the future.[3]

Within the context of the narrative, however, one thing stands out about Hannah's prayer. Unlike Sarah's poem, hers deals not with the joy of giving birth or of nursing children, but with triumphing over one's enemies. "While the barren woman bears seven, the mother of many is forlorn," Hannah chants (2:5). The Rabbis interpreted that to mean that each time Hannah gave birth to another child in later years, two of Peninnah's ten children died, until, at Peninnah's humble request, Hannah saved her last two children by praying for them (Pesikta Rabbati 43). Vindictive as such an interpretation might be, its tone picks up, again, on Hannah's deepest motive for wanting a child: as an answer to Peninnah's mockery. With Samuel born, Hannah can hold her head up in pride and thank God for her changing fortune. "I have triumphed through the Lord," she sings, "I gloat over my enemies" (2:1). Having a son who will be in God's service is Hannah's best revenge against Peninnah.

Yet even in this moment of glory and vengeance, Hannah has begun to change. If her longing for a child had been less about maternal wishes than about defending herself against Peninnah, actually having the child seems to turn her away from self-protection and toward maternity. Hannah, we notice, is becoming attached to her baby.

When the time comes for the family to make its annual pilgrimage to Shiloh, she holds back while she nurses the child, whom the text for the first time refers to as "her son" (1:23). She would like to keep him at home until he is weaned, she tells Elkanah, for once he appears at Shiloh "he must remain there for good" (1:22). We can feel the heavy sadness in those words and know that Samuel's weaning will not be the great celebration Isaac's was. Hannah will uphold her vow at that time and suffer the loss of her son for it.

The loss Hannah feels after relinquishing her child touches us through an exquisitely sensitive detail. Each year when she and Elkanah make their pilgrimage to Shiloh, she brings the young Samuel a little robe that she has made herself (2:19). She sees her son just once a year, we learn from this detail, and her only way of measuring his growth is through the new robe she sews for each visit. Hannah had promised her child away before she knew how quickly she would fall in love with him; now the robe is her ongoing embrace.

Sons

Sarah loves and protects her only child, Isaac, her laughing boy. Abraham's protection is more equivocal, and his greatest test of faith becomes the central trauma of Isaac's life. In the second part of the Rosh Hashana Torah reading, Abraham follows the voice he hears from God commanding him to sacrifice Isaac, and Isaac follows unquestioningly his father's directions.

Sarah's voice is unheard, a silence that growing numbers of contemporary women have filled with their own imaginings. In tradition, Sarah's death, recorded in Scripture almost immediately after the binding of Isaac, results from it. In one midrash, Sarah dies of shock when Satan misinforms her that Abraham has actually killed Isaac. In another, the shock comes from Satan's telling her the truth: how Abraham had almost sacrificed their son.[4]

But the midrash that is most telling about Sarah and her son has Isaac, prepared to be slaughtered on the altar, requesting that Abraham not give Sarah the news of his death when she is standing near a pit or on a rooftop. In despair, she might jump down and kill herself (Tanchuma, Vayera, 23). Isaac knows what he means to his mother, knows that without him she would not be able to live.

It is Isaac, however, who must go on living without Sarah. His grief at her death seems overwhelming, unconsoled, until some three years later when, at age forty, he marries his distant cousin Rebecca. He takes her into his mother's tent to consummate their marriage, and, we read, "Isaac loved her and thus found comfort after his mother's death" (Genesis 24:67). In marrying Rebecca, Isaac makes a new beginning in a world without his mother.

It's easy to regard Isaac as a weak character, a mama's boy—in Freudian terms still tied in an Oedipal knot to Sarah. Certainly he is overshadowed by the other two patriarchs, his father, Abraham, and his son Jacob. Yet Isaac is exceptional in ways the others are not. His is the first Biblical marriage described by the term "love"—it is not a word we hear in regard to Abraham and Sarah. He is the only patriarch who does not take a concubine or more than one wife. And he is the only one who prays for his wife when she, like the other matriarchs, suffers infertility (25:21). In one scene we see Abimelech, king of the Philistines, looking out his window and catching a glimpse of Isaac "fondling" Rebecca (26:8). The Hebrew word used is, again, *metzachek*, from the "laughter" root. Isaac laughingly sports with Rebecca, unselfconsciously showing his affection.

Isaac had brought laughter into Sarah's life, and her joy in him continued to permeate his. He may not have attained the heights of his father or son, but his inner strength allowed him both to survive the ordeal of his youth and to remain in the promised land of Canaan even in difficult times, in that way tightening the family's attachments there. Although he suffered difficulties with his sons, Jacob and Esau, in his old age, he lived much of his adult life working the land and at peace with his neighbors and himself. Not unworthy achievements for Sarah's son.

And how does Hannah's son's life unfold? Strong and determined like his mother, and given to her by God, Samuel becomes one of Israel's outstanding leaders—a judge, priest, and prophet. In his influence and importance in Jewish history, he is often compared to Moses.

But Samuel lacks one quality Moses had in abundance—compassion. Though Moses chastised the people for their sins, invariably he pleaded with God to forgive them. Samuel chastises the people, but only once does he mention praying on their behalf, and then we don't hear the prayer (I Samuel 12:23). He is a stern and lonely leader, qualities that may well reflect the austere and lonely life he led growing up among priests in a sanctuary.

If laughter is the thread that runs through Isaac's existence, the name *Shaul,* or Saul, reverberates through Samuel's. Hannah had defined Samuel's name from the root that forms Saul's, almost as if she had foreseen that the lives of the two men would be intertwined. They are, but with a constant tension.

Samuel anoints Saul as king after the people clamor for a monarch to replace him in his old age. From the start he seems to resent the new king. When Saul commits what appears to be a minor offense— before going into battle he offers a sacrifice himself, without Samuel's presence—Samuel declares that his action has lost him his kingdom (13:8–14). Later he breaks completely with Saul because the king did not obey his command to utterly destroy the Amalekites, Israel's long-standing enemy. As if to demonstrate his strength as opposed to Saul's weakness, Samuel has King Agag of Amalek, whom Saul had spared, brought before him and personally hacks him to pieces (15:33).

What is the source of Samuel's animosity toward Saul? Unbending in his religious devotion, he argues that by establishing a monarchy Israel is rejecting the only king it should have—God. What he doesn't say openly, but what we quickly surmise, is that he feels personally rejected by the demand for a king. "Whose ox have I taken? . . ." he asks defiantly in recounting his life to the people. "From whom have I taken a bribe?" (12:3). Here is a man who spent his childhood and youth deprived of the dailiness of family living, his life donated to God before he was even conceived. He is not prepared to give up any of his hard-earned leadership, let alone to a person whose name itself sounds like a usurpation of his own.

Samuel dies several years after the Amalekite incident, without speaking to Saul again. We don't know when his mother, Hannah, dies. Having set her son on his life's path, she disappears from it. He remains one of Israel's heroes, a man to be admired for his courage and uprightness, but not easy to like.

The Laughter and the Prayer

"Why were the mothers so long barren?" some sages asked. And they answered: "Because the Holy One, blessed be He, longed to hear their prayer. He said to them: 'My dove, I will tell you why I have kept you childless; because I was yearning to hear your prayer.' As it is written, 'For your voice is sweet and your face is comely.' " (Song of Songs Rabba 2:14).[5]

On one level this rabbinic explication of a verse in the Song of Songs seems coldly dismissive of the Biblical mothers' sufferings, as if God's enjoyment of their prayers justifies their long years of misery. Below the surface, however, this midrash also recognizes the special intimacy that exists in the Bible between God and the mothers.

When Sarah first laughs at the improbability of having a child in her old age, God complains to Abraham about her seeming lack of faith. Somewhat frightened, Sarah lies and says, "I did not laugh," to which God answers directly, "You did laugh" (Genesis 18:13–15). The incident ends there. Sarah is not punished for lying, nor does God seem angry. In fact, one can almost read a playfulness into God's response, a kind of "I caught you, but it's okay" attitude. The passage has the tone of an informal exchange between God and Sarah, in which each ultimately understands the other.

Hannah's sense of closeness to God is more fully developed. She pours her heart out, not needing any intervention by the priest Eli. In rabbinic terms she seems to know instinctively that God longs to hear her prayer.

Although these women, and others in the Bible, do not relate to God on the monumental scale of the Biblical men, they often have more clear-cut insights into divine goals than the men and a more steadfast determination to achieve those goals. Distant, detached Abraham is ready to make Ishmael his heir. Strong, single-minded Sarah knows that the future must belong to her son, Isaac. Loving but ineffective Elkanah essentially gives up on Hannah's having children. Decisive and dignified Hannah uses prayer not only to gain a son, but to shape his life to the needs of his nation.

Sarah and Hannah are individuals whose lives run different courses and whose hero sons might have little in common, were they to meet. Sarah desperately seeks motherhood, revels in it when she gains it, and raises a child deeply attached to her. Hannah, talented and inventive, may be more ambivalent about motherhood but is determined to stand up against Peninnah's barbs. She triumphs over her rival by vowing her child away, then suffers the emptiness of his absence.

Yet for all the differences in their lives and experiences, Hannah and Sarah resemble each other in their attachment to God and their celebration of divine possibilities.

Sarah's laughter, questioning at first, rises to a crescendo of joy and gratitude to God after her son is born. Hannah's prayer, conditional at first—"if You will grant Your maidservant a male child, I will dedicate him to the Lord"—swells into a poem of exultation in God. And underlying both the laughter and the prayer is a glorying in reversals, in impossibilities becoming actualities.

"Who would have said to Abraham that Sarah would suckle children!" (Genesis 21:7), the aged matriarch asks amid her laughter. The natural world has been turned upside-down. "The barren woman bears seven . . . ," sings Hannah; "The bows of the mighty are broken, and the faltering are girded with strength" (I Samuel 2:5,4). The weak win over the strong, the poor are raised from the dust. Each reversal is a victory of belief over despair and of the remarkable over the ordinary.

Reversals and renewals hold special power on Rosh Hashana. Contemporary women struggling with problems of infertility may find themselves identifying with the stories of Sarah and Hannah and inspired by them. Or they may find these stories difficult for them, when their own maternal dreams are unrealized. But these narratives encompass more than the birth of children, as basic as that is to them. Sarah's song of laughter and Hannah's prayer of success alert us to the unexpected, the changes and wonders that can spark our lives as a new year and new season come upon us.

The Power of Prayer: Hannah's Tale[1]

NEHAMA ASCHKENASY

Prayer is at the heart of our spiritual experience during the High Holy Days, the catalyst of the self-purification that we hope to undergo.[2] It is also at the very core of the tale of Hannah, mother of the prophet Samuel (in Samuel I), which is assigned as the *Haftara* reading of the first day of Rosh Hashana.[3] The story of Hannah's journey from the heartbreak of childlessness to the glory of motherhood exemplifies the power of petitionary prayer, giving us hope that our prayers, too, will be answered. Further, the tale exhibits the broad spectrum of the prayer modality: from the simplest, perhaps even primitive, request for a favor from God to the more sophisticated meditation on the glory of divine providence, crafted in brilliant verse.

But this tale is connected to the very essence of the High Holy Days in more ways than the obvious. Of all the petitions, prayers, and psalms in the Bible, mostly uttered by men, it is the woman's heartfelt plea to God that was singled out by our sages as a model and proto-type of all prayers to come. There must be something deeper in this seemingly predictable tale and its deceptively familiar heroine that has made it so appropriate for us to revisit during our Days of Awe. In fact, the story of a woman entering into a daring dialogue with God speaks to us today in even more ways than it did to our ancestors once we realize the subtle countercultural elements it contains.[4]

The contours of the tale's plotline are familiar within the Biblical tradition, repeating the known formula of the barren wife remembered by God and giving birth to a man who will distinguish himself in the community of Israel. The basic tenet of the tale, that a woman's redemption comes through motherhood, is a major Biblical concept as well as literary motif. The woman serves history by contributing a great leader to the people of God, but it is the male son, Samuel, whose deeds we then follow and who will give his name to the entire Biblical collection. At its very core, so it seems, this tale is a classic example of the Biblical attitude to women conceptually and literarily:

the woman's story is quickly abandoned and the text resumes its "male" concerns regarding proper leadership, the laws of the cult, acquisition of land and territory, and the history of the people.

Yet this tale is in fact rife with contradictions. The initial recounting of events confirms the familiar precepts of the culture, but some of the rhetoric reveals an attempt to reach out to a different, distant vision, one that introduces a set of values generally alien to Biblical man. This is accomplished by verbal statements made by some of the main players as well as by the shifting of narrative focus from the desired son and the miracle of his conception to the linguistically talented woman and the power of her speech.

The tale at its outset reinforces the patriarchal view of the woman's role and functions. We encounter Hannah in the polygynous household, one of two wives of the wealthy, God-fearing patriarch Elkanah. Hannah's anguish in her childless state is not only a typical Biblical situation, it also reinforces some modern theories about women's biological destiny. Hannah seems perfectly to illustrate Erik Erikson's theory of the tyranny of the woman's inner "empty space."[5] Overwhelmed by her biological "inner space," and controlled by her powerful physiological needs, to use Erikson's paradigm, Hannah can appease her sense of emptiness and deprivation only by pregnancy and motherhood. Not even her husband's love can compensate for the vacuum stemming from the roots of her femininity, which can be filled only in the most literal and physical sense, when the woman's painfully "empty" inner space, her womb, finally lodges an embryo. Hannah's lonely, unfulfilled state at the opening of the tale seems to confirm Erikson's theory that the very existence of the inner reproductive space exposes women early to a specific sense of loneliness, to a fear of being left empty or deprived of treasures as well as of remaining unfulfilled. Here, then, is an ancient legend whose underlying presumptions would appear in our times in the form of a psychiatric paradigm of women that locates the core of feminine existence in the woman's internal feminine organ and narrows the parameters of the female experience to a response to a mere physical urge.

The initial thrust of the story, to be sure, clearly accords with the code of a male-dominant society by offering a glimpse of the vast expanses of space and time that are part of the male existence and are closed to the woman. If the woman is defined by her "natural" functions, the man is seen as occupying a niche in history. Elkanah's family tree, recorded through the male line in the tale's very first verse, places the man within a long, respectable continuum of time and history. The tale's patriarch is introduced in terms of his place in the territory, "of Ramatayim-Tzofim, in Mount Efrayim," as well as in history ("son of . . . son of," and so on).

The man's life is defined as a presence in a geographical territory allocated to the family by God himself and as a link in a historical chain, while the women are removed from the sacred geography as well as divinely controlled history; they move only within the four walls of the polygynous home, their lives defined as looking inward, immersed in their biological cycle and the call of their empty inner space.

The man's mobility in space is further illustrated in the pilgrimage that Elkanah undertakes every year, when he leaves his home in Mount Efrayim and travels to Shiloh to worship God. Here mobility in space is tied to the sanctification of time. The territory of the land, within which the patriarch journeys to the holy site, and the historically significant holidays coalesce to reflect the man's essence. True, it is implied that Elkanah's wives and children also accompany him on his journey to Shiloh, yet it is the man whose religious experience this is: "And this man went up out of his city year by year to worship and to sacrifice to the Lord" (1:3).

The patriarch is seen in the glory of his religious and familial authority: he is the one who leads the family on the pilgrimage, offers the sacrifice to God, and then divides portions of it for his wives and children. The women, on the other hand, are introduced in terms of their reproductive abilities: Peninnah has been blessed with many children, while Hannah is childless. Within the confines of the women's environment, we find the co-wives engaged in rivalry, with the fecund Peninnah taunting Hannah for her barrenness or, rather, for having been singled out by God for misery "because the Lord had shut up her womb" (1:6). Twice in rapid succession is Hannah's childlessness attributed to divine intervention: once in the context of Elkanah's love for his wife and his attempts to compensate her for her barrenness (1:5); and then as a means for Peninnah to taunt Hannah (1:6).

Hannah slowly emerges from her position as the passive object of her husband's love and her rival's torment to become the tale's unde-niable axis. It seems that with verse 5 the narrator suddenly shifts gears. Having bowed to patriarchal tradition in his introductory statements, our storyteller now feels more at ease pursuing a different line of narrative and makes the woman Hannah the unquestionable pivot of the plot. Clearly the narrator has seen in Hannah the person a legitimate subject of his story. He intends to immortalize her not through her mere function as the progenitor of the prophet Samuel, but through the character traits that she manifests as a person. The beauty of her character is accentuated in her name (in Hebrew related to the noun "grace") and is dramatically displayed in her dignified conduct throughout her ordeal. Her noble bearing in the face of her adversary's constant teasing is the first expression of the dignity and grace she exemplifies.

The Bible does not provide the exact words that Peninnah uses to hurt Hannah, but it makes clear that Peninnah torments Hannah with the latter's childlessness. Within the context of the Biblical text it is not Peninnah's lexicon of teasing, but Hannah's noble mien, her un-willingness to stoop to Peninnah's level and respond to her badger-ing, that is important.

Elkanah's household represents a female community divided. Han-nah and Peninnah find themselves unwillingly and reluctantly under one roof, vying for the attention of the same man. They enact, or rather foreshadow, the stereotypical female community in literature, which is characterized by mutual betrayal and intrigue.[6] But while Peninnah conforms to the stereotype and views this "community" as a battleground for winning the man's favors, Hannah transcends it. She does not stoop to fight for her man, and male approval alone does not satisfy her. Hannah's lack of response to her adversary's provoca-tions ultimately points to a personality whose sights rise above the petty domesticity that is Peninnah's boundary. In fact, given Han-nah's eloquence later, it seems that in her silent presence here Hannah communicates her respect for language; it is not lack of words, but rather concern for the right and dignified use of words that lies be-hind Hannah's verbal restraint.

Elkanah's love for his wife functions as character testimony about Hannah, and is amply illustrated, surprisingly so against the Bible's usual stylistic rule of economy and terseness. It is first displayed through action: Elkanah gives his wife a "worthy" (or a "double") portion (1:5) in the sacrificial festival in Shiloh. This act is doubly significant: since the childless woman's economic position was precarious, Elkanah indicates that Hannah should not worry on that account, that she will always be amply provided for. The vital need for a child as the future economic security for the parents, coupled with the high rate of infant mortality in ancient times, was a factor that determined much of the ancient family's culture. The custom of polygyny was undoubtedly fueled by the family's need for male children as an assurance that if one wife were barren, then another wife would most likely be fertile. A childless woman like Hannah might have been concerned about her future survival, and the husband's double portion was no doubt a symbolic act of promise that she would never suffer deprivation. Hannah's wish for a child, then, is not to be taken simply as a tactic for survival.

Elkanah's love for his wife is both symbolically enacted and explicitly stated by the narrator: "for he loved Hannah" (1:5). His love is further confirmed through verbal communication: "Am I not better to thee than ten sons?" (1:8). The husband's words are exceptional not only in their comforting tone, but in their rejection of sexist norms. In ancient Israel the wife's primary contribution to the family was her sexuality, both her ability to please her husband as a woman and to present him with children.[7] In such a climate Hannah undoubtedly felt that she had disappointed her husband. One could expect a loving husband to solace his barren wife by assuring her that she satisfied him in other ways. Instead Elkanah's attitude is surprisingly modern; he views himself not as the patriarch who has magnanimously forgiven his wife for not having done her duty to his family, but as the loving partner whose duty it is to make his wife happy. "Love is primarily giving, not receiving," says Erich Fromm, and in his relationship with Hannah, Elkanah indeed seeks to give, not receive.[8] He does not define his relationship with his wife in terms of *her* familial or sexual duties, in terms of what she has or has not given him, but in terms of *his* contribution to her contentment: "am *I* not better to thee than ten sons" (1:8).

In several ways, through action and language, Elkanah indicates that while in his matrimonial practices he conforms to the polygynous culture, in his attitude to Hannah he has been able to rise above the familiar and accepted norms. Fromm's description of love as an active practice rather than a passive experience applies to Elkanah in a deeper sense: Elkanah must actively overcome the prejudices of his culture to be able to address his wife in this manner.[9] The giving of the double portion is an act intended to comfort, but the words come from a consciousness that has transcended the mind-set of Elkanah's generation.

Elkanah's extraordinary character introduces an egalitarian, non-patriarchal tone into the story, yet it is significant that after his initial intrusion, Elkanah recedes to the background, reappearing only later, in his capacity as the impregnator of Hannah (1:19): Elkanah "had intimacy with his wife." While it was Abraham who first received the good news about Sarah's pregnancy, and Isaac prayed for his barren wife, Elkanah is not the one who turns to God. Rather, Hannah is the sole architect of her redemption. From the start, Hannah seems determined not to involve her husband in her misery. Her self-containment may be contrasted with Rachel's petulant outburst to Jacob: "Give me children or else I die" (Genesis 29:1).

Hannah's silence, while adding nobility and dignity to her person, may also indicate a certain emotional numbness. Hannah's muteness, her failure to respond either to her husband's kind words or her adversary's taunting, may bespeak quiet desperation, even depression. In her speechless presence early in the tale Hannah cuts the figure of an introverted, preoccupied person, oblivious of her surroundings.

Until she finds her voice, Hannah's presence in the tale is inscrutable and impenetrable to us. Only when Hannah finds the courage to address God directly does her vocal dam finally collapse and her words, though soundless, flow freely and eloquently. Though humiliated and embittered, Hannah feels confident enough to approach God alone and without an intermediary. It seems that Hannah finds the appropriate address and the right addressee at one and the same time, so that the first sentence that comes out of her mouth is a prayer to God. Hannah's introspective state turns out to have been the ideal state of mind for praying. The Hebrew verb "to pray," which conjugates the root *pll* in the reflexive form, suggests in its very grammar that prayer begins with introspection.

Hannah's prayer first takes the form of wordless cries (1:10), with the Hebrew text offering two variations of the verb "to cry," thus implying the large volume of sobs and tears that flows out of Hannah. This cry is different from the previous cries, which were a reaction to Peninnah's taunting (1:7). This time the cry is already part of the act of prayer: "And she was in bitterness of soul, and prayed to the Lord, and wept bitterly" (1:10).[10] But the woman does not remain within the self-absorbed act of weeping; behind the grieving exterior there is a determined woman able to verbalize her request to God and enter the realm of hope and expectations for the future. When Hannah finally talks, she does not wallow in her sorrow, nor does she elaborate on her grief, but she states her request clearly and effectively. The heretofore voiceless Hannah turns out to be a master of language and a shrewd negotiator.

Hannah's negotiating tactics are cleverly made up of several clearly defined steps. First, her address to God is couched in the language of an oath, thus endowing it with the sanctity of a promise made to God. Instead of asking, Hannah frames her request within a sacred vow that she makes to God. She displays humble deference to God that is nevertheless combined with great tenacity. While prefacing her entreaty to God with the conditional, tentative "if," and modestly referring to herself as God's "handmaid," Hannah seems to be resolved not to leave God empty-handed. In fact, she actually wills her child into being by proceeding to describe the kind of life that she maps out for him before there is any indication from God that God has agreed to his end of the bargain. Hannah moves from the lexicon of the tentative to the clear vision of a certain future. Once she has verbalized her request for a male child, that child, at least in Hannah's mind, has already come into being: "I will give him to the Lord all the days of his life" (1:11). Hannah's word has created a world, and the certainty of a male child born to her is so undeniable that she can already describe the kind of life that he will have as a man of God; more specifically, she can even visualize him physically "and no razor shall come upon his head" (1:11).

If the son is now a reality for Hannah, then the lengthy prayer that follows (1:12) is no longer within the realm of a plea to God. Rather, it is an expression of a heart overflowing with emotions, of a soul that has suddenly found a way to talk to God freely and openly and thus feels gratified already. The mere spiritual experience of praying is for Hannah the beginning of her reward, for, as the philosopher Judah

Halevi suggested, prayer is a form of nourishment for the soul;[11] and Abraham Heschel has said: "Through prayer we sanctify ourselves, our feelings, our ideas."[12] Further, the mere attempt of communicating with God involves daring and, as such, is in itself an act of self-empowerment leading to spiritual growth.

Hannah's tactics have been to use the larger framework of a vow within which she petitions God, negotiates with God, proceeds to make God a promise, and then goes on to delineate the details of her "contract" with God. Hannah's address to God thus covers that whole gamut of the prayer modality; it consists of the pouring out of the soul, followed by a petition, a pledge, and thanksgiving, which culminates in a hymn of praise to God. No wonder that the ancient rabbis saw in Hannah's prayer a paradigm and a prototype of the prayer activity.[13]

Hannah's prayer not only serves to comfort her, but boldly declares her intention to persuade God to change her lot. If, as the Biblical narrator assumes and explains, it is God who has "closed Hannah's womb" so that Hannah's infertility is divinely mandated, then Hannah indeed sets out to change God's decree. God is viewed as a protagonist who, though invisible and uncommunicative, does enter into some kind of discourse with a woman and becomes a party to the negotiations. In fact, Hannah's faith in the power of her prayer is so strong that it seems now that God has no choice but to follow suit and comply with her request. Hannah has made a one-sided bargain with God, but she has cleverly involved God in such a way that it seems she has imposed her will on God and made God an active partner in bringing her wish to successful fruition.

Further, Hannah's petition to God involves pleading for a change not in the past, but in the future. This proves Hannah's nonfatalistic state of mind, her faith that no matter what the past and present have been, the future is always open to change and progress. Hannah views time as a redemptive mechanism and the human existence as a journey within changing history, rather than as an entrapment within the vicious cycle of nature. This attitude ties Hannah to the very core of Biblical thinking and may explain her sense of freedom and independence not only as a character trait, but as a philosophical attitude toward life and its immense possibilities and choices.[14]

Hannah's communication with God is an inner experience; therefore her monologue is soundless. But when Eli the priest confronts her, the tongue-tied Hannah proves that she possesses passionate eloquence. The experience of prayer has unlocked Hannah's tongue; she can now reply to the priest's harsh reprimand whereas before she was unable to respond either to her husband's kind words or to her adversary's taunts. Eli is so impressed with her delivery that he changes his initial impression of her as a drunk and sends her away with a blessing. Eli's blessing only supports what Hannah's own language has achieved for her. Once she has made the bargain with God and created for her son a destiny and a way of life, Hannah is visited by an inner peace, born of a certainty that she never possessed before. And when she has succeeded in turning the awesome, forbidding priest into an ally, Hannah is able to rejoin the family at the celebratory meal and appear calm and undisturbed (1:18).

Hannah's powerful command of language is demonstrated again later, when her son is born. Her manipulation of the verb "to ask" (*sh'l*), exploring all of the verb's possible conjugations, illuminates the tragedy of the woman who "asked" or "borrowed" a child from God but will have to make good on her promise to let God "borrow" the child from her. She calls her son Samuel, "because I have asked [or "borrowed"] him of the Lord," implying the temporariness of his stay with her as a "borrowed" gift. Hannah thus concedes the child's unique origins as part of a bargain made between herself and God, implying that she will not renege on her part of the agreement. Yet her actions belie her words; Hannah is a normal mother who clings to her long-awaited son and delays going on a pilgrimage to Shiloh to postpone the fulfillment of her promise to God. In one brief statement to Elkanah, Hannah encapsulates her painful predicament: she explains to her husband that when she goes to Shiloh with Samuel, it will be only for the purpose of leaving him there "for ever" (1:22).

When Hannah finally brings her child to Shiloh, her gratitude is somewhat tinged with regret, reflected in a small speech in which she again utilizes the various possibilities of the verb "to ask": "For this child I prayed; and the Lord has granted me my *request* [the noun is of the root *sh'l*] that I have *asked* [the root *sh'l*] of Him. Therefore also I have *lent* [the root *sh'l*] him to the Lord, for all his life he will be "borrowed" [*sh'l*] by the Lord" (1:27). In other words, the "borrower" is now God, and the "lender" is the woman. When the child was born and the process of bonding was just beginning, it may have been easier for the woman to admit that the child was, in a sense, a "loan" from God. Yet after a few years of nursing and rearing the child, Hannah will concede only that she is "lending" the child to God (1:28). The changes in Hannah's moods and the journey that she makes from the heartbreak of barrenness to the joys of motherhood to the sorrow of parting from her young child are thus transmitted to us through Hannah's ingenious play on the verb "to ask," which she uses for praying, asking, borrowing, and loaning.

Hannah's spiritual journey, as well as her walk through the whole range of the prayer modality, culminates with the psalm attributed to her (2:1–10), the Song of Hannah.[15] As a hymn of praise to God, Hannah's psalm is the ultimate, most sublime form of prayer. The psalm cautions humans against excessive pride, the sin of hubris, and celebrates God's benevolence and redeeming powers, God's ability to bring about change in human fortunes and lift people out of misery and suffering. The hymn does not focus exclusively on Hannah's personal salvation, or on the salvation of the barren woman in general. Even in the very first verse, where Hannah expresses her jubilant spirits and exults in her personal victory, she does not specify the feminine nature of this victory, her triumphant journey from barrenness to motherhood. Rather, Hannah revels in her good fortune and the elevated status that her experience has conferred on her as a person remembered by God and therefore exalted by God. As the psalm unfolds, Hannah offers a catalog of reversals of fortunes that covers a wide range of human experiences; the barren woman who gives birth to seven children and the "mother-of-many-sons" who ends up in misery (2:5) embody just one example, out of many, that God's "actions are weighed" (2:3). Hannah demonstrates a far-reaching vision that transcends the parameters of her own particular situation and goes beyond the stereotype of the barren woman. Her song shifts her predicament from the traditional feminine orbit to that of a dialogue between humanity and God, placing Hannah's particular situation within the larger pattern of justice with which God rules the human world.

Abraham Heschel's description of prayer applies perfectly to Hannah when she utters this psalm. Heschel explains that prayer, as an act of worship, lifts people out of the triviality of existence, giving

them a sense of living "in ultimate relationships."[16] In her psalm, as
in her conduct throughout the tale, Hannah rises above the circumscribed female boundaries of her generation. It is a measure of Hannah's delicate personality, as well as her great respect for language,
that she does not now confront Peninnah directly and flaunt her own
victory and Peninnah's defeat. The domestic situation is an occasion
for Hannah to make a general philosophical observation on the nature
of life and its changing fortunes, but she does not use the opportunity of her victory for the articulation of feelings of revenge and the
denigration of the loser. The verse "while the barren woman has born
seven \ and she that has many children has become wretched" (2:5)
might be seen as an oblique reference to Peninnah's increased unhappiness, now that Hannah has become fulfilled not only as a wife, but
as a mother, and to her status at home as the fertile wife who is nevertheless not loved by her husband.

The breadth of Hannah's vision is made clear, too, by the future
she paints for her child. In fact, she anticipates God in her determination that her son will dedicate his life to God. In a telling revision
of the story of Samson's origins (Judges 13), wherein the angel of God
defines the future son's role for the barren woman, here the woman
carves out for her son a role in the religious and cultic history of the
Israelite people. One might say that Hannah uses the prospect of a son
dedicated to holy work as a bait to God, but her tragedy is that she
begets a son only after she offers to lose him. Hannah could have
made a satisfactory bargain with God that would not involve losing
the desired child. The terms of her bargain in fact express Hannah's
ambition, her craving to cross over from the constricted existence of
the woman in polygyny to the exciting life of history making and
dedication to God.

Our storyteller has endowed Hannah the individual with diversi-
fied talents: verbal dexterity and poetic gifts, a powerful influence on
men (her husband and the high priest Eli), strong determination, and
great ability to bargain and negotiate. He has also attributed to her
views that mark a departure from accepted norms; Hannah interprets
the successful outcome of her struggle to become a mother as a victory that is existential and moral rather than feminine and biological.
Therefore, within the context of the tale, Hannah's son is not seen as
an instrument to appease and fill the woman's inner "empty space," a

means to satisfy the woman's raging biological needs. We might say that Elkanah's unusual view of his relationship with his wife has empowered Hannah and increased her self-esteem and ability to perceive herself as an individual rather than an instrument of procreation. Or we may conclude that it is Hannah's unusual presence that has bred in the polygynist Elkanah ideas and attitudes not shared by most men and the general culture of his time.

But if Hannah's presence radiates an understanding of feminine existence that is so different from that of Peninnah, for instance, and the rest of the culture, then it is also incongruous with the heart of the tale, which is the woman's monolithic pursuit of motherhood. Perhaps it is anachronistic to apply modern attitudes to a woman who, albeit charismatic, is still steeped in patriarchal traditions. But the question is one of narrative choice: if Hannah's function is only that of the mother of Samuel, why did the storyteller digress from the course of his tale to build up a personality of dignity and memorable talents, a woman who is the sole architect of her son's glorious career; and why does Elkanah reveal a consciousness that is ahead of his time in a remark that is jolting in its implications?

That a woman like Hannah would center her total being on producing an offspring indicates the paucity of opportunities that existed in ancient times for creative expression. For Hannah, the only opportunity to exercise her creative talents and eloquence within the tight social system could have been by educating her son, directing his life, and instilling in him that spiritual grandeur that she possesses.[17] In a system where the burden of educating the children fell often on the able mother, Hannah could have channeled her frustrated, unused gifts into the intellectual and spiritual nurturing of a son.

We may safely say that the vision of her son's future as the leader of the people as well as of his glorious place in the history of Israel is a source of great satisfaction for Hannah. With the force of her will she carved out for her son a place in the space outside the immediate and the domestic, in the history of the Hebrew nation and their sacred text. In turn, Hannah herself is placed in an important spot in that historical and textual space by occupying the center of a story that launches an important Biblical narrative, the Book of Samuel. The narrow domestic parameters in which the tale and its heroine are anchored in the opening verses are thus transmuted to envelop the expansive arena of the future both in time, the epic history of the Israelites, and in script, the eternal text; and it is the charismatic woman who makes it happen.

Thus what seems at first sight to be the prototypical story of maternal yearnings and their ultimate gratification turns out to be a different story. Its crux lies in the universally recognized human aspiration to make a mark that would live forever and in a person's iron-willed ambition to go beyond the temporal, to make an impact on history, if not for herself, then for her son. That this individual's particular aspirations take the form of maternal longings is not biologically determined. Our charismatic heroine is indeed subjugated by powers beyond her control, but she is under the tyranny of cultural and historical circumstances, not of her biological fate.

This literary gem, the Hannah tale, may be viewed as a dramatic treatise on prayer and its various manifestations and functions; as such it is not surprising that it was assigned as the *Haftara* reading for the first day of Rosh Hashana. A tale that illustrates the power of prayer to cleanse our soul as well as actually change the course of our destiny reinforces the spirit and theme of the High Holy Days. Like Hannah, we, too, hope that our entreaties will reach the gates of heaven and be heard by God.

But beyond the obvious, there is a deeper message in this tale. Why has our tradition chosen a woman, Hannah, not only to illustrate the efficacy of prayer, but to chart out the model of all prayers to come? It wanted to give us a message of equality, telling us that in the experience of prayer, gender differences do not exist. The High Holy Days are the most extraordinary days in the Jewish calendar, marking a time in the year when we are most preoccupied with our relationship with God as well as with our own human limitations. Through the medium of prayer we look into the depths of our soul as well as into the secret of our creation and creator. At that moment of mystery and awe, we are all like Hannah: desperate, needy, riddled with a sense of incompleteness, and, most of all, alone. In particular, the tale teaches us that women can and should address God directly and freely. Their status in the eyes of God is not inferior to that of men. When we stand naked before God, all worldly features that divide us from our fellow human beings—wealth, knowledge, status, and gender—are dwarfed.

Further, Hannah's courage in approaching God directly in an environment where she might have felt lacking in worth and significance is more meaningful to us as modern people. All too often we feel unable to connect with God, too distant from our Maker, lost in the overwhelming complexity of contemporary life. Hannah shows us that even the deepest sense of loneliness and worthlessness can be overcome through prayer and that we should not be afraid to initiate a discourse with God. Prayer is miraculous in that it allows us to express and unburden ourselves as well as transcend the narrow confines of human existence. In exemplifying these sublime qualities of prayer, Hannah represents every human being, not just the barren woman. By incorporating into the ritual and liturgy a tale of a woman who communicates successfully with God, our ancient sages have encouraged us to open our hearts to God. They further directed us to view everything that separates us as petty and insignificant and to recognize our common humanity, our shared existential loneliness and frailty, as we stand before our Maker during the Days of Awe.

Second Day
Introduction

The Biblical readings for the second day of Rosh Hashana begin with Genesis 22, in which God commands Abraham to sacrifice his beloved son Isaac. Traditionally understood as the culminating test of Abraham's faith, the *Akeda* (the Binding of Isaac) ends with Isaac's redemption from death and the acknowledgment of Abraham's devotion to God. As we call upon God to "remember us for life," the reading of the *Akeda* is meant to remind us that even when the knife is already raised, God has the power to redeem. This message is further reinforced by the sounding of the *shofar,* the most familiar ritual of Rosh Hashana. According to tradition, the ram's horn recalls the ram sacrificed in place of Isaac, reminding God of Abraham's faithfulness in hopes that it will redound to our benefit so that we too will be redeemed.

For the women writers in this section, the story of the *Akeda* and the sounding of the *shofar* have other associations. The *Akeda,* in which Sarah is conspicuously absent, reminds them of the many stories from which women have been left out. In the sounds of the *shofar* they hear the wails of the mother who has birthed the child she is ultimately powerless to protect. Drawing on midrash that connects the binding of Isaac with the death of Sarah recorded in the very next chapter of Genesis, they are acutely aware that the glorification of the father takes place at the mother's expense. They question Abraham's readiness to sacrifice the son Sarah has spent a lifetime waiting for and wonder why, though Isaac is redeemed, Sarah must die alone and uncomforted. As women searching to hear the women's voices hidden within Biblical texts, they probe the possibilities suggested by midrashic dramatizations of Sarah's responses and unveil a tragic figure who confronts the deepest existential questions of the human condition.

In a famous essay on this text, the literary scholar Erich Auerbach emphasizes the silences of this narrative, noting that the wealth of things not said creates a story "fraught with background." Like the creators of classical midrash, contributors to *Beginning Anew* fill those gaps in ways that express their values, intellectual commitments, and personal experience. They turn their attention to the dependent members of this male-headed family, trying to grasp not only Sarah's perspective, but also Isaac's. Some see this drama as a heightened and concentrated version of Abraham's troubling actions toward Ishmael in the previous chapter. But the excruciating moral and spiritual dilemmas inherent in the figure of Abraham occupy a central place in writers' consideration. Rejecting the traditional praise of Abraham's obedience or any simple notion of "faith" expressed through him, they emerge with a less transcendent and more human Abraham.

Tikva Frymer-Kensky articulates questions that trouble modern readers and subvert any simple embrace of the traditional reading of the story and its role in the experience of Rosh Hashana. Does this story really teach us to sacrifice people for God? Was Abraham's trial a test of submission or of his capacity to act as a moral agent, arguing on behalf of justice? What kind of religious heroism can we find in him now? Drawing on the resources of Biblical scholarship, she uncovers the ambiguous, even contradictory, possibilities of interpretation inherent in the language and structure of the story itself. Her own language pushes us into confrontation with both the horror and the richness of this text because it forces us into awareness of our own values. "We cannot remain neutral." She both demands that we actively "wrestle" with this text and shows us how to do that, by entering the text on its own terms as fully as modern scholarship can, while straining against it with all the power of a contemporary woman's values and spiritual consciousness.

As a teacher of law, Martha Minow tells us, she often ends her courses with stories because she sees that final moment as a last chance to "remind budding lawyers both to question authority and to bear responsibility for the power they will wield." For her, the story of the binding of Isaac resonates deeply with contemporary dilemmas involving conflicts between what the state perceives as the good of children and parents' sincere religious beliefs. Imagining Abraham on trial in a modern court of law, she speaks for both prosecution and defense, from secular and religious points of view. But it is not enough, she suggests, to respond to this story out of professional experience alone. Intertwining the lawyer's arguments with responses generated by her identification, as a woman and a mother, with Sarah and Sarah's child, she summons us to reflect on the theme of sacrifice, whether of children by parents or of parents for children.

Rebecca and Yael Goldstein address Tikva Frymer-Kensky's questions about Abraham's apparent abandonment of moral agency within the context of their spirited dialogue on the *Akeda*. They offer us the remarkable opportunity to hear a mother and daughter grappling with this quintessential father-son story in Jewish tradition. Their written dialogue grows out of their ongoing study partnership, the traditional practice of studying sacred texts *bechevruta*, an intense, interactive mode of discussion and argument involving two people committed to long-term study of a particular text. Rooted in the totally male world of the yeshiva, *chevruta* study, which assumes that insight flourishes most through dialogue, seems a particularly congenial mode for women and has been appropriated by many women engaged in traditional study. Here Rebecca and Yael Goldstein bring to their dialogue wide-ranging knowledge of traditional Jewish texts and the questions and responses aroused by training in philosophy and literature. They raise the issue of moral agency not only in relation to Abraham, but also as it concerns Isaac and Sarah. Reenvisioning the story within a wider Biblical context and responding to poignant midrashic traditions, they find in the text painfully difficult and crucial existential problems for which the only solutions are more dialogue.

We end our section on the *Akeda* with an edited version of Avivah Zornberg's *shiur* (oral presentation about traditional Jewish texts) on the cry of the *shofar*. Zornberg pursues the connection intimated by the Rabbis between "the death of the mother of the Jewish people, Sarah, and the plangent, penetrating notes of the *shofar*-cry." In probing the meaning of Sarah's death, understood by rabbinic midrash to be caused by the binding of Isaac, she draws us, in her unique intellectual style, into a journey in which we encounter classical Jewish sources and more recent texts steeped in rabbinic culture alongside ideas generated by existentialist philosophy, contemporary literature, and history of religion. In the midrashic traditions that also captured the attention of Rebecca and Yael Goldstein, she finds a confrontation with human mortality and with the possibility of meaninglessness that offers a profound challenge to faith. Ironically, that challenge arises from the very text conventionally cited as a demonstration of faith. Zornberg uses the traditional mode of the *shiur* to pursue radically new interpretations that are nevertheless deeply embedded in traditional texts and scholarship. Guided by her, we can understand the cry of the *shofar* as the paradoxical articulation of both radical doubt and affirmation, both of which are rooted in the experience of our mother Sarah.

The *Haftara* portion for the second day of Rosh Hashana is taken from the prophet Jeremiah (chapter 31). As Tamar Frankiel points out, the last Biblical reading of each holiday traditionally focuses on the promises of the messianic era, "reminding us that each holiday (*yom tov*) is a foretaste of the day that is *kulo tov,* completely good." The prophet speaks, in the name of God, a language of "eternal love" (*ahavat olam*) for the people of Israel, figured as "maiden Israel" (*betulat yisrael*) dancing with joy over the rebuilding and renewed fruitfulness of her land. He offers the promise of return (*teshuva*) and reconciliation after exile and destruction to the whole people, the "remnant of Israel . . . the blind and the lame among them, those with child and those in labor—in a vast throng they shall return here." The themes of turning and return, of the people to God and God to the people, sound powerfully in this chapter. As the metaphor for the people shifts to the figure of the "firstborn son," the beloved son, Ephraim, the voice of God promises to "remember him with affection, even when I rebuke him." Women may notice with particular sensitivity the prophet's fluid movement between female and male images for the people of Israel. Even the figurative language for God evokes God as both father ("For I am ever a Father to Israel, Ephraim is my firstborn") and mother (verse 20, translated "I will surely be merciful toward him, says the Lord," uses a doubled form of the verb, "to be merciful," *racheim arachamenu,* suggesting a connection to *rechem,* the womb). But women readers especially highlight three verses in which we suddenly hear the voice of a woman in dialogue with God, "Rachel weeping for her children." Hearing this poignant cry after a Torah reading in which the woman's voice, the mother's cry, was conspicuously, even outrageously, absent, we may perceive in the Rabbis' choice of this chapter a response to the need for a "return" of women's presence.

Tamar Frankiel asks, "Why Rachel?" Why was Rachel, rather than any of the other matriarchs, chosen by Jeremiah to represent the quintessential mother who weeps in prayer over the Jewish people? By exploring the Biblical narratives about Rachel as well as *midrashim* and other traditional commentaries, Frankiel creates a portrait of Rachel that unveils a deeper and more compelling figure than the conventionally noted rival to her sister Leah and favorite wife of Jacob. Rachel becomes "our mother of sorrows," a woman to whose voice God responds because her deep compassion is generated by sharing the pain of the human condition. She becomes, in Frankiel's depiction of her, a source for our own hopes of redemption and response to our prayers.

In a lyrical and learned meditation on the theme of the "first-born" in the Rosh Hashana readings, Nessa Rapoport reflects on the permutations of Jeremiah's image of Israel as God's firstborn son. Noting the pervasive significance of firstborn status and its connection to chosenness for males in the Bible, she asks what this means for daughters, silent and unnamed in most of our sacred stories. Reinterpreting the themes of the Rosh Hashana liturgy as "sovereignty" (*malkhuyot*), "memory" (*zikhronot*) and "summoning" (*shofarot*), she explores not only the problematics of firstborn children, but the meaning of God's transformation of "barren" women and the wider possibilities implied in the idea of "chosen-ness." Speaking as a daughter seeking her "rightful portion" in our heritage, she creates a language suffused with echoes and responses to Biblical narrative and imagery. In the last of this book's Rosh Hashana readings, she transforms Jeremiah's promises into a contemporary woman's vision of redemption.

"Binding of Isaac"
(Genesis 22)

TORAH READING—SECOND DAY ROSH HASHANA

22 And it came to pass after these things, that God did prove Abraham, and said unto him: 'Abraham'; and he said: 'Here am I.' ²And He said: 'Take now thy son, thine only son, whom thou lovest, even Isaac, and get thee into the land of Moriah; and offer him there for a burnt-offering upon one of the mountains which I will tell thee of.' ³And Abraham rose early in the morning, and saddled his ass, and took two of his young men with him, and Isaac his son; and he cleaved the wood for the burnt-offering, and rose up, and went unto the place of which God had told him. ⁴On the third day Abraham lifted up his eyes, and saw the place afar off. ⁵And Abraham said unto his young men: 'Abide ye here with the ass, and I and the lad will go yonder; and we will worship, and come back to you.' ⁶And Abraham took the wood of the burnt-offering, and laid it upon Isaac his son; and he took in his hand the fire and the knife; and they went both of them together. ⁷And Isaac spoke unto Abraham his father, and said: 'My father.' And he said: 'Here am I, my son.' And he said: 'Behold the fire and the wood; but where is the lamb for a burnt-offering?' ⁸And Abraham said: 'God will *provide Himself the lamb for a burnt-offering, my son.' So they went both of them together. ⁹And they came to the place which God had told him of; and Abraham built the altar there, and laid the wood in order, and bound Isaac his son, and laid him on the altar, upon the wood. ¹⁰And Abraham stretched forth his hand, and took the knife to slay his son. ¹¹And the angel of the LORD called unto him

כב

א וַיְהִי אַחַר הַדְּבָרִים הָאֵלֶּה וְהָאֱלֹהִים נִסָּה אֶת־אַבְרָהָם וַיֹּאמֶר אֵלָיו אַבְרָהָם
ב וַיֹּאמֶר הִנֵּנִי: וַיֹּאמֶר קַח־נָא אֶת־בִּנְךָ אֶת־יְחִידְךָ אֲשֶׁר־אָהַבְתָּ אֶת־יִצְחָק וְלֶךְ־לְךָ אֶל־אֶרֶץ הַמֹּרִיָּה וְהַעֲלֵהוּ שָׁם לְעֹלָה עַל אַחַד הֶהָרִים אֲשֶׁר אֹמַר
ג אֵלֶיךָ: וַיַּשְׁכֵּם אַבְרָהָם בַּבֹּקֶר וַיַּחֲבֹשׁ אֶת־חֲמֹרוֹ וַיִּקַּח אֶת־שְׁנֵי נְעָרָיו אִתּוֹ וְאֵת יִצְחָק בְּנוֹ וַיְבַקַּע עֲצֵי עֹלָה וַיָּקָם וַיֵּלֶךְ אֶל־הַמָּקוֹם אֲשֶׁר־אָמַר־לוֹ
ד הָאֱלֹהִים: בַּיּוֹם הַשְּׁלִישִׁי וַיִּשָּׂא אַבְרָהָם אֶת־עֵינָיו וַיַּרְא אֶת־הַמָּקוֹם מֵרָחֹק:
ה וַיֹּאמֶר אַבְרָהָם אֶל־נְעָרָיו שְׁבוּ־לָכֶם פֹּה עִם־הַחֲמוֹר וַאֲנִי וְהַנַּעַר נֵלְכָה עַד־כֹּה וְנִשְׁתַּחֲוֶה וְנָשׁוּבָה אֲלֵיכֶם:
ו וַיִּקַּח אַבְרָהָם אֶת־עֲצֵי הָעֹלָה וַיָּשֶׂם עַל־יִצְחָק בְּנוֹ וַיִּקַּח בְּיָדוֹ אֶת־הָאֵשׁ וְאֶת־הַמַּאֲכֶלֶת וַיֵּלְכוּ שְׁנֵיהֶם יַחְדָּו:
ז וַיֹּאמֶר יִצְחָק אֶל־אַבְרָהָם אָבִיו וַיֹּאמֶר אָבִי וַיֹּאמֶר הִנֶּנִּי בְנִי וַיֹּאמֶר הִנֵּה הָאֵשׁ
ח וְהָעֵצִים וְאַיֵּה הַשֶּׂה לְעֹלָה: וַיֹּאמֶר אַבְרָהָם אֱלֹהִים יִרְאֶה־לּוֹ הַשֶּׂה לְעֹלָה
ט בְּנִי וַיֵּלְכוּ שְׁנֵיהֶם יַחְדָּו: וַיָּבֹאוּ אֶל־הַמָּקוֹם אֲשֶׁר אָמַר־לוֹ הָאֱלֹהִים וַיִּבֶן שָׁם אַבְרָהָם אֶת־הַמִּזְבֵּחַ וַיַּעֲרֹךְ אֶת־הָעֵצִים וַיַּעֲקֹד אֶת־יִצְחָק בְּנוֹ וַיָּשֶׂם אֹתוֹ עַל־הַמִּזְבֵּחַ מִמַּעַל לָעֵצִים:

out of heaven, and said: 'Abraham, Abraham.' And he said: 'Here am I.' ¹²And he said: 'Lay not thy hand upon the lad, neither do thou any thing unto him; for now I know that thou art a God-fearing man, seeing thou hast not withheld thy son, thine only son, from Me.' ¹³And Abraham lifted up his eyes, and looked, and behold behind him a ram caught in the thicket by his horns. And Abraham went and took the ram, and offered him up for a burnt-offering in the stead of his son. ¹⁴And Abraham called the name of that place ᵇAdonai-jireh; as it is said to this day: 'In the mount where the LORD is seen.' ¹⁵And the angel of the LORD called unto Abraham a second time out of heaven, ¹⁶and said: 'By Myself have I sworn, saith the LORD, because thou hast done this thing, and hast not withheld thy son, thine only son, ¹⁷that in blessing I will bless thee, and

ªHeb. *jireh; that is, see for Himself.*
ᵇ That is, *The LORD seeth.*

in multiplying I will multiply thy seed as the stars of the heaven, and as the sand which is upon the sea-shore; and thy seed shall possess the gate of his enemies; ¹⁸and in thy seed shall all the nations of the earth be blessed; because thou hast heark-ened to My voice.' ¹⁹So Abraham re-turned unto his young men, and they rose up and went together to Beer-sheba; and Abraham dwelt at Beer-sheba.

²⁰And it came to pass after these things, that it was told Abraham, say-ing: 'Behold, Milcah, she also hath borne children unto thy brother Nahor: ²¹Uz his first-born, and Buz his brother, and Kemuel the father of Aram; ²²and Chesed, and Hazo, and Pildash, and Jidlaph, and Bethuel.' ²³And Bethuel begot Rebekah; these eight did Milcah bear to Nahor, Abraham's brother. ²⁴And his con-cubine, whose name was Reumah, she also bore Tebah, and Gaham, and Tahash, and Maacah.

10 וַיִּשְׁלַ֨ח אַבְרָהָ֤ם אֶת־יָדוֹ֙ וַיִּקַּ֣ח אֶת־
11 הַֽמַּאֲכֶ֔לֶת לִשְׁחֹ֖ט אֶת־בְּנֽוֹ׃ וַיִּקְרָ֨א
אֵלָ֜יו מַלְאַ֤ךְ יְהֹוָה֙ מִן־הַשָּׁמַ֔יִם וַיֹּ֖אמֶר
12 אַבְרָהָ֣ם ׀ אַבְרָהָ֑ם וַיֹּ֖אמֶר הִנֵּֽנִי׃ וַיֹּ֗אמֶר
אַל־תִּשְׁלַ֤ח יָֽדְךָ֙ אֶל־הַנַּ֔עַר וְאַל־תַּ֥עַשׂ
ל֖וֹ מְא֑וּמָה כִּ֣י ׀ עַתָּ֣ה יָדַ֗עְתִּי כִּֽי־יְרֵ֤א
אֱלֹהִים֙ אַ֔תָּה וְלֹ֥א חָשַׂ֛כְתָּ אֶת־בִּנְךָ֥
13 אֶת־יְחִידְךָ֖ מִמֶּֽנִּי׃ וַיִּשָּׂ֨א אַבְרָהָ֜ם אֶת־
עֵינָ֗יו וַיַּרְא֙ וְהִנֵּה־אַ֔יִל אַחַ֕ר נֶאֱחַ֥ז בַּסְּבַ֖ךְ
בְּקַרְנָ֑יו וַיֵּ֤לֶךְ אַבְרָהָם֙ וַיִּקַּ֣ח אֶת־הָאַ֔יִל
14 וַיַּֽעֲלֵ֥הוּ לְעֹלָ֖ה תַּ֥חַת בְּנֽוֹ׃ וַיִּקְרָ֧א
אַבְרָהָ֛ם שֵֽׁם־הַמָּק֥וֹם הַה֖וּא יְהֹוָ֣ה ׀
יִרְאֶ֑ה אֲשֶׁר֙ יֵֽאָמֵ֣ר הַיּ֔וֹם בְּהַ֥ר יְהֹוָ֖ה
15 יֵֽרָאֶֽה׃ וַיִּקְרָ֛א מַלְאַ֥ךְ יְהֹוָ֖ה אֶל־
16 אַבְרָהָ֑ם שֵׁנִ֖ית מִן־הַשָּׁמָֽיִם׃ וַיֹּ֕אמֶר בִּ֣י
נִשְׁבַּ֖עְתִּי נְאֻם־יְהֹוָ֑ה כִּ֗י יַ֚עַן אֲשֶׁ֤ר עָשִׂ֙יתָ֙
אֶת־הַדָּבָ֣ר הַזֶּ֔ה וְלֹ֥א חָשַׂ֖כְתָּ אֶת־בִּנְךָ֥
17 אֶת־יְחִידֶֽךָ׃ כִּֽי־בָרֵ֣ךְ אֲבָ֣רֶכְךָ֗
וְהַרְבָּ֨ה אַרְבֶּ֤ה אֶֽת־זַרְעֲךָ֙ כְּכֽוֹכְבֵ֣י
הַשָּׁמַ֔יִם וְכַח֕וֹל אֲשֶׁ֖ר עַל־שְׂפַ֣ת הַיָּ֑ם
18 וְיִרַ֣שׁ זַרְעֲךָ֔ אֵ֖ת שַׁ֥עַר אֹֽיְבָֽיו׃ וְהִתְבָּֽרְכ֣וּ
בְזַרְעֲךָ֔ כֹּ֖ל גּוֹיֵ֣י הָאָ֑רֶץ עֵ֕קֶב אֲשֶׁ֥ר
19 שָׁמַ֖עְתָּ בְּקֹלִֽי׃ וַיָּ֤שָׁב אַבְרָהָם֙ אֶל־
נְעָרָ֔יו וַיָּקֻ֛מוּ וַיֵּֽלְכ֥וּ יַחְדָּ֖ו אֶל־
בְּאֵ֣ר שָׁ֑בַע וַיֵּ֥שֶׁב אַבְרָהָ֖ם בִּבְאֵ֥ר
שָֽׁבַע׃ פ

20 וַיְהִ֗י אַֽחֲרֵי֙ הַדְּבָרִ֣ים הָאֵ֔לֶּה וַיֻּגַּ֥ד
לְאַבְרָהָ֖ם לֵאמֹ֑ר הִ֠נֵּה יָֽלְדָ֨ה מִלְכָּ֥ה
21 גַם־הִ֛וא בָּנִ֖ים לְנָח֥וֹר אָחִֽיךָ׃ אֶת־ע֥וּץ
בְּכֹר֖וֹ וְאֶת־בּ֣וּז אָחִ֑יו וְאֶת־קְמוּאֵ֖ל
22 אֲבִ֥י אֲרָֽם׃ וְאֶת־כֶּ֣שֶׂד וְאֶת־חֲז֔וֹ וְאֶת־
פִּלְדָּ֖שׁ וְאֶת־יִדְלָ֑ף וְאֵ֖ת בְּתוּאֵֽל׃
23 וּבְתוּאֵ֖ל יָלַ֣ד אֶת־רִבְקָ֑ה שְׁמֹנָ֥ה אֵ֙לֶּה֙
יָֽלְדָ֣ה מִלְכָּ֔ה לְנָח֖וֹר אֲחִ֥י אַבְרָהָֽם׃
24 וּפִ֙ילַגְשׁ֤וֹ וּשְׁמָ֣הּ רְאוּמָ֔ה וַתֵּ֤לֶד גַּם־הִוא֙
אֶת־טֶ֣בַח וְאֶת־גַּ֔חַם וְאֶת־תַּ֖חַשׁ וְאֶת־
מַֽעֲכָֽה׃

126

AKEDA: THE VIEW FROM THE BIBLE

TIKVA FRYMER-KENSKY

The story of the *Akeda* (Binding of Isaac) is an icon of Jewish life. Every year on the High Holy Days, we read the story and use it as the coinage of our relationship to God. "Forgive us, love us," we say to God, "because of the wondrous deed of our father Abraham, who was willing to give you his son" (Genesis 22). "Look what Abraham did," we say, "surely the merit he gained through this act will apply to us!" Abraham has been our hero, the one whose love for God was steadfast despite the ten trials the Rabbis discerned in his story. The first two of these trials entailed leaving his father's house and his homeland (Genesis 12:3–6); the third and fourth the taking of Sarah by Pharaoh (Genesis 12) and by Abimelech (Genesis 20); the fifth the war to rescue Lot (Genesis 14); the sixth the covenant among the carcasses (Genesis 15); the seventh Abraham's circumcision at ninety-nine (Genesis 17); the eighth, derived midrashically from the name of his city of origin, Ur Casdim, his passing unharmed through a fiery furnace; the ninth giving up Ishmael (Genesis 21); and the tenth and final trial the binding of Isaac (Genesis 22:1–14).

Some of us read this story somewhat differently now. We are not quite as ready to honor Abraham for being prepared to sacrifice the members of his family. We no longer view things only from the perspective of male heads of household and are just as apt to identify with the dependent members of his family. We read the story through the eyes of Sarah: "The giving of Sarah to Pharaoh and Abimelech was a trial of Abraham? What about me? I was the one who became no more than a slave-wife in these foreign rulers' households and had to be rescued by God. What right did Abraham have to just give me away to spare his life?" We read with the voice of Hagar and Ishmael: "Where is the love and loyalty that wives and children should be able to expect from a father?" And we read with the voice of Isaac: "Don't I count as a person? How can my own father be prepared to kill me without even consulting me?" Viewed through their eyes, the actions of Abraham in these events look less like loyalty to God and more like disregard for the human beings dependent on his benevolence; only in rescuing Lot did Abraham show himself to be someone on whom his family could rely.

Does the *Akeda* really tell us we should sacrifice people for God? When we look directly at the *Akeda* with eyes removed from the nostalgia of our religious teaching, it looks like a horrific story. And the horror is wrapped in enigmatic language, for the tale is told formally, with carefully controlled structure, and laconically, with every word carrying meaning. The story is notorious for what it does not contain, telling us nothing of Abraham's reactions or emotions, or those of Isaac, and thus leaving the story "fraught with background," to use Erich Auerbach's famous phrase.[1] These gaps force the reader to enter the scene to try to make sense of it. But not all details are omitted: some are given and even repeated. And these repetitions form a tight structure in which events at the beginning of the story are closely matched by ones at the end.

Genesis 22

1) *It came to pass after these things that God tested Abraham* and He said to him "Abraham" and he said, *"Here I am."*
2) He said, "Take now *your son,*
   your only son whom you love,
   Isaac
   and get you going to the land of Moriah
   and *offer him there as a burnt offering* on the one *mountain*
   that I will tell you."
3) He got up early
   and cinched his ass
   and took *his two lads* with him
   and *Isaac his son*
   and he split the WOOD *for the burnt offering*
   and he got up and went to the *place of which God had told him.*
4) On the third day Abraham lifted his eyes and saw the *place* from afar

5) Abraham said to *his lads,* "Stay here with the ass,
and I and *the lad* will go to there and bow down
and we will *return* to you."

6) Abraham took the WOOD *for the burnt offering* and placed it
on *his son*
and he took the fire and the slaughtering knife
and the two of them went together.

7) Isaac spoke to Abraham his father
and he said "my father" and he said, *"Here I am, my son."*
and he said, "Look, the fire and the WOOD,
but where is the *lamb for a burnt offering?"*

8) Abraham said, *"God will see* to (God will provide) the *lamb
for a burnt offering, my son."*
and the two of them went together.

9) They came to the *place of which God had told him.*
and Abraham built an altar there
and placed the WOOD in order
and he bound *Isaac his son*
and placed him on the altar on top of the WOOD.

10) Abraham stretched out his hand
and took the slaughtering knife
to slay *his son.*

11) The angel of the Lord called to him from heaven
and said, "Abraham, Abraham,"
and he said, *"Here I am."*

12) He said, "Do not lay your hand on *the lad*
and do not do anything to him,
Indeed I know that you fear God
but (now) you have not held back your son, your only son, from
me."

13) Abraham raised his eyes and looked
and look! A ram caught in the thicket by his horns!
and Abraham went and took the ram
and *raised him as a burnt offering* instead of *his son.*

14) Abraham called the name of the *place "the Lord has seen.*
(The Lord provided)"
for it is said today, "On the *mount* of the Lord it shall be
seen."

19) Abraham *returned to his lads*
   And they *arose*
   and they went together
   to Beer Sheba
   and Abraham settled in Beersheba

An Ambiguous Test

The very first words of this horrific story demand that we pay attention. "After these matters, God tested Abraham." Tested him for what? God doesn't say, the narrator doesn't tell us, and Abraham speaks only twice, to tell his servant lads, "We will return to you," and to answer his son's pointed question, "Where is the lamb?" with "God will see to the lamb, my son." The story is often interpreted as a test of faith, which Abraham passed. Once again, we must ask: Faith in what? If Abraham had faith in the ultimate goodness of God, why did he not argue for his son as he argued for Sodom: "Will God have me kill my innocent son? Will the judge of the world not act justly?" The Abraham who argued for Sodom and Gomorra says nothing to spare his son's life. Or was Abraham's faith a conviction that God would stop him from killing his son? Abraham's first statement, to his servants—his promise to return with the lad—could be a lie; this is, after all, the same patriarch who passed Sarah off as his sister in Egypt and in Gerar. And his second statement in response to Isaac's question is completely enigmatic, for it could also be read "the lamb: my son." If Abraham was really confident that God would stop him and that Isaac would be safe, then there is no real horror, and the whole affair is a colossal game of "chicken" in which God blinked first. But the story is crafted to elicit horror, and we must not make a mockery of our own horrified reactions.

The traditional Jewish suggestion is that God was testing steadfastness and loyalty to God, and Abraham proved himself to be "Eitan," the steadfast one, the name he is called in the medieval *piyyutim* (liturgical poems). But this interpretation creates enormous theological problems: Is God so insecure that God keeps questioning Abraham's loyalty even after Abraham's lifetime of devotion? A more recent idea that God was testing Abraham's willingness to submit to God's demand also has problems. Submission is not necessarily a value. Abraham intercedes for Sodom and Gomorrah on the basis of justice and could have done so here. Moses intercedes to save Israel using the argument that the nations would scoff at God if Israel died in the desert; Abraham could have done so here. Later prophets consistently intercede on behalf of Israel, and these intercessions are the mark of their intimate relationship to God. Surely it would not have angered God if Abraham had argued for his son's life!

The test itself is mysterious and may correspond to human emotions: when we feel that we are being tested, we often have no clear idea of what the test might be for. Nor do we know whether we have passed our "test"—or whether Abraham passed his. The results of Abraham's "test" are apparently announced in verse 12 when "the angel of the Lord" says, "Do not touch the lad and don't do anything to him" *ki atah yadati ki yare Elohim atta velo chasakhta et binkha et yechidkha mimmeni.* Our English Bibles translate "For now I know that you fear God since you have not withheld your son, your only son from me." But the "since" is a translator's interpretation of the all-purpose Hebrew *ve,* normally translated "and" and, more rarely, "but." And "withheld" is also a choice; *chasakhta* could also be translated as "held back": at the Exodus, God does not "hold back from death" the Egyptians (Psalm 78:50);[2] holding back your son from certain death may be a good thing to do.

But is it God-fearing? Does "fear of God" demand submission and obedience? In Deuteronomy, this seems to be its meaning. But in the Jonah story, which we also read on Yom Kippur, Jonah defies God's command to go to Nineveh and runs away to sea. Nevertheless, when the storm comes and the sailors wake him, he identifies himself: "I am a Hebrew and a God (of Heaven) fearer" (Jonah 1:9). Here, our translations say, "I worship the God of heaven," but the Hebrew is the same as in the *Akeda.* Other examples also show that the word can imply loyalty to God without question of "obedience." The Assyrians sent an Israelite priest to teach them "how to fear God" and "they worshiped God" and also served their own gods; despite repeated admonition they continued to worship God and serve their idols "till this very day" (II Kings 17:27–41). All these examples use the same form of the verb, *yare,* that God uses to describe Abraham as "God-fearer; one who worships God."[3]

Another important connotation of this verb *yare* is "to behave morally." Joseph promises to let his brothers live, "because I am a God-fearer" (Genesis 42:18), with the same grammatical form and syntactical structure as God's statement to Abraham. Verbal forms are also used. The midwives in Egypt "fear God" and do not kill the boy children despite Pharaoh's decree (Exodus 1:7); and when Israel heard how Solomon resolved the dispute between two prostitutes, "they 'feared' the king because they saw that the wisdom of God was in him to do justly" (I Kings 3:28). They already feared Solomon's royal power to punish; this new "fear" of Solomon is a recognition of the moral rectitude that accompanies true authority. To "fear God" is to acknowledge the moral order of God's ways.

"Fear God," says the proverb, "and avoid evil" (Proverbs 3:7); and the psalmist asks God to teach the God-fearer what to do (Psalm 25:12). The essence of such God-fearing is part of the puzzle of the book of Job, which begins when Satan declares that no one is a true God-fearer. When God boasts that Job is "One who fears God and avoids evil," Satan suggests that Job's God-fearing has all been in expectation of reward (Job 1:4–5). After all, Psalms often states that those who fear God will be rewarded.[4] God tests Job's God-fearing by taking away all the blessings of this world and at the end rewards Job by restoring the good life. Job has passed the test: he is a true *yare Elohim!*

But what has Job done? He has spent thirty-four chapters arguing with God and questioning God's judgment. By arguing for a moral order, by demanding that God do justly, he has proved himself a true *yare Elohim,* a true God-fearer. Could this have been Abraham's test? Was Abraham supposed to fight for Isaac the way he had fought for Sodom and Gomorrah? Was he supposed to demand that God not demand the death of an innocent child and, in addition, that God not break God's own covenant but keep the divine promise of a future for Abraham? If so, maybe Abraham failed the test!

Passed or Failed?

The beginning of God's statement in verse 12, *ata yadati* ("now I know"), seems to imply that the purpose of the test was to discover whether Abraham truly feared God. But surely Abraham had proved his devotion to God during a lifetime of allegiance—how many times does a human being have to reassure God? Did God really not know this before the test? Perhaps that *ata yadati* does not imply that the knowledge is newly determined, now (and not before). This becomes clearer if we look at Psalm 20, where the same phrase appears. Psalm 20 begins with reassurance that God answers in the time of trouble. In verses 2–6, all the verbs that describe God's actions[5] and the verbs that describe the people's activities[6] are in the imperfect, which may be translated "God answers" or "God will answer":

(LEADER)

The Lord will answer you on a day of trouble
the name of the God of Jacob will defend you.
(God) will send your help from holiness
and will support you from Zion,
(God) will remember all your gifts
and will accept your offering, selah.
(God) will give you as your heart('s desire)
and will fulfill all your wishes.

(ASSEMBLY)

we will rejoice in your salvation
and be draped in the name of our God

(LEADER)

The Lord will fulfill all your wishes.

But suddenly, verse 7 uses the perfect *hoshia* (has saved) preceded by *ata yadati: ata yadati ki hoshia YHWH Meshicho*—"that God has saved his anointed," or perhaps a prophetic future, "that God will indeed save." The psalm immediately goes back to imperfect forms— *ya'anehu mishmei qodsho bigvurot yesha yemino* ([God] answers you from (God's) holy heaven, (God's) right hand saves with mighty deeds")—and then continues in this mode:

(ASSEMBLY)

Some with chariots and some with horses
but we recite the name of the Lord our God
They are bowed and fallen
but we stand heartened

(LEADER)

> The Lord Saves,
>> the king answers us on the day we call.

In order to understand *ata yadati* as a temporal phrase implying "now I know (what I did not know before)," people have had to construct elaborate scenarios to explain why it appears in the middle of the psalm. These scenarios imagine that a prayer is recited, then interrupted, then resumed. A leader is answered by a chorus of worshipers, *then a cultic prophet speaks unrecorded words promising a future victory,* and then the leader and worshipers continue their prayer. Alternatively, the leader and people are praying for victory in battle, *then unknown words arrive from the battlefield announcing that the victory has been won,* then the leader and people affirm God's saving response. But these scenarios are unconvincing. Why wouldn't the words of the prophet or runner be recorded? Instead we should understand the phrase *ata yadati* in Psalm 20 and the *Akeda* as a strong assertive clause, like English "now (then)." In Psalm 20:7 the petitioner says, "Indeed I know that God saves his anointed—(now) let him answer from his holy Heaven." In Genesis 22:12 the angel says, "Indeed I know that you are a God fearer—but (now) you have not held back your son from me."

This crucially ambiguous sentence leads to utterly different conclusions—one, that binding Isaac for sacrifice is a mark of Abraham's special virtue and fidelity; and the other, that binding Isaac was a failure of Abraham, who was after all only human and who missed his opportunity to rise in defense of justice. The first explanation places a high value on submission, the second on God-wrestling. In modern philosophy the latter position has been identified with Kant, who argued that the moral is the ultimate; and the former with Kierkegaard, who proclaimed Abraham as a "knight of faith" who operated in a realm beyond morality. The story can support *either* position. We who believe that humans are supposed to be responsible moral agents can explain that Abraham did not act appropriately without doing violence to the text. We have no need to be angry at the Bible's values, for the story allows us to see our own position reflected in it. At the same time, we must acknowledge that the *Akeda* does not resolve the question of submission/moral agency, for verse 12 also allows the more traditional interpretation. The story holds two very different attitudes toward moral agency and total submission in suspension. Part of the impact of this story lies in the fact that it makes us aware of our own values as we read it. We cannot remain neutral.

An Older Question: Is It Wrong to Sacrifice Children?

The *Akeda* story multiplies its moral ambiguities. The pass/fail interpretations both rest on the assumptions that killing one's child in devotion to God is a horrible thing to do and that Abraham nevertheless was ready to do it because God had commanded it. They differ only on whether God wanted Abraham to obey the horrible demand. The artistry of the story's highly stylized and tightly organized telling reveals what question is most central to the narrator. The telling has nine scenes:

I. 1) announcement of test
      1–2 call; answer; command : "Take your son, go to Moriah, sacrifice him"

II. 3) To go to place of which God spoke:
      Abraham arises early
      cinches the ass, chops wood
      takes lads and son

III. 4) Abraham arrives within sight on third day
      5) leaves servants and ass

IV. 6) loads wood on Isaac
      takes fire and slaughtering knife

V. The two go together
      7) dialogue: Isaac—my father
                 Abraham—here I am
                 Isaac—where is the ram?
      8) Abraham:—the Lord will see to the lamb, my son
      the two go together

VI. 9) At the place of which God told
      Abraham builds altar
      arranges wood
      binds Isaac
      loads Isaac on wood

VII.   10) Abraham takes slaughtering knife to slaughter Isaac
VIII.   11–12) call; answer; command: "Do not lay hand on lad"
          12) pronouncement on result of test
          13) ram for burnt offering
          14) Abraham names place
  IX.   18) Abraham returns to the lads
          they go together

In this structure, section I (the test and God's command) and section VI (the second command and the *ata yadati* results) contain the same elements: command for sacrifice, place, and sacrificed object. Section II (the beginning, preparing wood, and starting journey) is echoed in section V (ending the journey and arranging wood). Section III (leaving the servants) achieves closure in IX (rejoining the servants). Section IV (beginning the last stage with Isaac, wood and slaughtering knife) culminates in VII (with Isaac and slaughtering knife). The story is written in a structure (sometimes called "ring structure" or "chiastic order") that highlights the center: the center is where the story crafter puts the essential meaning of the story. The center is the dialogue between Abraham and his son in verse 9, and the center of that is Isaac's question: "Where is the ram?" For the crafter of this story, the ultimate issue was not whether Abraham should have been submissive or confrontational, but which sacrifice God wants.

In the world of ancient Israel, the horror of child sacrifice was not obvious, for not everyone believed that it was wrong to kill one's child. The sacrifice of children was well-known in the ancient Mediterranean, celebrated in mythic writings, recorded by historians, and confirmed by archaeological excavation. Of the Greek stories about men who were prepared to sacrifice their offspring, the most famous (to us) is the tale of Iphigenia. In one version (the Cypria), Agamemnon was commanded to sacrifice his daughter Iphigenia, but at the last minute Artemis substituted an animal and Iphigenia became a priestess. In another version (Euripides), Agamemnon took an oath that would have been fatal to Iphigenia, but in this version, too, Artemis substituted an animal and Iphigenia became a priestess. In the most famous version (Aeschylus), Agamemnon actually kills Iphigenia and sets off a chain reaction of revenge murder.[7]

Child sacrifice is identified most closely with the Phoenicians. Philo of Byblos, who is quoted by the church father Eusebius, relates that the Phoenicians had an ancient custom: in order to save the city in great emergencies, the ancient rulers sacrificed their most beloved sons as an expiation to the avenging gods.[8] The Roman historian Quintus Curtius writes that at Alexander the Great's siege of Tyre (in 333–332 B.C.E.), the Phoenicians almost renewed the ancient custom by offering up the child of a nobleman as a sacrifice to the god Saturn and were stopped only by the opposition of the elders of the city; the people of the Phoenician colony of Carthage held to this custom until the destruction of the city.[9] Another Roman historian, Deodorus Siculus, relates that after Hannibal's death Hamilcar sacrificed a boy to Kronos.[10] The Romans were not above slandering their enemies the Carthaginians, but these reports of Carthaginian child sacrifice are confirmed by the finding of large child-graveyards, now called "Tophets" in Carthage and in Phoenicia itself, and by the discovery of a large stele at Puzo Moro, a Phoenician colony on the coast of Spain, which shows a monster-headed god lifting his knife to slaughter a child while another monster-headed figure in the background has body parts coming from his mouth.[11]

Child sacrifice was known to Israel. In the period of the settlement, the judge Jephthah sacrificed his only daughter as a result of his vow to sacrifice the first creature to greet him as he came home victorious (Judges 11:29–40). Later, the king of Moab, besieged by a joint Judeo-Israelite force, sacrificed his eldest son and heir apparent on the walls of the city. The drastic method worked: "a great fury" came out into the Israelite camp, and they abandoned the siege (II Kings 3). In the century of the destruction of the first Temple, in the days of Manasseh and Ahaz, child sacrifices, the "abomination of the peoples that God kicked out of the land before Israel" were performed in Judah, in Jerusalem itself.[12]

The idea that the people of Jerusalem sacrificed their children is so shocking that some scholars would like to believe that "passing children through fire" was an initiation ordeal in which only some children died. But the Bible has no doubt that people sacrificed their children. Post-exilic Biblical writings refer to the pre-exilic "slaughtering" (*shcht*) of children,[13] and evidence is mounting that "passing through fire"—despite our fervent wish for denial—actually refers to child sacrifice. "Passing through fire" is often characterized as *lmlk*, often translated as "to Molech" and explained as the name of a foreign god. Some people in Judah may have sacrificed their children to foreign gods, for Psalm 106 talks about the Israelites' sacrificing (*zbch*) their sons and daughters to demons, and Ezekiel mentions their slaughtering their children to idols. But the people "passing their children through fire" in the valley of Hinnom were sacrificing their child not to a foreign deity, but to God. The command in Leviticus "You shall not give your seed for passing *lmlk*" explains "You shall not profane the name of your God, I, YHWH."[14] Child burning profanes God's name because it is a horrendous sacrifice to God. *Mlk* is the very word used on the tombs of children in the child-graveyard of Carthage. It refers to a sacrifice and is sometimes specified as *mlk'mr*, the sacrifice of a lamb (instead of a child). Our standard theories of sacrifice would predict that first the people sacrificed children and then lambs, but the archaeological evidence from Carthage shows just the opposite. As time went on, more and more children were sacrificed and fewer and fewer lambs. It seems that as conditions got worse, people tried to become more intensely devoted. The same process may have happened in Israel. The time of Manasseh was a time of emergency, and Manasseh may either have imported the custom or revived an ancient one, but from the time of Manasseh until Josiah contaminated the Tophet, people "passed their children through fire" in the Tophet (furnace) in the valley of Hinnom.[15]

This "passing through fire" was the subject of harsh dispute, with only the anti-voices surviving. From Jeremiah's diatribe against the people who "built the 'bamot of the master' in the valley of Hinnom to pass their sons and their daughters through the fire as a *mlk*— which I didn't command them, which it didn't even enter my mind to do this abomination to cause Judah to sin" (Jeremiah 32:35), we can infer that the people in the valley of Hinnom believed that God commanded them to sacrifice their children. They seem to have attributed the worsening political situation of Israel to God's anger that they had not been sufficiently pious. They had only been sacrificing animals, not children! In an effort to be ever more devout, they started sacrificing their children to God.

Ezekiel in Babylonian exile believed that the sacrifice of children was a horrendous abomination and that Jerusalem was a "city of blood." But, unlike Jeremiah, he believed that God really did command it, or at least caused it intentionally by the wording of the divine commands. Ezekiel 20 is the most horrifying chapter of the Bible, ultimately even more horrifying than the *Akeda*. Here Ezekiel tells the story of Israel's lack of fidelity and God's retributive anger. According to Ezekiel, Israel sinned in Egypt, but God was obligated to redeem them by the promises to Abraham. Israel sinned in the desert, but God could not destroy them because it would profane the divine name. Even the generation of the desert sinned, but God could not destroy them because of God's name and the promise of Canaan. God had to bring them into the land, but God made sure that they would have to be exiled by giving Israel "laws that are not good, statutes that one can not live by" (20:25). In this way, God made sure that they would get contaminated even when they were bringing God gifts. The "not-good" law to which Ezekiel is referring is the law of the firstborn as it is stated in Exodus 22:8, ". . . the firstborn of your children you shall give me," and also in Exodus 13:15, "You will pass every womb-opener child to YHWH, and every first born of one of your beasts, the males are for God." Exodus 22 requires the child to be redeemed by substituting a lamb. Leviticus suggests that the father substitute a gift of silver and (elsewhere) considers the Levites' service as the substitute for Israel's obligation to give their children to God. But some Judeans believed that these substitutions in the Temple were the lesser options and that true devotion meant sacrificing the children. And according to Ezekiel (in this one passage) God wanted them to think so.

In the context of this dispute, telling the story about how Abraham was ready to sacrifice Isaac at the command of God (or listening and transmitting it) takes on a whole new character. Abraham is commanded—just as the sacrificers in the valley of Hinnom believe that they were commanded. The child sacrificers are not monsters; they are trying to obey the command of God as they understand it.

Plot and Polemic

Abraham's answer to the question "Where is the ram?" is cryptic: is "my son" his address to his son, or is it the answer, as in "the burnt offering: my son." We cannot be sure what Abraham believed God wanted of him, but the *Akeda* story tells us what God wants by the change in the parallel sections I and VIII, which contrast sacrificing son with sacrificing ram, which further identify Moriah with Abraham's naming the place "God will provide," and which emphasize that it is on the mount of the Lord that God has provided (or God's wishes are seen). It is on the Temple mount, identified as Moriah, that Abraham's answer is realized: God provides a ram for the sacrifice. The Temple is right, not the Valley of Hinnom, and the Temple's answer is confirmed; God wants animal and not human sacrifice.

The careful choice and repetition of words in this laconic story intensifies the message that Temple sacrifice is the proper sacrifice. One can see this just by following the repeated words:

I. "Here I am:" says Abraham to God (1), to Isaac (7), to angel of God (11)

II. your son: "Take your son" (2); "didn't withhold your son" (12)

III. your only son: "Take your only son" (2) didn't withhold "your only son" (12)

IV. his son: took his son (3); put wood on Isaac his son (6); bound Isaac his son (9); to slaughter his son (10); instead of his son (13)

V. my son: "Here I am, my son" (7); God will see to the lamb, my son (8)

VI. offer up a burnt offering: God to Abraham (2); Abraham offered (13)

VII. mountain: to the mountain I will tell you (2); on the mount of the Lord (14)

VIII. place: Abraham goes to the place God tells him (3); sees the place from afar (4); comes to place God tells him (9), names the place (14)

IX. wood: Abraham splits (3), loads on Isaac (6), arranges on altar (9), loads Isaac on top of (9)

X. burnt offering: offer him there as (2); Abraham splits wood for (3), loads wood for on Isaac (6); where is lamb for (7); God will see to lamb for (8); offered ram as (13)

XI. will see (provide): God will see to the lamb (8); Abraham names the place "the Lord has seen" (14)

The identifying word of the drama, the binding of Isaac (*akad*), appears only once. But the word *ben*, "son," used nine times in the fourteen verses,[16] emphasizes the relationship of Isaac to Abraham and the horror of what Abraham is about to do. We never hear that Abraham prepares the knife or the rope or brings them to the place, but ordinary sacrificial words are repeated often. *Olah*, "burnt offering" six times, twice with the phrase "offer him up as an *olah*" (when God commands and when Abraham offers), twice in the phrase "wood for the *olah*" (which Abraham splits and loads upon Isaac), and twice in the phrase "lamb for the *olah*," the subject of Isaac's question and Abraham's answer. The wood is mentioned four times: we see Abraham splitting the wood for the *olah* and loading it on Isaac, then we see him arrange the wood and place Isaac on the altar above the wood. The place is also repeated four times: when he sets out for it, when he sees it from afar, when he arrives, and when he names it. Twice it is specified as "the place God designates (tells to him)," a term also used for the mountain.

"The place God tells him" is reminiscent of Deuteronomy's "the place God chooses to place His name." Both ultimately prove to be the Temple mount in Jerusalem. And the text closely follows the procedure that must have been observed in the Temple. The individual had to bring wood as well as the animal, for Jerusalem could never have had enough wood for all the sacrifices. From this story we see the Temple process: the offerer must have brought the wood on an ass, then left his entourage and his ass and gone up alone to the Temple mount with the sacrificial animal. After the sacrifice, he would rejoin the family.[17] With the repetitions of precisely these terms the story conveys the message that the sacrifice of son was proceeding just like an ordinary sacrifice, which means that it (and all subsequent sacrifices of sons) should be done at the Temple by the substitution of an animal.

This narrative leaves no doubt about what God wants by telling the story in a way that makes the test of Abraham the paradigm for Temple sacrifices and the legitimating foundation legend for the superior holiness of the Temple's practice of honoring God's claim over children by sacrificing a substitution animal sacrifice. The portrait of an Abraham willing to sacrifice his son in obedience to God's command gives appropriate honor to the devotion with which the child sacrificers offer their children to God. At the same time, the intensity of God's statement to Abraham reflects the urgency with which God stops the killing. God does not only say "don't sacrifice the boy"; God says, "Don't touch the lad," and then repeats, "Don't do anything to him." There is urgency in this statement. If Abraham wasn't acting to spare his son, God would. The child must not be killed!

We will never know when the story of the binding of Isaac began to be told in Israel, whether the devout sacrificers in the valley of Hinnom had their version of the story, or what form their version might have taken. But the careful dramatic telling of this story in Genesis speaks with the voice of the priests and the prophets who believed that God did not want people to slaughter their children. Acknowledging that Abraham (and the child sacrificers) were truly devout, God provides a ram and stops Abraham at the critical moment.

After the Fall

Soon after this period, the Temple was destroyed. Child sacrifice was a dead issue, and the central issue of the day was salvaging Israel's relationship with God and assuring her survival. Deuteronomy and the pre-exilic prophets justify the troubles to come as just punishment for Israel's sins, and the exilic prophet Ezekiel claims that all Israel's suffering was deserved. But the destruction involved the suffering of many innocents, the killing of many children. To some, this must have seemed excessive retribution, and even to the exilic prophet Isaiah, the troubles were "double for all your sins" (Isaiah 40:2). At this time, the *Akeda* story looked very different, and Abraham became the paradigm of loyalty in the face of horror, of steadfastness despite an evil decree.

This may have been the time that the "second speech" of the angel was added to the story to create the "final form" of Genesis 22. This speech, written in a totally different style, offers a resolution to the question that the tautly told *Akeda* leaves ambiguous: Did Abraham pass or fail the test? Was he right in submitting, or should he have argued to save his son? This "second" speech resolves the ambiguity with two clearly unambiguous phrases ya'an asher (22:16) "because," and *ekev asher* (22:18) "in the wake of the fact that," and the specification that what Abraham did was "listen to my voice." The result is a grammatically redundant statement: "I swear, says God, that because you have done this thing and not withheld your son, your only son, indeed I will bless you and multiply your seed greatly as the stars of heaven and the sands on the shores of the sea and your seed will take over the gate of its enemies and all the nations of the world will be blessed by your seed in the wake of the fact that you have listened to my voice" (verses 26–28). It offers a very clear answer, removing all ambiguity. The *Akeda* was a test of obedience, Abraham has passed the test, and therefore God gives Abraham's seed the same blessing God gave Abraham at the beginning of the saga. This clarification is really the first commentary on the story, a commentary written early enough to be incorporated in the Bible itself.[18]

As Time Goes On

Later, as troubles increased and magnified in Israel's history, many Abrahams arose in Israel. In the Greek period, Hannah exhorted her seven sons to die rather than renounce God; in the Roman period, Pinchas ben Yair and the other zealots on Masada killed themselves and their children rather than allow them to fall into Roman hands. Many Isaacs arose, willing martyrs to the divine decree, and midrash began to portray Isaac as the willing accomplice to Abraham's sacrifice, neither struggling nor protesting, but submitting himself to God's demands for his death. The legend of the *Akeda* became the central story of Israel's spiritual formation, teaching the value of sacrifice to God during the millennia of persecution and martyrdom, teaching the value of steadfastness to Jews who stayed faithful when God did not stop their many sacrificial martyrs.

It is even later now. The commands of God are faint, and history teaches us the horrors that can be perpetrated by those who "hear" God's command. To many, the old values hold true, along with the readings that arose from them. But to many of us the story once again looks different. We want "no more killing," as Yitzhak Rabin said at the beginning of the peace accords. We do not want to march our children off to be killed in wars. And we have learned from Yitzhak Rabin's murder that the road from Pinchas ben Yair to Yigal Amir is very short. We are acutely conscious of Abraham's silence. Our religious ideal is not submission, but moral agency. When people suffer because of what some perceive as God's command, we protest in the name of justice and of life, prepared to wrestle with God, with the Bible or the rabbinic texts, or with those, dead or alive, who interpret the law. Our horrified reaction to the traditional reading of the *Akeda* shocks us into awareness of our religious rejection of obedience to harmful decrees and "laws that are not good." In its stark horror and ambiguous statements, the story of the *Akeda* remains the central text in the formation of our spiritual consciousness.

Child Endangerment, Parental Sacrifice: A Reading of the Binding of Isaac

MARTHA MINOW

What should I think about, when I think about the Binding of Isaac? The question, of course, arises each year during the Days of Awe. But it is a more persistent question for me as a teacher of law, as a woman, as a parent, and as a child. Should I respond with awe, horror, admiration, anger, relief? Any of these responses may be justifiable, but I worry that I mainly will feel a familiar perplexity. I wrestle for a fresher, deeper response. The knife Abraham uses almost to kill Isaac reminds me of the comment ascribed to Rabbi Moshe Leib: "The way in this world is like the edge of a blade. On this side is the netherworld, and on that side is the netherworld, and the way of life lies in between."[1] Can the Binding give us clues about how to live in this in-between?

As a teacher of law, I have often ended courses with stories and parables because that final moment feels like my last chance to remind budding lawyers both to question authority and to bear responsibility for the power they will wield. For these occasions, I used to use Woody Allen's version of the Binding of Isaac. In that version, Abraham, in his underwear, hears a deep, resonant voice directing him to sacrifice Isaac; Isaac asks why Abraham did not discuss the matter with God, and ultimately the angel of the Lord stops Abraham and admonishes him for having no sense of humor or ability to resist deep, resonant voices. I liked Allen's effort to remind us to be critical of authority and to resist even authoritative commands when they contravene fundamental values. But I do not use this story anymore. Since Allen faced charges of child abuse and then left his longtime companion for her adopted daughter—sacrificing his family relationships—his words are not the ones I want to leave with students.

The Binding of Isaac always resurfaces for me when I teach and write about parents who refuse medical treatment for their children because of religious conviction. These refusals sometimes turn into court disputes. Parents may be prosecuted for homicide or aggravated child abuse if their refusal of medical treatment leads to the child's death. For example, Ginger and David Twitchell were charged and tried for manslaughter after their two-and-a-half-year-old son, Robyn, died from a medically curable bowel obstruction. The Twitchells had turned to a Christian Science practitioner and to spiritual healing rather than taking Robyn to a doctor. The tenets of Christian Science do not forbid conventional medical treatment but view it as a weakness and as a failure to pursue the spiritual method of casting out the error in thought that is believed to have caused the problem. The jury convicted the Twitchells; the judge sentenced them to ten years' probation, conditioned upon their obtaining medical checkups for their other children and medical attention if any of them became seriously ill. Massachusetts' highest court later overturned the conviction because the jury was not permitted to view a Christian Science handbook used by the couple during the time that they decided that they lawfully could treat Robyn's illness without seeking medical care.[2]

Other cases go to court because parents invoke religious grounds to refuse particular medical treatment for a child already under a doctor's care.[3] Judges commonly authorize blood transfusions for a child over parental religious objections, such as those expressed by Jehovah's Witnesses, who believe that receiving blood prevents resurrection and everlasting life after death.[4] Or a court may consider ordering chemotherapy against religiously inspired views such as these: "We would love for [the child] to have a full and long life. But it is more important to us that his life be full instead of long, if that [is] the way it [has] to be."[5] A parent who deprives a child of food because of religiously inspired directions also risks state intervention.[6]

The director of a Massachusetts study that documents cases of children who died because their parents refused to seek medical treatment explained, "It's just bloodcurdling how these kids suffered. There are kids with diabetes who got no insulin. They died slow, painful deaths. There are kids with operable cancer who went through suffering that was really unnecessary."[7]

Who could respond to these descriptions without wanting the state to protect vulnerable children against such harms? Yet I cannot help but worry about state power wielded with indifference or hostility to religious beliefs. What if my sincere religious beliefs pitted me against the intervening, intermeddling state? What if state officials decide that male circumcision is child abuse? Circumcision, practiced by Jews since Abraham circumcised Isaac, is a model of human obedience to God's will that reminds us of the Binding of Isaac.[8]

Courts can acknowledge the intensity of parents' religious beliefs and even declare respect for those beliefs while stepping in over the parents' objections to protect the child or punish the parents.[9] Judges may themselves feel torn between respecting parents who love their children and secular medical experts who say they know better. The almost universal result, however, is to prefer the medical experts.[10] When asking how much parents may impose their religious beliefs on their children, state officials tend to neglect how much the state imposes its secular beliefs on parents. When the legal question is what serves a child's best interests, religious conceptions of faith and redemption vie with secular notions of health and longevity. If I were a judge faced with charges of child neglect or homicide, I wonder how I would, and how I should, evaluate parental defenses based on religious belief or inspiration.

Perhaps it is ludicrous to take another step in imagination, but what would a contemporary secular court in the United States do if Abraham's attempt to sacrifice Isaac were brought before it? How would he defend himself?

Heat of passion could provide no excuse; Abraham had three days to think about it. Perhaps Abraham would testify, "The Master of Time and Space commanded me to take my son, the long-awaited child with my wife, to a mountaintop, to tie him with restraints, and offer him as a burnt-offering to the Almighty by sacrificing him mortally." To contemporary ears, this testimony is more likely to signal psychosis than religious devotion. Hearing voices increasingly falls in the psychiatric domain, while communication with the Divine is generally thought to be more subtle or indirect.[11] That Abraham never heard directly from the Almighty after this event might be of some help, at least in establishing Abraham's competency to stand trial.

With a lawyer's advice, he might then defend himself as follows: "I acted in my child's best interests because I demonstrated for him and all of his descendants what the love and fear of the Divine demands."[12] If Søren Kierkegaard, the philosopher, were the lawyer, Abraham might defend his action as a crucial moment of self-definition by having faith in the impossible, faith that despite his own act of killing his beloved son, Isaac would be restored to him. With Kierkegaard as counsel, Abraham might even acknowledge that no one can understand his act, which in its unique particularity becomes an absolute relation to the absolute.[13] Maybe Abraham, or his lawyer, would maintain that Abraham protected his child by testing the Almighty and revealing the All-Merciful, or by giving Isaac himself the chance to act heroically and to accept the role of sacrificial lamb.[14] Perhaps, Abraham would argue, Isaac not only survived, but became a different Isaac; no longer Abraham's, but the Lord's; or perhaps a stronger, more independent Isaac who could become a patriarch himself. Abraham might claim Isaac was not a child; at the age of thirty-seven (or sixteen?) he could have resisted the climb to Mount Moriah and what transpired there. Or the lawyer's investigation might reveal that it was not the Almighty, but Satan who inspired the test, and thus Abraham should be excused.[15] Even with hindsight, Abraham would have difficulty persuading a judge that he took his action in order to free humankind of child sacrifice. It was Abraham, after all, who cast his first son, Ishmael, out in the desert to die. Different modus of operation, but same intent, the prosecutor would argue.

In defending himself, Abraham might find it difficult to decide whether to claim that he acted without a hope of reward or fear of punishment.[16] He might argue, in the alternative, that he acted precisely because of hopes for his child's well-being or out of fears of greater harms. Would Abraham be better off indicating that he knew it was a test or an initiative rite for Isaac—implying confidence that the Master of the Universe would not let harm come to the precious child? Or might this reveal Abraham's own misunderstanding of the nature of the test, a test that had to terrify, not reassure? Isn't the point of belief to leap before there is confidence or proof?

Lillian Smith, the acutely perceptive white Southern civil rights activist, once said, "To believe in something not yet proved and to underwrite it with our lives: it is the only way we can leave the future open."[17]

Perhaps only if Abraham knew with confidence that Isaac would emerge alive could he as the loving father wield the knife against his son. This would not be a powerful defense at a secular trial if somehow the son nonetheless died. Many religious parents evidence sincere shock when their children die without medical treatment. Yet this tends only to confirm the secular view that these parents failed in their duties to protect their children's best interests. God does not always come out well in tests of faith.[18] The extensive commentaries suggesting that Abraham did indeed slay Isaac may be evidence of this or may be evidence of the possibility of danger requisite for the test of faith.[19]

❖

To imagine Abraham's defenses in a secular court is to expose anew the terrifying incomprehensibility of his action. The text's silences about Sarah underscore terror and incomprehension. Sarah, who already has sacrificed herself by arranging the liaison with Hagar to assure Abraham's progeny, and Sarah, who finally with joy has a son, Sarah is missing from the entire chapter on the Binding of Isaac. Abraham takes Sarah's long-wanted, beloved son to be sacrificed without any discussion; the next we hear of Sarah, she has died. No wonder the Rabbis tried to fill in the silences about Sarah. One commentary has Abraham lying and telling Sarah he will take Isaac to study the ways of the Lord. Sarah replies, "Thou hast spoken well. Go, my lord, and do unto him as thou hast said, but remove him not far from me, neither let him remain there too long, for my soul is bound within his soul."[20]

Another commentary shows Isaac concerned with Sarah just when Abraham is not. Isaac tells Abraham to take his ashes to Sarah so that she can keep them and weep for him.[21] Sarah's death, to the commentators, is entirely linked to the incident: Sarah dies while Abraham lifts the knife over Isaac or when she hears that Abraham did sacrifice

Isaac.[22] Alternatively, Sarah dies of joy after learning that the Almighty had spared Isaac[23] or in response to the terrible truth that her son was all but killed.[24] If Sarah, the first observer to learn of the Binding of Isaac, dies upon hearing the story, is this a clue about how we should respond? Sarah would be unavailable to serve as a witness in court if Abraham were to face charges after the event. Perhaps he was estranged from her, as they lived apart before the incident. Some would say that the charges against Abraham should include causing Sarah's death.

Sarah's absence would not tell a secular court how to rule on Abraham's defenses. But perhaps Sarah's response tells me at least in part how I—yes a lawyer, but also a woman, a mother—should react to the Binding of Isaac. Whether she died of grief or joy, or instead screamed silently,[25] Sarah's response reminds me not to ignore the real, human connections and intense emotions implicated by the story of Abraham and Isaac, as well as by the stories of contemporary parents and children.

As a parent, I sympathize with the parents who face secular trials for adhering to religious beliefs that expose their children to harms. Despite my professional work defending rights for children, becoming a mother has given me pause about claims that children should have rights. It is not so much a vivid encounter with a totally dependent being that makes me question rights for children. We lawyers have not shied away from the language of rights for people who cannot speak—people who are comatose or severely disabled—just as we have not refrained from according rights to corporations and other artificial "persons." In these situations, and perhaps particularly in these situations, rights establish boundaries and bargaining chips where otherwise sheer power might prevail.

My doubts arise from the barely articulable but fierce resistance I have to anyone interfering with my care for my child. The idea that someone else—and, more worrisome, some stranger—could tell me how to raise my child is far more disturbing than all the strangers who dared to touch my pregnant belly. I do not trust those beyond my immediate sphere of family, friends, and tested teachers and physicians to know and understand my child, much less to cherish her and shield her from harm.

It is at these points in my reflections, though, that I hear echoes of a parent's shout aimed at me nearly two decades ago when I served as a court-appointed advocate for her child in a custody investigation. "Just wait until you have a child of your own," she leveled as if it were a curse. "Then you'll know how wrong it is for you to come in and stand between me and my child." The comment stung then, and it reverberates now that I have a child. Yes, it would be painful to have to deal with anyone else claiming to stand up for my child and, especially, to stand against me. If that someone else is a government official, a bureaucrat, or a social worker, my comfort level does not increase.

Yet some parents do abuse their children. Some adults, including public employees, inflict violence on children. Some parents expose their children to dangers with irreversible consequences. Denying medical care critical to the child's life may honor the parents' religious beliefs, but this permits parents to martyr a child without giving that child the chance to embrace or reject those beliefs.

So I do not disagree with the Supreme Court and state courts that have announced secular rights for children in judicial procedures, freedom of speech, education, and medical care. Rights for children necessarily involve relationships between children and adults and depend on adults for assertion, enforcement, and responsibility. Children's rights represent not their autonomy, but their connection with others; not their isolation, but their membership in a community with others who care about them. If their rights cut into parents' autonomy, perhaps that is because some parents, left alone, hurt their children. That risk is threatening enough that we all should embrace a system that checks parental power.

Even with my fierce resistance to interference with my child, I have come to face this basic truth: My responsibilities to my child include living under a system of laws that assure her more than me. If I fail her, the society—through laws and customs—will step in. I must sacrifice some of my control in order not to sacrifice my child.

If the fearsome story of the Binding of Isaac only reminded us not to sacrifice our children for our own beliefs, crusades, needs, or wants, it would be enough.[26]

I reread the Binding of Isaac as law teacher, as woman, as mother—
and as child. I feel a kind of helplessness in the face of the story that
I associate with childhood: a sense of overpowering events beyond
my control, obedience demanded without rationale; hope and en-
durance eked out because of a naive lack of alternatives rather than
common sense.

I confess that I worry less about my own parents sacrificing their
children than sacrificing themselves for their children. Maybe I
should understand that not only Sarah, but also Abraham, or a crucial part of him, died because of the events on Mount Moriah.[27]
Maybe he was too willing to give what he cared most about—his
son—for the ironic promise of his descendants.

I am reminded of these thoughtful musings on sacrifice within
families: "The capacity to sacrifice, like any skill, always needs some
fine tuning. It is one thing to sacrifice briefly one's sleep to comfort a
child with a bad dream; it is quite another for a mother to sacrifice her
whole career for a child. It is one thing for a father to sacrifice his desire to go fishing today because he needs to go to work to feed the
family; it is quite another to work for forty years at a job he hates. Often such massive sacrifice, if not a result of cowardice, comes from an
inability to discriminate between giving that is necessary and life-
giving and giving that brings death to the Martyr and hence to those
around him or her."[28]

Learning to fine-tune sacrifice seems contrary to Abraham's willingness to give the utmost. Yet the story gives us not only the model
of Abraham's initial obedience, but also the concluding lesson: he
need not sacrifice the utmost. The willingness to do it, but the recognition that it is not necessary: this, too, may be a lesson, especially in
the complex negotiations between parents and children who have
been in the habit of sacrificing for one another.

Sacrifices of parent for children are closely connected to the sacrifices of children by parents. I think about the extreme circumstances—Sethe, the tormented parent of Toni Morrison's novel
Beloved, who kills her child rather than let her be recaptured into
slavery and, in so doing, sacrifices part of herself;[29] the parent who

must cast out one child in order to save others;[30] or the parent forced by war, economics, or terror to choose to live while a child dies or to die so a child may live.

Life is the edge of a blade. Elemental stories may horrify and terrify. But, like the Binding of Isaac, they may also remind us to try to see our worlds, our families, our beliefs—our very lives—anew.

The *Ashes* of the Akeda, the *Ashes* of Sodom: A Mother-Daughter Dialogue

REBECCA GOLDSTEIN AND YAEL GOLDSTEIN

The practice of studying the sacred texts with a partner, or *chavruta,* is deeply entrenched in Jewish tradition. The need to find the right *chavruta* is one of the foremost priorities of a student. The right *chavruta* doesn't have to be someone who shares your ideas, or even your style of forming ideas; after all, the adversarial stance is also deeply entrenched in Jewish tradition. An important requirement, however, is that the positions of explainer and explainee be fluid and easily reversible.

We two have been studying together, on and off and on, for six years now, and, oddly, our primary relationship as mother and daughter has not proved an (insurmountable) obstacle in maintaining the required fluidity. Flux seems, as well, to be just about the only permanence adhering to the attitudes with which we approach the texts. There is something about this mother's skepticism that stirs the latent piety in this daughter, just as there is something about this daughter's pious stirrings that can provoke spasms of cynicism in this mother. But it is not unknown for these reactions suddenly to reverse themselves.

Within these contrary currents we thrash out our responses, sometimes coming, astonished, on the sweetness of a jointly reasoned interpretation. So it happened in our discussion of the binding of the son Isaac by the father, Abraham, even though the *Akeda,* the Binding, had been an issue over which we had been prepared to suffer nothing but dissension. After all, the parent-child bond is almost severed in the binding of the son. . . .

REBECCA: It *is* severed. Or at least some substantial strand of it is. The fact that the ultimate tragedy is averted by the deus ex machina ploy at the end—

YAEL: Deus ex machina . . . in *Genesis?*

REBECCA: —doesn't at all change the fact that something was irrevocably altered—altered in the sense of broken, ruptured—from that moment that found Abraham prepared to sacrifice his son. This preparedness—this *awful* preparedness—is an irrevocable alteration in the world they inhabit, whose structure is given in their relationships. It's an alteration that spreads itself out beyond the events of those three days that the two spend traveling to the slaughter site, out far beyond the actual hideous binding itself—hands tied together to the feet behind the body so that the neck is arched back, fully exposed, just as the sacrificial animal was bound: imagine. Imagine what that preparedness entailed. How could the world ever again be the same for them? Abraham's preparedness seeps outward, insinuating itself into everything he will ever do. All the preoccupations with family—finding a burial place for his wife, a wife for his son—every detail of his domesticity has to be apprehended now within the strange slanting light that emanates from that awful preparedness, a light that imposes distances between him and the objects of his attention. The text tells us that they went up together, leaving the servants below; but it doesn't have them coming back down together. I try to picture that—how it was for each of them to descend from Mount Moriah in one another's company—or alone. For one can easily imagine that each might very well have chosen to descend the mountain by himself.

YAEL: I'm tempted to interpret that sentence, that the two of them went up together, to mean that Isaac knew precisely what was happening, and that, in the silence of his heart, he assented.

REBECCA: I agree that that's tempting, if only to rescue Isaac from the utter moral obliteration he's subjected to here—on top of everything else! He's not even allowed the chance for moral failure, let alone moral triumph. He's a bound sacrificial animal—there's no question of his moral agency. His life is threatened, ultimately reprieved—but his humanity? It's obliterated in the very act of binding—making of him the consummate tragic victim. And remember, according to rabbinic tradition Isaac was no kid here. He was thirty-seven. So I too, like you, would love to rescue his human dignity and have him sharing in whatever heroism there was to be found on that mountain. But it's hard to reconcile that interpretation with the text. The text treats this as exclusively Abraham's trial, and that means that Isaac has to be denied his moral agency. He's not choosing to be bound. He has all the choice of the sacrificial lamb. I think perhaps I find this the most disturbing aspect of all, that Abraham's moral triumph deprives Isaac of his moral dimension, grounded in choice. He's *literally* brutalized, reduced to the level of an animal.

YAEL: That's exactly why I'm not ready to give up my view that Isaac does preserve his humanity, that he infers why it is that he's being summoned to go up to Mount Moriah. Nothing of what he silently knows and invisibly chooses can be voiced by him because that would cancel out the meaning of the sacrifice his father is being asked to perform. Isaac's self-sacrifice would nullify his father's.

REBECCA: Isaac has to keep his transcendence covert, in order to preserve the grounds of his father's transcendence? That would make him doubly sacrificial!

YAEL: "Thus the two of them went up together." This sentence is repeated twice, bracketing Isaac's direct questioning of his father: "Father . . . Here are the fire and the wood, but where is the lamb for the offering-up?"

REBECCA: And then the masterful parental evasion: "God will see-for-himself to the lamb for the offering-up."

YAEL: I like to imagine that Isaac almost immediately infers the truth from the little that Abraham says, but even more from what he doesn't say. Children are masters at interpreting not only their parents' words, but also their silences, their evasions and ellipses.

REBECCA: Mmmm.

YAEL: From which I infer that you don't agree.

REBECCA: Right you are. I don't agree, I can't agree, because if you have it your way, then Isaac's moral triumph completely surpasses and outshines his father's, and this just doesn't jibe with the text. It's Abraham who ends up with all the kudos, with God's blessing: "Because you have done this thing, have not withheld your son, your only-one, indeed I will bless you, bless you." But if Isaac knew why he was being summoned, and he concurred—if that's what the text is signaling in the repeated sentence "thus they went up together"—then he deserves far more praise than his father. His triumph would be far greater precisely because he never brings it out into the open—just as the highest form of charity, according to Jewish tradition, is the kind that keeps itself hidden. Isaac's transcendence, his deliverance of his will over to the will of God, would also contain within itself, within its kept covertness, an act of supreme love toward his father, something altogether lacking in Abraham's transcendence—which, quite the contrary, demands that his son be rendered a moral nonentity. If Isaac participates, as an agent, in this trial, then his triumph completely eclipses Abraham's. And how can that be squared with the text's insistence that this is Abraham's trial?

YAEL: I see what you mean—regretfully—though notice which of the two of us is pushing here for the more traditional interpretation!

REBECCA: It's simply a matter of text, of preserving the integrity of the text. I don't intend any implications as to truth or falsity or—

YAEL: Sounds suspiciously like deconstructionism to me. Of course you *are* the official definer of deconstructionism—the new *American Heritage Dictionary,* wasn't it'?

REBECCA: It was.

YAEL: Okay, on *such* authority I'll accept that this is exclusively Abraham's trial. Traditionally, that's been the explanation for why only Abraham is mentioned as descending from the mountain.

REBECCA: The theme of the bound animal, the non-agent, is perpetuated so that at the final curtain Isaac doesn't even appear. His obliteration, insofar as this particular episode is concerned, has been completed. So although God stays the hand, there's a hideous sacrifice all the same. Perhaps that's a possible meaning of that enigmatic rabbinical statement, to which Rashi, the foremost Biblical exegete in Jewish tradition, refers [22:14], namely that "Isaac's ashes were left piled there on the slaughter-site."

YAEL: And Isaac's sacrifice means that Abraham acts as the sole moral agent in this drama. Abraham's life was dominated by a series of trials, and this one is obviously the culmination, and it has a transfiguring power. God's words to Abraham: "Take your son, your only one, whom you love, Isaac, and go forth to the land of Moriah and offer him there for a burnt-offering"; those words were meant to make possible the appearance of something new, what you call

Abraham's awful preparedness. What's so awful—so awe-full—about Abraham's preparedness is that it exists side by side with a love undiminished. "Your son . . . whom you love." This is the very first time that the word "love" is used in Genesis. Love is first named in the very sentence that asks for the ultimate violation of that love.

REBECCA: Another interesting thing about that sentence. It repeats the *lekh lekha*—the go-you-forth—with which Abraham was first introduced in 12:1: "God said to Avram: go-you-forth, from your land, from your kindred, from your father's house, to the land that I will let you see." What a cruel déjà vu for Abraham! God's commanded him before to disregard the ties of blood in order to fulfill God's intentions for him. In Genesis, that's how God announces himself to Abraham. But when God first tells Abraham to go forth, it's to a new and better life, a life that will involve in its essence a covenant with God and the founding of a covenantal legacy. But the *lekh lekha* of the *Akeda* contains no promise of a yet better life, no new "land that I will let you see." This *lekh lekha* would seem to contain nothing but negation—even of the covenant itself! For God had promised Abraham that it would be "through Isaac that seed will be called by your [name]" (21:12).

YAEL: So what we're seeing is how many motives Abraham would have for not obeying this *lekh lekha,* or at the very least how many reasons he would have for very actively questioning it. His total absence of questioning is, on any reading, remarkable and seems now, as we discuss it, to become so remarkable, it's . . .

REBECCA: Baffling. First and foremost, in terms of a strong psychological motive for disregarding this *lekh lekha,* is Abraham's love as a father. But okay, let's say that in the very first trial that was presented to him, the one that was represented by that first *lekh lekha,* God had already let it be known that the ties of blood were not to constitute sufficient reasons for Abraham in determining his actions. The love he presumably had as a son had to be violated, and now the love that he has as a father has to be violated. He's been taught that his blood-conditioned feelings are not the final arbiters. So what does he have left?

YAEL: He has the word of God. But how can he trust that word to be the right reason for acting, since if he fulfills that word, then God's previous promise to him is ipso facto falsified? Reason itself would seem to demand that Abraham disregard or, at the very least, question this *lekh lekha,* since God's words have become suspect—

REBECCA: Riddled with self-contradiction, more hole-y than holy. So on the one side, pushing Abraham toward the fulfillment of this *lekh lekha,* what we have are nothing but these God-given words—

YAEL: These words that don't manage to satisfy the very least requirement for believability, namely self-consistency—

REBECCA: Yes, so that Abraham's triumph of belief is all the more exalted for being in stark defiance of logic, at least according to Kierkegaard: "Everyone shall be remembered, but each became great in proportion to his expectation. One became great by expecting the possible, another by expecting the eternal, but he who expected the impossible became greater than all."

YAEL: How extraordinary. Was Kierkegaard referring there specifically to Abraham?

REBECCA: To none other. That line is from the first chapter in *Fear and Trembling,* called "A Panegyric upon Abraham." Kierkegaard's attempt to imagine himself inside of the hidden drama of the *Akeda* was what inspired his *Fear and Trembling.*

YAEL: Fascinating. Fascinating, too, to hear a philosopher, of all people, lauding the defiance of logic—

REBECCA: Well, he was a philosopher of religion.

YAEL: Shall I read *Fear and Trembling?*

REBECCA: Immediately. Now where were we?

YAEL: On the one side, compelling Abraham's obedience to the *Akeda's lekh lekha,* there exists nothing but the words of God, words flimsy with inconsistency.

REBECCA: Yes, while on the other side, holding Abraham back, there exists such a hefty bunch of ponderous considerations that had he behaved differently, we would have had our choice among an abundance of entirely adequate alternative explanations. It would have been what philosophers call a case of causal overdetermination. We would have had the description of him as loving father to explain him to us. Or our explanation might just as well have been based on the description of Abraham as reasoner and moral philosopher—both of which descriptions justly fit him. As a reasoner, he would have placed his trust in logic and rejected the impossible, seen the inconsistency of God's words as sufficient cause to push them away.

YAEL: And as moral philosopher, he would have known that the murder of Isaac was wrong, was objectively, morally wrong. Abraham *was* a moral philosopher, and as a moral philosopher he had already arrived, previous to the *Akeda,* at his own God-independent moral intuitions, that had flowed out of the compassion that was fundamental to his being. His moral intuitions were so strong, and so strongly God-independent, that he actually took it upon himself to argue with God, *on moral grounds,* when God informed him, among the oaks at Mamre, of the decision to destroy the sinful city of Sodom (18:23–33).

REBECCA: That is one extraordinary passage, isn't it—starting even further back, right from the point at which we overhear God deciding to take Abraham into his confidence (18:17–19): "Shall I cover up from Avraham what I am about to do?"

YAEL: It's as if Abraham had somehow taken on moral substance enough so that God has to keep him informed of significant ethical happenings.

REBECCA: Just as it is with the angels. And, interestingly, Abraham responds a bit like the angels, who are also sometimes given to taking exception with God. Abraham doesn't seem at all overwhelmed by the high regard God shows him. In fact, he responds by telling God that He's wrong!

YAEL: We know that Abraham didn't just passively receive his notions of good and evil, but rather arrived at them actively, for how else could he have engaged God Himself in moral debate? It was for the quality of his mind that God chose him as the progenitor of the covenantal legacy. Abraham is the first person to reencounter God in the very different world that exists after the Flood. It's a world in which God is far more removed, remote, in which a person who hopes to know God has to assert himself in the knowing. It's Abraham's own efforts that induce God to reacquaint with humanity.

REBECCA: And now—how much more paradox can one heap around this slaughter-site?—what this culminating trial is all about is this moral philosopher's surrender of his moral intuitions. He's prepared to commit an act that—well, if he's ever known anything to be wrong, then he knows this to be wrong. So what his awful preparedness entails—besides the unspeakable binding itself—is his surrender of that moral substance of himself for which he was originally singled out in the first place. There's nothing with*in* him that can move him toward this horrific deed. Everything he passionately feels and everything he morally and rationally knows would hold him back. The sole impetus is held within God's words— God's self-negating words! Talk about a leap of faith! How could Abraham convince himself that what God was asking him to do was right, was morally justified? How could he have gotten himself into that state, when in chapter 18, in that very same *Parasha* [Torah portion], *Vayera,* he was cocky enough to call God to a moral reckoning, there among the oaks at Mamre?

YAEL: In its own way the drama at Mamre is quite as extraordinary as the drama up there on Moriah, though of course it's a much quieter drama, consisting purely of dialogue, no outward actions at all.

REBECCA: At Mamre, Abraham had been quite willing to entertain the possibility that God might be guilty of injustice. Upon being informed of the fate of Sodom, Abraham assumes the high ground *in relation to God:* "Heaven forbid for you to do a thing like this, to deal death to the innocent along with the guilty, that it should come about: like the innocent, like the guilty. Heaven forbid for you! The judge of all the earth—will He not do what is just?" What an extraordinary way for Abraham, of all people, to address God! I very much like your point that the encounter at Mamre is high, although quiet, drama.

YAEL: It begins with a soliloquy by God: "Now YHWH had said to himself: Shall I cover up from Abraham what I am about to do?" He goes on to describe Abraham in moral terms. "I have known him, in order that he may charge his sons and his household after him: they shall keep the way of YHWH, to do what is right and just. . . ." He then speaks of the evil in those cities: "And their sin—how exceedingly heavily it weighs!" and announces His intention: "If they have done according to its cry that has come to me—destruction!" And then the text says that Abraham "came close," which is suggestive, and then he launches into that moral inquisition of God. It begins, as you say, with Abraham assuming an almost stridently self-assured tone of moral superiority to God. But his tone becomes progressively less sure of itself. He keeps asking God if He would save the evil cities for the sake of the innocents who live there, progressively lowering the magic number, and obviously something is being communicated to him in between—

REBECCA: At the very least that there are not that many innocents living there—

YAEL: At the very least. But perhaps far more. I definitely want to say far more. Don't you think far more?

REBECCA: You mean in order to explain why Abraham becomes so much less confident as the exchange continues.

YAEL: Yes, to explain that. He starts out trying to shame God into doing the right thing, but by degrees he becomes less and less confident—mentioning along the way that he is but earth and ashes—until in the end he's reduced to utter hesitancy: "Pray let my Lord not be upset that I speak further just this one time." What a change in tone!

REBECCA: It's almost as if the passage actually puts a diminishing quantitative measure on Abraham's confidence by speaking in terms of those hypothetical innocents: fifty, forty-five, forty, thirty, twenty, ten. . . . The real issue, you're saying, is something far different, far more significant, than this hypothetical head count.

YAEL: What occurs to me is that each of those decreasing numbers is correlated with an increase in something else: in Abraham's vision of the vastness of moral and spiritual reality that escapes him. He's glimpsing something, something that can't be articulated.

REBECCA: Glimpsing. It's interesting how many forms of the Hebrew verb "to see" are packed into this *Parasha*. And sight is that faculty of perception that most lends itself to metaphors of ethics, metaphors of knowledge.

YAEL: The *Parasha*'s Hebrew name is itself a form of the verb: He (God) was seen, seen by Abraham here at Mamre. And it seems to me he sees Him by degrees, in progressive stages.

REBECCA: Or perhaps what Abraham progressively sees is how much he's not seeing, can never see. William James talks about the belief in the "reality of the unseen" as fundamental to the religious outlook. Abraham may be developing here a progressively deeper appreciation for the reality of the unseen, its density and vastness, stretching off into the boundlessly unreachable.

YAEL: And he's progressively more confounded, more hesitant in his own grasp of moral truth.

REBECCA: So here he is, Abraham, the very best that humankind can offer in the way of a moral philosopher, the first person who actually made his way back to a knowledge of God by using his own faculty of moral reasoning, and what *he* sees, when he is suffered to "come close," ends in the undermining of all his moral certitude. We're witnessing his passage toward absolute doubt, just the sort of doubt that would issue in that awful preparedness.

YAEL: Look at how the passage at Mamre ends: "YHWH went, as soon as he had finished speaking to Abraham, and Abraham returned to his place." You have the sense that God had graciously *suffered* Abraham's interrogation and that Abraham has gradually come into the full realization of this grace, so that, by the end, he is literally quaking, possessed by his fear and trembling.

REBECCA: There's something reminiscent of Descartes' first Meditation in this reconstruction you're offering of the inward drama at Mamre. There's a sort of parallel passage toward absolute doubt, the systematic corrosion of epistemic confidence. Maybe if the Torah gave voice to Abraham's state of confoundment, it would sound something like Descartes. "The Meditation of yesterday filled my mind with so many doubts that it is no longer in my power to forget them. And yet I do not see in what manner I can resolve them; and, just as if I had all of a sudden fallen into very deep water, I am so disconcerted that I can neither make certain of setting my feet on the bottom, nor can I swim and so support myself on the surface."[1] Only of course Descartes here is discussing his knowledge of the external world, whether he knows anything at all to exist, whereas Abraham's loss of certainty is moral. Descartes assumes the position of the ideal knower, someone who's in the best position to know and reduces that knower to absolute uncertainty. And what you're suggesting is that at Mamre the ideal moral agent experienced a reduction to absolute moral uncertainty.

YAEL: After the destruction of Sodom is described, including the incident with Lot's wife, the text returns to Abraham, showing him silently surveying the devastation, perhaps lost in his moral astonishment. "Abraham started early in the morning to the place where he had stood in YHWH's presence, he looked down upon the face of Sodom and Amora and upon the whole face of the plain-country and saw: here, the dense-smoke of the land went up like the dense-smoke of a furnace." He goes to stand in that very place where he had had the temerity to challenge God on moral grounds, and he contemplates this scorched earth. Perhaps that's when the final confoundment occurs, beyond all speech, even that of Descartes.

REBECCA: And then a few pages after this, in the very same *Parasha Vayera*—And He (God) Was Seen—we have the drama on Mount Moriah/Seeing. It's almost as if the *Akeda* is the externalization of that entirely inner drama that occurred between the lines of spoken text at Mamre. Its externalization would allow us to infer the enormity of Abraham's confoundment, without seeing the grounds of that confoundment, without glimpsing whatever it was that Abraham was suffered to glimpse.

YAEL: This unthinkable act that Abraham was prepared to commit is the only one, perhaps, that could convey to us something of the magnitude of the domain that God inhabits—

REBECCA: Which is to say that this terrible externalization was, in its terrible way, necessary.

YAEL: Exactly. There's something vast and otherwise incommunicable that's conveyed in our seeing that Abraham, the most perfect moral agent, was prepared to do *this!*

REBECCA: Descartes, at the end of the first Meditation, is at a loss because up until then he's assumed all his knowledge of the world has come from his senses, and now he's convinced himself that all beliefs founded on that evidence are subject to doubt. He has to uncover a new faculty of mind to deliver him from his absolute doubt. Abraham's in something of an analogous situation as regards the moral realm.

YAEL: What Abraham will have to rely on is his capacity to receive God's words—

REBECCA: Which arguably isn't an active faculty of his mind at all, though it was prompted by his active faculties. It's his moral and reasoning faculties that originally led him to a knowledge of God—to a knowledge of God in the abstract. But then God speaks, God reveals.

YAEL: And what He reveals, no matter how sketchily, how incompletely, is sufficient to subvert the very grounds that had first made possible Abraham's abstract knowledge of God.

REBECCA: And so we find Abraham in that state of awful preparedness, that mute and non-argumentative receptivity to God's most outrageous behest. The very enormity of its outrageousness is a measure of the vastness of the unarticulated truth. This, after all, is a great theme in Genesis, the great hiddenness of the bulk of ethical/spiritual reality. If I could wax learned for a moment—

YAEL: Wax away—

REBECCA: —and quote from this truly wonderful essay by Erich Auerbach, "Odysseus' Scar." "Let no one object that this goes too far, that not the stories, but the religious doctrine, raises the claim to absolute authority; because the stories are not, like Homer's, simply narrated 'reality.' Doctrine and promise are incarnate in them and inseparable from them; for that very reason they are fraught with 'background' and mysterious, containing a second, concealed meaning. In the story of Isaac, it is not only God's intervention at the beginning and the end, but even the factual and psychological elements which come between, that are mysterious, merely touched upon, fraught with background; and therefore they require subtle investigation and interpretation, they demand them. Since so much in the story is dark and incomplete, and since the reader knows that God is a hidden God, his effort to interpret it constantly finds something new to feed upon."[2]

YAEL: The drama of the *Akeda* is introduced in 22:1 with the open-ended "Now after these things it was that God tested Abraham." The Hebrew word, translated here as "things," is *devarim,* which also means words. There is a tradition of rabbinical interpretations, to which Rashi refers, that understands *devarim* in this way—that is, as meaning words—and that try to supply the extratextual words that were responsible for God's testing Abraham. One tradition plays around with the possibility that it was the words of Satan, denouncing Abraham to God, that caused God to test Abraham—

REBECCA: Analogous to what precipitates the action in Job—

YAEL: Right. Satan as agent provocateur. Another tradition has the relevant words being spoken in a squabble between Ishmael and Isaac over which one better loves his father. Ishmael, according to this midrash, brags that he loved his father so well that he allowed himself to be circumcised at age thirteen, whereas Isaac was circumcised, less painfully at eight days.

REBECCA: And people think Freud was the first to notice how that particular male preoccupation gets tangled up with the family drama.

YAEL: Anyway, according to this midrash, Isaac is provoked into uttering the *devarim:* " 'With one organ you intimidate me? If God said to me, "Sacrifice yourself before Me," I would not hold back' "—

REBECCA: Which would buttress your original—and discredited— intuition that this was Isaac's supreme test, as well as Abraham's—

YAEL: Right. But what if the *devarim* aren't extratextual at all, but the very words that are spoken a few passages back in Genesis, in the description of the exchange at Mamre? What if those are the words that eventually lead to the events at Moriah?

REBECCA: What's so completely horrible about this interpretation— something we're glossing over in referring to the *Akeda* as the externalization of the drama at Mamre—is that the *Akeda* is not only Abraham's drama. He may be the sole moral agent here, just as Descartes is the sole knower in that first Meditation, but since this isn't just an epistemological drama, since this is a moral drama, there are others besides Abraham who are intimately involved, and who suffer, suffer egregiously—first and foremost, of course, Isaac, and then—

YAEL: Sarah. According to rabbinic tradition, Sarah dies as a result of the *Akeda.*

REBECCA: This is where the parallelism between Descartes' first Meditation and the *Akeda* completely breaks down. Descartes' descent into epistemic doubt has no implications for action, but God forces Abraham's inner drama of doubt out into the sphere of action: "And it was after these things/words that God tested Abraham." And this God-forcing demands—quite literally—the sacrifice of Isaac. There's no way to palliate the horror of it: what Isaac is forced to undergo is tragic. He's sacrificed to our moral edification!

YAEL: Neither Isaac nor Sarah had undergone the corrosive seeing at Mamre. They hadn't been brought to that state of awful preparedness and so couldn't participate as agents—

REBECCA: Only as victims. Isaac is the most tragic figure among the patriarchs. If the repeating theme of Abraham's life was his God-forced moral trials, then the repeated theme of Isaac's life is his self-effacing role in others' trials. Even at the very end of his life, in his dealings with his twin sons, Esau and Jacob, he's the duped non-agent in the moral drama of their rivalry. There simply are such figures in Genesis, from the very beginning, from the story of Cain and Abel; Isaac seems to belong to that Abelesque category of people—sacrificed, one way or the other, so that those who have been designated moral players—the Cains, the Abrahams—can make their way toward moral failure or triumph.

YAEL: Designated moral players. Arbitrarily?

REBECCA: Interesting question. In the case of Abraham, I guess we'd want to say not. His trial, at least the way we're looking at it, is the direct outcome of his moral strivings, of his pushing God with the force of his questions. And Cain, when you consider, went out of his way to engage God, too. He's the one who first sacrificed to God. His brother, Abel, just copied him. So Cain is the first to try to reengage with God after the banishment from the Garden. He's the founder of religion! So he too earns the right to undergo the moral test that God sets up when he chooses Cain's brother over him—

YAEL: A test Cain fails—

REBECCA: In spades. These trials are in some sense earned. The tested one presents himself or herself as a moral agent by some sort of superogatory engagement with God.

YAEL: Maybe that's one possible meaning of chosenness. It's terrible to be chosen to be tested, to be a Cain or Abraham—

REBECCA: But it can be even more terrible not to be chosen, to be an Abel or an Isaac.

YAEL: Isaac is diminished by his father's transcendence, bound throughout his life by passive non-agency. We always see him only in relationships with others—his father, his mother, his wife, and his sons—and in every case the drama is presented as really belonging to the other, not to Isaac. It's as if he's been deprived forever after of some essential vitality, that something in the position of the bound sacrifice sustains itself through his life—which again brings us back to that statement of the Sages, that "his ashes remain piled on the slaughter-site." Something was killed in him on Mount Moriah. Abraham pleads with God at Mamre that no innocents of Sodom be harmed by God's justice, and the ultimate outcome is that his own innocent son is irrevocably harmed. There's a sense in which the ashes of Sodom are mixed up into the ashes of Isaac that remain piled there on the Mountain of Seeing.

REBECCA: That's a profoundly sad statement you've just spoken. I hear it as a parent, and it breaks my heart. Abraham, in pursuing his own risky but fantastically exemplary life-project, kills off something vital and creative in his own beloved child. The ashes of Sodom mixed into the substance of Isaac, a legacy from the father he carries in him to his end. One of the traditional explanations of the blindness that Isaac suffered later in his life, that allowed his son Jacob to dupe him into giving him and not Esau the blessing of the firstborn, was that when he was lying there bound on the slaughter-site of that Mountain of Seeing, the heavens opened up and the ministering angels saw and wept, and their tears came down and fell into his eyes, dimming their sight. Those angels are weeping at a spectacle that's tragic beyond all attempts at explication. In the end, those explications are cold, and we're cold insofar as they satisfy us, soothe away our sense of horror. There's no consolation for the spectacle of sacrificed innocence. The only adequate response is the weeping of the angels.

YAEL: It violates our sense of justice that there should have to be this category of the sacrificial, as innocent as Abel, as innocent as Isaac. It's very hard to reconcile what moral intuitions we have with this presentation in Genesis of such a category as the Abelesque. In a sense we, too, like Abraham, would have to loosen our grip on our moral intuitions and trust to the existence of a vastly inaccessible moral reality, revealed, though darkly, in the words of God. We're asked, though in less stark and drastic terms than were presented to Abraham, to believe in the divine justice of what seems heartbreakingly unjust.

REBECCA: Difficult, no?

YAEL: Difficult, yes. Ultimately, I think that what we're told at the end of this drama, that arcs its way from Mamre to Moriah, is that there *is* validity in Abraham's compassion-based moral intuitions. Abraham is the best that humankind can offer because his being is based on *chesed*—on kindness—and this basis is perhaps as far as we can go as humans, even though it might be that going as far as we can go as humans takes us no very great distance.

REBECCA: Abraham was the only moral agent in the drama of the *Akeda* because he was the only participant who had undergone the requisite preparation. He doesn't tell his son what's happening, answering Isaac's poignantly direct question, "Where is the lamb for a burnt-offering?" with a pointedly vague "God-will-provide" evasion. And he, of course, doesn't enlighten Sarah either as to the true nature of this little outing. Yet Sarah's position, unlike Isaac's, isn't really Abelesque. She exists, here in the context of the *Akeda,* in a place intermediate between Abraham's full moral agency and Isaac's sacrificial passivity. Unlike Isaac, what Sarah suffers on account of the *Akeda* has everything to do with who she is, the bent of her mind and desires. She is a victim of the *Akeda*—

YAEL: Very much a victim. Rabbinical tradition interprets the fact that her death is recorded immediately after the account of the *Akeda* to mean that she died as the direct result of the *Akeda*. For example, Rashi, says: "The death of Sarah is narrated directly after the Binding of Isaac, because, as a result of the tidings of the *Akeda*—that her son had been fated for slaughter, and had been all-but-slaughtered—her soul flew away and she died."

REBECCA: Yes, very much a victim, even under the plainest interpretation, much less the various versions of the rabbinical interpretation to which Rashi is referring. Even on the plainest of interpretations we can imagine what that "all-but-slaughtered" would have meant to this mother—

YAEL: Who had already demonstrated her undeviating, even ruthless, determination to protect her son from any possible harm, demanding that Abraham's older son, Ishmael, whose mother, Hagar, was Sarah's maid, be banished—

YAEL: Banished simply because of the *possibility* that harm might come to Isaac through Ishmael. She's a mother who scans the future, seeking all and any possible dangers to her child so that she can remove them, childproof the future like a conscientious parent childproofs the home. In the fierceness of her love she imagines that this is really possible, that she herself can guard Isaac against the terrifying contingency of life.

YAEL: Oh, so the first Jewish mother really was the first "Jewish Mother."

REBECCA: I guess you could say that. With the birth of Isaac, with the fierceness of the mother-love that Sarah experiences when this miracle of a child who is, beyond all her expectations (18:12), given to her, Sarah can tolerate nothing less than the sense of certainty, the banishment of the condition of contingency. Here is her illusion, an illusion to which I think all mothers can relate: If only I am attentive enough, not only to the circumstances that exist, but to all those that might possibly arise, I can keep my child safe. Her world, under the severities of her strange belated motherhood, undergoes a powerful contraction.

YAEL: Both Abraham and Sarah had first laughed when they were told that this child would be born to them, born to a father who was a hundred years old and to a mother who was ninety. Their laughter is recorded in Isaac's very name. And it's the laughter of skepticism, of disbelief. They both—but most particularly, it seems, Sarah—can barely bring themselves to believe in the possibility of his birth. And then he *is* born, but given its previous unlikelihood, his very birth might have seemed to Sarah like the sheerest of contingencies. Isaac could so easily not have been! How horrible for Sarah to contemplate—

REBECCA: Too horrible, perhaps, for her to bear any increase to her sense of the tenuousness of his existence. She will drive out that tenuousness, as she drives out Hagar and Ishmael from her household.

YAEL: What if the illusion of certainty, in the sense of controlling the future, is linked with the illusion of a certain sort of moral certainty? Though she engages in actions that are, to say the least, equivocal, she's never shown to us as equivocating. Equivocating would have required her to see and give some moral weight to the conflicting claims of the son Ishmael, to take his well-being and rights into account—as well as to those of Abraham, who suffers for his eldest son's banishment. She can preserve her sense of moral certainty only by limiting her sight to the well-being of her son. So at the same time that she's busy seeing what she hopes are all the possible (and eliminable) circumstances that might harm her son, she's excluding from her vision any considerations that might bar her from eliminating those circumstances. Her maternal love makes her at once see a great deal and not see a great deal. It's a very focused kind of seeing.

REBECCA: Her illusion of certainty seems the very inverse of Abraham's awful preparedness. He's been brought to a state of no-confidence in his moral judgments, has given himself up entirely to the word of God, while Sarah, who even before Isaac's birth had always demonstrated a great deal of certainty and assertiveness—

YAEL: She's the one, after all, who sent Hagar to Abraham in the first place (16:1–4), thus precipitating the very birth of Ishmael that she will later believe threatens the future of Isaac—all of which might already have suggested to her the futility of controlling the future—

REBECCA: Has been brought, through the singular fierceness of her mother-love, to a state that tolerates no equivocation or doubt. And then comes the "tidings of the *Akeda*." If Abraham's passage to absolute doubt had brought him to a state of awful preparedness, able to withstand the full blast of unintelligibility in God's summons, then Sarah's illusion of absolute certainty brought her to the very opposite of such preparedness.

YAEL: Then comes the "the tidings of the *Akeda*," and with it Sarah knows the utter futility of her attempt to ensure Isaac's safety through her ever-vigilant maternal intervention.

REBECCA: For how could she ever have imagined *this* contingency, the most unthinkable: that the gravest danger to her son's life would issue from *Abraham?*

YAEL: "Abraham did not rejoice in My world and you seek to rejoice?" This is from *Vayikra Rabba,* one of the sources to which Rashi is referring when explaining the tradition that associates Sarah's death with the *Akeda*. *Vayikra Rabba* continues: "He had a son at the age of a hundred. And in the end, God said to him, 'Take your son. . . .' So Abraham took Isaac, his son, and led him up hill and down dale, and up to the top of one mountain, and he built an altar and arranged the wood, and took the knife to slaughter him.

And were it not that the angel called out from heaven, he would already have been slaughtered. Know that it is so, for Isaac then returned to his mother and she said to him, 'Where have you been, my son?' He answered, 'My father took me and led me up hill and down dale. . . .' She said, 'Woe upon the son of the drunken woman! Were it not for the angel, you would already be slaughtered?' He said, 'Yes.' At that she screamed six times, corresponding to the six *tekia* notes [of the *shofar* blowing]. She had not finished doing this when she died. As it is written, 'Abraham came to mourn for Sara and to bewail her.'" It's fascinating, I think, that the *shofar* blowing is doubly linked to the *Akeda*. The ram's horn is said to recall the animal that Abraham sacrificed in Isaac's stead: "Abraham lifted up his eyes and saw: there a ram, caught behind in the thicket by its horns!"

REBECCA: The notes that emanate from the *shofar* echo the despairing death cries of Sarah, "the drunken woman." "Woe upon the son of the drunken woman!" Her pity and her terror—even here in the cries of her final moments—are all for *him,* for Isaac, the beloved son whose existence was at first too wonderful to be believed in and then must be believed in as nothing else is. "Woe upon the son," who will be, as all of us are, left vulnerable to the terrors of the maddeningly opaque future, that unrelenting closed-up-ness that will yield itself to no one, not even the most keen-sighted of mothers, whose gift for prophecy had been God praised. "Know that it is so," the Sages tell us, and we believe them. My God, how we believe them. Her powerlessness, in the face of unrelenting contingency, is intolerable—made so by the unbounded force of her love for that son whose very name holds her doubt that such a wonder as he could come to be. She had possessed an acuteness of vision that had become bent inward under her too heavy love and had imagined herself into a place of drunken certitude. It's the sound of that certitude being shattered that we reproduce for ourselves in the Days of Awe, in that wailing of the *shofar* that cries out her last despair.

YAEL: It sounds like part of Sarah's illusion is the very modern, or perhaps very American, or Emersonian, idea of self-reliance. She doesn't trust to God. "Were it not for the angel you would already be slaughtered?" "Yes." "At that she screamed six times."

REBECCA: Can she trust God to love Isaac as she loves him?

YAEL: But if she were convinced of God's goodness, then she could be certain that whatever happened would be for the good—

REBECCA: But not necessarily for the good of Isaac, which is the only good she cares to consider. There does exist, after all—though we wish to God there didn't—that Abelesque category of people, the born-to-suffer whose suffering goes unexplained, even if this suffering is ultimately—that is to say inexplicably—compatible with God's goodness.

YAEL: The ram recalls the reprieve of Isaac and the ultimate validation of Abraham's compassion-based moral intuitions, his original certainty that murder is wrong, now tempered with the knowledge that absolute moral certainty will never be his. ·

REBECCA: And through this instrument, that recalls the soundness of Abraham's compassionate intuitions, comes Sarah's voice, crying out the limits of our human understanding—

YAEL: The terrifying limits placed on the degree of control we have over destinies—

REBECCA: And over the destinies of those we most love in this world. What Sarah saw, in her all-too-sober stare into the *Akeda*'s implications, is a sight that can inspire—when the love is as fierce as Sarah's love for Isaac—that sickness-unto-death that killed her, the despair that removed, in the brief few moments it took to form, the grounds of her existence. Those *tekia* notes, with their strangely piercing quality, cry out the truth—terrible, really— that we live, every day and every moment, *in extremis,* our situation no different from that which inspired Sarah's final desperate despair—

YAEL: Or inspired Abraham's just as desperate faith.

Cries and Whispers: The Death of Sarah

Avivah Gottlieb Zornberg

This is an edited transcript of a shiur, *a traditional Jewish form of teaching that offers oral reflections on classical texts. Avivah Zornberg, who teaches primarily in Jerusalem, gave this* shiur *in New York in 1995. The structure of the piece reflects its oral character. We are invited into it as listeners, participants in an ancient tradition of oral interpretation now being expanded by learned women such as Zornberg. Drawing upon her deep knowledge of the Biblical text and a wealth of related sources—midrashim, traditional commentaries, works of religious philosophy, and* halakha *(Jewish law)— Zornberg immerses us in a sea of quotations and interpretations as she moves from one point to the next. She often makes connections (as the sources themselves usually do) through an associative process, based on complex connections among words shared and explored within the texts. At the same time she creates her own mode of interpretation, bringing modern philosophy, scholarship, and literature into dialogue with traditional Jewish sources.*

THE EDITORS

Cries and whispers: we hear the cry of the *shofar* and we ask, "Why?" What is the nature of this sound? What is its effect? *Cries and Whispers* is the title Ingmar Bergman gave to his film about death, about the human apprehension of mortality. The Rabbis intimate a radical connection between the death of the mother of the Jewish people, Sarah, and the plangent, penetrating notes of the *shofar*-cry. It is this connection that I would like to pursue. The resonance from Bergman evokes an anguish, a sense of the absurd, that at first seems quite alien to the rabbinic sensibility. As we study a cluster of midrashic sources, however, we shall see that the Bergman connection is not as foreign as we might have thought.

Let's begin with the verse we recite as we blow *shofar,* a verse that raises the whole question of happiness and tragedy. *Ashrei ha'am yodei terua* (Psalm 89:16): Happy the people who know the *terua*—the *terua* sound, one of the characteristic clusters of sound when we blow the *shofar.* And when I say "we," I mean *we:* the person who blows the *shofar* blows it for us who listen. We should know that it is being done for us. Our bodies should participate, as well as the rest of us. Happy the people who know the *terua. Hashem, be'or panekha yehaleikhun:* O God, in the light of Your face they will walk. This is the next phrase in the psalm. The question is: What does it mean? What is this happiness that is being ascribed to a certain group who know the *terua?* Everyone knows the *terua,* in the most superficial sense. Everyone has heard it. Clearly the verse means something else. *Yodei terua*—those who *really* know the *terua,* those who empathize with the *terua,* who have blown it out of themselves, who have emitted it from themselves. It is this mysterious happiness that comes from knowing the *terua* that I want to talk about.

At the moment, we don't know what any of these words mean. *Ashrei* is a particular kind of happiness among many possible shades of happiness. *Ashrei* has to do with the idea of a firmly based, solid happiness—of an *ishur.* In modern Hebrew an *ishur* is a validation, a certificate that allows you to enter into a certain place. It makes you feel safe because it's a guarantee of some kind. It's also connected with the word for "footsteps"—you place your footsteps firmly down on the ground, and this too suggests the idea of firmness, of solidity. Happy—solidly happy—are the people who know *terua.*

Why do we blow *shofar?* Perhaps the most famous explanation is in the Talmud (Rosh Hashana, 16a). *Imru lefanai malkhuyot kedei shetamlikhuni aleikhem:* Say before Me that section of the Rosh Hashana prayer that's called *malkhuyot* (the section about God's kingship) for the purpose of crowning Me over you. *Uvema?:* And how do we really do it? How do we crown God? *Beshofar:* We do it through the *shofar.*

The Rabbis then quote I Kings 1:39: *Yitke'u beshofar veyomru kol ha'am: yechi hamelekh Shlomo.* This historical passage records the coronation of King Solomon where it was announced that there should be a blowing of the *shofar* and everyone should cry out, "Long live the king! Long live the King Shlomo!"

Here the Talmud suggests—and this is the classic explanation— that we blow the *shofar,* in a clarion call, to proclaim the kingship of God over the world. Now that sounds fine. But what does it mean? On some deeper level, *what* are we proclaiming? What difficult act are we doing? We assume difficulty here, for otherwise we could do it all of the time. Why do we need to wait for Rosh Hashana and expend great energy and great effort doing this thing that's called "crowning God" by blowing the *shofar*?

I now want to set this classic source against a much less classic, much less well-known, tradition that talks about the sound of the *shofar* not as a triumphal sound, but as a sound full of pain, a sound full of poignancy—hence my title, "Cries and Whispers"—which, of course, is only a loose description of the way the *shofar* sounds but one that brings into play the Bergman film of the same name that deals with subjects similar to the subjects I want to raise here.

I begin with a passage from Rambam (Maimonides, Laws of Shofar 3:2). He starts off by asking what the *terua* sounds like. Although the Torah calls Rosh Hashana *yom terua* (the day of *terua*), we no longer know how the *terua* sounds. With the passage of time, *nistapeik lanu basafeik* (we are now very dubious about exactly what it's supposed to sound like). The original traditions have been obfuscated. This means that in the time of the Rambam, many centuries ago, we already couldn't determine precisely what the *terua* should sound like. He suggests two possibilities. He first asks *im hi hayelala shemeyale- lim hanashim beineihen be'eit shemeyabvin:* Is it the wails, the howls (*yelala*) that women howl and wail among themselves at the time that they are *meyabvin,* crying with gasping, panting breaths? Women cry this way when they want to sob; that is the idea of *leyabeiv.* The word *yevavot* (from the same root) is also associated with the sound of the *shofar* in classic texts that technically describe the different sounds of the *shofar.* In some texts, the *terua* is assumed to be a *yevava,* a certain sobbing noise.

Perhaps the sound is not a *yevava,* but an *anacha,* a groan, which has a different quality and a different length of sound. *Kederekh sheya'anach ha-adam, pa'am achar pa'am, kesheyidag libbo midavar gadol:* In the way that a person, *adam* (and here there's no gender mentioned), in the way that a human being will groan when his heart is oppressed, when he's anxious about some great matter. I hear great significance in what the Rambam is saying here. What is the great matter that one, man or woman, groans about when one's heart is oppressed by it? The feeling that the Rambam calls *da'aga,* the existentialists call angst, which is associated with the same idea of anxiety, of worry. But the existentialists mean worry about something very particular. They are talking about what Heidegger calls the human being's sense that he is living unto death. The Rambam does not explicitly say anything like that. Rather he simply says that there are two kinds of cries that he's heard from people. He's a doctor; he must have heard many people cry. He has a clinical mind in the sense that he responds to empirical reality and has noticed that the *yevava/yelala,* and the *anacha* are sounds people make when they're in different kinds of trouble. One is associated with women; the other is associated with either sex.

The fact that the *yelala* is associated with women is very important. There's something special about the sound of women. Recently I happened to see a trailer on television about a film that's just come out. I was struck by one particular image of a group of men standing under a lamppost at night, in a kind of fascinated horror as a woman cries from a building. There was a certain panting, sobbing cry of a woman that could be expressing any one of many things. But there was something characteristically feminine about that cry. The men stand there, looking ashamed, even horrified, as they listen to what, apparently, only a woman can do. This particular kind of sound is her privilege and comes at her expense. It costs her a great deal.

The Rambam continues in a legal mode. Is the *terua* one of these two sounds, or is it both together, both the groan and the wail, one following the other? (He's heard that, too.) That would be called *terua* because that's the way of someone in a state of anxiety—first he (she) groans, and after that he (she) wails. *Lekakh, anu osim ha-kol:* Therefore, we do everything. It's a *halakhic,* a legal, technical point he's making here. Since we don't know which of the two sounds the *terua* is supposed to be, to be safe we do both. But he backs up his point by again relying on empirical observation. He says: In fact, that's the way we hear people cry very often. They groan and wail one after the other; the two sounds are associated.

One level the Rambam is addressing is technical. Since we have no musical notations, he wants to give an idea of how long the sounds go on and how many of them there are. At the same time, it's very clear that the Rambam means more than just the technical specifications of the length of the note, and so on. He keeps repeating the phrase *kederekh she*—the *way* that—men and women express pain. He's not talking *only* about the length of a note. He's also talking about the tone of the note, about what emotion you should assume is behind sounds of this kind.

In thinking about the *shofar* on Rosh Hashana, I want to bring in a very short statement from the Talmud (Yoma 86a): *Gedola teshuva, shemevia refua laolam:* Great is repentance which brings healing to the world. This is an important thread in the tapestry I want to weave. What is the function of repentance on Rosh Hashana? It's not masochistic; on the contrary, it brings healing to the world. But what does that mean? In what sense does *teshuva* bring healing to the world? The world has become sick, it needs repair, it needs healing. Perhaps inevitably in the course of a year, things really go out of sorts, the truly tuned instrument begins to go off, and we need, on Rosh Hashana, to retune. Something like that seems to be implied here.

This is universal, and the beginning of my subject proper. In the work of Mircea Eliade, the historian of religions, for instance, this is a very important theme. He points to society after society that celebrates either the New Year or a coronation. In all these societies the purpose of these rituals, of crowning a king or beginning a year, is basically to heal the world. The world has begun to crack, to shake; it's not so solid anymore. And every now and then we get together and try to make the world sit firmly again, take its place firmly in time and in space. We do this through reenactments of the primary strong condition of the world, reenactments of the beginnings when the gods first created the world. Coronations are also a re-creation of the world. Some of the examples in Eliade's book *Myth and Reality* are especially fascinating. In Australia people will walk over the song-lines, invisible lines on the ground that the great ancestors walked when they first lived in the world. There's a music that's associated with those lines, and the people walk singing over those same lines on their New Year as a way of saying, "We are reestablishing the world." Among the Yurok tribes in California the priest will climb to the top of a hill and drag a stick across the ground, across the dust, and say, "Now the cracks are filled up." Whatever cracks there had been in the world are now filled up. There's a healing, some kind of *refua,* here. Or he sits firmly on a stone and says: "Now the world will stop tipping." It's been tipping, it has gotten out of balance; and now I sit down and it's firmly in place again. These are all, in Eliade's terms, cosmogonic rituals. They reactivate the creative force of beginnings because the world needs *tikkun* (repair).

If I assume that something about that procedure, of trying to clock in to beginnings by way of putting the world right, is relevant to our traditions, where do we see it? What do we do that re-creates beginnings? In an obvious way, we don't have any such rituals. What I want to suggest (with all due modesty, because I don't know if I'm right in this) is that we look at a surprising source. In Isaiah 51:1–2 we read: *Shimu eilai rodfei tzedek mevakshei Hashem:* Listen to me, you who pursue righteousness, who seek God. *Habitu el tzur chutzavtem, ve'el makkevet bor nukartem:* Look to the rock from which you were hewn, the origin, and to the hole, the cavity, the cistern, from which you were hewn out.

⬌

Look to your origins; we seem to be talking about a rock and a hole in the rock. What is that rock? *Habitu el Avraham avikhem:* Look at, look to, Avraham your father *ve'el Sarah techolelkhem:* and to Sarah, who *will* give birth to you.

⬌

It's an extraordinary word, that *techolelkhem.* It's in the future tense, *te.* The root of the verb is *lecholel,* which means "to bring to birth." It means to go through birth pangs, pains of all kinds, and is used of the woman in birth, in labor. It also conveys the idea of hollowness: a *chalal* is a hollow, an empty space. That's the cave, the hole that you are to look to. And it is identified with Sarah. The *peshat*

reading, the most obvious reading, is that this is a biological statement. She is your origin, the first mother of this people. Look back to
that birth cavity, to where you came from in a biological sense.

But Rashi, the great medieval commentator, doesn't read it like
that. If I try to reconstruct how I came to put the things I am discussing here together, I think one of the early stages was when I saw
Rashi's comment on this verse. Rashi says *makkevet* is not actually a
hole. It does have the root *nkv,* one of whose forms is *nakuv,* meaning
a perforation, a hole. But a *makkevet* is that which creates a hole. It's
actually a hammer, in modern Hebrew usage. It's a hammer that ham-
mers out a hole from the rock. Suddenly we can't simply say that
we're talking about the birth cavity, nor are we simply talking biologically. We're talking about Sarah. Abraham is a *tzur* (rock). I don't
even want to touch that now since it requires much more time. Sarah
is not a rock, but a hammer that hammered a hole in the rock. And
out of that hole, you were hewn. That's the image here. She *will* give
birth to you, *techolelkhem*—she will ultimately generate you. But this
verb should be in the past tense; she already has given birth to you.
There's a sense here that while Sarah lived, she had not yet given
birth to the people. The meaning of her life will become clear retroactively when, ultimately, she will give birth to you.

At the moment that's mysterious. But it should become clearer as
we go on. I want to look first at the description of the death of Sarah
at the beginning of the Torah reading *Chayei Sarah* (Genesis 23). "The
life of Sarah was a hundred years and twenty years and seven years;
these were the years of the life of Sarah." A summary sentence like
that is always ominous. Once someone's life is summed up like that,
you expect the statement *vatamot Sarah* (and Sarah died) to follow.
Now, of course, in any literal reading, we don't know when she died
or why she died. We know only that at a certain point she dies, and
that she was a hundred and twenty-seven years old. But when we begin to look into Rashi and the *midrashim,* we will see a very specific
death narrative traced out. Neither willful nor arbitrary, this narrative relies on the context in which Sarah's death is recorded. It comes
straight after the story of the *Akeda* (the Binding of Isaac). Why?
Rashi and other commentators assume a logic to these sequences.

According to Rashi the contiguity occurs *al yedei besorat ha'akeida—*
as a result of the news of the *Akeda; shenizdamein bena leshechita uki-*

mat shelo nishchat—that her son had been made ready for sacrifice and had almost been sacrificed, *parcha nishmata mimena, vameta*—her soul flew from her and she died.

⌒⌒⌒

"As a result of the news of the *Akeda*"—very cryptic. Rashi reduces some very elaborate and vivid midrashic interpretations of Sarah's death to a bare minimum here. The news of the *Akeda* was that her son *nizdamein* (had been summoned, invited, called). *Nizdamein* (the passive form of the verb) makes it sound as though it all happened by chance. He'd just come up against slaughter and *kimat shelo nishchat*—had almost been slaughtered. *Kimat shelo;* that's the central expression that I want to focus on. As a result of that, Sarah's soul flew away (*parcha nishmata*). *Parcha nishmata* is the classic expression for a kind of instantaneous departure, when the soul can't bear the environment, the straits, of the body, and simply flies away. The tension for Sarah is too great. But why the tension? If the news was that her son was almost slaughtered, the bottom line was that he's alive. Why, then, does she die? In what sense does *kimat shelo* explain her death? What is Rashi calling our attention to when he says that Isaac was "all but" slaughtered?

A simple way of reading that phrase would be to say that Sarah died because of the shock, the suddenness, thinking on the one hand that her son is dead and then hearing the news that he's not dead. But I don't think Rashi or the midrash is interested in telling us about the physical flutterings of Sarah's heart. What is there to learn from knowing that Sarah was given a terrible shock and died as a result of a shock? Perhaps something physiological. But that is not of great interest from the Torah's point of view. So, what are we dealing with?

The Gur Aryeh (the sixteenth-century Maharal's commentary on Rashi) tries to answer our question about why she dies by considering the phrase *kimat shelo*. It is a mysterious phrase because literally it means he was almost *not* slaughtered, while you really should say, he almost *was* slaughtered. And this is the way he reads it. The normal human reaction to learning that one has escaped a terrible fate, *shechita* (slaughter), by a hair's breadth, by a *davar mu'at* (from the word *kimat*), by a little thing, by a nothing, is what the Gur Aryeh calls *behala*. That word too is important and critical to what I want to say.

What is *behala*? Again, one could say something like shock. But *nivhal* is not exactly shock. *Nivhal* is something like dizziness, even a kind of nausea. It's vertigo. It's not knowing where one is, a shock in the sense of the loss of orientation. I don't know at all where I am in the world. Gur Aryeh says that this is a universal. It's a very common reaction to a situation in which one is almost—almost—almost. Of course, there are people who would react differently. Once you are empirical about it, you would have to acknowledge that there are those naturally religious souls, people who would simply be grateful to God, who would simply say, Thank God I was saved. But one still wonders what these naturally religious souls think. "I was saved because" . . . what? What's the meaning of this special gesture that God has made for me? I'm better than everyone else? Surely not. So I have to begin again with the whole question of theodicy. It's a question of trying to understand: Why did God save me? Of course there are many answers, but the more common response is one the Gur Aryeh draws our attention to, that most people will react with a sense of *behala,* with a sense of what I want to call vertigo, a sense of dizziness. What does anything mean after this has happened? It's just a matter of a hair's breadth. Every now and then you read in the papers about "extraordinary examples" of this kind, which leave you feeling literally *nivhal* even though it's good news. I remember reading one unbearable story about two children who were playing with a bow and arrow. One shot the arrow through the head of the other child, and it came out the other side, with no vital centers affected. This must be an absolute freak. What we feel when we read such a story is an open question. Maharal (the author of the Gur Aryeh) says, very strongly— and gives me a foundation for pursuing a path that might be surprising to some of you—the reaction is a sense of theological vertigo, of asking what does anything mean in that case. If it's really just a matter of a millimeter—it could go this way, it could go that way—how do we understand God's providence? How do we understand anything, in view of such events? The interesting thing is that Rashi, as interpreted by the Maharal (and Rashi is *the* classic interpreter of the Bible), indicates that Sarah dies of something like this. She does not die thinking that Isaac is dead. She knows he's alive, but only by a hair's breadth. And that immediately sets everything awry, does something radical to her sense of order and coherence in the world.

I want to follow this up by looking at the source *midrashim*. These are *midrashim* that Rashi presumably knew, and they lie at the intellectual heart of what I'd like to talk about. I'll present three different versions of a midrash that basically tries to describe how Sarah died and through that description explain her death.

The midrash from *Pirke de-Rabbi Eliezer* (32) gives us what I want to call the simplest explanation. I'll paraphrase it. When Abraham came back from Mount Moriah, Samael (Satan) is frustrated and angry that he hasn't managed to do anything to prevent Abraham from confronting the test of the *Akeda*. The midrash is full of stories about how Satan tried to stop Abraham from going to the *Akeda*. Abraham comes back triumphant; Satan is cowed, but also very angry and frustrated. So he decides that the only way he can save face is to gain a minor victory, perhaps with Sarah. So he goes to Sarah and says to her: Have you been listening to the news? Have you heard what's been going on in the world? And she says, No. And he says, Your old man, your old husband, has taken your son—*ve-hikrivo le'ola*—and he offered him up for a sacrifice. No ifs and buts about it. No *kimat shelo*. That's why I say it's the simplest form of the midrash. Satan says, he offered him up for a sacrifice, and *hana'ar bokhe umeyaleil shelo yakhol lehinatzeil*—and the boy was crying and wailing (and here's that word *meyaleil* again) because he couldn't be saved. It's an unbearable moment for us; how much more so for Sarah. *Miyad hitchila bokha umeyalelet*—immediately she began to cry and wail—miming the sounds of her son (*meyalelet, meyaleil*), trying (as it were) to take on his pain. *Bakhta shalosh bekhiyot keneged shalosh tekiot*—she cried three cries, corresponding to the three *tekiot* of the *shofar*, three wails corresponding to the three sobbing short sounds. *Uparcha nishmata vameta*—and her soul flew away and she died. By saying that this is the simplest version of the midrash on Sarah's death, I am not in any way denigrating it. I think it's an extremely poignant midrash. It's simple only in the sense that it clearly states why she died. She is maliciously misled by Satan, who is doing his work in a masterly way. She dies thinking that her son has been sacrificed by her husband. There couldn't be a worse scenario, as she dies in *bekhiya* and *yelala*, in those two modes.

When the midrash uses the word *keneged* (corresponding to), it suggests an idea that we want to take very seriously. In fact, a whole cluster of *midrashim* teach that we blow the *shofar*—the *tekia* sound, the *terua* sound—to remember Sarah's cries when she died. Now, that's not the usual explanation of the *shofar* taught us in Hebrew school. We are generally taught that the *shofar* (made of a ram's horn) reminds us of the ram that was substituted for Isaac at the *Akeda*. I'm in no way overriding that. But here I am exploring a counterversion, which for some reason is not so well-known.

In regard to the phrase *keneged*, (corresponding to), I'll share with you a few sources very quickly, to show you how serious this idea is. *Hitchila bokha*—she began to cry and wail three *yelalot*, and she died. Therefore the Sages instituted three sobbing sounds, the three *tekiot*. (That's from a midrashic collection called *Or Ha'afeila*.) In another (both are quoted in Torah Sheleima [23,2]), we hear: *Tzavcha tzadi kol*—She cried out ninety notes, the ninety notes of the *shofar* (all the sounds of the *shofar* on Rosh Hashana). And then she died. *Velekakh* (and therefore) we blow the *terua* on Rosh Hashana, in order that the death of Sarah should be an atonement, *kappara*—because *terua* is groaning and wailing (the two expressions of the Rambam again, *ginu'ach veyelala*). Again, I'm baffled. In what sense is the death of Sarah an atonement for us? How can we understand what, on the surface, seems to be a very un-Jewish association with the idea of vicarious atonement?

Another source, the medieval commentator Abudraham, writes, *Vatitzchak vateyabeiv vateyaleil:* She laughed and she sobbed and she wailed. She laughed?!? This is one of those really surrealistic *midrashim*. There was a laugh and there was a cry and there was a sob. What kind of laugh can we have here? With a midrashic memory, one can remember the verse at the end of *Eishet Chayil* (Proverbs 31, describing the "woman of valor")—*vatitzchak leyom acharon*—and she will laugh at the last day—and its common midrashic connection with Sarah. In the midrash, Sarah is chosen as the exemplar of someone who *will* laugh—who died in crying and wailing, and who *will* laugh. And of course one must remember that original laugh of Sarah's when she overhears the angel, announcing that she is to give birth to Isaac, in her old age. Somehow, you know, the wires begin to vibrate. A statement of great tension is being made here. According to Abudraham, Rosh Hashana is called *yom yevava* (a day of sobbing), which is an Aramaic translation of the Bible's Hebrew phrase *yom terua*. On *yom yevava*, we remember the sobbing of Sarah.

The sources, including the Rambam we discussed earlier, talk about the sobbing sounds as *yevava* or *yelala*. What is this *yelala?* Let me try, very briefly, a phenomenological description. First of all, the very sound is an onomatopoiea. It's what is called ululation, from the Latin *ululare*. It conveys the wordless sound made by women, particularly at moments of birth or death, at extreme moments when all normal patterns and neat understandings of the world break down. Words, too, break down, and all one has are these wordless cries. That's a *yelala*, basically—a howl, a hoot—for there's something animal about the sound. It's a failure of articulation, a song without words, because there is no possibility of words. In Hosea (7:14) we find one of the rare places in Tanakh where the word is used. The prophet chastises the people: *Velo za'aku eilai belibbam* (They don't cry to Me in their heart); *Ki yeyeililu al mishkevotam* (What they are doing is wailing upon their beds). The Metzudat David commentary on Hosea takes that word "wailing" and says something very sharp. And I emphasize that this commentator is not fanciful but usually gives the basic, literal translation of the text. He says: *Yelala* is the sound that expresses loss of belief in providence (*mekachashim behashgacha*). It's the sound that is the opposite of crying to God in one's heart. To cry to God in one's heart means to be directed, to know where to turn, as in prayer. The other reaction that's referred to here, disapprovingly, of wailing upon their beds, is the reaction of *mekachashim behashgacha*, they deny providence. They really don't think there is anywhere to turn or that there is any meaning in reality. This is the basic meaning of *yelala*. At the end of Shakespeare's *King Lear*, Lear thinks that Cordelia is alive, and then at the last minute she dies. He comes in carrying her in his arms, and Shakespeare writes as the words of his speech: "Howl, howl, howl, howl, howl." This is not a stage direction. It's not meant to say, "Lear should howl." Rather we are meant to hear howling as a significant act of language. I don't know how the actor should act it; I can't remember actually having heard it. But one's imagination opens up at this point. What is the content of the howl? A little later, right at the end of the play, Lear will say (and it seems to me to be the content in words of the howl): "And my poor fool is hanged, no no no life, why should a dog, a horse, a rat have life, and thou no breath at all? Thou wilt come no more, never never never never never." That howl is: A dog, a horse, a rat have life, and you don't. What possible sense can there be in that? What possible sense of providence, of a caring God in the world, can there be in that?

If Lear expresses this, it's one thing. If *Sarah* expresses it when she dies, then it's really something quite different. It may reflect the same experience, but it arouses quite different reactions from the reader. We didn't expect the midrash to say such things about Sarah. Yet one has to note that she's clearly not being disapproved of. I want to make that point very strongly, because I think people sometimes misunderstand this. She is in no way disapproved of for this reaction. After all, we keep blowing the *shofar*, year by year. If the *shofar* sound, the *yelala*, helps us to atone for ourselves, there must be something at least not negative implied in Sarah's *yelala*—something that the midrash insists we should bear in mind. I would like to assume that what the midrash calls to mind is something that brings us back to significant beginnings, that understanding of New Year we saw as a universal phenomenon. But what is our significant beginning? Strangely and tragically, it's not the comfortable idea of filling in cracks and sitting on stones and so forth. It's actually reuniting, empathizing, with a moment of the worst anguish possible. And when we blow the *shofar*, we are reenacting something and drawing on a certain kind of strength, as Eliade would say. Although this is not yet very clear, two other *midrashim* can help us explore the area of ambiguity and difficulty.

According to a midrash in Tanchuma (Vayera, 23), *Be'ota sha'a*, At that time, Satan went to Sarah. And he appeared to her, *nizdamein la*, in the guise of Isaac. When she saw him, she said to him: My son, what has your father done to you? Now of course, that question is significant. You're meant to notice it. The midrash doesn't fill in the details, but the question rings: Why does she ask, "What has your father done to you?" I don't know if I want to answer it, except to say that the midrash imagines that there is something about the way he looks that makes her feel something has happened. Perhaps one could even go further and say that Sarah has a very deep intuition, that she never liked it when Avraham and Yitzchak disappeared so early one morning. The midrash makes a point of it: they disappear early so that Sarah should not change her mind about permitting her husband and son to go off on a journey of "initiation in the knowledge of God," as the midrash rather ominously puts it (Tanchuma, 22). Abraham had fears for her sanity, for her life—"lest she kill herself." Now, her question, "What has your father done to you" suggests that Satan-playing-Isaac crystallizes all the nightmare possibilities. He then answers her: My father took me up hill and down dale, up to the top of a certain mountain, he built an altar, arranged the wood, bound me on top of it, he took the knife to slaughter me, and if God had not said, "Don't stretch out your hand," I would already have been slaughtered. Notice it's God who speaks here; in the actual narrative in the Torah, it's an angel who calls out. He doesn't manage to finish the story, *lo hispik ligmor et hadavar,* before she died, *ad she-yatza nishmata.* In this version of the story, Sarah's death is more puzzling. After all, Isaac is standing in front of her, apparently. She is not aware that it's Satan dressed up as Isaac. So why does she die? The midrash tries to explain itself by saying there's a tragic irony here, that she doesn't manage to live to the end of the story. If she'd only heard the end of the story and heard the *kimat shelo,* the *kvar hayiti,* then she would have lived. One might think that we have here one of those ironic stories about tragic ends, where one moment more would have changed everything. But that's clearly not what we have here. Since it's apparently Isaac standing before her, she shouldn't need to hear the ending. What causes her to die, then, is not so clear.

The third version is the most mysterious: *Avraham lo samach be'o-lami, ve'atem mevakshim lismo'ach:* Avraham didn't manage to rejoice in my world, and you want joy? It's a very pessimistic midrash. People want joy. On a certain level, that's absurd. There is no such thing as *simcha sheleima*—complete joy—(as another version of the midrash puts it) in this world. Examples are given of moments of seeming great satisfaction, such as Avraham after the *Akeda*. He has his son back, he survived the test, all is well. He comes back feeling that the world is somehow coherent or resolved. But from what happens immediately afterward, we learn there is no such thing as *simcha sheleima*. He comes and finds Sarah dead. To explain how she died, the story is told again: Avraham took Yitzchak up hill and down dale, the whole story that we've just heard. If it hadn't been that the angel called out, he would have already been slaughtered. *Teida shekein*. Perhaps the most significant words in the midrash: Know that it is so. Know that what is so? What's the midrash saying here? On one level, it seems to me, the midrash is saying: Know that my story about the *Akeda* really was so. It really implies things that you're thinking. How do we know? Because Yitzchak actually came back to his mother afterward (no Satan anymore)—no deceptions, no malice. Yitzchak comes back to his beloved mother, and he appears in front of her, and she says to him, "Where have you been, my son?" And he says, "My father took me . . ." and tells the whole story. It's abbreviated. He took me up hill and down dale, and the whole story again. And if it hadn't been . . . And she reacts. She says: *Vay al berei derabita*. Woe to the son of a hapless woman, of an unfortunate woman (that's one translation). Another translation I came across has to do with the idea of drunkenness. Woe to the son of a drunken woman. Meaning: I am beside myself. I lost my sanity. I'm outside myself. It's a kind of ecstasy of anguish. But she doesn't die right away. First she asks him a question: *Kvar hayita shachut?* (Were you already slaughtered?) If the angel hadn't interfered—what would have happened? She wants to get it clear. It's almost like a legal interrogation. Are you saying that if the angel hadn't interfered, you would have already been slaughtered? And he answers: Yes. And at that point she cries out, she cries out six cries—this time corresponding to the *tekiot* rather than the *teruot* (there are different versions of the midrash)—and the sages said: She didn't manage to finish the thing, until she died. *Lo hispika et hadavar ad shemeita*.

What didn't she finish? In the previous version, it was Satan who didn't manage to finish the story, and that let us think, at least for a moment, that she died too soon to hear the happy ending. We saw that this explanation didn't quite work. And here it's *she* who doesn't manage to finish. The root of the word *lehaspik* (to complete) contains the word *safeik*, doubt. It suggests a sense of radical doubt—never resolved—*Lo hispika et hadavar*. She doesn't manage to go through it and come out at the other side; she dies in the middle.

This is such painful material that it's really hard to go on, but I feel it's important to press on and see what is being said in these *midrashim*. I don't think *Chazal* (the Rabbis) are here just turning the knife in wounds that are plentiful anyway. *Chazal* are saying something, with the greatest possible honesty—an honesty that's rarely paralleled—about how human beings really feel about their condition, about the experience of the human being headed toward death.

The notion of contingency, the sense of the absurd, the sense of vertigo, is an existentialist commonplace. Existentialist philosophers and psychologists are always talking about this vertigo. Sartre, in a famous statement, talks about the nothingness that lies coiled in the very core of being like a worm. (*L'etre et le néant*.) Paul Tillich in *The Courage to Be* talks about vertigo as the sense of not being able to preserve one's being. Not being able, from one minute to the next, to live longer than is destined, than is decreed. One can't do anything to extend one's being, even by a minute. Paul Ricoeur talks about vertigo as the sense that a human being has of being already born. As soon as one knows oneself, one becomes conscious, one is already born. That is: I have no control. I didn't give birth to myself; I didn't put myself into the world. Therefore, at the other end, I also have no control. There is only a sense of nothingness, which reveals to me the "non-necessity of having once been born" (*History and Truth*, 296). Non-necessity means absurdity. I didn't have to be here; I just found myself here. It's like the foam on top of the wave. It was, it's here for a moment, *haya ve'avad*. (Remember the end of Jonah? *Bin laila haya uvin laila avad*—The gourd appeared overnight and perished overnight.) Is that really all it is? For Ricoeur, that's what vertigo is.

Where do we find this idea in Jewish sources? I can think of two examples. One is in Job (26:7), of course. *Tole eretz al belima*. That's perhaps a very concise expression of the idea—that God hangs the world, suspends the world, over nothing, over the abyss. This sense of an abyss, *belima*, without a what, which is what *belima* literally means—may mean without all the intellectual questions, all the philosophical questions, the what, why . . . and so on. Even the questions are absurd, because ultimately the abyss is serious. We can get an inkling of that seriousness from a passage in Lionel Trilling's essays on humanist education (*The Liberal Imagination*, 221–222), where he describes ironically an assignment he gave at the beginning of the year. He was teaching modern literature and modern philosophy, and he told his students to be prepared to look into the Abyss. And, he says with a dry irony, "both dutifully and gladly they have looked into the Abyss." They studied, they read the works, they talked about them intelligently, they wrote papers, and they did what he asked them to do. Now, what is Trilling saying here? He's saying very clearly that the activity of discussing and thinking and writing in intelligent company—even the activity we're engaged in now—is *not* looking into the Abyss. It's talking about it. That's something else. It's not the nothing itself. As soon as we're talking, we're not in nothing. We're in a world of substance. The real Abyss is: *tole eretz al belima*. Or perhaps it is the curse in the *tokheicha* (Deuteronomy 28:66): *Vehayu chayekha teluyim lekha mineged*—Your life will be suspended in front of you. It will be hanging in front of you, as it were, hanging by a thread, *u-fachadeta laila veyomam,* and you'll fear by day and by night, *velo ta'amin bechayekha,* and you won't believe in your life. You won't believe that there's any necessity to it, that there's anything meaningful about it. Rashi asks: What is this *talu'i,* this hanging in front of you (which we encountered before in the verse from Job— *tole eretz al belima*)? And Rashi answers: *Kol safeik karu'i talu'i.* Any condition of doubt is called being in suspense, being suspended, as it were. If one's not sure, if one doesn't have a well-founded and coherent vision of one's world, that's called being in doubt. If one doesn't know, that's called being *talu'i*. It's a cursed condition. It's the condition basically of existential angst. *Shema amut hayom.* Lest I die today. That's the doubt. It's a constant sense of "I don't know" that puts into question one's whole life, the totality—how does Ricoeur put it?—the totality of one's existence. One looks on oneself as a threatened totality.

That threatened totality comes into play, I'm suggesting, in the death of Sarah. She dies of this radical angst, of this radical sense of doubt about the meaning and the coherence of her life, a kind of "mortal vertigo." *Lo hispika,* she didn't manage to come through. She absorbs it, she articulates it wordlessly, but she doesn't come through it and resolve it. She hasn't any wisdom to offer us about how one resolves it. Instead, in the most pure way, she dies in the middle, as it were, to give us something of the purity and the truth of a certain perspective. And it's a perspective that the religious person (I say with fear and trembling) cannot afford to be without. The religious person cannot afford to leap at ultimate bliss, ultimate theological statements about meaning and hope and a connection with God, without going through *this* perspective on reality—which, in spite of the fact that it's denied and undercut by religious statements of affirmation, will always remain a vital and a viable (ironically chosen words) perspective on reality. One can't entirely put it behind one.

Who says this? The religious existential philosophers—Paul Tillich, among others. But we hear it as well (and from my point of view this has great weight) from the traditional Jewish scholar Rav Isaac Hutner. He says it twice, in two different books (Rosh Hashana, 7; Sukkot, 19). Let me sum up very briefly his analysis (and he is someone who's concerned with the world of the Sages, with the world of rabbinic wisdom, and who tries to come at wisdom that way). On the one hand, the Sages will characteristically say that life is good and that human life, in particular, is unquestionably good. When God looked at the world after creating Adam, the world suddenly became *tov me'od*, very good (Genesis 1:31). Before, it had just been *tov* (good)—every night and morning it was *tov*. With the creation of human life, it suddenly becomes *tov me'od*. And the Sages point to an apparent anagram on the word *me'od*. If we switch the letters around, we have *adam* (human being) (*Yalkut Shimoni*, 16). What is *tov me'od*? It's the existence of the human being; the existence of the human being is a very good thing.

Rav Hutner then quotes a counterstatement that is quite unusual and very perturbing, for those who are used to the idiom of *Chazal* (the Rabbis). *No'ach lo le'adam shelo nivra mishenivra*—It would be more comfortable, easier, for a human being, not to have been created than to have been created (Eruvin 13b). It would have been better not to be at all. Basically, what we have here is a kind of rejection of life. Why this undermining skepticism, even nihilism? Rav Hutner offers a dialectical understanding. He uses the example of the Talmudic technique of the *hava amina*, wherein to come to a certain conclusion, the Talmud will always consider the opposite possibility on the way (that's what I mean by dialectical). In order to come to the conclusion that the world is good and the life of a human is good, Rav Hutner suggests, we must first treat the opposite reading, the opposite perspective, with full seriousness. We must relate to that perspective as if it's not just a rejected hypothesis, but as if it were the conclusion. Forget for a moment that you know the conclusion. Forget your credos, forget what you've learned with your mother's milk, the beliefs about life you've acquired in the course of a life. Contemplate this:

No'ach lo le'adam shelo nivra mishenivra. It leads to a more adult understanding of in what way, exactly, human life is good. The primary,
childish sense that human life is good won't do for an adult who lives
unto death, who begins to understand things. *No'ach lo le'adam,* certainly it would be more comfortable not to live in such a situation, in
the human situation of being the only animal who knows the end.

Rav Hutner insists that the only way of arriving at affirmative and
transcendental statements is by thoroughly confronting the statements that speak of vertigo, of apparent meaninglessness. Such statements destroy all the illusions about what would make the world or
human life worth living for. If we take this idea seriously, then we understand the verse about blowing the *shofar, Ashrei ha'am yodei terua*
(Happy the people who know the *terua*), to say: Happy, solidly happy,
realistically happy, are a people who know the *terua,* who know what
it's like to cry in the mode of *yelala* or *yevava,* who understand life on
that basis. Only such a people can go beyond that. The English poet
William Blake says, Without contraries, there's no progression. Without a sense of creative tension, without always understanding the
counterstatement, there's no way of moving onward or going beyond
a rather simplistic understanding of things. And Rav Hutner also
means to say that this process never ceases. He doesn't mean that just
for one moment you should consider the opposite and then fly off
into your blissful life of faith. He actually means that this tension has
to endure. If the conclusion of faith is to have muscles, some kind of
solid strength, one has to know the other perspective .

This other perspective is one that negates reality or meaning. Rav
Hutner quotes a verse from Isaiah (45:18): *Ko amar Hashem, borei ha-
shamayim*—Thus says God, the Creator of the heaven. He is God Who
forms the earth and He makes it; He establishes it firmly. *Lo tohu be-
ra'a; lashevet yetzara*—Not for nothing—not for emptiness and void,
not for absurdity—did He create it, but rather to sit in firmly, to live
in, to have children in, to set up civilizations in, He created it. Rav
Hutner reads this verse provocatively. He interprets it to say: You
can't make the statement *lo tohu,* not for nothing did God create the
world, until you've understood the meaning of the word *tohu,* until
you've understood the possibility of looking at the world and seeing
it as possibly created *letohu* (for nothing). Only then can we see the
full meaning of God's statement *Lo tohu.* It's what Ricoeur calls "de-

negation." The only affirmatives are a confrontation with the negation, with the nothing, and then—only then—a de-negation, lo tohu
[*not* nothing]. *Not* as you think, but . . . you have to think it first! You
have to be there before you can understand the force of that *lo tohu*.
God created the world for what look like very superficial purposes: to
have children—like the animals! To set up a post office and a school
and a law court, all this stuff that sub specie aeternitatis is really just
the froth on the wave. If that's the case, why should we care about all
these things? But Isaiah says: God created the world precisely for all
these things, but in the view of *lo tohu*—that is, in a sense that goes
beyond, not precedes, the mode of experience, as Blake would call it.
Isaiah is talking about a different stage altogether, beyond the songs
of experience that come after the songs of innocence.

Take this notion and move a step further with it. It leads to a very
serious, metaphysically pessimistic understanding. According to
Midrash Rabba, *Vatamot Sarah mei'oto hatza'ar*—Sarah died of that
pain. "Of that pain"—a pain that the midrash does not spell out. It's
a way of gesturing at something that can't be put into words. She dies
from the reality of the *Akeda* in spite of the fact that the *Akeda* is superseded. It's highly paradoxical. And you find in *midrashim* exactly
this idea that Rav Hutner tries to proclaim. On one level, a cheerful
level, we can say that the *Akeda* doesn't make any demand in the end.
In the end it's canceled, it's neutralized, and the value of life, the
value of the world, is reaffirmed. The implication of the text is, Don't
ever do anything like this again, no human sacrifice. That's the way
we'd like to read it. But the midrash that Rav Hutner is working with
says, really unbearably, that although Isaac got up off the altar and
came down and had children and lived a successful life, even a wealthy
life, from another perspective, *efro tzavur al gabei hamizbei'ach*—his
ashes are gathered on the altar. There *was* a playing out to the end of
a tragic perspective on truth. It wasn't a game in which you are taken
almost to the finishing post and then you get saved. What is developed here is a paradigm for all situations in which there was no redemption, in which things got played out to the end. Sarah is the
clearest actual realization of this "to-the-endness." She dies in the full
force of what I'm calling a kind of metaphysical pessimism, a sense
that can be expressed only in the *yelala*. We express it by blowing the

shofar. And then we say, ironically, paradoxically, only such a people is happy.

Ricoeur and many other existentialists point out that negation—nothing, holes, not having, not being—is actually the perspective that allows human beings to use language in the first place. We begin to use language when we notice that things are not what they're supposed to be, what we'd hoped they would be, what we desire they be. If the world were full of positives, simply full of things the way they're supposed to be, or the way that human beings would like them to be, then a human being would never open his mouth. Henri Bergson, the great French philosopher, talks about language as granting the peculiar possibility of a negative ("The Idea of Nothing" in *Creative Evolution*). Language expresses the peculiar possibility that a human being has, of saying: No; not; it's *not* the way I expected it to be, this is not the way I would have it. Ricoeur writes: "Is not value this lack, this hole, which I hollow out before me, and which I fill by acts" (*History and Truth,* 322). We talk about fulfilling a wish, completing a program. Every human action has, as its starting point, a dissatisfaction and thereby a feeling of absence (Bergson). All human actions, human language, human projects, have to do with filling an emptiness, with providing something in a place of absence. Ricoeur says pointedly, "Volition is nolition" (312). When we *will* to do something in the world, actually what we're saying is: No. We're saying "no" to a prevailing state of affairs that we don't like, that we disapprove of. Therefore we gather our will together, and we say, No. I mention these notions because it seems to me that we're dealing with exactly this idea of holes and hollows, of empty spaces as created by Sarah, created for all time by Sarah. She is Sarah *techolelkhem* (who will give birth to you), Sarah who is the first hammer, the one who creates hollows. She's the first one who, because of an uncompromising strength of spirit, pursues to the end a certain way of seeing reality. She doesn't draw back. She's unflinching. She goes to the end, she dies in *yelala,* and she doesn't have a chance to resolve the paradox in any way.

At the most basic level we create hollows when we breathe out. Of course, if we blow the *shofar,* we have to breathe out. But more generally, breathing out is our response to God's creation of the human being. *Va-yippach be'apav nishmat chayyim:* God blows into the first human being the breath of life (Genesis 2:7). The word *nishmat* (breath) is clearly also the soul (*neshama*), not just the breath. *Kol haneshama tehalel Kah*—Every soul, every breath, should praise God (Psalm 150:6). The phrase from the liturgy, *nishmat kol chai* (the soul/breath of every living being), is interpreted by the midrash: human beings should praise God with every breath. The midrash means literally—with every expiration, the experience of breathing out should lead to an act of praising God. Why? Just because it creates a hollow. If you've ever done any breathing techniques like yoga, you'll know that if you want to take in a very good breath, a good, life-giving breath, the first part of the technique is to breathe out very well, to experience the expiration, what it's like to be a body without breath. Although it's actually a reflex to take in breath, for as long as we are alive, the midrash reacts to it as an act of will. It's the *will* of the human being to live, against reality, against negations. *Lo tohu.* That is the act of de-negation.

The Torah is given in a place of *yelala*. In an extraordinary moment in Moses' last song, spoken just before he dies, he says (Deuteronomy 32:10): God found this people in a desert land, and in *tohu*, in emptiness, howling (*yeleil*) *yeshimon* (waste). And that was where God gave this people the Torah: in a place of howling and waste, emptiness. Rashi's comment on this verse sketches it out very clearly. In this howling place of nothing, the hyenas, the jackal, the sounds of the *midbar* (desert), where there's no meaning, no human civilization, nothing to give structure to the experience—*af sham nimshekhu achar ha'emuna*—yea there, indeed to there, precisely there, into the wilderness, the people were drawn toward faith. Rashi sees in the verse not just obedience to a commandment of God, but almost an existential attraction. The people are drawn to that place of nothingness because they're looking for faith. And you can't look for faith where there's complete plenitude. Where everything is self-explanatory, or good, and full, then there's no need for faith. Perhaps one can eventually come back to plenitude with faith. But the primary impulse of faith has to do with the *yelala*, with the *midbar*—a very difficult perception.

All this brings us back to the point we started from. How can one crown God? Apparently only by affirming coherence as against a real understanding of incoherence, a real understanding of what I'm calling vertigo. This is our natural condition with all the holes and cavities that ring hollowly from it. A famous Talmudic statement (Sanhedrin 37a) tells us: *Chayav adam lomar: bishvili nivra ha'olam.* A person should say: for *my* sake the world was created. Why? Because man was created alone. There's a certain aloneness inherent in the possibility of validating the creation of the world. A human being alone has to understand why the world is worthwhile. It cannot be done in any dogmatic way or through masses but only in a solitary attempt to come to grips with the basic issues.

Rav Hutner, in a further essay (Rosh Hashana, 11), points to a famous passage in the Talmud (Pesachim 50a). It starts with a verse from the prophetic book of Zechariah (14:9): *Vehaya Hashem lemelekh al kol ha'aretz*—And God will be king over the whole earth. *Bayom hahu yihye Hashem echad ushemo echad*—On that day, the Lord will be one and His name will be one. This familiar verse is often recited as part of the liturgy. The Talmud asks the obvious question. On *that day* God's name will be one? and *now* He's not one? But then what do we mean when we say: *Shema yisrael . . . Hashem echad* (Hear Israel . . . the Lord is one)? The Talmud goes on to say: This world is not like the world-to-come. In this world, if one gets good news, one makes one *berakha* (blessing). One says, *Barukh hatov vehameitiv,* Blessed be the good One who does good. And if one gets bad news, one also makes a *berakha,* but it's a different kind of *berakha.* One says, *Barukh dayyan ha'emet,* Blessed be the judge of truth. This blessing is a pure act of language, a pure act of accounting for a tragic narrative. Rav Hutner comments, "The two blessings evoke two realities." There is good and there is bad. There are moments when we experience coherence and goodness and plenitude, and there are moments when we experience *barukh dayyan ha'emet,* in the larger sense. And, Rav Hutner says, there is no healing of that chasm in this world. What moves me is his uncompromising realism. It would be very easy to try to say something else. Instead he insists that, in this world, the two don't converge. At most, when we say *shema yisrael,* we press our hands very tight against our eyes and we close our eyes very tight and we try to concentrate on the possibility of *echad* (one), on the possibility of things coming together. In the world-to-come, it will be quite different. In the world-to-come, the Lord will be king; on that day the Lord will be one and His name will be one. And in that world, there will be only one *berakha*. That's the way the Talmud puts it. Whatever we hear, it will all be *barukh hatov vehameitiv*. But that's a perspective, a vision, that is by definition otherworldly. It doesn't belong in this world. In this world, we struggle with the two and at rare moments, perhaps, at least try to see them as converging, in one form or another.

In this perspective, what does it mean to say that Sarah is the one who *will* generate us? Why is Sarah the one? Perhaps we haven't yet succeeded in retroactively justifying her life. In what sense could we justify the way she dies, a death that apparently gives a terrible inner architecture to her whole life, a shape that no one would choose? What good is she doing her children through this? It's hard to say glibly. But the point I'm trying to make is that she, for all time, made it clear that there are holes and cavities, and that one shouldn't fool oneself about it. The act of faith, the life of faith, of affirmation and value, acts that really are acts, arise out of what Sarah left, what Sarah bequeathed unresolved. We will try to resolve it, but here we experience a moment that is unabated in any way, not equivocal, which we then must deal with. In dealing with it, we become who we're supposed to be. That's *techolelkhem*. Through much pain, she *will* give birth to you. She invents longing. She invents the sense of a negative, a sense of *yelala*.

I want to finish with one of the classic stories of the Chasidic master Rabbi Nachman of Bratslav, "The Seven Beggars." Seven beggars come to a young couple at their wedding, one after the other, and each one is more crippled and more disabled than the other. Each of these beggars tells a story as their present to the couple, and each one finishes his story by saying: And I wish you to be like me. The one we're concerned with is the fourth beggar, who has a twisted neck. This is actually a very strange description: *tzavar akum, akum hatzavar,* he has a twisted neck. The connotations of this description in Hebrew are all negative. *Akum* is not a good word in Hebrew contexts of all kinds. *Vehaya he'akov lemishor*—In the end, everything twisted shall be made straight (Isaiah 40:4). Or the idea embedded in the name Ya'akov (Jacob), which can suggest deceit—that *akov/akum* idea is clearly an idea that's supposed to be superseded when the name Ya'akov is changed to Yisrael. There was a time when he was like this, and then he became Yisrael. *Akov* is *galut* (exile), and afterward there will be redemption. It's not the desirable state of affairs. A twisted neck in the physical sense is not a pretty thing. Although references to necks in the Tanakh are not too plentiful, there is a verse in *Song of Songs* (4:4) describing the beloved's neck, presumably defining what makes a neck beautiful. *Kemigdal David tzavareikh, banu'i letalpiot*—Like the tower of David is your neck, built *letalpiot*, for some very beautiful structure, straight. The idea is straight, erect. And Rashi comments that when a neck is straight, it draws the eye. It has a fascination. If someone has a very straight neck, it makes people look at them, because it says something about the coherence of the whole body. And I think that's exactly what many modern body movement disciplines really are about. The angle at which this neck is held says something about the organic working of the whole body, that this is a healthy, erect body.

But here we have a twisted-necked beggar, and he is a great musician, he says. In fact, he boasts: I am greater than everyone else. I had a competition with all the other musicians and they claimed they were greater than I was, but I told them what I could do. What I can do is throw my voice. Because I've got this twisted neck, I can ventriloquize. I can let out a sound that no one near me will hear, but at a distance, people will hear it. I can do this magic thing. And then, I wanted to prove to my fellow musicians what my talents are, so I told them a story. There is a country in which, at night, there are great *yelalot. Meyalelim* to the point where no one can sleep. All night long there's great wailing. There's a kind of contagion of wailing that goes on, and not a person is exempt from it in that country. This makes it unbearable to be there. But it's just as unbearable to be there during the day when there is great joy. There's a strange joy during the day and great sorrow during the night. And the joy of the day has to do with people giving each other hope, trying to make each other feel that the matter of the night is not the final word. Either way it's unbearable, he says. You can't be there in that world, either by day or by night. It's just too much. But the musicians insist on being invited. They want to go there to see if they can heal this disease. They're very confident. And they arrive there and find that immediately they start wailing. In other words, they're immediately overtaken by the disease. They can't cure it, except for our musician, of course. And our musician then explains to them the source of this illness. He knows what caused it, and it's two birds. Two birds who love each other but are separated from each other. *Ne'evdu ze mize, avad*. They cease to be to one another, they're out of reach. One makes its place near one kingdom and one makes its place near another kingdom, and at night these two birds set up a human cry, a wailing for a lost one, which affects the whole kingdom nearby. So in the end, there are these two kingdoms where everyone is wailing and crying at night. That's the story. Can you heal this situation? the musicians asked. He says, Oh yes, very easily. No problem. You know my crooked neck? It's actually a very straight neck, he says. It can do just what it's supposed to do. It's perfect for this world, coordinated well with this world. He goes to one of the birds and imitates the wailing. He's not overcome by it, but he imitates the wailing and throws his voice so that it reaches the other bird. The other bird had never heard the wailing of the partner. But he throws his voice in his imitation so the other bird can hear. And he does the same with the other bird. He goes to the place where the other bird is and radios back, so that now the two birds, in their wailing, hear the other wailing. And that, already, is a form of comfort and a form of therapy—the understanding that somewhere there is a corresponding wailing going on, in this exiled world.

It implies the idea of *galut*, the exile of this world, yet there is a God who wails for us. That's a very characteristic Chasidic idea—that as we mourn for God, so God mourns for us. It may not help us with our immediate problems, but it does somewhere put a frame around it. Somewhere, it says, the frame contains more than what I immediately observe. Somewhere, there's a God who wants us, too.

How is that achieved? It's achieved simply by someone who knows how to imitate the wail—that is, how to take the wail, without putting it down, without any disrespect to it, and do it faithfully, but in a mode that already (as it were) enters into the world of art. Such a person tries to achieve a certain directionality through the wail. He's throwing his voice using his twisted neck, which is an entirely appropriate neck for this twisted world, for a world that is out of joint, dislocated, and not in connection with the other world that gives meaning. The twisted neck is exactly right for such a dislocated place, for it has the capacity to take the *yelala* and, as it were, to broadcast it to the place where it needs to be heard and then to enable us to hear a reply. This is the capacity of our beggar. In the end he says to the couple: I wish you, I bless you, that you should be like me—a dubious blessing; or perhaps the basic blessing, the premise that underlies the verse that we started from: *Ashrei ha'am yodei terua* (Happy the people who know the *terua*).

The possibility of *ashrei,* difficult as that might be, comes from being a people that knows the *yelala,* that knows the *terua,* that blows it, even performs it through the *shofar,* reenacting the death of Sarah, but with a difference. The difference is that I'm now using a *shofar;* I'm not using my own voice. The *shofar* is crooked. In fact, according to Jewish law, it *must* be crooked, it may not be straight. We don't want to use an instrument that could give a false impression of the immaculateness and coherence of the world. It's a crooked *shofar,* but it's *mekhuvan lema'ala*—we blow it directed—directed upward. And that, of course, is exactly the same expression that the beggar uses. He says: *Ani yodei'a lekhavein et hakolot*—I know how to direct the sounds. I know how to make of them something that has a direction and an imagined and almost experienced recipient. I know that I can reach something invisible, something imperceptible, in a very serious performance—and I mean both those words—of the *yelalot,* of the *shofar,* of the *terua.* Only in that mode, with all its paradoxes, is it possible to talk about the *ashrei,* a certain measure of solid affirmation, even solid happiness, of a whole nation who found the roots of their being in Sarah and the particular inner architecture of her life.

"Rachel Weeps for Her Children"
(Jeremiah 31:2–20)

HAFTARA READING—SECOND DAY ROSH HASHANA

²Thus saith the LORD:
The people that were left of the sword
Have found grace in the wilderness,
Even Israel, when I go to cause him to rest.
³'From afar the LORD appeared unto me.'
'Yea, I have loved thee with an everlasting love;
Therefore with affection have I drawn thee.
⁴Again will I build thee, and thou shalt be built,
O virgin of Israel;
Again shalt thou be adorned with thy tabrets,
And shalt go forth in the dances of them that make merry.
⁵Again shalt thou plant vineyards upon the mountains of Samaria;
The planters shall plant, and shall have the use thereof.
⁶For there shall be a day,
That the watchmen shall call upon the mount Ephraim:
Arise ye, and let us go up to Zion,
Unto the LORD our God.'

⁷For thus saith the LORD:
Sing with gladness for Jacob,
And shout at the head of the nations;
Announce ye, praise ye, and say:
'O LORD, save Thy people,

כֹּה אָמַר יְהֹוָה מָצָא חֵן
בַּמִּדְבָּר עַם שְׂרִידֵי חָרֶב הָלוֹךְ
לְהַרְגִּיעוֹ יִשְׂרָאֵל ׃

מֵרָחוֹק יְהֹוָה
נִרְאָה לִי וְאַהֲבַת עוֹלָם אֲהַבְתִּיךְ
עַל־כֵּן מְשַׁכְתִּיךְ חָסֶד ׃

עוֹד אֶבְנֵךְ
וְנִבְנֵית בְּתוּלַת יִשְׂרָאֵל עוֹד תַּעְדִּי
תֻפַּיִךְ וְיָצָאת בִּמְחוֹל מְשַׂחֲקִים ׃

עוֹד תִּטְּעִי כְרָמִים בְּהָרֵי שֹׁמְרוֹן
נָטְעוּ נֹטְעִים וְחִלֵּלוּ ׃

כִּי יֶשׁ־יוֹם
קָרְאוּ נֹצְרִים בְּהַר אֶפְרָיִם קוּמוּ
וְנַעֲלֶה צִיּוֹן אֶל־יְהֹוָה אֱלֹהֵינוּ ׃

כִּי
כֹּה אָמַר יְהֹוָה רָנּוּ לְיַעֲקֹב שִׂמְחָה
וְצַהֲלוּ בְּרֹאשׁ הַגּוֹיִם הַשְׁמִיעוּ הַלְלוּ
וְאִמְרוּ הוֹשַׁע יְהֹוָה אֶת־עַמְּךָ אֵת

201

The remnant of Israel.'
8Behold, I will bring them from the
north country,
And gather them from the utter-
most parts of the earth,
And with them the blind and the
lame,
The woman with child and her that
travaileth with child together;
A great company shall they return
hither.
9They shall come with weeping,
And with supplications will I lead
them;
I will cause them to walk by rivers
of waters,
In a straight way wherein they shall
not stumble;
For I am become a father to Israel,
And Ephraim is My first-born.

10Hear the word of the LORD, O ye
nations,
And declare it in the isles afar off,
and say:
'He that scattered Israel doth
gather him,
And keep him, as a shepherd dot .
his flock.'
11For the LORD hath ransomed Jacob,
And He redeemeth him from the
hand of him that is stronger than
he.
12And they shall come and sing in the
height of Zion,
And shall flow unto the goodness of
the LORD,
To the corn, and to the wine, and
to the oil,
And to the young of the flock and
of the herd;
And their soul shall be as a watered
garden,
And they shall not pine any more at
all.
13 Then shall the virgin rejoice in the
dance,
And the young men and the old
together;
For I will turn their mourning into
joy,

8 שְׁאֵרִית יִשְׂרָאֵל: הִנְנִי מֵבִיא אוֹתָם
מֵאֶרֶץ צָפוֹן וְקִבַּצְתִּים מִיַּרְכְּתֵי־אָרֶץ
בָּם עִוֵּר וּפִסֵּחַ הָרָה וְיֹלֶדֶת יַחְדָּו
קָהָל גָּדוֹל יָשׁוּבוּ הֵנָּה:

בִּבְכִי יָבֹאוּ
9 וּבְתַחֲנוּנִים אוֹבִילֵם אוֹלִיכֵם אֶל־
נַחֲלֵי מַיִם בְּדֶרֶךְ יָשָׁר לֹא יִכָּשְׁלוּ בָּהּ
כִּי־הָיִיתִי לְיִשְׂרָאֵל לְאָב וְאֶפְרַיִם
בְּכֹרִי הוּא:

שִׁמְעוּ דְבַר־יְהֹוָה
10 גוֹיִם וְהַגִּידוּ בָאִיִּים מִמֶּרְחָק וְאִמְרוּ
מְזָרֵה יִשְׂרָאֵל יְקַבְּצֶנּוּ וּשְׁמָרוֹ כְּרֹעֶה
עֶדְרוֹ:

11 כִּי־פָדָה יְהֹוָה אֶת־יַעֲקֹב
וּגְאָלוֹ מִיַּד חָזָק מִמֶּנּוּ:

12 וּבָאוּ
וְרִנְּנוּ בִמְרוֹם־צִיּוֹן וְנָהֲרוּ אֶל־טוּב
יְהֹוָה עַל־דָּגָן וְעַל־תִּירֹשׁ וְעַל־יִצְהָר
וְעַל־בְּנֵי־צֹאן וּבָקָר וְהָיְתָה נַפְשָׁם
כְּגַן רָוֶה וְלֹא־יוֹסִיפוּ לְדַאֲבָה עוֹד:

13 אָז תִּשְׂמַח בְּתוּלָה בְּמָחוֹל
וּבַחֻרִים וּזְקֵנִים יַחְדָּו וְהָפַכְתִּי אֶבְלָם
לְשָׂשׂוֹן וְנִחַמְתִּים וְשִׂמַּחְתִּים מִיגוֹנָם:

And will comfort them, and make
them rejoice from their sorrow.
¹⁴And I will satiate the soul of the
priests with fatness,
And My people shall be satisfied
with My goodness,
Saith the LORD.

¹⁵Thus saith the LORD:
A voice is heard in Ramah,
Lamentation, and bitter weeping,
Rachel weeping for her children;
She refuseth to be comforted for her
children,
Because they are not.

¹⁶Thus saith the LORD:
Refrain thy voice from weeping,
And thine eyes from tears;
For thy work shall be rewarded,
saith the LORD;
And they shall come back from the
land of the enemy.
¹⁷And there is hope for thy future,
saith the LORD;
And thy children shall return to their
own border.
¹⁸I have surely heard Ephraim be-
moaning himself:
'Thou hast chastised me, and I was
chastised,
As a calf untrained;
Turn thou me, and I shall be turned,
For Thou art the LORD my God.
¹⁹Surely after that I was turned, I
repented,
And after that I was instructed, I
smote upon my thigh;
I was ashamed, yea, even confounded,
Because I did bear the reproach of
my youth.'
²⁰Is Ephraim a darling son unto Me?

Is he a child that is dandled?
For as often as I speak of him,
I do earnestly remember him still;
Therefore My heart yearneth for
him,
I will surely have compassion upon
him, saith the LORD.

וְרִוֵּיתִי נֶפֶשׁ הַכֹּהֲנִים דָּשֶׁן וְעַמִּי 14
אֶת־טוּבִי יִשְׂבָּעוּ נְאֻם־יְהוָה׃

כֹּה 15
אָמַר יְהוָה קוֹל בְּרָמָה נִשְׁמָע נְהִי
בְּכִי תַמְרוּרִים רָחֵל מְבַכָּה עַל־בָּנֶיהָ
מֵאֲנָה לְהִנָּחֵם עַל־בָּנֶיהָ כִּי אֵינֶנּוּ׃

כֹּה ׀ אָמַר יְהוָה מִנְעִי קוֹלֵךְ מִבֶּכִי 16
וְעֵינַיִךְ מִדִּמְעָה כִּי יֵשׁ שָׂכָר
לִפְעֻלָּתֵךְ נְאֻם־יְהוָה וְשָׁבוּ מֵאֶרֶץ
אוֹיֵב׃ וְיֵשׁ־תִּקְוָה לְאַחֲרִיתֵךְ נְאֻם־ 17
יְהוָה וְשָׁבוּ בָנִים לִגְבוּלָם׃

שָׁמוֹעַ 18
שָׁמַעְתִּי אֶפְרַיִם מִתְנוֹדֵד יִסַּרְתַּנִי
וָאִוָּסֵר כְּעֵגֶל לֹא לֻמָּד הֲשִׁיבֵנִי
וְאָשׁוּבָה כִּי אַתָּה יְהוָה אֱלֹהָי׃

כִּי 19
אַחֲרֵי שׁוּבִי נִחַמְתִּי וְאַחֲרֵי הִוָּדְעִי
סָפַקְתִּי עַל־יָרֵךְ בֹּשְׁתִּי וְגַם־נִכְלַמְתִּי
כִּי נָשָׂאתִי חֶרְפַּת נְעוּרָי׃

הֲבֵן יַקִּיר 20
לִי אֶפְרַיִם אִם יֶלֶד שַׁעֲשֻׁעִים כִּי־
מִדֵּי דַבְּרִי בּוֹ זָכֹר אֶזְכְּרֶנּוּ עוֹד עַל־
כֵּן הָמוּ מֵעַי לוֹ רַחֵם אֲרַחֲמֶנּוּ נְאֻם־
יְהוָה׃

Our Mother of Sorrows

TAMAR FRANKIEL

The events of women's lives occupy a special place in the Rosh Hashana readings. In Judaism women represent renewal of life, not only in the biological sense, but also in the sense of the fertile power of wisdom from which all created things ultimately derive.[1] The *Haftara* for the second day of Rosh Hashana, Jeremiah 31:1–19, promises the ultimate redemption of the Jewish people, but it too mentions a woman: *Rachel Imeinu,* our mother Rachel. The passage focuses on the promises of the messianic era, as is traditional for the last reading of *yom tov* (holiday), reminding us that each holiday is a foretaste of the day that is *kulo tov,* completely good. But surely, in selecting the last reading for this holiday of renewal, our Sages were interested in Jeremiah's invocation of the figure of Rachel.

> So said the Lord: "A voice was heard on high—wailing, bitter weeping—Rachel weeps for her children, she refuses to be consoled for her children, for they are gone." So said the Lord: "Restrain your voice from weeping and your eyes from tears, for there is a reward for your accomplishment—the words of the Lord—and they shall return from the enemy's land. (Jeremiah 31:14–15)

Jeremiah was either recording his own visionary perception of Rachel or, more likely, alluding to a folk tradition already known when he wrote in the sixth century B.C.E., that Rachel is the mother who weeps in prayer over the Jewish people. According to that tradition, later recorded in a midrash, she was buried "on the road" so that people passing by her grave on the way to exile would recall her tearful prayers and beg for her blessings to hasten the redemption. What lies behind this portrait of Rachel weeping?

To put it another way, why Rachel? What was the traditional perception of this woman that allowed her to be chosen for this role rather than Sarah, Rebecca, or Leah (who, according to midrash, had "weak eyes" from weeping)? Let us explore some of the various facets of Rachel's life in hopes that it will lead us to an understanding that can deepen our own prayers for the redemption on Rosh Hashana.

Rachel's story extends over several chapters in Genesis (29:1–31:47, 35:9–20). In the first part of the story, Jacob encountered Rachel when he arrived in the city of Haran, home of his mother's brother Laban. Rachel, Laban's younger daughter and the shepherdess for a small flock of his sheep, was at that very moment bringing the animals to water at the well. As our commentators note, the well, a symbol of feminine wisdom, was the location for several important meetings of future husband and wife. Isaac and Rebecca met at a well, as did Moses and his Midianite wife, Tzippora.[2]

When Jacob learned of Rachel's identity, he kissed her and wept. She ran to tell her father of his arrival. Jacob asked for Rachel's hand in marriage and, in return, offered to work for Laban seven years, "and they seemed to him a few days because of his love for her" (29:20). Although Laban agreed, when the wedding day arrived seven years later, he substituted her older sister, Leah, later explaining his deceit by the custom that the younger daughter should not be married before the elder. Jacob was understandably upset but arranged to marry Rachel anyway, with the provision that he would afterward work another seven years.

A midrash explains that Rachel, suspecting her father would try to deceive Jacob, had arranged signs and passwords with him so that, at the wedding, he could be sure that, under the veils, she was the bride. (The Jewish custom of having the groom himself veil the bride just before the wedding is traced to this event.) However, just before the wedding took place, Rachel took pity on Leah, who would have been terribly embarrassed if the deception were discovered, and revealed the signs to her.

This, explains a midrash cited by the medieval commentator Rashi, is the main reason that Rachel's prayers were listened to on high. Rachel's kindness toward her rival gave her special merit. Even when the prayers of Abraham, Isaac, and Jacob had no effect on the heavenly decree that the Jews would have to be in exile, Rachel's pleas would arouse God's mercy.

When King Manasseh of Judah set up an idol in the Temple, God made the decision that the Temple would be destroyed and the people exiled. The souls of the Patriarchs and Matriarchs pleaded with God to rescind His decree, but He rejected their pleas.

Then Rachel came weeping before God. She said, "Surely Your mercy is greater than the mercy of a mortal human being! Nevertheless, look at the mercy I displayed. Jacob labored seven years only for the right to marry me. Still, when my father Laban substituted my sister Leah for me under the marriage canopy, not only did I remain silent, I even gave her the passwords Jacob and I had devised. Thus I allowed a rival to come into my [future] household. You, O God, should do the same. Although Your children have brought a rival [i.e., Manasseh's idol] into your Temple, may You be silent."

God told her, "You have defended them well."[3]

The midrash suggests a lovely metaphor for the relationship of the Jewish people to God. Rachel's soul perceived God's suffering over the fickle affections and loyalties of the Jewish people. But she understood that, in a deeper sense, the Jews were not really attached to the Canaanite idols. Just as Jacob was deceived by Laban and given another wife, so the Jewish people had idols thrust in their faces, so to speak, and succumbed to the deceit. But like Jacob, they still had in their hearts only one true love, the God of Israel.

There is more to understand about Rachel. After marrying Jacob, she had no children for many years. Leah, in the meantime, was very fertile, bearing Jacob four children in four years. Rachel gave Jacob her handmaid, who bore him two children; but then Leah followed suit and her handmaid brought forth two as well. In despair, Rachel cried out to Jacob, "Give me children, or I die!" The commentators tell us that because she had the spirit of prophecy, Rachel knew that she was supposed to be the mother of two of Jacob's twelve sons. Perhaps she suspected Jacob of trying to thwart that design.[4] Jacob became angry with her and informed her in no uncertain terms that God was the one who had closed her womb. Finally, in response to her prayers, "God opened her womb" and Rachel gave birth to one son, Joseph. At this point she had been married to Jacob for nearly fourteen years.[5]

Jacob contracted with Laban to continue working for him, but after six more years, he had become so wealthy that Laban's family was very resentful. A prophecy came instructing him to return to the land of Israel. When he and his family left Laban's territory, Rachel took her father's *terafim,* which were either idols of the household deities or oracular devices.[6] According to Rashi, Rachel wanted to wean her father from idol worship by showing him that the idols had no power to protect themselves. But if we understand *terafim* to be oracles, Rachel's theft might indicate her belief that she could make better use of them than her father. As a result of her act, Laban pursued the family and accused Jacob of taking his daughters, his sheep, and his gods. Jacob was indignant at the accusations but allowed Laban to search for the idols, vowing indiscriminately, "With whomever you find your gods, he shall not live!" (v. 32).

Of course, Jacob had no idea that Rachel had stolen the *terafim.* When Laban searched her tent, she put them under a camel's saddle and sat on it, excusing herself from rising by saying that "the way of women is upon me." Laban had to leave without finding the idols, but Rachel was left with the unintended curse of Jacob upon her. Because, according to rabbinic tradition, the words of a *tzadik* (holy man) are always fulfilled in some manner, Jacob's words cast a shadow over Rachel's future.

Jacob's journey homeward took nearly two years. Several months before reuniting with his father, Isaac, who lived in Hebron, he stopped at Beit-El to establish a site of worship, thereby fulfilling his vow of twenty-two years before. For Jacob, this act would reestablish him in that special relationship to God that could emerge only in the land of Israel. He therefore ordered everyone in his entourage to destroy their idols and purify themselves. At this time, if not before, the *terafim* were presumably destroyed, too.

But Rachel was not destined to share in the ultimate reunion. On the journey, she had become pregnant again. After leaving Beit-El, as the caravan approached Efrat (just north of Beit-Lechem), she went into a very difficult labor. As she was giving birth, the midwife consoled her, "Don't be afraid; this also is a son for you." Rachel knew then that she had fulfilled her destiny of bringing forth two of the twelve sons who were the foundation for the Jewish people. But she herself would not live. Our Sages say that a woman is often judged when she is giving birth, and the judgment for her sin of taking the *terafim*—however well intentioned it was—became apparent in her dying at that powerful moment.

With her last breath, she named the boy Ben-Oni, "son of my mourning," for the family would be mourning for her even while they celebrated his birth. Jacob, however, changed the name to Ben-Yamin (Benjamin), "son of the right-hand." Some commentators read this in its simple meaning as "son of the south," that is, born south of Padan-Aram, Laban's territory, while others read it as "son of my days," from a variant spelling of *yamim* (days), referring to Jacob's old age.

This tragic ending to the life of Rachel, Jacob's favored wife, is amplified by subsequent events. Jacob decided to bury her immediately, at Efrat, rather than take her body with him to Hebron. While the custom was to bury quickly a woman who died in childbirth,[7] the party was so close to Hebron, site of the burial cave of the Patriarchs and Matriarchs, that it is difficult to explain why they could not delay burial for another day or two. After all, at the end of his own life, Jacob would ask that his bones be transported all the way from Egypt, delaying burial for weeks. The medieval commentator the Ramban (Nachmanides) understands the hasty burial of Rachel as a shift in the level of holiness expected of Jacob: when settling in Israel, he was required to behave according to Torah standards. Because marriage to two sisters would be forbidden once the Torah was given, his second marriage, to Rachel, was now in question. Therefore Rachel not only had to die, but also had to be buried separately so that Jacob would not be "embarrassed before his ancestors."[8]

It is difficult for modern readers to understand Jacob's apparent abandonment of Rachel as based on spiritual purity. Rather, we are drawn to Rachel in compassion and sorrow. Why did she deserve this double separation from the husband she loved and who loved her so much? Jacob's love and respect for her to the end are demonstrated by the fact that he set up a monument to her grave, whereas in Biblical times graves were usually unmarked. He wanted his descendants to be able to remember her by visiting her grave. Moreover, according to traditional commentaries, he separated himself from all his wives after Rachel died as another indication of his devotion.[9] But he accepted, as a judgment on her and himself (for his thoughtless curse), that she had to be buried in a separate place.

Yet in every judgment there is mercy, if only we can look with clear eyes. Jacob burying her on the road set Rachel apart among the Patriarchs and Matriarchs, as being especially accessible. Travelers who passed by could ask for her blessing, whether they were exiles on their way to Babylon or women praying for a healthy pregnancy. She was placed close to the people because she could be deeply involved with them.

Rachel's words and actions always expressed deep feelings toward others. She loved and was loved passionately by her husband. Her mercy toward her sister overcame any rational assessment of her evil father (remember, Laban is described in the Passover *Haggada* as the opponent worse than Pharaoh, who would have liked to "uproot" Jacob). The explanation of the theft of the *terafim* in terms of her desire for her father's repentance suggests her love for him and her enduring hope that he would turn from his sins. Rachel had a passionate desire for children, so much that she cried, "Give me children or I die!" In her death, too, she was caught up in the passion of the event, when she breathed out her son's name, "son of my sorrow, my mourning."

We should take care not to read this deathbed scene lightly as simply the cry of a woman exhausted by pain and realizing her own life's breath was passing from her. The "sorrow" was not momentary, but the essence of Rachel's life. If we look into it further, we can see Rachel's experience of sorrow was profound and unique.

Rabbi Samson Raphael Hirsch, in commenting on Rachel's use of the word *oni* ("my sorrow") here, notes that it has to do with a pervasive sense of loss. He relates *oni* to a word that appears in Numbers 11:1 as a description of the Israelites' unhappiness in their desert wanderings: *mitonenim*. This expression is usually translated "murmuring," but Hirsch renders it "as if in mourning over themselves." The Israelites were disturbed, worried, grieved.[10] This *on* was a feeling that came over them despite being completely taken care of, surrounded in their travels by clouds of divine protection. The commentaries make clear that this murmuring or mourning was different from mere complaint. It was a specific kind of disturbance, an existential sorrow over the suffering present in human experience, a suffering caused by a spiritual lack. Despite the care God was giving and the blessings heaped on the people, they remained unconnected to their souls.

This disconnection happens to everyone some of the time, and to some people most of the time. Rachel seems to have been a person with such an intense soul-hunger, yet so connected to the realities of earthly life, that she always felt the human world's lack of connection to something beyond the mundane. She could not be satisfied unless earth and heaven were truly connected. This soul-hunger is usually regarded negatively by society, and today Rachel might be treated as chronically depressed and given a prescription for Valium. But the Torah tells us that a monument was erected to her so that we all could remember her, and our prophet says that Rachel's prayers, her crying out in despair, will be answered.

Rachel knew the truth that in every moment of existence, even the happiest, there is suffering. She learned this early. Married at fifteen, as the midrash suggests, she had the most ideal husband anyone could imagine—the saintly Jacob, who combined the best traits of Abraham and Isaac and who loved her completely. One might think, from a modern perspective, that she was just one of those people who can't be satisfied with their lot in life. Wasn't it enough to have a devoted husband; she had to have children, too? (Imagine the pain of the husband at this situation. Would he not, like Elkanah in the *Haftara* for the first day of Rosh Hashana, cry out, "Am I not more to you than ten sons?") But for Rachel, the pain of childlessness was the manifestation in her own personal life of *on,* a broader existential pain only partially relieved when God gave her Joseph.

We see this more clearly when we recognize that she also felt deeply the pain of others. The midrash tells us that Rachel was aware of Leah's fear that she might be wed to Esau: a fear that made her eyes red from weeping. Rachel realized that, even when Leah learned she would be married to Jacob, it would humiliate her to be married in deep veils as a decoy, so Rachel had mercy on her and shared the secret signs she had arranged with Jacob. Rachel even felt such deep compassion for her father's spiritual state that she endangered herself by taking the *terafim* into her possession. Her sense of the sorrow and suffering of life was not selfish, but universal. Because Rachel's compassion overcame all feelings of personal hurt, disappointment, and revenge, she was the one who could evoke the mercy of God when she prayed for the redemption of her people.

Rachel is the embodiment, in Jewish tradition, of the weeping mother—not unlike the *mater dolorosa* embodied in Michelangelo's *Pietà*, or the compassionate Kuan-yin of East Asian tradition. No wonder Jews have flocked to her grave for more than three thousand years. Rachel represents the deep compassion that, as we say, "only a mother" can feel.

Even more important, the weeping mother enables us to transform our sorrow. In the midst of her deepest sorrow, the passage into death, Rachel named her child Benoni, "son of my sorrow." But as she died, Jacob looked on the child and saw something else: Benyamin, "son of the right hand," associated with the south and the summer sun. He seems to have recognized that Rachel's word *on* could mean "strength." Out of Rachel's sorrow came strength—the strength that would complete the twelve tribes.[11]

How is it that strength comes from sorrow? Although we have suffered collectively for centuries, our tradition does not advise us to focus on the sad elements of existence in order to be strong. We can and should feel sorrow deeply, in its own time, as the traditional mourner does when "sitting *shiva*" for seven days and observing restrictions on joy for a year, or when we collectively mourn the destruction of the Temple on Tisha b'Av. There is a "time to weep and a time to laugh" (Ecclesiastes 3:4). But sorrow should not become deeply embedded in our character. Even our reflective sorrow, in regret for our own sins and errors, should be limited in scope. Many of the Chasidic masters advised that we set aside a certain time each day to examine our lives and search out our sins, but during the rest of the day we should make every effort to be happy. Melancholy and depression, taught Rabbi Nachman of Bratslav, is a tool of the *yetzer hara,* the evil inclination. Strength comes from joy. "It is a great *mitzvah*," he said, "to be always happy," always *besimcha*. As King David sang, "You have turned my mourning into dancing" (Psalm 30).

If so, then why did Rachel name her second son for her sorrows—couldn't she just as easily have named him for her joy, her completion? After the midwife told her she had a son, fulfilling her matriarchal destiny, she might have named him "Shalom," symbolizing the completion of a passionate life.

Rachel knew, however, that no earthly experience could be truly complete. Only at the end of the journey of the whole people through all time could one hope for completion. Her own incomplete journey reminds us of this: as the commentary to the *Stone Chumash* observes almost in passing, Rachel was on her way to the home she had never seen, and would now never see.

Let us imagine the last period of her life. Since she was a child, betrothed to Jacob, she had been hearing about the Land of Israel, about his birthplace, the places holy to his father and grandfather. Finally they departed the land of Padan-Aram and started on the long journey home. Two long years followed, with the party facing Esau and suffering through the sad episode of Dina, then finally approaching the goal, as Rachel was daily heavier with child. In the last month the whole company purified themselves, discarded the relics of their past, worshiped at Beit-El, and prepared for the climax of the journey, their arrival in Hebron.

Then Rachel went into labor. She and Jacob must have recognized that it was no mere happenstance that labor began before they could reach home. They must have realized that it was her destiny to die on the road, before seeing the goal. God would let her bring forth her child, but she would become a poignant reminder that even when our individual destinies are complete, we are not fulfilled until we are all home.

Rachel becomes for us the mother of sorrows because she knew the passionate struggle for life, for completion—and the sense of loss or failure we feel when what we sought, what seemed just within our reach, is suddenly taken away. How apt that she should be the one whose prayers reach to heaven for our redemption! Her life tells us there is a taste of this lack in every moment, even the greatest moment, even when we achieve our personal goals. For our souls are not only ours. We have a deep connection with our whole people and the whole earth, and these must all reach fulfillment for us to feel complete. We remind ourselves of this less-than-whole existence when we break a glass at weddings or when we recite Psalm 137 before grace after meals on weekdays, saying: "If I forget you, O Jerusalem, let my *right hand* forget its skill!" Strength, the strength of the right hand, comes, like Benjamin, from sorrow, because this is part of living completely a full human life. We must be connected to our souls and to the souls of all others; then we are strong. But it also means we cannot regard our task as finished until all are redeemed.

Chasidic tradition tells of certain great *rebbes* who pledged that when they left this earth and went to the world beyond, they would refuse to enter Gan Eden (Paradise) until God agreed to redeem the world. They would stand outside the gate, praying for their people. Rachel is this kind of saintly figure, a woman whose heart is totally connected to her people. She prays for return, return from exile and redemption, because she knows how hard we struggle for completion, how much we want to do *tikkun olam* (repair of the world), how deeply we yearn to make the earth a better place, how much we want to do God's will, how much we love his creation, how much we truly love one another. Rachel's passion is for this earth, for human beings, and for their ultimate redemption. If we detach ourselves from that passionate desire, we lose a part of ourselves, we lose our right hand, our strength. Rachel teaches us to live with sorrow, not with detachment but with passion and prayer, never giving up the ultimate hope. "There is hope for you—words of the Lord—and your children shall return to their border" (Jeremiah 31:16).

On Rosh Hashana let us be single-minded, like Rachel, begging and pleading with God that we be allowed to see our dreams and the beautiful dreams and visions of all the prophets fulfilled. May we all return and be returned, may our mourning be turned into joy, and godliness be fully revealed in the world, soon and in our days.

Firstborn to You: Remembering the God of Mercy

NESSA RAPOPORT

As God is gracious, so be you also gracious;
As God is merciful, so be you also merciful.

Sifre, Deuteronomy 10:12

The yearning of the firstborn to be the chosen one, to continue to dwell in the light of the parents' love after the others come: this is known to any child who was first to enter the world.

On the birth day of the world, we who came first contemplate the sacred readings of Rosh Hashana with longing hearts. On the first day, we read the Torah narrative of the birth of Isaac, Sarah's firstborn son, whom Abraham is soon willing to sacrifice; and of Abraham's firstborn son, Ishmael, whom Sarah is willing to expel.

That story is followed, in the *Haftara,* by the tale of Hannah's first-born son, Samuel; as soon as he is weaned, Hannah offers him to God.

The second day's Torah reading describes the near sacrifice of Isaac. Augmenting the poignancy for readers who are firstborn children, Isaac is called here Abraham's only, beloved son, although we have read a mere day ago of Ishmael's near death.

We then read, in the *Haftara,* Jeremiah's lyrical invocation of God's love for the nation of Israel: "For to Israel I am a father, and Ephraim is my firstborn." But later in the reading, we hear Rachel weeping for her exiled children, "refusing to be comforted." And Ephraim is heard, chastised, punished, pleading to return to the God who calls him "my favorite son, my beloved child."

It appears that firstborn sons are singled out for both love and sacrifice, given by God only to be given back. Yet these stories resist the predictable privilege of the firstborn son's anointment for inheritance and blessing. Ephraim, most beloved and named God's firstborn, is not his father Joseph's firstborn. And Joseph, most beloved of sons and firstborn to his mother, Rachel, is not his father Jacob's firstborn.

Rather, in these stories of our beginnings, God chooses the children most beloved of mothers, often children firstborn of their mothers rather than their fathers. In these tales of birthright and blessing, God sides with the mothers, the bearers of children, aligning the choice of the sons who will father a nation with those who give birth, with the mothers and their *rechamim,* wombs.

In fact, *rachamim,* mercy, comprising the same letters as the word for womb (*rechem*), is the first attribute of God we invoke throughout the liturgy of these Holy Day: *Adonai, Adonai, El rachum*—Lord, Lord, Merciful God. In the Rosh Hashana readings, merciful love is the arc between human and divine.

Thus the final words of Jeremiah, in the second day's *Haftara,* are in God's voice and spoken of Ephraim, divinely cherished child who stands in for the people Israel: *"Racheim arachamenu,"* God says of Ephraim. "I will have mercy upon him."

Sovereignty

In my status as the firstborn of four daughters, I read these stories of firstborn sons with a frisson of danger averted and the solitude of invisibility.

To be favored as eldest is an equivocal blessing. It represents the honor of being sacrificed or offered to God: first fruits of the vine, first yield of the crops, firstborn of the animals belong to God and are therefore returned to God. And firstborn sons are dedicated to God, too; they would be consecrated to serve in the Temple were it not for the *kohanim,* priests, taking their place.

To this day, the *pidyon haben* ceremony redeems month-old sons who are firstborn of their mothers from the obligation of holy service. (Only sons born of a Kohen or Levite father or of a mother who is the daughter of a Kohen or Levite need not be "bought back" from the priesthood.) Firstborn sons, animals, and crops belong to God in a more proprietary way than those who follow them.

Singled out for destruction in the Tenth Plague, the firstborn sons of Egypt evoke a shiver of recognition, too. Indeed, on the day before Passover, firstborn adult Jewish men are meant to fast, to remember their having been "passed over," spared the death that befell their Egyptian counterparts.

This firstborn daughter notes the uneasiness of such a day. Why are the firstborn sons, albeit of another people, singled out for death? What is the connection between death and chosenness, between sacrifice and choice fruit? And how do we, firstborn daughters of this tradition, join "the kingdom of priests and holy nation" (Exodus 19:6) into which we were born? How can we be consecrated to God?

The word *bekhor,* for firstborn son, is not simply a description, but a status; a firstborn daughter, called *bekhira,* eldest, is recognized merely by the order of her birth. No status attaches to daughters born first in any Biblical narrative.

On the contrary, in most of our sacred stories, daughters are silent, unnamed. Firstborn or last, we usually have no voice. And so it is striking to hear the talk of women in three of the four Rosh Hashana readings. We hear Sarah, as well as Hagar, on the first day. We hear Hannah uttering her vow to God, speaking to the priest, Eli, and concluding with a long, poetic prayer of exultation. Significantly, only in the story of Isaac's near sacrifice do we hear no woman's voice. And in the second *Haftara,* "a voice is heard in Ramah—lamentation, bitter weeping; it is Rachel weeping for her children; she refuses to be comforted, for they are gone." Perhaps she is also weeping for Sarah, whose child disappeared early one morning, who disappears herself, mute forever in the narrative that will next record her death.

Memory

The first words of the first day's reading are: "The Lord remembered Sarah as promised." And in the *Haftara* of that day we read: "Elkanah was attached to Hannah, his wife, and the Lord remembered her."

What is God remembering in transforming the weeping of barren women into fertility? Perhaps in the infinite Present in which God dwells, there is still the memory of solitude—not the solitude of God's glorious splendor, which cannot be replicated, but of the world that was without life, the *tohu vavohu* of barrenness before creation, before humankind was made in God's image, male and female at once, keeping God company in the first creation story and both named "very good"; before the second story of creation and the birth of the woman who is needed as companion, without whom Adam is not complete, the one to whom man must cleave to know and be known in the act that creates new life.

The wordless solitude of *tohu vavohu*, darkening chaos, an undifferentiated world: this is a solitude that longs for "the spirit hovering over the water" to turn the darkness of the fostering womb into a living child. This is a solitude that longs to be named, that longs for the recognition between the Creator and the created that culminates in "male and female created God them"—parity, presence, an end to loneliness.

Perhaps God can be merciful to us by remembering that loneliness and knowing its opposite—the love of the Creator for us, and ours for the One who gave us life, the immortality of that life flung forward, generating a future known to God, unknown to us, a future to which, despite God's omnipotence, we in our humanity are absolutely necessary.

Summoning

If status is not necessarily assessed by rank of birth, to what status might we be summoned? On this day of our hearing the horn's call, how might we be heard and measured?

One response to readings about favorite children is to banish privileges granted by birth order so that everyone enters the world equally. Indeed, many Jews have abolished the laws of the *kehuna* (priesthood), the language of "chosen people," or even the bequeathing of Jewish status by matrilineal descent because of the arbitrary nature of such birth- and blood-conferred honors.

Yet anyone born into a family or forging one knows that the dream of a child is not to be treated as the precise equal of his or her sibling, but to be unique, incomparable, in the parents' eyes. Love does not reach its apotheosis in an even-handed neutrality. Rather than deny the random privileges of firstborn or favorite sons because they seem to come at the expense of others, we might imagine a world in which each of us can be the beloved, chosen, favorite child, consecrated to a God with an infinite capacity to love not one of us over another, but each of us as first. We can imagine taking shelter under the wings of such a God or re-creating our world in the image of that particular love.

If we are re-creating the world, we might think about the way God designated us as the chosen, beloved people and imagine a world where every created being belongs to "a kingdom of priests and a holy nation," a world in which no one need be redeemed from priesthood because each of us can be anointed as sovereign, remembered uniquely by our Creator, eternally summoned by name.

And when we are summoned, shall we flee, like Jonah? Or shall we laugh, like Sarah, half-skeptical, half-longing to dwell in the living voice, speaking directly to us, to whom we can speak in return, without intermediaries, without angels, priests, prophets, or kings, because we remember not only our exile and redemption, but the days of our youth in relation to God; we remember our creation, before one human being was chosen over another to receive favor.

What does God tell us in Jeremiah on the second day of this New Year? "With everlasting love I love you," gathering every one—blind, lame, and laboring—until we are like a garden sated with water, until God has satisfied us, "the priests," with abundance, sustaining us with bounty.

What is the note of sorrow, of suffering, alongside this vision of the end of days? It is a woman's voice, Rachel's lamenting, refusing comfort in the absence of her children. There is hope for your future, says God in response. "The children will return to their own land."

To which land need Jewish women return? What is our inheritance, our rightful portion?

When the daughters of Tzelofchad appeared before Moses (Numbers 27:1) to demand their portion of land as their father's inheritors, Moses brought their case before God, who responded: "The plea of Tzelofchad's daughters is just."

The midrash in *Sifre Bemidbar* adds: "When the daughters of Tzelofchad heard that the land was being divided according to tribes, but not according to women, they took counsel with one another. And they said: The mercy of God is unlike the mercy of flesh and blood. For flesh and blood are more merciful to men, while God—who spoke, and the world came into being—is different, compassionate to men and women, to all humans, as it is written: 'God is good to all and merciful to all God's creation.'"

God's mercy for us is bound up in our inheritance. The spiritual mantle we grant ourselves in the absence of status and favor is not sufficient. All of us want the double portion Hannah received from her husband out of love, the largest portion of the firstborn. We are greedy for love, greedy to bequeath it to those who follow us because we flourished within the love of those who came before us, leading us back to the garden and to the One who longed life into being and gave it to us as a gift. We learn mercy from those who are merciful to us, wrought in the image of the Source of all mercy.

Now the daughters want their rightful portion. We seek it in our holy words so that we can live the holy lives asked of us. As male Israelites, so all Jews. And, messianically, as all Jews, so all peoples of the world.

We taste that expansive possibility in the final reading on Rosh Hashana morning, when God names an entire people "my *bekhor*," favored, beloved, firstborn to You.

As for our invisibility, it, too, bears fruit. For God, it emerges, does not want the blood of daughters, not for circumcision and not for sacrifice. And out of our invisibility, out of the place without words for our status, without language for what we are or could become, we can take our place as life bearers and creators, bearing in our blood the nourishment of life—and not death.

Instead of seeing our foremothers as reduced to their biological utility, let us read their stories as expressions of their affiliation with the God who can make life, choose life, choose a people, and ally God's self with the mothers who choose their destiny, who subvert the hierarchies of the world into which their children are born.

When we read these stories on the birth day of the world, we can say: Take me back to the beginning, to the time when God created humankind and named male and female very good. Take me back to the narratives when women could hear God speak and could address God directly, have their wishes granted and the blessing bestowed upon their chosen ones. Take me back to Eve and Sarah, to Hannah and to Rachel, efficacious in their spheres of fertility and nationhood, in active engagement with their Creator—and unheard in the narrative of near sacrifice, when life was almost taken in the name of the One who bestows life. Transform Abraham's willingness to sacrifice his son, Sarah's firstborn, into Hannah's offering of her child to serve God while alive, because a life devoted to serving God is a greater tribute than the most dramatic death in God's name.

We who were children, who have children, who long for children, who offer our gifts to redeem the world for coming children and for the unblemished child within us know that the women's bleeding that separates us as ritually impure in these ancient texts is the same blood from which children grow and are nourished in wombs of mercy. These ancient texts understand that the firstborn child of the father and the consecrated *peter rechem,* firstborn of the womb of the mother, are not the same. The *peter rechem,* first fruit of the mother, is allied with priesthood, with those chosen to serve.

On the day of our redemption, earthly society will recognize the power of our being made in God's image. On that day, all will see in mothers, sisters, aunts, wives, and daughters the capacity for immortality, the "watered garden," the "never-failing spring" of the Yom Kippur prophetic reading (Isaiah 58:11) that follows the readings of Rosh Hashana set in this world.

And so God may say: "As the world was barren, I was barren. As I created each of you, beloved, chosen, firstborn, so you may create and be re-created on this birth day of our world, the one we inhabit together, transcendent and transient, immanent and imminently to be redeemed. As I am holy, so shall you be holy. As I am sovereign, so shall you be sovereign. As I remember Ephraim eternally, so shall you remember the infinite within you. And as I call you, so shall you, like your foremothers, hear my voice and summon me into your lives."

Yom Kippur

The Day of Atonement

Yom Kippur Morning
Introduction

The readings chosen by the Rabbis of the Talmud for Yom Kippur offer us, in layers, our people's history of observance of this holiday. The traditional morning Torah reading (Leviticus 16) draws us back to the most ancient ritual in which the first *kohen gadol* (high priest), Aaron, acts alone in the mysterious, awe-filled inner space of the *mishkan* (tabernacle) to effect atonement for the entire people's sins and impurities. This ceremony, which we take to represent the Yom Kippur observance during the time of the First Temple as well, involves animal sacrifice, acts of purification using water and incense, symbolic "laying of hands" on a scapegoat that then "carries" the people's sins off to the wilderness—all ritual acts that have become completely foreign to us. As Naama Kelman suggests, this text describes (and prescribes) a mode of atonement that other ancient peoples could more easily identify with than we can, even though we are the descendants of its practitioners. It is not only the foreignness of this ritual mode that distances us. This oldest form of Yom Kippur observance itself kept everyone but the male priestly elite outside the sanctuary as passive spectators to a stark, silent ritual done on their behalf.

Nevertheless, the Rabbis' decision to start the Yom Kippur readings with this text offers us, from their point of view, a way to participate. They are asking us to take with utmost seriousness the Torah's prescriptions for sacrificial worship as a "service" (*Avoda*) pleasing to God. They call us to experience our inability to worship in that way as a profound loss. But rabbinic texts also tell us that the words we speak by reciting (and studying) the Torah's prescriptions of sacrifice will be received by God as though we had performed them. We can still offer what the prophet Hosea calls the "bull [offerings] of our lips" (14:3). They become an essential part of the "service of the heart" (Ta'anit 2a) we now offer instead of sacrifices. Although many modern Jews, including some of the contributors to *Beginning Anew*, are no longer moved by this rabbinic perspective and look for other ways into the reading from Leviticus, the Rabbis' rationale for choosing this text can begin to draw us toward it.

In the Biblical text, the only observances that involve the entire people are "afflicting" ourselves and ceasing from work. Precisely those rituals preoccupy the prophetic voice in the *Haftara* chosen to accompany the reading from Leviticus (Isaiah 57–58), in which Isaiah powerfully denounces ritual practices divorced from ethical striving. Its impassioned poetry speaks to the whole people, who confine themselves to their long-established observances, fasting and bodily affliction, expecting to achieve atonement, reconciliation with God, through physical performance alone. Isaiah calls for an inner transformation that, for him, must be manifested in just action and deeds of lovingkindness as much as in ritual observance. Through the juxtaposition of this prophetic text with the Torah reading, we deepen our sense of the meanings Yom Kippur has held historically. It seems clear that the Rabbis who made this choice saw the need to reflect on the complex relationship between ritual and ethical action, between external performance and inner experience, as an essential dimension of this day.

Within the Reform movement the sense of distance from the sacrificial ritual described in Leviticus 16 and the absence of explicitly moral or inward-looking dimensions to the prescribed observances led to the choice of an alternative Torah reading. Reform congregations read Deuteronomy 29 and 30 on the morning of Yom Kippur. Even though this text is not specifically set on Yom Kippur, its explicit insistence that the entire people "stand before" God who constantly offers us all a choice—life and goodness or death and evil—and its exhortation to choose life led to the decision to read it on the day on which we try to make ourselves worthy of continued life.

Contributors to *Beginning Anew* expand and reinterpret our understanding of the spiritual and existential issues raised by these texts through feminist analysis and their own experiences as women. Naama Kelman, a rabbi in Jerusalem, brings her immersion in the land itself, its historical and personal associations, to address the problem of "drawing near" to Leviticus 16. Because the Biblical passage "keeps us at a distance," she asks how we can read it and "feel God's closeness." Kelman chooses to "read it with all the bleakness and promise of the wilderness." The wilderness, both as recurring motif in the historical experience of the Jewish people and as present reality for a Jewish woman living in Israel today, becomes the prism through which she invests the mystery of the high priest and the scapegoat with personal and contemporary meanings.

Bonna Haberman, in the next essay in *Beginning Anew*, sees the Torah reading through the lens of the much more elaborate and dramatic account of the ritual recited during the *Musaf* (additional) service. Haberman offers us the "challenge to experience the service of the high priest (the *Avoda* service) on Yom Kippur as a reenactment rather than a mere recitation—"inspiring and evocative like other Jewish festival reenactments that invite us to celebrate and transcend our finite lives." In order to achieve this goal, we must move beyond the Biblical text into the description of the Yom Kippur rituals performed in the Second Temple to be found in the liturgy of the Yom Kippur *Musaf* (additional) service. Although the Torah reading from Leviticus prepares us, Haberman explains, the actual reenactment occurs in the *Musaf Avoda*, a more elaborate text based on descriptions found in the Talmud. She therefore analyzes the Biblical text as a first step and then leads us into the reenactment itself. She seeks to "make the text relevant to our own experience," despite its remoteness from "contemporary notions of holiness." In a bold and provocative interpretation of the meaning of Jewish sacred spaces, Haberman associates "holy enclosures"—tabernacle, temple, and, by derivation, the synagogue sanctuary—with the body of a woman. This radical interpretive move opens to her the possibility of understanding the *Avoda* service, in which the high priest enters the innermost holy space, through the erotic metaphor of "a climax of intimacy between the Jewish people and God." Even more radically, she uncovers metaphors of the cycles and processes of female sexuality within the enacted rituals. For her, both male and female sexuality are sanctified and given meaning through the metaphors and symbols embedded in the *Avoda* text, while the ritual itself takes on vital connection to the deepest dimensions of our existence. She reclaims what appears to be the most exclusively male dimension of Yom Kippur, by showing that "the

Avoda offers all women a unique expression and affirmation of our embodiment and of our identities as women members of the prayerful community."

Laura Geller creates a Yom Kippur sermon by interweaving the reading from Deuteronomy chosen for Yom Kippur morning by the Reform movement with her experience as rabbi, mother, wife, and daughter. When the text "tells its story" of a whole people standing before God, from "the heads of your tribe" to "the one who chops your wood . . . and draws your water," she hears "a story about me . . . as I do the twentieth-century equivalents of chopping wood and drawing water." But she also hears "all of us in the story . . . standing before God . . . as Jews with our own stories." She calls on us to find the connections between the "Torah of our lives" and the "Torah of tradition." Claiming that "all theology is autobiography," she shows us how we can tell our own stories so as to "discover the divinity that is present in our lives" and how to "hear our stories as part of the cosmic Jewish stories."

Alice Shalvi hears the prophetic voice of Isaiah in the *Haftara* with an understanding permeated by her many years of activism as a Jewish educator and feminist leader in Israel, as well as by her personal observance. She directs our attention to the prophet's powerful critique of mere outward observance, an indictment that leads to a call for "action designed to relieve the suffering of others." In her analysis of what constitutes "true contrition" in this text, she emphasizes the connections between fulfilling our obligations to "our fellow beings" and "personal and national redemption." But she draws us just as strongly toward her own appreciation of Isaiah's holistic vision of transformation, in which both impassioned activism for social justice and the ritual of Sabbath observance are essential components of a transfigured life. Shalvi moves from reflection on the text of Isaiah to creation of her own religious language, drawing on the model of *techines,* prayers written as personal supplications specifically for women in central and Eastern Europe. Her *techine,* like the traditional women's prayers, speaks to personal concerns and needs but equally resonates with the broad scope of her concerns as a modern woman.

We can think of Isaiah's words as a powerful sermon, stirring up a congregation on Yom Kippur. Rachel Cowan preaches a sermon based on Isaiah, addressing a contemporary congregation in a language that both echoes and interprets the prophet's language and ideas. Her interaction with Isaiah and with a text written by Rabbi Abraham Isaac Kook, the first Ashkenazic Chief Rabbi of Eretz Israel, is the springboard for her articulation of the two dimensions of Isaiah's sermon—the critique and the vision. The very modern voice of a woman and a rabbi speaks with depth and powerful resonance because of its immersion in and independent response to these traditional texts.

"To Seek . . . Atonement"
(Leviticus 16)

Torah Reading—Morning Service

16 And the LORD spoke unto Moses, after the death of the two sons of Aaron, when they drew near before the LORD, and died; ²and the LORD said unto Moses: 'Speak unto Aaron thy brother, that he come not at all times into the holy place within the veil, before the ark-cover which is upon the ark; that he die not; for I appear in the cloud upon the ark-cover. ³Herewith shall Aaron come into the holy place: with a young bullock for a sin-offering, and a ram for a burnt-offering. ⁴He shall put on the holy linen tunic, and he shall have the linen breeches upon his flesh, and shall be girded with the linen girdle, and with the linen mitre shall he be attired; they are the holy garments; and he shall bathe his flesh in water, and put them on. ⁵And he shall take of the congregation of the children of Israel two he-goats for a sin-offering, and one ram for a burnt-offering. ⁶And Aaron shall present the bullock of the sin-offering, which is for himself, and make atonement for himself, and for his house. ⁷And he shall take the two goats, and set them before the LORD at the door of the tent of meeting. ⁸And Aaron shall cast lots upon the two goats: one lot for the LORD, and the other lot for Azazel. ⁹And Aaron shall present the goat upon which the lot fell for the LORD, and offer him for a sin-offering. ¹⁰But the goat, on which the lot fell for Azazel, shall be set alive before the LORD, to make atonement over him, to send him away for Azazel

א וַיְדַבֵּר יְהֹוָה אֶל־מֹשֶׁה אַחֲרֵי מוֹת שְׁנֵי
בְּנֵי אַהֲרֹן בְּקָרְבָתָם לִפְנֵי־יְהֹוָה וַיָּמֻתוּ:
ב וַיֹּאמֶר יְהֹוָה אֶל־מֹשֶׁה דַּבֵּר אֶל־אַהֲרֹן
אָחִיךָ וְאַל־יָבֹא בְכָל־עֵת אֶל־הַקֹּדֶשׁ
מִבֵּית לַפָּרֹכֶת אֶל־פְּנֵי הַכַּפֹּרֶת אֲשֶׁר
עַל־הָאָרֹן וְלֹא יָמוּת כִּי בֶּעָנָן אֵרָאֶה
ג עַל־הַכַּפֹּרֶת: בְּזֹאת יָבֹא אַהֲרֹן אֶל־
הַקֹּדֶשׁ בְּפַר בֶּן־בָּקָר לְחַטָּאת וְאַיִל
ד לְעֹלָה: כְּתֹנֶת־בַּד קֹדֶשׁ יִלְבָּשׁ
וּמִכְנְסֵי־בַד יִהְיוּ עַל־בְּשָׂרוֹ וּבְאַבְנֵט
בַּד יַחְגֹּר וּבְמִצְנֶפֶת בַּד יִצְנֹף בִּגְדֵי־
קֹדֶשׁ הֵם וְרָחַץ בַּמַּיִם אֶת־בְּשָׂרוֹ
ה וּלְבֵשָׁם: וּמֵאֵת עֲדַת בְּנֵי יִשְׂרָאֵל יִקַּח
שְׁנֵי־שְׂעִירֵי עִזִּים לְחַטָּאת וְאַיִל אֶחָד
לְעֹלָה:
ו וְהִקְרִיב אַהֲרֹן אֶת־פַּר
הַחַטָּאת אֲשֶׁר־לוֹ וְכִפֶּר בַּעֲדוֹ וּבְעַד
ז בֵּיתוֹ: וְלָקַח אֶת־שְׁנֵי הַשְּׂעִירִם
וְהֶעֱמִיד אֹתָם לִפְנֵי יְהֹוָה פֶּתַח אֹהֶל
ח מוֹעֵד: וְנָתַן אַהֲרֹן עַל־שְׁנֵי הַשְּׂעִירִם
גֹּרָלוֹת גּוֹרָל אֶחָד לַיהֹוָה וְגוֹרָל אֶחָד
ט לַעֲזָאזֵל: וְהִקְרִיב אַהֲרֹן אֶת־הַשָּׂעִיר
אֲשֶׁר עָלָה עָלָיו הַגּוֹרָל לַיהֹוָה וְעָשָׂהוּ
י חַטָּאת: וְהַשָּׂעִיר אֲשֶׁר עָלָה עָלָיו
הַגּוֹרָל לַעֲזָאזֵל יָעֳמַד־חַי לִפְנֵי יְהֹוָה
לְכַפֵּר עָלָיו לְשַׁלַּח אֹתוֹ לַעֲזָאזֵל

into the wilderness. [11]And Aaron shall present the bullock of the sin-offering, which is for himself, and shall make atonement for himself, and for his house, and shall kill the bullock of the sin-offering which is for himself. [12]And he shall take a censer full of coals of fire from off the altar before the LORD, and his hands full of sweet incense beaten small, and bring it within the veil. [13]And he shall put the incense upon the fire before the LORD, that the cloud of the incense may cover the ark-cover that is upon the testimony, that he die not. [14]And he shall take of the blood of the bullock, and sprinkle it with his finger upon the ark-cover on the east; and before the ark-cover shall he sprinkle of the blood with his finger seven times. [15]Then shall he kill the goat of the sin-offering, that is for the people, and bring his blood within the veil, and do with his blood as he did with the blood of the bullock, and sprinkle it upon the ark-cover, and before the ark-cover. [16]And he shall make atonement for the holy place, because of the uncleannesses of the children of Israel, and because of their transgressions, even all their sins; and so shall he do for the tent of meeting, that dwelleth with them in the midst of their uncleannesses. [17]And there shall be no man in the tent of meeting when he goeth in to make atonement in the holy place, until he come out, and have made atonement for himself, and for his household, and for all the assembly of Israel. [18]And he shall go out unto the altar that is before the LORD, and make atonement for it; and shall take of the blood of the bullock, and of the blood of the goat, and put it upon the horns of the altar round about. [19]And he shall sprinkle of the blood upon it with his finger seven times, and cleanse it, and hallow it from the uncleannesses of the children of Israel. [20]And when he hath made an end of atoning for the holy place, and the tent of meeting, and the altar, he

11 הַמִּדְבָּרָה: וְהִקְרִיב אַהֲרֹן אֶת־פַּר הַחַטָּאת אֲשֶׁר־לוֹ וְכִפֶּר בַּעֲדוֹ וּבְעַד בֵּיתוֹ וְשָׁחַט אֶת־פַּר הַחַטָּאת אֲשֶׁר־לוֹ:

12 וְלָקַח מְלֹא־הַמַּחְתָּה גַּחֲלֵי־אֵשׁ מֵעַל הַמִּזְבֵּחַ מִלִּפְנֵי יְהֹוָה וּמְלֹא חָפְנָיו קְטֹרֶת סַמִּים דַּקָּה וְהֵבִיא מִבֵּית לַפָּרֹכֶת:

13 וְנָתַן אֶת־הַקְּטֹרֶת עַל־הָאֵשׁ לִפְנֵי יְהֹוָה וְכִסָּה | עֲנַן הַקְּטֹרֶת אֶת־הַכַּפֹּרֶת אֲשֶׁר 14 עַל־הָעֵדוּת וְלֹא יָמוּת: וְלָקַח מִדַּם הַפָּר וְהִזָּה בְאֶצְבָּעוֹ עַל־פְּנֵי הַכַּפֹּרֶת קֵדְמָה וְלִפְנֵי הַכַּפֹּרֶת יַזֶּה שֶׁבַע־ 15 פְּעָמִים מִן־הַדָּם בְּאֶצְבָּעוֹ: וְשָׁחַט אֶת־שְׂעִיר הַחַטָּאת אֲשֶׁר לָעָם וְהֵבִיא אֶת־דָּמוֹ אֶל־מִבֵּית לַפָּרֹכֶת וְעָשָׂה אֶת־דָּמוֹ כַּאֲשֶׁר עָשָׂה לְדַם הַפָּר וְהִזָּה אֹתוֹ עַל־הַכַּפֹּרֶת וְלִפְנֵי הַכַּפֹּרֶת: 16 וְכִפֶּר עַל־הַקֹּדֶשׁ מִטֻּמְאֹת בְּנֵי יִשְׂרָאֵל וּמִפִּשְׁעֵיהֶם לְכָל־חַטֹּאתָם וְכֵן יַעֲשֶׂה לְאֹהֶל מוֹעֵד הַשֹּׁכֵן אִתָּם בְּתוֹךְ טֻמְאֹתָם: 17 וְכָל־אָדָם לֹא־יִהְיֶה | בְּאֹהֶל מוֹעֵד בְּבֹאוֹ לְכַפֵּר בַּקֹּדֶשׁ עַד־ צֵאתוֹ וְכִפֶּר בַּעֲדוֹ וּבְעַד בֵּיתוֹ וּבְעַד כָּל־קְהַל יִשְׂרָאֵל:

18 וְיָצָא אֶל־ הַמִּזְבֵּחַ אֲשֶׁר לִפְנֵי־יְהֹוָה וְכִפֶּר עָלָיו וְלָקַח מִדַּם הַפָּר וּמִדַּם הַשָּׂעִיר וְנָתַן 19 עַל־קַרְנוֹת הַמִּזְבֵּחַ סָבִיב: וְהִזָּה עָלָיו מִן־הַדָּם בְּאֶצְבָּעוֹ שֶׁבַע פְּעָמִים וְטִהֲרוֹ 20 וְקִדְּשׁוֹ מִטֻּמְאֹת בְּנֵי יִשְׂרָאֵל: וְכִלָּה מִכַּפֵּר אֶת־הַקֹּדֶשׁ וְאֶת־אֹהֶל מוֹעֵד

shall present the live goat. [21]And
Aaron shall lay both his hands upon
the head of the live goat, and confess
over him all the iniquities of the children of Israel, and all their transgressions, even all their sins; and he shall
put them upon the head of the goat,
and shall send him away by the hand
of an appointed man into the wilderness. [22]And the goat shall bear upon
him all their iniquities unto a land
which is cut off; and he shall let go the
goat in the wilderness. [23]And Aaron
shall come into the tent of meeting,
and shall put off the linen garments,
which he put on when he went into
the holy place, and shall leave
them there. [24]And he shall bathe
his flesh in water in a holy place
and put on his other vestments,
and come forth, and offer his burnt-
offering and the burnt-offering of the
people, and make atonement for himself and for the people. [25]And the fat
of the sin-offering shall he make
smoke upon the altar. [26]And he that
letteth go the goat for Azazel shall
wash his clothes, and bathe his flesh
in water, and afterward he may come
into the camp. [27]And the bullock of
the sin-offering, and the goat of the
sin-offering, whose blood was brought
in to make atonement in the holy
place, shall be carried forth without
the camp; and they shall burn in the
fire their skins, and their flesh, and
their dung. [28]And he that burneth
them shall wash his clothes, and
bathe his flesh in water, and afterward he may come into the camp.
[29]And it shall be a statute for ever
unto you: in the seventh month, on
the tenth day of the month, ye shall
afflict your souls, and shall do no
manner of work, the home-born, or
the stranger that sojourneth among
you. [30]For on this day shall atonement be made for you, to cleanse you;
from all your sins shall ye be clean
before the LORD. [31]It is a sabbath of
solemn rest unto you, and ye shall
afflict your souls; it is a statute for

וְאֶת־הַמִּזְבֵּחַ וְהִקְרִיב אֶת־הַשָּׂעִיר

2 הֶחָי: וְסָמַךְ אַהֲרֹן אֶת־שְׁתֵּי יָדָו עַל־
רֹאשׁ הַשָּׂעִיר הַחַי וְהִתְוַדָּה עָלָיו אֶת־
כָּל־עֲוֺנֹת בְּנֵי יִשְׂרָאֵל וְאֶת־כָּל־
פִּשְׁעֵיהֶם לְכָל־חַטֹּאתָם וְנָתַן אֹתָם
עַל־רֹאשׁ הַשָּׂעִיר וְשִׁלַּח בְּיַד־אִישׁ

22 עִתִּי הַמִּדְבָּרָה: וְנָשָׂא הַשָּׂעִיר עָלָיו
אֶת־כָּל־עֲוֺנֹתָם אֶל־אֶרֶץ גְּזֵרָה וְשִׁלַּח

23 אֶת־הַשָּׂעִיר בַּמִּדְבָּר: וּבָא אַהֲרֹן אֶל־
אֹהֶל מוֹעֵד וּפָשַׁט אֶת־בִּגְדֵי הַבָּד אֲשֶׁר
לָבַשׁ בְּבֹאוֹ אֶל־הַקֹּדֶשׁ וְהִנִּיחָם שָׁם:

24 וְרָחַץ אֶת־בְּשָׂרוֹ בַמַּיִם בְּמָקוֹם קָדוֹשׁ
וְלָבַשׁ אֶת־בְּגָדָיו וְיָצָא וְעָשָׂה אֶת־
עֹלָתוֹ וְאֶת־עֹלַת הָעָם וְכִפֶּר בַּעֲדוֹ
וּבְעַד הָעָם:

25 וְאֶת־חֵלֶב

26 הַחַטָּאת יַקְטִיר הַמִּזְבֵּחָה: וְהַמְשַׁלֵּחַ
אֶת־הַשָּׂעִיר לַעֲזָאזֵל יְכַבֵּס בְּגָדָיו
וְרָחַץ אֶת־בְּשָׂרוֹ בַּמָּיִם וְאַחֲרֵי־כֵן

27 יָבוֹא אֶל־הַמַּחֲנֶה: וְאֵת פַּר הַחַטָּאת
וְאֵת ׀ שְׂעִיר הַחַטָּאת אֲשֶׁר הוּבָא אֶת־
דָּמָם לְכַפֵּר בַּקֹּדֶשׁ יוֹצִיא אֶל־מִחוּץ
לַמַּחֲנֶה וְשָׂרְפוּ בָאֵשׁ אֶת־עֹרֹתָם וְאֶת־

28 בְּשָׂרָם וְאֶת־פִּרְשָׁם: וְהַשֹּׂרֵף אֹתָם
יְכַבֵּס בְּגָדָיו וְרָחַץ אֶת־בְּשָׂרוֹ בַּמָּיִם

29 וְאַחֲרֵי־כֵן יָבוֹא אֶל־הַמַּחֲנֶה: וְהָיְתָה
לָכֶם לְחֻקַּת עוֹלָם בַּחֹדֶשׁ הַשְּׁבִיעִי
בֶּעָשׂוֹר לַחֹדֶשׁ תְּעַנּוּ אֶת־נַפְשֹׁתֵיכֶם
וְכָל־מְלָאכָה לֹא תַעֲשׂוּ הָאֶזְרָח וְהַגֵּר

30 הַגָּר בְּתוֹכְכֶם: כִּי־בַיּוֹם הַזֶּה יְכַפֵּר
עֲלֵיכֶם לְטַהֵר אֶתְכֶם מִכֹּל חַטֹּאתֵיכֶם

31 לִפְנֵי יְהוָה תִּטְהָרוּ: שַׁבַּת שַׁבָּתוֹן הִיא

ever. ³²And the priest, who shall be anointed and who shall bé consecrated to be priest in his father's stead, shall make the atonement, and shall put on the linen garments, even the holy garments. ³³And he shall make atonement for the most holy place, and he shall make atonement for the tent of meeting and for the altar; and he shall make atonement for the priests and for all the people of the assembly. ³⁴And this shall be an everlasting statute unto you, to make atonement for the children of Israel because of all their sins once in the year.' And he did as the LORD commanded Moses.

לָכֶם וְעִנִּיתֶם אֶת־נַפְשֹׁתֵיכֶם חֻקַּת
32 עוֹלָם: וְכִפֶּר הַכֹּהֵן אֲשֶׁר־יִמְשַׁח אֹתוֹ
וַאֲשֶׁר יְמַלֵּא אֶת־יָדוֹ לְכַהֵן תַּחַת אָבִיו
וְלָבַשׁ אֶת־בִּגְדֵי הַבָּד בִּגְדֵי הַקֹּדֶשׁ:
33 וְכִפֶּר אֶת־מִקְדַּשׁ הַקֹּדֶשׁ וְאֶת־אֹהֶל
מוֹעֵד וְאֶת־הַמִּזְבֵּחַ יְכַפֵּר וְעַל הַכֹּהֲנִים
34 וְעַל־כָּל־עַם הַקָּהָל יְכַפֵּר: וְהָיְתָה־
זֹּאת לָכֶם לְחֻקַּת עוֹלָם לְכַפֵּר עַל־בְּנֵי
יִשְׂרָאֵל מִכָּל־חַטֹּאתָם אַחַת בַּשָּׁנָה
וַיַּעַשׂ כַּאֲשֶׁר צִוָּה יְהוָה אֶת־
מֹשֶׁה:

"To Seek . . . Life"
(Deuteronomy 29:9—14, 30:11—20)

TORAH READING—MORNING SERVICE
(REFORM CONGREGATIONS)

⁹Ye are standing this day all of you before the LORD your God: your heads, your tribes, your elders, and your officers, even all the men of Israel, ¹⁰your little ones, your wives, and thy stranger that is in the midst of thy camp, from the hewer of thy wood unto the drawer of thy water; ¹¹that thou shouldest enter into the covenant of the LORD thy God—and into His oath—which the LORD thy God maketh with thee this day; ¹²that He may establish thee this day unto Himself for a people, and that He may be unto thee a God, as He spoke unto thee, and as He swore unto thy fathers, to Abraham, to Isaac, and to Jacob. ¹³Neither with you only do I make this covenant and this oath; ¹⁴but with him that standeth here with us this day before the LORD our God, and also with him that is not here with us this day—

¹¹For this commandment which I command thee this day, it is not too hard for thee, neither is it far off. ¹²It is not in heaven, that thou shouldest say: 'Who shall go up for us to heaven, and bring it unto us, and make us to hear it, that we may do it?' ¹³Neither is it beyond the sea, that thou shouldest say: 'Who shall go over the sea for us, and bring it unto us, and make us to hear it, that we may do it?' ¹⁴But the word is very nigh unto thee, in

⁹ אַתֶּם נִצָּבִים הַיּוֹם כֻּלְּכֶם לִפְנֵי יְהֹוָה אֱלֹהֵיכֶם רָאשֵׁיכֶם שִׁבְטֵיכֶם זִקְנֵיכֶם ¹⁰ וְשֹׁטְרֵיכֶם כֹּל אִישׁ יִשְׂרָאֵל: טַפְּכֶם נְשֵׁיכֶם וְגֵרְךָ אֲשֶׁר בְּקֶרֶב מַחֲנֶיךָ מֵחֹטֵב ¹¹ עֵצֶיךָ עַד שֹׁאֵב מֵימֶיךָ: לְעָבְרְךָ בִּבְרִית יְהֹוָה אֱלֹהֶיךָ וּבְאָלָתוֹ אֲשֶׁר יְהֹוָה אֱלֹהֶיךָ כֹּרֵת עִמְּךָ הַיּוֹם: ¹² לְמַעַן הָקִים־אֹתְךָ הַיּוֹם לוֹ לְעָם וְהוּא יִהְיֶה־לְךָ לֵאלֹהִים כַּאֲשֶׁר דִּבֶּר־לָךְ וְכַאֲשֶׁר נִשְׁבַּע לַאֲבֹתֶיךָ לְאַבְרָהָם ¹³ לְיִצְחָק וּלְיַעֲקֹב: וְלֹא אִתְּכֶם לְבַדְּכֶם אָנֹכִי כֹּרֵת אֶת־הַבְּרִית הַזֹּאת וְאֶת־ ¹⁴ הָאָלָה הַזֹּאת: כִּי אֶת־אֲשֶׁר יֶשְׁנוֹ פֹּה עִמָּנוּ עֹמֵד הַיּוֹם לִפְנֵי יְהֹוָה אֱלֹהֵינוּ וְאֵת אֲשֶׁר אֵינֶנּוּ פֹּה עִמָּנוּ הַיּוֹם:

¹¹ כִּי הַמִּצְוָה הַזֹּאת אֲשֶׁר אָנֹכִי מְצַוְּךָ הַיּוֹם לֹא־נִפְלֵאת הִוא מִמְּךָ וְלֹא־רְחֹקָה ¹² הִוא: לֹא בַשָּׁמַיִם הִוא לֵאמֹר מִי יַעֲלֶה־ לָּנוּ הַשָּׁמַיְמָה וְיִקָּחֶהָ לָּנוּ וְיַשְׁמִעֵנוּ אֹתָהּ ¹³ וְנַעֲשֶׂנָּה: וְלֹא־מֵעֵבֶר לַיָּם הִוא לֵאמֹר מִי יַעֲבָר־לָנוּ אֶל־עֵבֶר הַיָּם וְיִקָּחֶהָ ¹⁴ לָּנוּ וְיַשְׁמִעֵנוּ אֹתָהּ וְנַעֲשֶׂנָּה: כִּי־קָרוֹב

thy mouth, and in thy heart, that thou mayest do it.

¹⁵See, I have set before thee this day life and good, and death and evil, ¹⁶in that I command thee this day to love the LORD thy God, to walk in His ways, and to keep His commandments and His statutes and His ordinances; then thou shalt live and multiply, and the LORD thy God shall bless thee in the land whither thou goest in to possess it. ¹⁷But if thy heart turn away, and thou wilt not hear, but shalt be drawn away, and worship other gods, and serve them; ¹⁸I declare unto you this day, that ye shall surely perish; ye shall not prolong your days upon the land, whither thou passest over the Jordan to go in to possess it. ¹⁹I call heaven and earth to witness against you this day, that I have set before thee life and death, the blessing and the curse; therefore choose life, that thou mayest live, thou and thy seed; ²⁰to love the LORD thy God, to hearken to His voice, and to cleave unto Him; for that is thy life, and the length of thy days; that thou mayest dwell in the land which the LORD swore unto thy fathers, to Abraham, to Isaac, and to Jacob, to give them.

אֵלֶיךָ הַדָּבָר מְאֹד בְּפִיךָ וּבִלְבָבְךָ לַעֲשֹׂתוֹ: ס

15 רְאֵה נָתַתִּי לְפָנֶיךָ הַיּוֹם אֶת־הַחַיִּים וְאֶת־הַטּוֹב וְאֶת־הַמָּוֶת וְאֶת־ 16 הָרָע: אֲשֶׁר אָנֹכִי מְצַוְּךָ הַיּוֹם לְאַהֲבָה אֶת־יְהוָה אֱלֹהֶיךָ לָלֶכֶת בִּדְרָכָיו וְלִשְׁמֹר מִצְוֹתָיו וְחֻקֹּתָיו וּמִשְׁפָּטָיו וְחָיִיתָ וְרָבִיתָ וּבֵרַכְךָ יְהוָה אֱלֹהֶיךָ בָּאָרֶץ אֲשֶׁר־אַתָּה בָא־שָׁמָּה לְרִשְׁתָּהּ: 17 וְאִם־יִפְנֶה לְבָבְךָ וְלֹא תִשְׁמָע וְנִדַּחְתָּ וְהִשְׁתַּחֲוִיתָ לֵאלֹהִים אֲחֵרִים 18 וַעֲבַדְתָּם: הִגַּדְתִּי לָכֶם הַיּוֹם כִּי אָבֹד תֹּאבֵדוּן לֹא־תַאֲרִיכֻן יָמִים עַל־הָאֲדָמָה אֲשֶׁר אַתָּה עֹבֵר אֶת־הַיַּרְדֵּן לָבוֹא שָׁמָּה 19 לְרִשְׁתָּהּ: הַעִידֹתִי בָכֶם הַיּוֹם אֶת־הַשָּׁמַיִם וְאֶת־הָאָרֶץ הַחַיִּים וְהַמָּוֶת נָתַתִּי לְפָנֶיךָ הַבְּרָכָה וְהַקְּלָלָה וּבָחַרְתָּ בַּחַיִּים לְמַעַן תִּחְיֶה אַתָּה 20 וְזַרְעֶךָ: לְאַהֲבָה אֶת־יְהוָה אֱלֹהֶיךָ לִשְׁמֹעַ בְּקֹלוֹ וּלְדָבְקָה־בוֹ כִּי הוּא חַיֶּיךָ וְאֹרֶךְ יָמֶיךָ לָשֶׁבֶת עַל־הָאֲדָמָה אֲשֶׁר נִשְׁבַּע יְהוָה לַאֲבֹתֶיךָ לְאַבְרָהָם לְיִצְחָק וּלְיַעֲקֹב לָתֵת לָהֶם:

Journey into the Wilderness

NAAMA KELMAN

Yom Kippur is the day set aside in the Jewish calendar for collective atonement. A process of inner cleansing and renewal begins late afternoon on the eve of Yom Kippur and concludes the next day at sunset with the sounding of the *shofar*. Our ancestors, like ourselves, commemorated this day with fasting and abstinence. Unlike us, they also offered sacrifices in the wilderness. On Yom Kippur morning, in traditional services, the story of that ancestral commemoration is recounted.

The brightness of the light is overwhelming. The beauty of the Sinai wilderness is staggering. The high priest stands before the children of Israel. He is wearing his linen tunic, sash, and turban. He is fully prepared to enter the Shrine, for God's presence is within. He enters with the bull of the herd for a sin-offering and a ram for a burnt-offering. He will also take two he-goats, one marked for God and the other for Azazel, chosen by lots; and then he will take another ram for a burnt-offering (Leviticus 16).

The first bull is offered to atone for the sins of Aaron and his household. Then one goat for God is offered for the people's sins. The blood of these two offerings purges the Shrine, the Tent of Meeting, and the altar. At the climax of this ritual the high priest lays his hands on the live goat, the one destined by lots for the wilderness of Azazel. Only then does he speak, making confession for all the sins and transgressions of the House of Israel. The goat is sent off, carrying with it the sins of the whole people, accompanied by a "designated man," into the wilderness. The service concludes some time later, when the high priest has removed his linen, bathed, and offered the two remaining rams for the burnt-offering.

In Leviticus 16:1–34, we enter a distant and strange world. The first verses contain a short synopsis of the entire ritual. Intricate details of the sacrifices and ceremony follow. The final verses specify the day of the year to be set aside for testing one's spirit, cessation from

work, repentance, and cleansing. The chapter ends with a recapitula-
tion of the rituals conducted by the priest, delineated in the previous
verses.

This is the chosen text for Yom Kippur morning. The obvious reason we read this text is the retelling, the rendering of the most ancient Jewish rite of expiation performed in the wilderness on Yom
Kippur—the prototype of an ancient people seeking forgiveness
through the agency of the high priest.

This text might be read with the sweep of all the High Holy Day
Torah and *Haftara* texts. Stories of expulsion, banishment, sacrifice
and near sacrifice, repentance, forgiveness, and sinning: each text
echoes and foreshadows the other. Ishmael is banished to the wilderness. Does he serve as scapegoat precursor? Jonah, who cannot take
the enormity of God's compassion, is willing to die in the wilderness.
Has he taken on himself all the sins of Nineveh in an attempt to truly
purify himself? Does Isaac—who, by his willingness to be offered to
God, purges Abraham and reaffirms the covenant—serve as a symbolic scapegoat? And why is it necessary to mark a chosen one? Isn't
Yom Kippur about our collective guilt and atonement?

Yom Kippur, the Day of Atonement, the day we correct ourselves
before God—we speak only in the collective before God, yet each individual takes stock and begins anew. We come before God only after
we have made amends with our fellow men and women. The reading
of the Leviticus text prescribed by the Rabbis joins us with our earliest ancestors. But the very act of reading a text, of focusing on words,
differentiates our Judaism from Biblical Judaism, the highly central-
ized, ritualized form of worship where words are secondary. Instead
of rituals of atonement being performed by every individual in the
community, only those privileged to be born into the priestly tribe
act in the holy places. Men, of course, whose birthright determines
their eligibility.

Where are the words, where are the women, where is the community? Where can we possibly find ourselves in this text, as we do in the
other High Holy Day readings, where the rich narrative gives us so
many possibilities for identification, empathy, and self-understanding?
When, where, and how do we cleanse ourselves?

The wilderness of Sinai, brown and red rocks jut out from every
direction, reaching heavenward. The beauty is astounding. One can

climb to a jagged cliff and peek out to the sea. I am sitting on the beach, looking far off to Saudi Arabia, past the blue, green, turquoise waters of the Red Sea. Behind me are the red brown mountains. The sea is salt water. Somewhere deep in the mountains, there is vegetation where water might be found. The conditions are harsh, but the overwhelming power of nature fills one with such awe.

Eleven women are journeying south to the Sinai wilderness. These four days are billed as a spiritual retreat, but for most of us it is just a chance to take time out from the demands of work, loved ones, family, and other assorted hassles. With each bend in the road we strip ourselves of the layers of stress. The crystal blue sky frames every breathtaking view of mountain or sea. We are entering Egypt, but we feel free.

We go walking into the canyon. We are surrounded by rock and sky. Is this where the he-goat was sent carrying our sins? The medieval commentator Rashi explained the meaning of Azazel: a high, jagged mountaintop. Were our ancestors frightened of these high rocks and deep canyons? We know of their great thirst, physical and spiritual. Were they purged, knowing that the wilderness conditions took their sins far away, never to return?

I feel cleansed by this scenery, this climate, this place. I gather my sins and fears and walk into the wilderness.

Our ancestors were surrounded by those who worshiped many gods. The children of Israel knew of foreign priests whose secret rites were far from view. Abraham and Sarah left a land where children and virgins were sacrificed to the gods. The One God of Abraham and Sarah who could not be seen or touched demanded faith and responsibility. Was this ancient rite of expelling a scapegoat a throwback to darker days? Two rabbinic references, one in the Talmudic tractate Yoma and the other in the midrash, indicate that Azazel was a demon, a seducer. The "sacrifice" might be understood as a form of appeasement to evil powers never quite understood or controlled.

Are the other High Holy Day texts the narrative of the human story, while the elaborate rite of Aaron belongs to the holy world that only male priests may enter? In this world each animal and each object symbolizes a process of purification and renewal, whose meaning is lost to us. Just like our ancestors in the wilderness, we listen to these passages as passive observers, mere spectators. We, who are not priests, cannot hope to fully understand. Ironically, other ancient peoples would more easily identify with this kind of practice, for, as historians tell us, it originates in practices of the ancient Near East.

And what of our goat destined to Azazel? Does he die on the way, or is he merely released to the endless wilderness? While all the other animals are sacrificed, this goat carries our sins to a mysterious destiny with an even more mysterious end. Is this because our collective sins cannot be "killed"? They may be cast off, released to the wilds, sent away to secret destinations. Is this because as human beings we may encounter these sins again? The sacrificial killing of rams and bullocks offers a certain finality of cleansing, while the casting off of the he-goat is a "work in progress." We release our sins knowing full well that next year we will need to do the same. But with each passing year comes improvement, a deeper awareness of our frailties. We transfer our sins to the he-goat, yet we understand that we share this burden.

The stark, silent ritual detailed in the Torah stands in dramatic contrast with the ritual from the Second Temple period described in the *Avoda* ceremony, reenacted through words and prostration during the *Musaf* (additional) service of Yom Kippur. Over the course of Yom Kippur, we move from this most ancient ritual to Temple worship to Isaiah's compassionate appeal for real human change, which comes only through acts of compassion and caring. We end with the story of Jonah, suggesting the universal possibility of repentance and renewal.

We travel from vicarious expiation of Jews in the wilderness to universal acts of repentance in the city of Nineveh. The *Avoda* ceremony is a station along the way, describing the people gathered at the Temple. They are no longer merely passive witnesses. They speak out with the high priest. This service, read after the Leviticus and Isaiah portions, is based on the description found in the Mishna (edited in 200 C.E.) of the Second Temple Yom Kippur ritual. This service is so much more dramatic and engaging that it overshadows the Torah reading.

Or perhaps it influences our reading of the Torah portion from Leviticus, which we embellish through the lens of the *Avoda* service. In our minds we add the words of confession, we fall to the floor as a collective community, asking for forgiveness. Yet the Biblical passages keep us at a distance. In Leviticus the people of Israel are spectators. We are purged of our sins through the act of the high priest and the sacrificial agents. In this wordless, mysterious unfolding of blood, fire, and motion, our sins, transgressions, vanities, and profanities are burned, drained, and sent off.

Not far from the synagogue of which I am a member, there is a magnificent promenade overlooking the Old City in Jerusalem. On a clear day I can see the southern steps leading to the Temple and follow the trail toward the Judean wilderness. Right beyond the Mt. of Olives or Mt. Scopus, the rolling green hills slope drastically to beige mountainous, arid hillsides. The contrast is startling. I imagine the throngs gathered outside the Holy of Holies, as the community is led in public confession again and again. Finally the he-goat is led out toward the wilderness, to be thrown off the cliff, killed for our sins.

So many have wandered that wilderness in search. Minutes from Jerusalem toward Jericho and the Dead Sea, the wilderness calls.

Our ancestors knew the wilderness, though they never quite mastered it—always complaining about lack of water, always fearful of the future. Even when the children of Israel were settled in the Land of Israel, their spirit wandered. They looked for tangible gods—gods that insured the rain and the bounty.

Our prophets came to know God in the wilderness of uncertainty. Abram leaves a major city to start his journey. Moses encounters God in the burning bush in the wilderness. The ultimate encounter is at Mt. Sinai, in the wilderness of Sinai, when the people of Israel receive the Torah. We are asked to believe, when the sense of the unknown, the mysterious, is most felt.

In this wilderness encounter on Yom Kippur we look to God for forgiveness, but what do we ask of ourselves? We assume that the he-goat is the innocent victim. What does he symbolize for us? Blame and guilt, self-blame and undiminished guilt. Women, who have been marginalized and blamed since the creation of Eve, tend to blame themselves first. We readily scapegoat ourselves, taking all blame, while wishing secretly we were the high priests, masters of all fates. Is this tension possibly played out in the Rosh Hashana reading on the first day? Sarah, acting as high priest, convinces Abraham to cast out Hagar, the willing scapegoat. Both these roles are problematic and reflect women's lack of power, real influence, and self-esteem.

How often do we blame ourselves when it is nowhere near our "fault"? How often have we been scapegoated as Jewish mothers, Jewish princesses, source of all Jewish male neuroses? Most recently, Jewish women's success is singled out as the cause of communal breakdown. What did our foremothers think as they watched the goat cast out? Did they allow their sins to go, too, or did they hold them close?

On our spiritual retreat in Sinai, there are no high priests or scapegoats. As Jewish women struggling for balance, we know that extreme dichotomies are harmful. We talk, we pray, we create art, we dance, we laugh. Most of all, we own up. We admit our weaknesses, we question authority, we are skeptical. We are no longer willing to take all the blame, nor are we intoxicated with power. The wilderness reminds us of our limitations and our strengths. We want to take this with us. On Yom Kippur we again address the balance. We own up. We cleanse ourselves, reminded through fasting and prayer of our weaknesses and our strengths. On Yom Kippur we re-create the wilderness.

The Reform movement has long had trouble with the passage from Leviticus. Indeed, in Reform synagogues this passage is not read on Yom Kippur morning. As Rabbi Gunther Plaut points out in his commentary:

> This holy day as we know it was created by the Jewish people in the past two thousand years. The biblical section now before us hardly suggests anything of inwardness or of moral aspiration. One may feel disappointed when reading in Leviticus, chapter 16, the outline of a complicated sacrificial service performed by the High Priest on behalf of the community, with the people as passive spectators. At the end of the chapter—almost as an afterthought—they are commanded to fast and abstain from work on the sacred day, but nothing is said about inner contrition, self-discipline, or higher standards of conduct. For this reason, the leaders of Reform Judaism replaced this chapter by selections from Deuteronomy, chapters 29 and 30, which they deemed more appropriate.[1]

The alternative reading from Deuteronomy appeals to all the children of Israel to choose life, acknowledging that God has put before us life and goodness, death and evil. This reading affirms the closeness of God's Torah and commandments. The Leviticus reading, in its distant remoteness, gives us one message, while Deuteronomy gives another. Yet they are part and parcel of our one Torah.

How do we merge these perspectives? How do we read Leviticus and feel God's closeness? The Reform movement chose to delete it. Other Jews hear it with the overlay of the *Avoda* service. I read it with all the bleakness and promise of the wilderness.

The wilderness belongs to no one. The wilderness belongs to everyone. According to one midrash, God gave us the Torah in the wilderness so that no tribe could claim exclusive possession of it, saying, "The Torah was given on my land, therefore it is mine." Something happens to us in the wilderness. In the face of the toughest elements, we let go. In the silence of the wilderness, we listen. In the expanse of the wilderness, we call out.

Repeatedly in the Jewish calendar year we are asked to recall the trials of our wilderness experience. With the Exodus from Egypt, we began our journey through the wilderness, entering as slaves and finding our freedom there. On Yom Kippur we remove all excesses; we live a physical wilderness for twenty-five hours. We are left to our own resources. On this day we recall the paradigm of expiation and atonement. Through the casting out of the scapegoat, our ancestors were cleansed.

In the wilderness rite blood from the he-goat, the one not cast out, was used to cleanse the sanctuary, the outer Tent of Meeting. The blood from the sin offering cleansed the altar. Thus not only were the family of the high priest and the children of Israel cleansed, so were the vessels. The entire House of Israel is released through these acts. This process was critical for insuring God's presence in the Sanctuary.

This idea of purifying the shrine and its inner spaces is critical to the entire procedure. Since the priest could be a source of impurity for the Shrine, he must be pure, and the same is true for the Israelites. For this reason, only the high priest will go inside the Sanctuary. In fact, we read in verse 20: "When he was finished purging the sanctuary, the Tent of Meeting, and the altar, the live goat was brought forward." In other words, only when all the elements have reached the state of purity was the confession made. *Vehitvada* (he shall confess)—we do not know what the priest confessed in the Biblical passage, although in the rabbinic rendering, the *Avoda* service, his confessions are detailed. *Vehitvada*—and the goat is released.

Here, too, the dynamic tension holds us in suspense. While all else has been purged, a single goat carries all the sins and transgressions, transmitted through the hands of Aaron. According to the commentary of the Jewish Publication Society, "The ancient view of Yom Kippur is somewhat different from that which came to predominate in later Judaism. . . . Atonement for the sins of the people eventually replaced the purification of the sanctuary per se as the central theme of Yom Kippur."[2] The idea of cleaning up your house before you can truly release your sins may be a point we miss in the flow of the elaborate ritual.

We cannot really cleanse ourselves if we haven't prepared ourselves, our space, our community. Real cleansing comes when the entire process is completed. In that great shining moment, when all is purged, the goat is sent off with the weight of the community's transgressions. It is momentary, fleeting, like the goat.

On Friday afternoon, every Friday afternoon in Jerusalem, just after public transportation has stopped and before the sun has set, a slow hush falls over the city. The beige stones of the buildings and the Old City walls turn pink, then peach, and, finally, gold. It seems as if the city takes in its breath and then releases it on the arrival of the Sabbath. We have cleaned our homes, prepared our sanctuaries, readied ourselves to let go of the week.

In Leviticus, the tenth day of the seventh month is called *Shabbat Shabbaton,* the quintessential Sabbath, a day of complete abstinence and rest, cleansing and renewal. Each week we can have a little taste of this, from frenzied preparation to release. As we enter the Sabbath, we let go of the past week, we release the tensions and stress for twenty-five hours. As on Yom Kippur, we stop to look inward, to review, and to refresh ourselves.

The privilege of living in Jerusalem is the ability to hold homeland and wilderness in one view. Throughout the centuries we kept it in our prayer books and hearts. Jerusalem, eternal symbol of hope and homeland, throughout Jewish history. To the east, the Judean wilderness beckons. Jerusalem holds the promise of security and comfort, *tzur yisrael,* the rock of Israel. The wilderness calls out to our fears and our stirrings. For our souls and bodies to be relieved, we need that wilderness, that mysterious powerful unknown. To live and work the everyday we need the concrete place, the actual sanctuaries, where we can do our holy work. Jerusalem reminds us of those sanctuaries, large and small, where in our own way we tend the world.

On Yom Kippur, the children of Israel, the high priest and the goat destined for Azazel bring these pieces together.

The Yom Kippur Avoda within the Female Enclosure

BONNA DEVORA HABERMAN

On Yom Kippur day, the *Avoda*—service of the *kohen gadol* (the high priest)—is one of the central pieces of the traditional liturgy. From the vantage point of our cultural experience, this ritual is remote and inaccessible. The ritual functions of the once holy Temple have little to do with our contemporary notions of holiness. Animal sacrifice and the ritual use of blood strike us as activities belonging to a barbarous past. The synagogues in which we congregate are clean and orderly. From our perspective, the smells and sounds, feed and excrement, of live goats, lambs, and bullocks belong on the farm. Animals are slaughtered far from us, cleaned and packaged neatly for consumption, betraying by name and appearance as little as possible the violent and bloody acts that precede the cellophane wrappings. How do we reconcile the textual focus on Temple ritual at the center of the Yom Kippur liturgy with our contemporary lives and concerns? How can we participate meaningfully in the recitation of texts that recount acts we find repulsive? How can we identify with or comprehend the community of our people who once thronged to the Temple precinct to witness the high priest's entry into the Holy of Holies? I propose a challenge: to experience the service of the high priest on Yom Kippur as a reenactment rather than a mere recitation—inspiring and evocative, like other Jewish festival reenactments that invite us to celebrate and transcend our finite lives.

My willingness to respect the process by which the *Avoda* became part of the Yom Kippur liturgy combines with my expectation that my struggle with the blood and rituals contained therein will yield moving and powerful results for our experience on Yom Kippur. My concern here is not to ascertain the intentions of those who included the *Avoda* in the *Musaf* (additional prayer). I also don't expect the *mach-*

zor (High Holy Day prayer book) to straightforwardly articulate our most profound feelings and prayers on the awesome day of reckoning, for these are complex and many. To make the text relevant to our own experience, we must actively engage the text with our life, our thoughts, our feelings, and our bodies. That effort opens the possibility of finding sublime meaning in the reenactment of an ancient experience, part of the repertoire of our people.

Enactments

Jewish festivals regularly invite us to enter a historical experience, to relive events, and to become part of an expanded context that is not the one we habitually occupy. On Passover we are taught to see ourselves as slaves in Egypt whom God leads to freedom. On Shavuot we are the recipients of the Torah at Mount Sinai. On Sukkot we dwell in temporary booths on our journey to Israel, the promised land, and celebrate the fruits of our harvest, which once "we" took to the holy Temple in Jerusalem. Holiday rituals reinforce our identification with the original historical actors: we eat *matza,* which resembles the unleavened bread eaten by our ancestors who were rushing on their path to redemption. We spend the night of Shavuot in study, preparing ourselves, as did our ancestors, for the great moment when "we" will accept the Torah. By means of these reenactments, the holidays enliven our bodies and our consciousness. They invite us to participate in, and to be affected by, awesome experiences that transpired at other times and locations during our people's history. They enable us to transcend the boundaries of our individual time and place, joining with other participants in a celebrating community.

The locus for the *Avoda* is the desert Tabernacle/Jerusalem Temple. The synagogue sanctuary in which we find ourselves as we recite the *Avoda* is the metaphoric equivalent of these historic sites of Jewish worship. This equivalence between the Temple and our synagogue creates a poignant simplicity. We can identify more easily with the original worshipers and experience our prayer leader in the place of the high priest. The *Avoda* service that we perform follows one unswerving line from the desert Tabernacle to our synagogues and engenders the potential for an unparalleled intensity of synagogue experience.

The Avodah Context

Preparation for the reenactment of the *Avoda* begins with the Torah reading of the morning service (Leviticus 16:1–34). The reading draws us into the desert, where the children of Israel, liberated from Egypt, wander for years en route to the Land of Israel. The sere clarity of desert sky forms the backdrop for a rugged and challenging terrain, barren rock, sand. Against the vastness of creation, imposing mountains, and quiet, unremitting landscapes, the human form is humbled. This is the locus for encountering God.

In this arid climate, our body is exposed to the harshness of elements: searing sun, sweeping dry and eroding winds, penetrating night chills, when no soothing moisture or mediating vegetation retains any of the scorching heat of day. In this desert we are helpless and impotent to provide for our own basic needs. Our daily life is wholly in the hands of God, by whose lovingkindness we are sustained. Mouth dry, we find our consciousness altered by the unrelenting heat. We gather for the Yom Kippur assembly. In our synagogues too we are dry-mouthed, reminded by our empty bellies of our dependence, our destiny undetermined.

Leviticus 16 recalls the imminent danger involved in approaching the holiest enclosure to serve God. By invoking Nadav and Avihu, two of Aaron the priest's sons who died when they brought a "strange fire" before God (Leviticus 10:1–2), we heighten our awareness of the mortal dangers involved in serving God. We grieve the fate of the two children whose service failed, praying for the success of our own. We understand that Aaron must be extremely cautious when he enters the holy place lest he too die (Leviticus 16:2). By emphasizing that life itself is at stake, the text creates an identification between each Jew whose life is weighing in the balance on this day of divine judgment and the high priest.* The high priest performs the *Avoda* on behalf of each member of the community. The fate of the entire congregation is bound up with successful completion of the ritual. Reciprocally, the high priest is relying upon the prayers and supplications of the assembled congregation. From the people the high priest draws strength to approach God on their behalf.[1]

*Throughout this essay, I refer to the high priest using gender-inclusive language. My aim is to call into question the gender tradition and stereotypical imagery of the Temple functionaries.

The Biblical text elaborates the rituals that were performed by Aaron, the first high priest, on the Day of Atonement: a sequence of ritual baths, dressing in special white linen garments, confessions, offerings, and incursions into the inner sanctuary of the Tabernacle. Through these rituals the high priest aspires to absolve the sins from the children of Israel that have interfered with God's holiness among them.

The Biblical account later formed the basis for the Yom Kippur rituals performed in the Second Temple and described in detail in the *Avoda* liturgy of the additional service. On Yom Kippur our reading of the Biblical version precedes and prepares us for the reenactment that actually occurs in the *Avoda*. The text of the reenactment draws on the Levitical source but elaborates it in accordance with descriptions of the Second Temple service found in the Talmud. The versions of the *Avoda* that we use today developed from the tradition of replacing the rites performed in the destroyed Temple with meaningful reenactments in diaspora synagogue contexts. The contributors to these texts had a tacit goal of replicating the Temple service through recounting, studying, interpreting, and teaching it. These activities became spiritually equivalent to performing the actual services in the Temple. The *Avoda* liturgy, therefore, is not a nostalgic account of long defunct rituals for the purpose of reminding ourselves of our history. Rather, this active recounting of the ritual performed by the high priest is intended to draw us into an atemporal Temple experience.

The Musaf *Avoda*

The *Avoda* is introduced by the recitation of an alphabetical acrostic that summarizes the entirety of history, from the Creation of the world through to the appointment of the high priest and the preparation to perform the *Avoda*.[2] We learn from the Mishna (Avot 1:1) that the high priest had been instructed to eat little at the final meal before the fast, in order to avoid sleepiness, and was kept up all night reviewing the services. The day begins at sunrise with washing and immersion in the *mikveh* (ritual bath). While performing the daily offerings and services, the high priest wears the eight priestly golden garments. Before beginning the *Avoda*, s/he washes hands and feet and immerses again in the *mikveh*. For the *Avoda*, four special single-thread white-linen garments were worn. The introductory *piyyut* (prayer-poem) ends with the laying of hands on the head of the bull, the *chatat* (sin-offering), upon which s/he utters a confession for personal and familial sins. The intense supplication in the first-person singular echoes the *viddui* (confession), the leitmotiv of Yom Kippur. This confession is repeated on the successive sacrifices, in the first-person singular on behalf of the priestly tribe and in the plural on behalf of the entire People of Israel. After each confession, the high priest offers the sacrifice according to an elaborate ritual, then enters the Holy of Holies. When s/he first enters, s/he burns incense on coals to create a cloud, which hides the ark cover over the testimony to protect him/her from the mortal danger of seeing it. Each of the three times that the high priest emerges from the Holy of Holies, s/he utters the ineffable Name of God, the tetragrammaton. As the people hear the Name, they prostrate themselves, exclaiming, "May the Name of the glorious majesty be blessed forever." In many congregations the community reenacts the prostration performed in the Temple each time the prayer leader intones this momentous passage, falling to the floor in supplication.[3] The cantorial melodies to the *vehakohanim* ("and the priests") section of the *Avoda* are among the most richly embellished in the entire synagogue liturgy. Upon completion of each set of the confessions, as the people rise to their feet, the high priest pronounces, "You shall be purified."

The prayer leader then describes the precise rituals involving the slaughter of the offerings, collection of the blood in special vessels, and sprinkling of it by the high priest within the Holy of Holies on the ark and outside upon the curtain and altar. Like the high priest, the prayer leader counts each sprinkling: "one"; "one and one"; "one and two"; up to a total of eight, in specified upward and downward directions. The blood is poured at the base of the altar, from where it flows down to the Kidron Brook.

Turning to the remaining goat, the high priest confesses on its head all of the sins of Israel. S/He dispatches the goat "to Azazel" with an appointed messenger, who leads it to a high cliff in the desert from which it was pushed to its destruction. The high priest then gathers the remains of the bull and kid offerings and sends them out of the compound to be burnt. News of the goat reaching its destined destruction were speedily relayed to the Temple, where a crimson thread would turn white to symbolize the success of the purification.[4] The high priest then reads from the Torah the Levitical sexual prohibitions (chapter 18). In the traditional liturgy this Torah chapter is read at the synagogue afternoon service. The high priest then recites the eight blessings of the *Avoda*, washes and immerses in the *mikveh*, and dons the golden vestments to continue with the services. After these offerings, s/he again washes and immerses in the *mikveh* and dresses in the Yom Kippur white linen garments in order to enter the Holy of Holies for the last time, removing the shovel and ladle that had been left since the burning of the incense.

The high priest concludes the *Avoda* by washing and immersing one last time to dress again in the golden garments, to burn the daily incense and light the candles of the *menora* (candelabrum). The prayer-poem that closes the *Avoda* replaces the joyous parade accompanying the high priest after the successful service and emergence from the Holy of Holies. It celebrates the special privilege enjoyed by those who had the opportunity to experience the *Avoda* while the Temple was standing.

During the recitation of the *Avoda*, the prayer leader[5] becomes unambiguously identified with the high priest. In the paraphrase above, it was difficult to convey a separation of the recitation by the prayer leader and the acts of the high priest. The description becomes the act. Nevertheless it is important to emphasize that though the prayer leader stands for the high priest, the identification remains symbolic because the medium of the reenactment is verbal. The prayer leader does not lay her hands on a bull, a ram, or goats; she does not sprinkle blood; she does not enter the Holy of Holies. Indeed, she does not displace her two parallel touching stocking feet even when fully prostrating herself on the ground as part of the *Avoda*. She is absorbed in a standing prayer as the representative of the community. Recounting the acts with the intentionality of prayer substitutes for performing them. The community joins with her in utterances and prostrations. The *Avoda* is a symbolic representation of the service performed first in the desert Tabernacle, then in the holy Temple in Jerusalem through a gesticulated, cantillated community prayer experience.

Holy Enclosures

My understanding of the significance of the *Avoda* ritual is rooted in my association of the holy enclosures—the Tabernacle, the Temple, and, derivatively, the synagogue sanctuary—with the body of a woman.[6] Enclosed space is often understood to indicate a female aspect of the material world. The holy space of the Jewish people, the Tabernacle, then, later, the Temple, and, even later, synagogues, are located in the center of the encampment, surrounded and protected by the people. They are nested chambers that enclose holy objects. Only a select few are permitted to enter the innermost sanctuary, the sacred spaces that are the ritual locus for the Jewish people's interactions with God. As one moves toward them, one is closer to a concentration of holiness.[7] Approaching and entering the confines of God's house *(bayit)* are Biblical metaphors for attaining intimacy with God. Greatest intimacy is found in the Holy of Holies, the deepest internal space within the Tabernacle and Temple. In our synagogues, the Holy of Holies corresponds to the holy ark, containing the Torah scrolls.

It may seem extraordinary to suggest an analogy between the Tabernacle, Temple, and synagogue and the female body; between the Holy of Holies and the womb. But this analogy arises from my deep reverence for the holy place of our prayer and my sense of our bodies as formed in God's image, partaking in the holiness of Creation. Sexuality, in particular, is an exalted facet of the divine Creation, a climactic fulfillment of God's will for union through which Creation is perpetually renewed. To perceive this metaphor at work in the Yom Kippur ritual contributes not only to our understanding of the Temple on Yom Kippur, but also to our appreciation of the exalted dignity of our bodies. With this experimental and provocative approach to the *Avoda*, I hope to open layers of symbol and metaphor that can deepen our experience of this ancient ritual.

If the inner sanctuaries of the Jewish people are uterine, to them I attribute uterine functions. The cycles of daily, monthly, and festival offerings in the Tabernacle and Temple replicated the cyclical functions of the womb. Regular rites of sacrifice were performed, expiations accomplished, and blood drained. The *Avoda* enacts in a concentrated form the entire cycle of embodied functions of the divine womb. It is also the single opportunity we have for perfect intimacy with God, expressed through the metaphor of consummation in sexual union, accompanied by the articulation of the ineffable Name.[8] Yom Kippur day becomes both a microcosm and a climax of intimacy between the Jewish people and God.

In the Temple service, only one individual per year is privileged to have intimacy with God, to enter the deepest recesses of the holy enclosures of sacred space. Yom Kippur is the sole appointed day when only one specific priest, the high priest, actually penetrates into the Holy of Holies. Our recitation of the *Avoda* in the synagogue liturgy reenacts that awesome experience. The high priest prepares for the *Avoda* with an elaborate meticulousness comparable to the detailed preparations for marital intercourse in traditional Jewish society. S/He reviews the laws and protocol intensively, focusing his/her intentions purely. S/He takes particular caution not to have a seminal emission, which would disqualify him/her from the service, as a menstrual emission would disqualify a woman from sexual intercourse. S/He removes the golden priestly garments that have an implicit association with the sin of the golden calf in which Aaron had taken a significant part. S/He bathes and then, like the traditional bride, immerses in the ritual bath and dons simple white linen garments.

When s/he first enters the Holy of Holies s/he burns the incense. According to Aryeh Kaplan, a modern interpreter of Jewish texts, the ten sweet-smelling ingredients that the Rabbis tell us compose the incense represent what the midrash calls the ten statements of the Creation of the world. The tenth statement, "God saw everything She had made, and it was good" (Genesis 1:31), is followed, in the midrashic understanding, by an eleventh statement, "It is *not good* for man to be alone" (Genesis 2:18). This last statement corresponds to the one foul-smelling ingredient in the incense, *chelvana* (galbanum). Loneliness is "not good," but, burned with the other ingredients, galbanum contributes to the special aroma.[9] The eleventh statement expresses the loneliness of the Creator, who then conceives the desire to create woman, who will imitate the Creation act through her union with man.[10] The incense is the aphrodisiac of the *Avoda*. It arouses the lonely beloved.

Penetrating the womb, the Holy of Holies, the high priest symbolizes the phallus in the act of lovemaking.[11] The high priest is the sexual organ of the Jewish people, an instrument of excitement and desire for intimacy with God. There is a tradition that Yom Kippur is the anniversary of Abraham's circumcision, the preparation of the male member of the Jewish covenant. Abraham, according to the midrash, performed the circumcision during the heat of the day, at the approximate hour of the *Avoda*, on the stone on Mount Moriah that was to become the foundation of the Temple.[12] This midrashic elaboration inaugurates the sexual symbolism of the Temple as a site for covenantal rituals involving blood.[13] The high priest's preparations and ultimately his/her incursions into the Holy of Holies are intended to stimulate theo-erotic mechanisms, to elicit God's response to the supplications of the people, to inspire God's reciprocal arousal, attention, and love. The high priest may be understood as the symbolic instrument for attaining union of the Jewish people with the One, an acceptance of the body of the people into God's house, a climactic merging of lovers. The choreography of the rituals that s/he performs with his/her body reflects the sensuality aroused in the relationship, which culminates in orgasmic penetration into the holiest space. Because of the erotic energy unleashed in this communal act, the boundaries of human sexual expression must be carefully affirmed. The consummated sexual intimacy of God and the Jewish people during the *Avoda* could explain why the afternoon Torah reading consists of the Levitical sexual prohibitions (chapter 18).

Bearing in mind that the sanctuary is an inanimate symbol of the divine enclosure or home, the source of its animation is the performance of the services by those who minister there. Created by human beings, human beings also give it the semblance of life by symbolically replicating life functions in it. I interpret the priests and ancillary workers, all those who labor in the Temple, as the equivalent of the physiological systems of a woman's body. On Yom Kippur the high priest serves not only the phallic function; as a regularly employed minister of the Temple, s/he is also a caretaker and one who enacts the functions of the Temple's female body. Of course I am speaking symbolically, not literally. This will become clearer as I look at the menstrual symbolism of the *Avoda*.

The Biblical and Mishnaic texts specifically record that the sprinkling of blood expiates the holy place from sin. The assumption is that the holiness of the inner sanctum has been "stained" by the transgressions of the people. Holy objects have somehow absorbed an impurity as a consequence of the people's sins, which threatens the holy domain and dominion of God. By the ritual sprinkling of blood, the stains of iniquity and sin are removed, and with them God's vulnerability in the earthly dwelling. The relationship between God and the people is an interdependent one. God has a sensitivity to the acts of the people expressed by the staining of the sanctum. The people, in turn, rely on God to expiate their transgressions. Expiation is one of the cyclical requirements for ongoing fulfillment of the covenantal relationship between God and the Jewish people. The blood of Yom Kippur accomplishes this essential *kappara* (cleansing, expiation).

Throughout the Torah blood plays a crucial role in maintaining the covenant between God and the people. We find it in the Sinai context (Exodus 24), where it functions to repair the damage caused to the covenantal relationship by the sins of the people. And we find it again in the investiture of Aaron into the priesthood and in the relationship between God and the house of Aaron (Leviticus 8; Numbers 25:12–13).[14] The *Avoda* expiation also has this covenantal nuance. The sins of the people somehow interfere with God's holiness and disable the relationship. Through the sprinkling of blood, atonement is offered. The continuation of the covenantal relationship with God requires a regular sprinkling of blood that purifies.

In this context the blood stands for life; it is in lieu of life itself. The blood runs down to the earth from the corners of the altar. It functions in the Tabernacle as menstrual blood does in a woman's body. We can see the enactments of the *Avoda* as replicating the menstrual cycle of purification.[15]

Within the bodies of women, during their fertile years, the cycle of ovulation and menstruation continually renews the potential for the creation of life. There the activities of re-creation occur: ovulation, intercourse, conception, gestation, birth, and initial sustenance. Menstruation is not the opposite of the holy creative function, but an inextricable part of the cycle that enables human creation, imitating the initial creation of humanity by God. The menstrual period marks the transition from lost opportunity, whereby the unused fluid of life-giving nourishment is discharged and the woman prepares for another cycle of potential life-giving. The ovum is released into a woman's womb in which the fertile conditions for life are continuously regenerating. The very fluids that are usually unused and flow outward from within, at first soaking, then spotting, are the ground in which new life might take root. In the event of conception, those fluids fulfill their function of nourishing the embryo. When there is no conception, the passing fluids cleanse and revitalize the inner sanctum, the womb.

The shedding of menstrual blood calls our attention to an essential characteristic of the created world. Much life potential is latent in the world, yet only a minuscule portion ever attains fruition. Millions of seeds are shed, yet only a relatively small number germinates and grows into mature trees. Millions of sperm and thousands of ova are produced, yet few merge in conception. The loss of the overwhelming potential life latent in Creation is essential to sustaining life in the finite world. I see this loss as analogous, though not identical, to human acts of transgression. The imperfection of our behavior is part of the finitude of Creation. God's desire for our freedom of will, granting us unlimited potential to act though we are finite human beings, necessitates error and transgression. I am not associating menstruation with sin. The menstrual blood flow is purification from loss of potential life, as the flow of blood in the Tabernacle is purification from sin. The shedding of menstrual blood is a symbol of the inexorable cycle of death and renewal. Menstrual blood is a quintessential material of God's Creation of humanity.

The blood carries away existential ruin and danger; it also heralds new possibility. Though inevitable, each unfulfilled conception is a loss, a miss. This cycle is expressed in plant and animal life and in the relationships of men and women. Though it occurs principally in the woman's body, the man's sexuality is implicit in the cycles so that man as well as woman is implicated in the loss of potential life.

The time of menstrual bleeding is a time of separation, a boundary marking the transition between loss and renewed possibility to conceive. The atmosphere of Yom Kippur reflects this dramatic life and death tension, the dangerous confrontation with harsh judgment, and the longing for renewal and re-creation. Menstrual blood is the transitional blood, the lubricant and nutrient of passage, the recycling of potential into the earth from which we are ultimately born and to which we ultimately return. The blood of the Yom Kippur *Avoda* represents the cyclical purification of the holy relationship between God and the Jewish people. This relationship involves the same cycles of holiness that apply to male-female intimate relationships in society: the observance of a rhythm of approaching and receding. Our mistakes and transgressions produce separation, alienation from God, loss. Longing for acceptance and reconnection, we bring our offerings, transferring to them our remorse. Their blood represents a shedding of the lost potential we recognize in our lives and bodies and in the world, as well as our yearning for renewal. The goat to Azazel is a stillborn or a discarded ovum, who bears not only our iniquities, but the inadequacies of Creation. Few are destined to attain fulfillment relative to the nearly boundless potential to create new life. And so the menstrual blood drains down from us, washes into the Kidron Brook, down into the earth. Again and again the high priest washes and immerses in the waters of life, returns to the blood of sacrifice and back to the water. Identifying with him/her, we emerge from God's inner sanctum reborn from the primordial blood and water of Creation.

I have proposed that the *Avoda* of Yom Kippur, one of the central rituals of our liturgical life, resonates with metaphors of human sexual embodiment. Recognition of these metaphors affects our experience of the synagogue service. Our awareness of the structures of gender relations that are expressed by our liturgy is heightened. Our fascination with the sheer multiplicity of latent meanings in the text is intensified. This recognition is relevant to our experience of synagogue ritual in general. It suggests a way of understanding the systematic exclusion of women from our central ritual functions in holy space. If these rituals are at some level replications of female embodiment, then men may well find the presence of actual women profoundly threatening to their full and equal participation in the symbolic representation of women's bodies and functions.

But to view the *Avoda* and our sexuality in a mutually sustaining and sublime relationship grants women the possibility of forging a unique identification with the rituals. Our bodies are the edifice of the Temple; our blood, the medium of life and death, of Creation and expiation. The *Avoda* represents a purifying union whereby the high priest participates in the functions of woman and enacts the holiness of the female regenerative cycle. S/He also readily represents male sexuality, entering into God's precinct on behalf of the Jewish people.

The high priest thus performs both male and female functions, representing a fully engendered human reminiscent of the original *adam rishon,* the first human who was created male and female in God's image (Genesis 1.26–27).

Traditionally the male aspect of the high priest and the *Avoda* has been emphasized. Male members of the congregation can identify with the high priest in the phallic function. Women in synagogue who sit apart from men and do not lead prayers are replicating the Temple practice of assigning the priestly function to males. Women who sit among men in unsegregated sanctuaries or who pray in women's-only groups can more easily explore the female aspects of the high priest as well as of the *Avoda.* A woman prayer leader symbolically highlights the regenerative power of woman through blood and the consequent purification and renewal of the covenant. Regardless of our seating arrangements, the *Avoda* offers all women a unique expression and affirmation of our embodiment and of our identities as women members of the prayerful community.

Offerings of Prayer and Study

On Yom Kippur, as on every day since the Temple was destroyed, our offerings are words, words of prayer and interpretations of Torah.

In the Talmudic tractate Yoma, while discussing the sprinkling of the blood by the high priest (Yoma 54a–b), the Rabbis become concerned with the possible disappearance and subsequent hiding of the ark that contained the Ten Commandments after the destruction of the First Temple. The ark was meant to be housed within the Holy of Holies. The Talmud cites Lamentations (1:6), "And gone from Zion is all her glory," and interprets "her glory" to mean "that which is enclosed within her." The implication is that the tablets are in exile. The discussion of the mystery and danger that engulfs the location of the tablets prompts a sequence of statements that blatantly portray the Temple enclosure erotically as a woman's body. They describe the ends of the staves by which the ark was transported: "They tore through the curtain, and showed forth; they pressed and protruded out as the two breasts of a woman, as it is said 'My beloved is to me as a pouch of myrrh that lies between my breasts (Song of Songs 1:13)'" (Yoma 54a). According to Rabbi Kattina, the curtain was removed for the people of Israel when they came to the Temple on festivals in order to show the cherubim whose bodies were intertwined with one another. The assembly would be told, "Look! You are beloved to God as man and woman are to each other." Answering some rabbis' concern with the danger of viewing the holy objects, Rabbi Nachman relates an allegory. "It is like with a bride. When she is in her father's house, she must behave modestly and discreetly with her spouse, but at home with him, she does not need to behave modestly" (Yoma 54a). This suggests an understanding of the Tabernacle period in the desert as prenuptial: there the intimacy was circumscribed. But in the Temple in Jerusalem, and at home with God in the synagogue enclosures of our people, we can engage in the most intimate encounters with the One.

It is striking that precisely at the moment of describing how the high priest counts the blood as s/he sprinkles it, the Rabbis embark upon a discussion of the eroticism of the inner sanctum, the intermingling of the cherubs in their sexual embrace. The myrrh mentioned in the verse from *Song of Songs* alludes to the first ingredient in the incense that the high priest brought during his/her first incursion into the Holy of Holies.[16] The choice of this blatantly erotic proof-text corroborates my perception of the eroticism of the high priest's acts. The Talmudic passage, driven by wonder at the hidden mystery of the enclosure, articulates the mortal danger of the holy space and its secrets. It also conveys the desire of the Rabbis to enter the enclosure and their fantasies about its female eros. I believe that the Rabbis are responding to the same evocative aspect of the *Avoda* that I have been discussing in this essay. The sanctuary enclosure is where the body of Israel engages in intercourse with God. The wedded God and people observe the menstrual cycle of ritual purification and engage in a relationship of embodied holiness. The Yom Kippur *Avoda* is the climax of our intimacy.

Every year on Yom Kippur, as we approach the synagogue sanctuary, we have the possibility of entering into the holiest, most sensitive, and erotic union of our people with the Creator. The entire Jewish people is assembled on this same day, as once we were at the Tabernacle. Deprived of water and food, we stand barefoot before God. Identifying with the high priest in our simple white garments, with our prayers and prostrations, we reenact the *Avoda*. Desert dryness in our mouths, we count the drops of blood, issue of our bodies, offering of our souls, the flow of life and death. At this supreme moment of our Yom Kippur encounter with God, our ritual affirms our fully human female embodiment, intertwined with male, we and God, cherubim in the inner sanctuary of Creation. In Temple times, upon successful completion of the powerful *Avoda* services, the high priest celebrated among a joyous parading congregation. Relieved and exhausted, the weary bride/groom was feted in the streets of Jerusalem.[17] May life potential be renewed by our service.

The Torah of Our Lives

Laura Geller

The Torah portion we read on Yom Kippur morning in Reform congregations stands in stark contrast with the prayer most identified with Yom Kippur, the *kol nidre*. *Kol nidre* intones, in its haunting melody, a troubling and confusing message: "Our vows shall not be our vows; our bonds shall not be our bonds; our oaths shall not be our oaths."

No wonder the Rabbis discouraged the recitation of this prayer. They were afraid people would misunderstand from it that vows could be easily made and broken or that the word of a Jew could not be taken seriously. But the prayer has a power that withstood rabbinic opposition, a power that gives the day its existential holiness.

On its most fundamental level, Yom Kippur is a day lived without bonds, without the obligations created by our vows and oaths. On this day what matters is not that we are mothers or fathers, daughters or sons, sisters or brothers, wives or husbands, not that we are rabbis or professors, homemakers or teachers, auto mechanics or bus drivers. On Yom Kippur what matters is that we stand naked and alone before God. We are disembodied souls, confronting the reality of our mortality.

Yom Kippur is a symbolic encounter with death. We are supposed to refrain from life-affirming activities—eating, drinking, bathing, making love, and adorning ourselves. Because leather is viewed as adornment, we are instructed to take off our leather shoes, to stand barefoot, resembling the shoeless corpses we will someday be. We are to wear white; many male Jews even wear the white garment in which they will someday be buried, their *kittel*.

No wonder the *kol nidre* sings about untying our bonds. As we face death, the social roles we inhabit seem unimportant. As we face death, the vows we made that turned us into wives or husbands are as ephemeral as a passing shadow.

I think about all this as I race around the house on Yom Kippur morning, trying to get the kids up, dressed, and fed in time for me to get to synagogue for the early service. My vows are still vows—I'm a wife, with a supportive husband who doesn't want to spend the whole day at temple. I'm a mother of two kids who are both proud and ambivalent that their mother is the rabbi of a large congregation. I'm the grateful daughter of wonderful parents who come out from Boston every year to help me get through the holidays.

I think about all this as I wrestle with the Torah portion for Yom Kippur morning. While the traditional reading focuses on the ancient ritual of the sacrifices of the two goats, the scapegoat exiled to Azazel with all of our sins, the other goat slaughtered for a sin-offering, the Reform reading evokes a different story.

> You stand this day, all of you, before the Lord your God—the heads of your tribe, your elders and officers, every one in Israel, men, women and children and the strangers in your camp, from the one who chops your wood to the one who draws your water, that you should enter the covenant which the Lord your God makes with you this day, in order to establish you henceforth as the people whose only God is the Lord, as you have been promised and as God has sworn to your fathers, to Abraham, Isaac and Jacob. (Deuteronomy 29:9–14)

This is a story about me, I think to myself, as I do the twentieth-century equivalents of chopping wood and drawing water, those tasks essential to keeping a family fed, clothed, and ready for synagogue. All of us are in the story: my husband and my father, my mother and me, my son and daughter. And all the Jews who usually feel so left out of Jewish religious life are in this story too—the "strangers in our camp," the gays and lesbians who don't feel comfortable in so many of our synagogues, the single people, the widows and widowers, or those who can't afford to buy High Holy Day tickets or to belong to a temple. All of us are standing before God—not as the disembodied souls we were during *kol nidre,* but as Jews with our own stories.

Part of the story is what happened to us at Mt. Sinai, the first time we all stood together before God. We were all there. We stood together at the bottom of the mountain, "every Jew who ever was or ever will be," says the tradition. We heard the lightning and saw the thunder; we felt the mountain tremble. Then, with our own ears, we heard God speak.

But what did we hear? Some say we heard the Ten Commandments; others say we heard only the first two, those commandments in the first person. Still others say all God spoke was the first word—*Anokhi* (I); just that word alone was so powerful, we couldn't withstand the intensity. Finally, others teach that all we heard was the first letter of the first word: the silent *alef*.

The content of revelation is revelation itself; then a person writes down the story. Each of us heard God in his or her own way. Each of us tells the story. As we tell the story we discover that there is a Torah of our lives as well as a Torah of tradition.

All theology is autobiography. As we tell our own stories we often discover the divinity that is present in our lives. And if we listen carefully, we hear our stories as part of the cosmic Jewish stories.

Listen: as we struggle with narrow places in our lives—we find ourselves in *mitzrayim* (the Hebrew word meaning Egypt that comes from the root "narrow place"). A moment of clarity as we wrestle with a problem whose solution has eluded us—we find ourselves at Sinai. The child we prayed for is born—we find ourselves echoing the words of Hannah: "For this child I prayed" (I Samuel 1:27). We hit bottom, our world feels destroyed—the words of Lamentations artic- ulate our pain. *Yetziat mitzrayim* (the going out from the narrow place, from Egypt), *matan torah* (the giving of Torah), exile and re- demption, alienation and *teshuva* (returning), returning to God— these stories are our stories.

The kids are ready now. We race off to temple. I see some people I haven't seen for a long time. The child who became Bar Mitzvah over a year ago is already a young man, the woman who knocked on my of- fice door furtively one afternoon without an appointment to share her story of spousal abuse was there without her husband.

I recall my last conversations with each of them. The boy, strug- gling with the challenges of adolescence, had discovered through his Torah portion in the Book of Numbers that he could be like Joshua and Caleb and face his fears or he could be like the other ten scouts from *Shelach Lekha* and say: "The land out there looks good, but the other people are so much stronger than we are. We look like grasshoppers to ourselves" (Numbers 13:33). That insight gave him an empowering moment of clarity, even though it didn't change his situation.

The woman told me that it was only after really hearing the story of Abraham's harsh treatment of Hagar a year ago Rosh Hashana that she had been able to confess her secret. Naming her pain was the beginning of finding the courage to change her life.

As I look out over the congregation, I don't see disembodied souls. I see mothers and fathers, aging great-grandparents, grown children—all of them with their own stories created out of the vows and obligations of their lives.

Many have shared those stories with me, stories of liberation from the Egypts of their lives, stories of the courage it took to leap into the forbidding seas of their lives, only to discover that the waters parted before them.

There are also stories of loss, the middle-aged woman whose husband left her for a younger colleague, surprised to see her pain echoed in the words of a psalm; the older woman afraid of chemotherapy, breathing in and out the words of the *Shema* as she imagined the healing liquid entering her veins.

And there are so many more stories I don't know. Many of these congregants come to temple only on Rosh Hashana and Yom Kippur. Something about being Jewish pulls at them, draws them closer, but not enough to make a deeper connection. Perhaps they have yet to discover the Torah of their lives.

> For this commandment which I command you this day is not too hard for you, nor too remote. It is not in heaven that you should say: "Who will go up for us to heaven and bring it down to us, that we may do it." Nor is it beyond the sea that you should say: "Who will cross the sea for us and bring it over to us that we may do it?" No, it is very near to you, in your mouth and in your heart and you can do it. (Deuteronomy 30:11-14)

On Yom Kippur morning we stand again at Sinai, hearing the voice that comes not from heaven, but from the quiet place inside of us. The Torah we receive is the Torah of our lives, the divinity we encounter

in our relationships with other people, the holiness of our own stories. Knowing that each of our stories is part of the Jewish story gives
us the power and the confidence to claim our tradition. We were
there; we can discover what God wants from us, we can learn how to
create lives of meaning and purpose.

It is not too hard for us, not something we must leave to experts or
even rabbis. It is not just for people who are fluent in Hebrew and
know all the words of prayer. It is part of each one of us because we
were there, the one who chops wood and the one who draws water,
the one who drives car pool and the one who makes dinner. It is in
our mouths and our hearts—and we can do it.

Before *kol nidre* begins, many congregants take off their shoes. It is
a new *minhag* (custom) that grows out of the prohibition against
wearing leather, a sign of adornment. Although many Reform Jews
don't observe this prohibition, the symbolism of taking off our shoes
remains powerful. We spend the day in synagogue; we have no place
to go—we don't need shoes. We are on the one hand like corpses and
on the other hand like angels—neither wear shoes. We face the possibility of our own death, untying all our social roles.

Yom Kippur morning, shoes again untied, we are confronted in the
Torah portion with a choice:

> I call heaven and earth to witness against you this day that I have
> set beside you life or death, blessing or curse: choose life, therefore,
> that you and your descendants may live—by loving the Lord your
> God, listening to God's voice and holding fast to the One who is
> your life and the length of your days. Then you shall endure in the
> land which the Lord promised to your fathers Abraham Isaac and
> Jacob. (Deuteronomy 30:19–20)

What kind of a choice is this, life or death, blessing or curse? Who
wouldn't choose life?

But have we chosen life? Are we truly alive or living a kind of
death, stuck in the *mitzrayim,* the narrow places, of our lives? Are we
alive to the holiness of our lives, the moments of wonder, the surprise
of listening to God's voice in the laughter of a child, the challenge of
God's voice as we listen to a homeless person's cry for help or to the
pain in our own families?

Choose life—by loving God, our Torah teaches. But it doesn't really tell us how. Standing there in our stocking feet at the end of the Torah portion, we know the questions to ask. We know the answers are close to us—in our hearts and minds and in our own stories—but the answers are still ephemeral.

Then we hear the words of the *Haftara*, clear and unwavering.

God says: Cry aloud, do not hold back, let your voice resound like a *shofar:* declare to My people their transgression and to the house of Jacob their sin. Yes, they seek Me daily as though eager to learn My ways as if they were a nation that does what is right and has not forsaken the teachings of its God.

They ask of Me the right way as though eager for the nearness of God. When we fast you say why do You pay no heed? Why, when we afflict ourselves, do You take no notice?

Because on your fast days you think only of your business and oppress all your workers! Because your fasting leads only to strife and discord and hitting out with cruel fist! Such a way of fasting on this day will not help you to be heard on high.

Is this the fast that I look for? A day of self-affliction? Bowing your head like a reed and covering yourself with sackcloth and ashes? Is this what you call a fast, a day acceptable to the Lord? Is not this the fast that I look for: to unlock the shackles of injustice, to undo the fetters of bondage, to let the oppressed go free and to break every cruel chain? Is it not to share your bread with the hungry and to bring the homeless poor into your house? When you see the naked to clothe them and never to hide your face from your own kin? (Isaiah 58:1–14)

"How do we love God?" asks the Torah portion. The answer of the *Haftara* is unequivocal: by unlocking the shackles of injustice, undoing the fetters of bondage, letting the oppressed go free. The prophet continues: by sharing our bread with the hungry and bringing the homeless poor into our houses.

The Torah portion begins with us standing together in community, a community that includes each one of us. It brings us back to Sinai, where we each heard the silent *alef*. It empowers us to write the Torah of our lives. We fashion our own stories out of our vows and promises, tying our lives to other people in our families. But that is only the beginning.

Our personal stories become the story of community, of responsibility to other people who need our help. Our stories are linked to the larger Jewish story of *tikkun olam,* the challenge to repair what is broken in the world. That's what it means to choose life, for ourselves and our descendants.

Yom Kippur has its own rhythm. From the loosening of our shoes and our vows at *Kol Nidre,* we slowly reconstruct our lives. The process begins in the morning as we claim our place in the story—we were there at Sinai, we are here now, listening to the Torah of our own lives.

We ask what God wants of us, and as we begin to tie together the loose ends of our lives, the circle expands beyond our own story to the larger community, the broken world calling us to *tikkun,* to repair.

There is still more to come. *Yizkor* (the memorial prayer), wresting a final amen from those who have come before us; afternoon Torah, demanding of us that we be holy; then the story of Jonah, who, like us, reluctantly leaves the claustrophobic belly of the big fish that resembles our synagogue crowded with people, to struggle with the possibility of change. There is the *Avoda* service, the story we tell about the old days when it seemed so easy to believe, and the martyrology, the horrific tale of those who died because they were Jews.

Finally there is *Ne'ila,* the closing service, the locking of the gates. *Ne'ila* is also the word for "tying," as in the tying of shoes.

This long day has moved us from death to life, from disembodied souls to people with stories that radiate out into larger and larger circles. We have retied our vows and our bonds, spoken the promises that create family and community. We are ready to put on our shoes, to venture outside into the broken world with the courage and the faith that we can make a difference.

Exhausted (but exhilarated), I, like all the other mothers, wives, and daughters, gather my family together to head home to break the fast. I feel ready to face the New Year and to recommit myself to the vows that make up the fabric of a life full of challenge and blessing.

"The Fast I Have Chosen"
(Isaiah 57:14–58:14)

HAFTARA READING—MORNING SERVICE

14And He will say:
Cast ye up, cast ye up, clear the way,
Take up the stumblingblock out of the way of My people.
15For thus saith the High and Lofty One

That inhabiteth eternity, whose name is Holy:
I dwell in the high and holy place,
With him also that is of a contrite and humble spirit,
To revive the spirit of the humble,
And to revive the heart of the contrite ones.
16For I will not contend for ever,
Neither will I be always wroth;
For the spirit that enwrappeth itself is from Me,
And the souls which I have made.
17For the iniquity of his covetousness was I wroth and smote him,
I hid Me and was wroth;
And he went on frowardly in the way of his heart.
18I have seen his ways, and will heal him;
I will lead him also, and requite with comforts him and his mourners.
19Peace, peace, to him that is far off and to him that is near,
Saith the Lord that createth the fruit of the lips;
And I will heal him.
20But the wicked are like the troubled sea;
For it cannot rest,
And its waters cast up mire and dirt.
21There is no peace,
Saith my God concerning the wicked.

14 וַיֹּאמַר
סֹלּוּ־סֹלּוּ פַּנּוּ־דָרֶךְ
הָרִימוּ מִכְשׁוֹל מִדֶּרֶךְ עַמִּי:

15 כִּי כֹה אָמַר רָם וְנִשָּׂא
שֹׁכֵן עַד וְקָדוֹשׁ שְׁמוֹ
מָרוֹם וְקָדוֹשׁ אֶשְׁכּוֹן
וְאֶת־דַּכָּא וּשְׁפַל־רוּחַ
לְהַחֲיוֹת רוּחַ שְׁפָלִים
וּלְהַחֲיוֹת לֵב נִדְכָּאִים:

16 כִּי לֹא לְעוֹלָם אָרִיב
וְלֹא לָנֶצַח אֶקְצוֹף
כִּי־רוּחַ מִלְּפָנַי יַעֲטוֹף
וּנְשָׁמוֹת אֲנִי עָשִׂיתִי:

17 בַּעֲוֹן בִּצְעוֹ
קָצַפְתִּי וְאַכֵּהוּ הַסְתֵּר וְאֶקְצֹף
וַיֵּלֶךְ שׁוֹבָב בְּדֶרֶךְ לִבּוֹ:

18 דְּרָכָיו רָאִיתִי וְאֶרְפָּאֵהוּ
וְאַנְחֵהוּ וַאֲשַׁלֵּם נִחֻמִים לוֹ וְלַאֲבֵלָיו:

19 בּוֹרֵא נִוב שְׂפָתָיִם
שָׁלוֹם שָׁלוֹם לָרָחוֹק וְלַקָּרוֹב
אָמַר יְהוָה וּרְפָאתִיו:

20 וְהָרְשָׁעִים כַּיָּם נִגְרָשׁ
כִּי הַשְׁקֵט לֹא יוּכָל
וַיִּגְרְשׁוּ מֵימָיו רֶפֶשׁ וָטִיט:

21 אֵין שָׁלוֹם
אָמַר אֱלֹהַי לָרְשָׁעִים:

265

58 Cry aloud, spare not,
Lift up thy voice like a horn,
And declare unto My people their
transgression,
And to the house of Jacob their
sins.
²Yet they seek Me daily,
And delight to know My ways;
As a nation that did righteousness,
And forsook not the ordinance of
their God,
They ask of Me righteous ordi-
nances,
They delight to draw near unto God.

³'Wherefore have we fasted, and
Thou seest not?
Wherefore have we afflicted our
soul, and Thou takest no knowl-
edge?'—
Behold, in the day of your fast ye
pursue your business,
And exact all your labours.
⁴Behold, ye fast for strife and con-
tention,
And to smite with the fist of wicked-
ness;
Ye fast not this day
So as to make your voice to be
heard on high.
⁵Is such the fast that I have chosen?
The day for a man to afflict his
soul?
Is it to bow down his head as a bul-
rush,
And to spread sackcloth and ashes
under him?
Wilt thou call this a fast,
And an acceptable day to the
LORD?
⁶Is not this the fast that I have
chosen?
To loose the fetters of wickedness,
To undo the bands of the yoke,
And to let the oppressed go free,
And that ye break every yoke?
⁷Is it not to deal thy bread to the
hungry,
And that thou bring the poor that
are cast out to thy house?

א קְרָא בְגָרוֹן אַל־תַּחְשֹׂךְ
כַּשּׁוֹפָר הָרֵם קוֹלֶךָ
וְהַגֵּד לְעַמִּי פִּשְׁעָם
וּלְבֵית יַעֲקֹב חַטֹּאתָם׃

ב וְאוֹתִי יוֹם ׀ יוֹם יִדְרֹשׁוּן
וְדַעַת דְּרָכַי יֶחְפָּצוּן
כְּגוֹי אֲשֶׁר־צְדָקָה עָשָׂה
וּמִשְׁפַּט אֱלֹהָיו לֹא עָזָב
יִשְׁאָלוּנִי מִשְׁפְּטֵי־צֶדֶק
קִרְבַת אֱלֹהִים יֶחְפָּצוּן׃

ג לָמָּה צַּמְנוּ וְלֹא רָאִיתָ
עִנִּינוּ נַפְשֵׁנוּ וְלֹא תֵדָע
הֵן בְּיוֹם צֹמְכֶם תִּמְצְאוּ־חֵפֶץ
וְכָל־עַצְּבֵיכֶם תִּנְגֹּשׂוּ׃

ד הֵן לְרִיב וּמַצָּה תָּצוּמוּ
וּלְהַכּוֹת בְּאֶגְרֹף רֶשַׁע
לֹא־תָצוּמוּ כַיּוֹם
לְהַשְׁמִיעַ בַּמָּרוֹם קוֹלְכֶם׃

ה הֲכָזֶה יִהְיֶה צוֹם אֶבְחָרֵהוּ
יוֹם עַנּוֹת אָדָם נַפְשׁוֹ
הֲלָכֹף כְּאַגְמֹן רֹאשׁוֹ
וְשַׂק וָאֵפֶר יַצִּיעַ
הֲלָזֶה תִּקְרָא־צוֹם
וְיוֹם רָצוֹן לַיהֹוָה׃

ו הֲלוֹא זֶה צוֹם אֶבְחָרֵהוּ
פַּתֵּחַ חַרְצֻבּוֹת רֶשַׁע
הַתֵּר אֲגֻדּוֹת מוֹטָה
וְשַׁלַּח רְצוּצִים חָפְשִׁים
וְכָל־מוֹטָה תְּנַתֵּקוּ׃

When thou seest the naked, that
thou cover him,
And that thou hide not thyself
from thine own flesh?
⁸Then shall thy light break forth
as the morning,
And thy healing shall spring forth
speedily;

And thy righteousness shall go
before thee,
The glory of the LORD shall be thy
rearward.
⁹Then shalt thou call, and the LORD
will answer;
Thou shalt cry, and He will say:
'Here I am.'
If thou take away from the midst
of thee the yoke,
The putting forth of the finger, and
speaking wickedness;
¹⁰And if thou draw out thy soul to
the hungry,
And satisfy the afflicted soul;
Then shall thy light rise in darkness,
And thy gloom be as the noon-
day;
¹¹And the LORD will guide thee continually,
And satisfy thy soul in drought,
And make strong thy bones;
And thou shalt be like a watered
garden,
And like a spring of water, whose
waters fail not.
¹²And they that shall be of thee shall
build the old waste places,
Thou shalt raise up the foundations
of many generations;
And thou shalt be called The
repairer of the breach,
The restorer of paths to dwell in.
¹³If thou turn away thy foot because
of the sabbath,
From pursuing thy business on My
holy day;
And call the sabbath a delight,
And the holy of the LORD honour-
able;
And shalt honour it, not doing thy
wonted ways,

הֲלוֹא פָרֹס לָרָעֵב לַחְמֶךָ ⁷
וַעֲנִיִּים מְרוּדִים תָּבִיא בָיִת
כִּי־תִרְאֶה עָרֹם וְכִסִּיתוֹ
וּמִבְּשָׂרְךָ לֹא תִתְעַלָּם:
אָז יִבָּקַע כַּשַּׁחַר אוֹרֶךָ ⁸
וַאֲרֻכָתְךָ מְהֵרָה תִצְמָח
וְהָלַךְ לְפָנֶיךָ צִדְקֶךָ
כְּבוֹד יְהֹוָה יַאַסְפֶךָ:
אָז תִּקְרָא וַיהֹוָה יַעֲנֶה ⁹
תְּשַׁוַּע וְיֹאמַר הִנֵּנִי
אִם־תָּסִיר מִתּוֹכְךָ מוֹטָה
שְׁלַח אֶצְבַּע וְדַבֶּר־אָוֶן:

וְתָפֵק לָרָעֵב נַפְשֶׁךָ ¹⁰
וְנֶפֶשׁ נַעֲנָה תַּשְׂבִּיעַ
וְזָרַח בַּחֹשֶׁךְ אוֹרֶךָ
וַאֲפֵלָתְךָ כַּצָּהֳרָיִם:

וְנָחֲךָ יְהֹוָה תָּמִיד ¹¹
וְהִשְׂבִּיעַ בְּצַחְצָחוֹת נַפְשֶׁךָ
וְעַצְמֹתֶיךָ יַחֲלִיץ
וְהָיִיתָ כְּגַן רָוֶה
וּכְמוֹצָא מַיִם אֲשֶׁר לֹא־יְכַזְּבוּ מֵימָיו:
וּבָנוּ מִמְּךָ חָרְבוֹת עוֹלָם ¹²
מוֹסְדֵי דוֹר־וָדוֹר תְּקוֹמֵם
וְקֹרָא לְךָ גֹּדֵר פֶּרֶץ
מְשֹׁבֵב נְתִיבוֹת לָשָׁבֶת:

אִם־תָּשִׁיב מִשַּׁבָּת רַגְלֶךָ ¹³
עֲשׂוֹת חֲפָצֶיךָ בְּיוֹם קָדְשִׁי
וְקָרָאתָ לַשַּׁבָּת עֹנֶג
לִקְדוֹשׁ יְהֹוָה מְכֻבָּד
וְכִבַּדְתּוֹ מֵעֲשׂוֹת דְּרָכֶיךָ

267

Nor pursuing thy business, nor
speaking thereof;
[14]Then shalt thou delight thyself in
the LORD,

And I will make thee to ride upon
the high places of the earth,
And I will feed thee with the heritage of Jacob thy father;
For the mouth of the LORD hath
spoken it.

מִמְּצוֹא חֶפְצְךָ וְדַבֵּר דָּבָר:

14 אָז תִּתְעַנַּג עַל־יְהֹוָה

וְהִרְכַּבְתִּיךָ עַל־בָּמֳתֵי אָרֶץ

וְהַאֲכַלְתִּיךָ נַחֲלַת יַעֲקֹב אָבִיךָ

כִּי פִּי יְהֹוָה דִּבֵּר:

Repentance, Responsibility, and Regeneration: Reflections on Isaiah

ALICE SHALVI

I

THE SYNAGOGUE is filled to capacity, particularly because we will soon be reciting the *Yizkor* (memorial prayer for the dead), a prayer that resonates with every Jew who has ever lost a parent. Once again we have chorused the confessional prayers, admitting—in the collective first-person plural, not merely as individuals, but as a people— that we have committed an appallingly comprehensive range of sins. We have beaten our breasts in rhythm to the alphabetically arranged transgressions: *ashamnu, bagadnu*—"We are guilty, we have betrayed, we have robbed . . ." Over and over again, we have begged to be forgiven for evil deeds and evil thoughts. We have listened to the Torah portion describing the sacrifices performed by Aaron the priest—sacrifices that conclude with the dispatch into the desert of the scapegoat laden with the sins of an entire nation. From the final section of the reading we have learned that this is the day on which— if we duly fast and subject our bodies to physical deprivation, mortifying the flesh—God will cleanse us of our sins.

But then the impassioned words of Isaiah burst upon our ears, clarifying what God *really* expects of us, what will and what will not suffice to satisfy God's terms for redemption. The lowly and humble in spirit, the truly contrite, will be revived, the mourners consoled with words of comfort, but for the wicked there is no safety.

II

One of the critical questions raised by this *Haftara* is what constitutes wickedness. For the people of Israel as they are described here, unlike the people of Nineveh, of whom we shall read later in the day when we come to the Book of Jonah, have not abandoned religious practice. On the contrary, they are eager to learn God's ways, eager for the "nearness of God." They starve their bodies on fast days, bow their heads in penitence like bulrushes before the wind, even lie in sackcloth and ashes. They engage in precisely such mortification of the flesh and affliction of the soul as the Torah portion has prescribed.

Yet Isaiah indicates that such outward show, such purely physical scourging of the body, is not the penitence God requires. *True contrition expresses itself in action designed to relieve the suffering of others.* He spells this out quite explicitly: it is "to let the oppressed go free" (58:6), specifically (as 58:3 indicates), to refrain from exploiting our servants and subordinates; not to fast, but rather to share our bread with the hungry; not to lie in ashes, but rather to take the wretched poor into our home; not to wear sackcloth, but to clothe the naked; not to be concerned solely with self, but to care for our kith and kin. In other words, God is more concerned with our behavior to other human beings, particularly those less fortunate than ourselves, than with acts of self-abasement designed to impress the Deity.

The structure and syntax of the text foreground the cause and effect of redemption: *when* we fulfill our duties to our fellow beings, perform the *mitzvot bein adam lechavero* (injunctions governing our behavior to others), *then* shall we achieve personal and national redemption.

An image of dawning light penetrating nightime gloom and midday sunshine replacing the dark, joy replacing sorrow (58:10), ushers in a further series of similes and metaphors that rise to a superb crescendo. The object of redemption becomes, in turn, a redeeming force. From being at first succored, with thirst slaked, like a watered garden whose withered blooms are restored to freshness, the people of Israel will themselves become an eternal source of life-giving water.

> The Lord will guide you always:
> He will slake your thirst in parched places
> And give strength to your bones.
> You shall be like a watered garden,
> Like a spring whose waters do not fail. (58:11)

With vigor renewed, the revived become revivers; restored, they will in turn restore:

> Men from your midst shall rebuild ancient ruins,
> You shall restore foundations laid long ago.
> And you shall be called
> "Repairer of fallen walls,
> Restorer of lanes for habitation." (58:12)

The transformative nature of redemption is not confined to one generation. Those who give shall, in turn, receive. The interpersonal, even intergenerational, nature of righteous living is what is primarily conveyed by Isaiah's inspired and inspiring prophecies.

III

Only after this soaringly lyrical passage, with its promise of what will result from proper observance of God's injunctions to behave humanely to our fellow human beings, does the prophet turn to the commandments that govern our relations with God (*mitzvot bein adam lamakom*). Now, as we might have guessed given the opening of the *Haftara,* it is not fasting, prayer, or sacrifice that are stressed. Significantly (to my mind), the commandment to which Isaiah relates almost specifically, even exclusively, is observance of the Sabbath. Unlike the other commandments in this God-related category, which stress the principle of monotheism and rejection of idolatry, the commandment of Sabbath observance is one that, when obeyed, brings palpable comfort and delight to the observers themselves. The weekly day of rest provides a relief from tension, a calm of mind, and relaxation of body that can be obtained only from the total setting aside of daily tasks, physical labors, financial transactions, and negotiations— the "getting and spending" that "lay waste our powers." No wonder it is said that the Sabbath was made for humans, not humans for the Sabbath.

In singling out this one practice, Isaiah (expressing God's promise) once again stresses the transformational nature of the observance of God's commandments. Since, in observing the Sabbath, we are imitating God, who also rested from His labors on the seventh day, it follows that this practice will be rewarded by we ourselves becoming godlike. The *Haftara* began with a description of God as *"high aloft . . . dwell[ing] on high."* Coming full circle, it ends with the promise that we too will be *"set astride the heights of the earth,"* not only rewarded with the fulfillment of God's territorial promises to our forefathers, but also, one may presume, spiritually uplifted to a state of heavenly bliss.

IV

In its stress on correct interpersonal relations as a vital and essential accompaniment to ritual worship, in fact even more important than the latter if we are to achieve redemption, the Yom Kippur *Haftara* enlarges upon one of the central messages of Rosh Hashana prayer, in the course of which we are assured that severe judgment and retribution for our sins can be averted by penitence (*teshuva*), prayer (*tefila*), and charity (*tzedaka*). The object (or target) of each of these activities is different.

Teshuva demands honest self-scrutiny and reflection. It is a process between me and my *own self.*

Tefila embodies my relationship with *God.*

Tzedaka regulates my relationship with my *fellow human beings.*

Together, these three elements—the individual, the divine, the societal—constitute our entire existence as believing beings.

None of these prescribed activities can *alone* bring redemption and renewal. It is precisely the combination of all of them and, most particularly, the practice of *tzedaka,* that the Yom Kippur *Haftara* presents as a model of human behavior. In that lies the essence and uniqueness of Judaism. For its part, the uniqueness of Yom Kippur is to be found in the way in which it provides an annual opportunity for us to combine the three elements of human existence and the three related activities, through a mortification of the flesh, which symbolizes penitence, and through prayer, which ideally combines confession of past sins with firm resolution to mend our behavior in everything relating to everyday human relations.

Jewish prayer has been formulated and codified in post-Biblical times, so that we regularly pray in a language and a fixed form that have been established for centuries and are to be found in our prayer books. Indeed, the very names of those books—*siddur* (order) and *machzor* (cycle)—stress the recurrent nature of Jewish liturgy, which is far from the improvisation and spontaneity of, for example, Methodist or Quaker practice.

Nevertheless, Jewish tradition allows for the very human desire for personal expression; for a variety of historic reasons, women have been the main beneficiaries of this awareness of personal needs. Even in the standard, fixed, and obligatory Hebrew liturgy, the central prayer, the *Amida,* which is couched throughout in the plural form, has a coda in the first person, which was originally a *techine,* a supplication, that was later incorporated into the canon.

Because women were excluded from public prayer and because they frequently lacked the skills (or the time) for reciting the standard prayers at their fixed times—and were, indeed, benevolently (?) exempted from the performance of such time-bound commandments—substitutes were created, usually in the vernacular, which related specifically to those commandments that are exclusive to women: *ner,* the kindling of the lights that usher in the Sabbath or a holy day; *challa,* the setting aside of a portion of dough in memory of the tithe paid to priests in Temple times; and *nidda* (marital separation during menstruation and ritual immersion after menstruation). Additional *techines* were created for pregnancy and childbirth. Many of these prayers appear to have been composed by women themselves. All of them make it possible for the reciter to insert her own name or other personal details—something for which the fixed liturgy does not provide.[1]

Today, when we are no longer confined to *Kinder,* and *Küche,* women can follow suit, to make the set liturgy more meaningful by adding their own improvised prayer to the standard ones. And because women are, on the whole, more concerned with personal and interpersonal relations, because they are linked so closely with the social issues that form the web of our daily lives, the precept and practice of *tzedaka* are probably the most natural theme for a woman's supplicatory prayer of repentance and resolution.

What I offer here is a personal version both of the recurring *al cheit* (For the sins . . .) and of *avinu malkeinu* (Our Father, our King . . .), the moving supplication with which we end the *Ne'ila* (closing) service before the gates of heaven close for another year.

A Techine for Yom Kippur

O God, creator of Heaven and Earth, creator of humankind and of all living things, grant me the power to feel as others feel, the power to listen and to hear, to behold and truly see, to touch and be touched.

Keep fresh within me the memory of my own suffering and the suffering of *clal yisrael* (the whole community), not in order to stimulate eternal paranoia, but rather that I may better understand the suffering of strangers; and may that understanding lead me to do everything in my power to alleviate and to prevent such suffering.

When I see streams of refugees bearing the pathetic belongings they have salvaged from ruined homes, may I recall the wanderings of the people of Israel and may I vow never to be the cause of loss and homelessness.

Enable me to be like Yourself—to feed the hungry, clothe the naked, tend the sick, comfort the bereaved. Guide me in the ways of *tikkun olam,* of mending the world. As I delight in a loving marriage of true minds, may I never forget the thousands of women battered and beaten by their spouses. As I rejoice in the bliss of my children and grandchildren, may I never forget the pleading eyes and swollen bellies of starving infants deprived of physical and emotional nourishment. May my woman's capacities for concern, compassion, and caring never be dulled by complacency or personal contentment. May my feelings always lead me to act.

Grant me the wisdom to discern what is right and what is wrong and inspire me with the courage to speak out whenever I see injustice, without shame or fear of personal retribution. Enable me to feel pity even for my enemies. Grant me the will and the ability to be a peacemaker, so that the day may soon come when all peoples will live in friendship and your tabernacle of peace will be spread over all the dwellers on earth. Amen.

God and God of our ancestors, forgive me my sins of pride and conceit, my obtuseness to the needs, desires, and ambitions of others, my lack of empathy, my ignorance and obliviousness to all that is going on in the world save what is directly related to my own experience and that of the Jewish people. Forgive us our arrogance and narrowness of vision; forgive us our readiness to inflict pain on those who have hurt us. Make us whole, make us holy.

Yom Kippur 1996

RACHEL COWAN

DURING the Days of Awe, the *shofar* calls us to awaken. Look up, think fresh, answer God's question to Adam in the Garden of Eden—*Ayeka?* Where are you? That call is sounded in a different mode by Isaiah in the magnificent *Haftara* read on Yom Kippur morning.

To what are we summoned? On one level, of course, we are called to personal *teshuva* (repentance). Tradition makes time for us to do the vitally important work of repairing our relations with each other, of reflecting on the year that has passed, of redirecting our lives so we will come closer to being who we want to be.

On another level, though, we are called to reexamine our soul. Today we have the time and occasion to reflect, to feel, to deepen our relationship to the spirit that is larger than all of us, deeper than all of us, within all of us, and within the cosmos. It is better to talk about it, however awkwardly, than to let it slide by another year. Let's take this opportunity to try to articulate our experience of the sacred.

The poetry of the liturgy is a wonderful tool, giving us multiple metaphors: we are clay in the hands of the potter, a vineyard guarded by a watchman; passing shadows; our days are as grass, we flourish as flowers in a field, and the wind passes over us and we are gone; the soul is Yours, the body is Your creation. But we are not passive. We are created in the image of God. We cannot limit our search for meaning to the borders of our individual domains. Our sense of our own lives is most complete when integrated with an understanding of the larger whole. We can open ourselves to the spirit that is both underlying and overarching.

Isaiah calls us to be much grander, much more powerful, yet much deeper and more humble than we imagine ourselves to be. This essential message is elaborated in a text written by Rabbi Abraham Isaac Kook, the first Ashkenazic Chief Rabbi of Eretz Israel, a true *tzaddik* (righteous person), who made *aliya* (immigrated) to Jerusalem in 1904, where he lived until his death in 1935. It is called "A Fourfold Song."

Rav Kook built his text by letting each stanza of the song well up from the one that precedes it. I have regendered his language so that it speaks clearly about all of us.

There is one who sings the song of her own life, and in herself she finds everything, her full spiritual satisfaction.

There is another who sings the song of his people. He leaves the circle of his own individual self, because he finds it without sufficient breadth, without an idealistic basis. He aspires toward the heights, and attaches himself with a gentle love to the whole community of Israel. Together with her, he sings her songs. He feels grieved in her afflictions and delights in her hopes. He contemplates noble and pure thoughts about her past and her future, and robes with love and wisdom her inner spiritual essence.

There is another who reaches toward more distant realms, and she goes beyond the boundary of Israel to sing the song of humanity. Her spirit extends to the wider vistas of the majesty of humanity generally, and its noble essence. She aspires towards humanity's general goal and looks forward to its higher perfection. From this source of life she draws the subjects of her meditation and study, her aspirations and visions.

Then there is one who rises towards wider horizons, until he links himself with all existence, with all God's creatures, with all worlds, and he sings his song with all of them. It is of one such as this that tradition has said that whoever sings a portion of song each day is assured of having a share in the world to come.

And then there is one who rises with all these songs in one ensemble, and they all join their voices. Together they sing their songs with beauty, each one lends vitality and life to the other. They are sounds of joy and gladness, sounds of jubilation and celebration, sounds of ecstasy and holiness.

The song of the self, the song of the people, the song of humanity, the song of the world all merge in her at all times, in every hour.

And this full comprehensiveness rises to become the song of holiness, the song of God, the song of Israel, in its full strength and beauty, in its full authenticity and greatness. The name "Israel" stands for *shir el,* the song of God. It is a simple song, a twofold song, a threefold song and a fourfold song.

It is the Song of Songs of Solomon, *shlomo,* whose name means peace or wholeness. It is the song of the Sovereign in whom is wholeness.

I believe that the point of the High Holy Days is to coach us into trying to sing that song—to aspire to hold in our hearts a vision and sense of self that transcends our worried, work-driven lives. And I believe that the Yom Kippur *Haftara* is one voice singing it loudly, echoing through time.

When the Rabbis gave Isaiah 57–58 center stage in the High Holy Day liturgy, they conveyed a vision akin to Rav Kook's. Well into the Day of Atonement, we have been focusing on ourselves—fasting, afflicting ourselves, confessing, humbling ourselves, criticizing ourselves. By now we are feeling discouraged, disempowered, self-absorbed. We are taking self-criticism a little too seriously. So Isaiah comes to arouse us: awake, rise, travel out into the world, and turn it to justice. Your soul will not find peace until it is attuned with the soul of the world!

Just to make sure we get the message, the Rabbis inserted the Book of Jonah toward the end of our liturgy, just before *Ne'ila* (the closing service). Jonah is the reluctant prophet of universalism. He teaches us that however deeply we travel into our souls, we must travel as widely out into the world.

I believe that Isaiah calls us to sing Rav Kook's "song of *Shlomo.*" It is not an easy one to sing. On the level of our individual lives, on the level of the Jewish people, on the level of the world as a whole, there is so much to criticize, and there are so many unfulfilled dreams of perfection. And on the level of the cosmos, of eternity, we have so many doubts, such lack of clarity about what we believe, and such skepticism that any ethical core is operating. We have to sing the song as aspiration and as inspiration. It can help us recognize the sacred in the profane, the extraordinary in the mundane, the holiness of detail. Isaiah helps us to sing the song of *Shlomo.*

And he shows us that the song of the self is important. He reflects to us God's care for the fate of the individual. God clearly loves us, feels for us—God dwells with the humble and contrite, God promises peace for those far and those near. But God has little patience for small-minded selves. Empty rituals, self-afflictions, don't move God.

Actions that change the real world do. Isaiah instructs us that ours is both the work of justice and the work of spirituality. Ours is the work of removing the yoke of oppression, speaking with a gentle tongue, delighting in the Sabbath. *Tikkun hanefesh,* repair of the soul, is meaningless outside a life devoted to *tikkun olam,* repair of the world.

Today, our struggle must be to find a center, to find balance between the needs of our self and the needs of others, the need for work, for beauty, for cultivating our soul. We need to grow spiritually in order to be able to link our inner selves to our people, to humanity, and to the infinite.

Our tradition offers many spiritual practices that can guide our inner growth. It is a resource that bears deep exploration. A few examples:

As we get out of bed each day, we can say the *moda ani* ("I thank you") prayer: "I am grateful to You, Sovereign of the Universe, for restoring my soul with compassion." Or we can recite Marcia Falk's new version of it: "The breath of my life will bless, the cells of my being sing in gratitude, reawakening." These blessings help us cultivate the skill of gratitude. They remind us that each day is a gift that we did not create for ourselves. Each day is a mini–Rosh Hashana, a chance to renew the center of our lives.

Before taking our first bite of food, we can say the *motzi* (the blessing over bread), connecting the gratification of our individual, specific needs with the awareness of our place in the universe. Tradition teaches that we should say one hundred blessings a day. The more we do, the more we allow gratitude room.

The *mikveh* (ritual bath) is an institution few of us ever think of using except perhaps before a wedding, certainly before a conversion. It is a spiritual treasure. It is a place of waters, a liminal space where borders melt and we can open to a new sense of ourselves as part of a sacred universe.

Jewish healing practices teach us to look for the meaning of our lives even in the midst of pain and fear. We pray for *refuat hanefesh,* healing of the soul as well as *refuat haguf,* healing of the body. They teach us to relinquish our story of suffering, to define ourselves as more than our illness, more than our loss. They teach an awareness of beauty as well as an acceptance of pain.

When we are spiritually nourished, we bring a stronger voice to the song of our people. What does Isaiah teach us about singing that song? It's interesting that this song seems as hard for God to sing as for us. God goes back and forth between wrath and compassion, between justice and mercy. God hides God's face, then offers to heal. God rages and despairs over our violations of the laws and instructions we have been given yet offers constant love and promises healing and comfort when we begin to repent. "Yet they seek me daily, and delight to know My ways. Like a nation that does what is right and forsakes not God's ordinance they ask me for righteous judgments, they delight to draw near to God."

For Isaiah, the individual exists fully within the context of a people, a nation. Our individual spirituality, our individual commitment to justice, is important because each of us bears responsibility for making our people an *am kadosh*, a holy nation.

Nowadays, when we are so focused on the individual self, individual boundaries, individual rights, we don't think much about our responsibility to the collective. But we are more than single Jews. We make up the Jewish people. And the quality of the people, and the light it brings into the world, depends on us. Our challenge is not so much overcoming parochialism or opening our eyes beyond the Jewish world. It is committing ourselves to participate in shaping the future of our people, here and in Israel.

We must, first and foremost, speak up in support of the peace process. We must let our government know that American Jews want Israel to negotiate seriously with Palestinians, that we believe peace is more important than territory. And we must let Israelis know that we care as well. We are often silent, so the minority appears the majority.

We also should be a much stronger voice in American Jewish life. Our community is becoming polarized between Orthodox and liberal, while most Jews yawn on the sidelines. They will stop yawning and join us when we stop fighting and create communities of passion and learning and caring.

As our community becomes more affluent, it is more distanced from its identification with the oppressed and vulnerable. We need to assert the centrality of Isaiah's words in our community's sense of mission. We know the needs of the hungry, the homeless, the immigrant. Though we can't solve their problems simply by collecting food and operating shelters, we must collect food and we must keep our shelters open every night. But beyond that we must urge our communal organizations to lobby for humane, progressive legislation. Our communal leaders need to know that we consider justice a central mission. Our children need to believe that they are the children of Isaiah.

Today we need to sing a more inspiring song of our people. We can sing more melodiously and more strongly when we are whole people, who work on the healing of our souls, who are anchored with a spiritual practice, who are committed to justice.

What can Isaiah teach us about singing the song of humanity? It's clear in the text:

> This is my chosen fast: to loosen all bonds that bind men unfairly, to let the oppressed go free, to break every yoke. Share your bread with the hungry, take the homeless into your home. Clothe the naked when you see him, do not turn away from people in need.

The quality of every life matters. The world is an arena in which we live, about which we care. All creatures are made in God's image, and all are important to us. Many of us live most of our lives in the secular world that we share with others. We contribute in important ways to its culture, its education, its health, its very functioning. We debate the issues it faces. We sing the song of its humanity. Our song is more melodious and more powerful when we sing it with a Jewish cadence.

What does Isaiah teach us about singing the song of the world. "For thus says the exalted One who inhabits eternity, whose name is Holy: Although I am exalted and holy, I also dwell with those who are humble and contrite, to revive the spirit of the humble and the heart of the contrite."

All is of concern to God. The eternal connects with the weakest human spirit. God inhabits eternity, God is infinite. God's domain is everywhere. As individuals, as Jews, as human beings, we are part of creation, we are not masters of creation. We have the Sabbath to remind us of our place in the world. We are stewards of this earth, an endangered planet. We can sing the song of the cosmos, but our song will be more melodious, more harmonious, if we sing it as many peoples working together to preserve, to rescue, and to restore God's creation.

How can we make our song stronger and clearer, yet also our own? We can sing it if our own spiritual practice opens us to a love of our own tradition and our own people, a compassion for humanity, and a sense of our integration into an eternal unity—which I call God— even if that sense is only partial, only momentary.

And Isaiah is saying we don't have to do that work alone. God yearns for us to open ourselves, to turn to God. His words offer us comfort, for sometimes we feel so alone:

> Do not turn away from people in need. Then cleansing light shall break forth like the dawn, and your wounds shall soon be healed. Your triumph shall go before you and the Lord's glory shall be your rearguard. Then you shall call and the Lord will answer: you shall cry out and God will say, *"Hineni,* Here I am."

Yom Kippur Afternoon
Introduction

THE TORAH and *Haftara* readings are the very core of the *mincha* (afternoon) service of Yom Kippur. Yet of all the Biblical texts chosen by the Rabbis of the Talmud for recitation during the Days of Awe, no selection seems more puzzling than Leviticus 18 and none more appropriate than the Book of Jonah.

Leviticus 18 begins with God's command to the Israelite people to avoid the practices of the Egyptians with whom they had dwelled and of the Canaanites to whose land God was bringing them. It is God's laws alone that they must follow. But this preamble to the articulation of a new set of laws does not specifically prepare us for the particular laws that follow. A detailed catalog of forbidden sexual relationships, including various forms of incest, adultery, male homosexuality, bestiality, and relations with a menstruating woman, the chapter focuses on a series of "abominations" that the people are warned to neither commit nor tolerate in their midst.

Traditional explanations for why this particular chapter was chosen for the afternoon reading range from the historical to the allegorical. Some suggest that it is rooted in ancient practice wherein the afternoon of Yom Kippur was a festive time, celebrated by young women with joyous dancing intended to catch the attention of young men in search of brides. While these activities were encouraged by the community, the Torah portion was chosen to caution the young not to lose control. In a similar vein, though from a psychological rather than historical perspective, others have suggested that this text was chosen to warn against the tendency toward excess and abandon that often follows periods of strict abstinence.

While for some commentators the experience of late Yom Kippur afternoon is mainly one of release, for others the afternoon service is central to the day's continuing prayers for forgiveness. These com-

mentators understand the selection of Leviticus 18 for the Torah reading as a reminder rather than a warning. As the day wanes, this particular catalog of sins may stir the listener to further repentance. As
the medieval commentator Rashi writes, "Since all people are subject
to strong passions from time to time, they should hear this chapter
and repent in case they have sinned in this manner" (Megilla 31a).

Yet another traditional explanation for the relationship between
this particular reading and Yom Kippur is that the reading is an implied prayer. We recall the prohibitions against uncovering physical
nakedness in an attempt to move God to forgive and protect us—and
not disclose the moral nakedness of our sins.

In our own time, many congregations have found these explanations unconvincing and the chapter itself not just puzzling but disturbing, and have replaced this chapter from Leviticus with the one
that follows it. Leviticus 19 speaks of loving one's neighbor and doing justice, themes that seem more appropriate and continue the call
to repentance sounded by Isaiah in the morning's *Haftara*.

Judith Plaskow was among those who "applauded the substitution
of an alternative Torah reading until," as she writes, "a particular incident made [her] reconsider the link between sex and Yom Kippur."
That incident, really a conversation between two women, led her to
rethink the connection between *teshuva* (repentance) and reading
about sexuality on Yom Kippur. She even came to value the chapter's
"disturbing concreteness" as more profoundly challenging than the
broader, foundational precepts of Leviticus 19. But while acknowledging the importance of addressing issues of sexual responsibility
during the day on which Jews gather together to reflect on themselves as individuals and as a community, Plaskow finds the actual
content of Leviticus 18 unacceptable. Its sexual ethic, she argues, reinforces negative religious and cultural attitudes toward women generally, toward women's bodies in particular, and toward gays and
lesbians. Disturbed by the reading and yet unwilling not to read, she
suggests that the way out of the dilemma is to transform the text, to
maintain its concern with a sexual ethic while reshaping that ethic to
reflect modern values and contemporary understanding of what constitutes both justice and holiness in sexual relations. Plaskow and
members of her *chavura* (prayer community) have engaged in this task
for several years, and she shares with the reader both the process of

her community's rethinking of Leviticus 18 and sections of the new sexual ethic they are developing. For her, such efforts at transforming Torah are critical acts of "communal *teshuva,* both in relation to those who are marginalized and anathematized by Leviticus 18 and those who are abandoned when it is abandoned without considered discussion."

In the afternoon Torah reading we hear God warning the Israelites against engaging in the evil practices of other nations. But in the *Haftara* that follows, God calls to an Israelite, the prophet Jonah, to address a foreign nation, Israel's neighbor and enemy, and warn its inhabitants of the consequences of their wickedness. To ask Jonah to proclaim against Nineveh, the capital of Assyria, is to ask Israel to assume moral responsibility for others as well as for itself. Distancing oneself from the immorality of others is but a first step, the step demanded of Israel in the Torah reading. The story of Jonah comes to remind us that we must also concern ourselves with others.

In further contrast with the Torah reading, the Book of Jonah suggests that other nations can serve as a positive rather than a negative example to the Israelites. When Jonah finally appeals to the Ninevites, their response is immediate and total. That response, according to tradition, serves as a model for us to repent our sins. As we move toward the final hours of Yom Kippur, facing our last opportunity to repent, we are offered, through the *Haftara* reading, an unusual example of successful and efficacious repentance. It is not one of "us" who teaches us how to repent, but one of "them."

The story of Jonah, of course, encompasses far more than Nineveh's repentance and God's forgiveness. It is also the story of a prophet, a human who, though called by God, is nevertheless very fallible. The book begins with Jonah's attempt to avoid the prophetic call. He takes refuge on board a ship, but when he reveals to its crew that he is the cause of the storm endangering their lives, they reluctantly follow his advice and throw him overboard. God then appoints a great fish to swallow Jonah and return him to shore safely. The Hebrew word used to describe how the fish rids itself of Jonah (vomited out) is the same word used in the Torah portion to describe how the land of Israel has treated and will treat inhabitants who indulge in abominations that contaminate it. Why the fish who has dutifully harbored the prophet might feel contaminated becomes clear only later in the story, when Jonah displays his utter lack of compassion for anyone other than himself.

Devora Steinmetz heightens our sense of Jonah's lack of compassion by comparing him with two earlier prophets, Moses and Elijah. She carefully traces the ways in which each one's story echoes the others', illuminating the dilemma of the prophet who stands apart. A loner "with an extreme commitment to what is right," the prophet must learn to temper his harshness with a concern for the people. His success is inextricably connected with his ability to join others, empathize with their suffering, and care for them. Jonah fails to learn this lesson, though ironically he "brings about more change than any other Biblical prophet." Steinmetz neither glosses over this contradiction nor attempts to explain it away. Rather, she suggests that "it is the very tension between the words of Jonah and the story of Jonah that gives the book its power and . . . that makes the book ring true to us as we read it each year on the afternoon of Yom Kippur."

For Steinmetz the "troubled prophet," resistant to change in others as well as in himself, gives voice to our own doubts about our potential for transformation at this critical moment when the Day of Atonement is drawing to a close. In Rachel Adler's playful reading of Jonah, the troubled prophet is transformed into a "curmudgeon of a prophet," who though he lacks "discernible gifts either of evangelism or of charm," nevertheless manages to leave "a trail of people beating their breasts and shouting halleluyah" wherever he goes. The irony for her is decidedly comic, and her essay highlights the abundance of comic and grotesque elements in this "most carnivalesque of Biblical books." Adler provocatively proposes that "the most religious response to the reading of Jonah would be a hearty guffaw." The laughter the book is meant to provoke not only protects us from excessive browbeating, but also leads us to appreciate the utter ridiculousness of the womanless world of Jonah, epitomized in the prophet's rigidity and rejection of life. The reading of Jonah thus liberates us to join laughter to repentance and embrace "a moral universe brimming with laughter" and characterized by compassion, caring, and persistent hope.

"Do Not Uncover Their Nakedness"
(Leviticus 18)

TORAH READING—AFTERNOON SERVICE

18 And the LORD spoke unto Moses, saying: ²Speak unto the children of Israel, and say unto them:

I am the LORD your God. ³After the doings of the land of Egypt, wherein ye dwelt, shall ye not do; and after the doings of the land of Canaan, whither I bring you, shall ye not do; neither shall ye walk in their statutes.

⁴Mine ordinances shall ye do, and My statutes shall ye keep, to walk therein: I am the LORD your God. ⁵Ye shall therefore keep My statutes, and Mine ordinances, which if a man do, he shall live by them: I am the LORD.

⁶None of you shall approach to any that is near of kin to him, to uncover their nakedness: I am the LORD.

⁷The nakedness of thy father, and the nakedness of thy mother, shalt thou not uncover: she is thy mother; thou shalt not uncover her nakedness.

⁸The nakedness of thy father's wife shalt thou not uncover: it is thy father's nakedness.

⁹The nakedness of thy sister, the daughter of thy father, or the daughter of thy mother, whether born at home, or born abroad, even their nakedness thou shalt not uncover.

¹⁰The nakedness of thy son's daughter, or of thy daughter's daughter, even their nakedness thou shalt not uncover; for theirs is thine own nakedness.

¹¹The nakedness of thy father's wife's daughter, begotten of thy father, she is thy sister, thou shalt not uncover her nakedness.

¹²Thou shalt not uncover the nakedness of thy father's sister: she is thy father's near kinswoman.

א וַיְדַבֵּר יְהֹוָה אֶל־מֹשֶׁה לֵּאמְר: דַּבֵּר
ב אֶל־בְּנֵי יִשְׂרָאֵל וְאָמַרְתָּ אֲלֵהֶם אֲנִי
ג יְהֹוָה אֱלֹהֵיכֶם: כְּמַעֲשֵׂה אֶרֶץ־מִצְרַיִם
אֲשֶׁר יְשַׁבְתֶּם־בָּהּ לֹא תַעֲשׂוּ וּכְמַעֲשֵׂה
אֶרֶץ־כְּנַעַן אֲשֶׁר אֲנִי מֵבִיא אֶתְכֶם
שָׁמָּה לֹא תַעֲשׂוּ וּבְחֻקֹּתֵיהֶם לֹא תֵלֵכוּ:
ד אֶת־מִשְׁפָּטַי תַּעֲשׂוּ וְאֶת־חֻקֹּתַי תִּשְׁמְרוּ
לָלֶכֶת בָּהֶם אֲנִי יְהֹוָה אֱלֹהֵיכֶם:
ה וּשְׁמַרְתֶּם אֶת־חֻקֹּתַי וְאֶת־מִשְׁפָּטַי
אֲשֶׁר יַעֲשֶׂה אֹתָם הָאָדָם וָחַי בָּהֶם אֲנִי
ו יְהֹוָה: ס אִישׁ אִישׁ אֶל־
כָּל־שְׁאֵר בְּשָׂרוֹ לֹא תִקְרְבוּ לְגַלּוֹת
ז עֶרְוָה אֲנִי יְהֹוָה: ס עֶרְוַת
אָבִיךָ וְעֶרְוַת אִמְּךָ לֹא תְגַלֵּה אִמְּךָ הִוא
ח לֹא תְגַלֶּה עֶרְוָתָהּ: ס עֶרְוַת
אֵשֶׁת־אָבִיךָ לֹא תְגַלֵּה עֶרְוַת אָבִיךָ
ט הִוא: ס עֶרְוַת אֲחוֹתְךָ בַת־
אָבִיךָ אוֹ בַת־אִמֶּךָ מוֹלֶדֶת בַּיִת אוֹ
מוֹלֶדֶת חוּץ לֹא תְגַלֵּה עֶרְוָתָן: ס
י עֶרְוַת בַּת־בִּנְךָ אוֹ בַת־בִּתְּךָ לֹא תְגַלֶּה
עֶרְוָתָן כִּי עֶרְוָתְךָ הֵנָּה: ס
יא עֶרְוַת בַּת־אֵשֶׁת אָבִיךָ מוֹלֶדֶת אָבִיךָ
אֲחוֹתְךָ הִוא לֹא תְגַלֵּה עֶרְוָתָהּ: ס
יב עֶרְוַת אֲחוֹת־אָבִיךָ לֹא תְגַלֵּה שְׁאֵר

287

¹³Thou shalt not uncover the nakedness of thy mother's sister; for she is thy mother's near kinswoman.

¹⁴Thou shalt not uncover the nakedness of thy father's brother, thou shalt not approach to his wife: she is thine aunt.

¹⁵Thou shalt not uncover the nakedness of thy daughter-in-law: she is thy son's wife; thou shalt not uncover her nakedness.

¹⁶Thou shalt not uncover the nakedness of thy brother's wife: it is thy brother's nakedness. ¹⁷Thou shalt not uncover the nakedness of a woman and her daughter; thou shalt not take her son's daughter, or her daughter's daughter, to uncover her nakedness: they are near kinswomen; it is lewdness. ¹⁸And thou shalt not take a woman to her sister, to be a rival to her, to uncover her nakedness, beside the other in her life-time. ¹⁹And thou shalt not approach unto a woman to uncover her nakedness, as long as she is impure by her uncleanness. ²⁰And thou shalt not lie carnally with thy neighbour's wife, to defile thyself with her. ²¹And thou shalt not give any of thy seed to set them apart to Molech, neither shalt thou profane the name of thy God: I am the LORD. ²²Thou shalt not lie with mankind, as with womankind; it is abomination. ²³And thou shalt not lie with any beast to defile thyself therewith; neither shall any woman stand before a beast, to lie down thereto; it is perversion.

²⁴Defile not ye yourselves in any of these things; for in all these the nations are defiled, which I cast out from before you. ²⁵And the land was defiled, therefore I did visit the iniquity thereof upon it, and the land vomited out her inhabitants. ²⁶Ye therefore shall keep My statutes and Mine ordinances, and shall not do any of these abominations; neither the home-born, nor the stranger that sojourneth among you—²⁷for all these abominations have

אָבִיךָ הִוא ס עֶרְוַת אֲחוֹת־ ¹³
אִמְּךָ לֹא תְגַלֵּה כִּי־שְׁאֵר אִמְּךָ הִוא׃
עֶרְוַת אֲחִי־אָבִיךָ לֹא תְגַלֵּה ס ¹⁴
אֶל־אִשְׁתּוֹ לֹא תִקְרָב דֹּדָתְךָ הִוא׃
עֶרְוַת כַּלָּתְךָ לֹא תְגַלֵּה אֵשֶׁת ס ¹⁵
בִּנְךָ הִוא לֹא תְגַלֵּה עֶרְוָתָהּ׃ ס
עֶרְוַת אֵשֶׁת־אָחִיךָ לֹא תְגַלֵּה עֶרְוַת ¹⁶
אָחִיךָ הִוא׃ ס עֶרְוַת אִשָּׁה ¹⁷
וּבִתָּהּ לֹא תְגַלֵּה אֶת־בַּת־בְּנָהּ וְאֶת־
בַּת־בִּתָּהּ לֹא תִקַּח לְגַלּוֹת עֶרְוָתָהּ
שַׁאֲרָה הֵנָּה זִמָּה הִוא׃ וְאִשָּׁה אֶל־ ¹⁸
אֲחֹתָהּ לֹא תִקָּח לִצְרֹר לְגַלּוֹת עֶרְוָתָהּ
עָלֶיהָ בְּחַיֶּיהָ׃ וְאֶל־אִשָּׁה בְּנִדַּת ¹⁹
טֻמְאָתָהּ לֹא תִקְרַב לְגַלּוֹת עֶרְוָתָהּ׃
וְאֶל־אֵשֶׁת עֲמִיתְךָ לֹא־תִתֵּן שְׁכָבְתְּךָ ²⁰
לְזָרַע לְטָמְאָה־בָהּ׃ וּמִזַּרְעֲךָ לֹא־ ²¹
תִתֵּן לְהַעֲבִיר לַמֹּלֶךְ וְלֹא תְחַלֵּל אֶת־
שֵׁם אֱלֹהֶיךָ אֲנִי יְהוָה׃
וְאֶת־זָכָר לֹא תִשְׁכַּב מִשְׁכְּבֵי אִשָּׁה ²²
תּוֹעֵבָה הִוא׃ וּבְכָל־בְּהֵמָה לֹא־תִתֵּן ²³
שְׁכָבְתְּךָ לְטָמְאָה־בָהּ וְאִשָּׁה לֹא־
תַעֲמֹד לִפְנֵי בְהֵמָה לְרִבְעָהּ תֶּבֶל הוּא׃
אַל־תִּטַּמְּאוּ בְּכָל־אֵלֶּה כִּי בְכָל־ ²⁴
אֵלֶּה נִטְמְאוּ הַגּוֹיִם אֲשֶׁר־אֲנִי מְשַׁלֵּחַ
מִפְּנֵיכֶם׃ וַתִּטְמָא הָאָרֶץ וָאֶפְקֹד עֲוֺנָהּ ²⁵
עָלֶיהָ וַתָּקִא הָאָרֶץ אֶת־יֹשְׁבֶיהָ׃
וּשְׁמַרְתֶּם אַתֶּם אֶת־חֻקֹּתַי וְאֶת־מִשְׁפָּטַי ²⁶
וְלֹא תַעֲשׂוּ מִכֹּל הַתּוֹעֵבֹת הָאֵלֶּה
הָאֶזְרָח וְהַגֵּר הַגָּר בְּתוֹכְכֶם׃
כִּי אֶת־כָּל־הַתּוֹעֵבֹת הָאֵל עָשׂוּ ²⁷

the men of the land done, that were before you, and the land is defiled— [28]that the land vomit not you out also, when ye defile it, as it vomited out the nation that was before you. [29]For whosoever shall do any of these abominations, even the souls that do them shall be cut off from among their people. [30]Therefore shall ye keep My charge, that ye do not any of these

abominable customs, which were done before you, and that ye defile not yourselves therein: I am the LORD your God.

אַנְשֵׁי־הָאָרֶץ אֲשֶׁר לִפְנֵיכֶם וַתִּטְמָא

[28] הָאָרֶץ: וְלֹא־תָקִיא הָאָרֶץ

אֶתְכֶם בְּטַמַּאֲכֶם אֹתָהּ כַּאֲשֶׁר קָאָה

[29] אֶת־הַגּוֹי אֲשֶׁר לִפְנֵיכֶם: כִּי כָּל־

אֲשֶׁר יַעֲשֶׂה מִכֹּל הַתּוֹעֵבֹת הָאֵלֶּה

וְנִכְרְתוּ הַנְּפָשׁוֹת הָעֹשֹׂת מִקֶּרֶב עַמָּם:

[30] וּשְׁמַרְתֶּם אֶת־מִשְׁמַרְתִּי לְבִלְתִּי עֲשׂוֹת

מֵחֻקּוֹת הַתּוֹעֵבֹת אֲשֶׁר נַעֲשׂוּ לִפְנֵיכֶם

וְלֹא תִטַּמְּאוּ בָּהֶם אֲנִי יְהֹוָה אֱלֹהֵיכֶם:

289

Sexuality and Teshuva:
Leviticus 18

JUDITH PLASKOW

OF ALL the readings for the High Holy Days, the Torah portion for the afternoon of Yom Kippur seems the most puzzling and even bizarre.[1] Coming after the awe-filled description of the service of the high priest and before the reading of Jonah, with its clear focus on repentance and forgiveness, Leviticus 18—a list of forbidden sexual relations—seems to bear little relation to the themes of the day. Yom Kippur is a time for self-examination, for reflection on one's sins and one's relationship with God. Of the many ways in which it is possible to transgress the divine commandments, why should sexual violations be singled out to be described in all their concreteness? How does reading Leviticus 18 forward the movement of the liturgy?

A possible historical explanation for the Torah reading is provided by a statement in the Talmud. Mishna Ta'anit 4.8 says that *Tu B'Av* (the fifteenth day of the month of *Av*) and Yom Kippur were the happiest days of the year. On the afternoons of these days, the daughters of Jerusalem would go out in white clothing and dance in the vineyards, while young men would come and choose their brides. Lamentations Rabba (33) comments on the appropriateness of Yom Kippur as a day for dancing, pointing out that it is a day of forgiveness and expiation. In light of these indications that the solemnity of the day once gave way to rejoicing by the afternoon, the reading of Leviticus 18 might be understood in one of two ways. It could be a strict warning not to get carried away by an excess of exuberance, or it could be a reminder to prospective spouses of what relationships are permitted and prohibited.

The existence of historical reasons for reading Leviticus 18 does not necessarily make the portion meaningful in the contemporary context, however. Not only is the notion of Yom Kippur as a day for choosing brides at best a distant memory, but the specific content of the chapter is in many ways disturbing. Its profound male-centeredness, its silences, its focus on purity, its condemnation of certain sexual practices that many Jews today find entirely acceptable, are more likely to provoke a sense of alienation from the service than to promote self-reflection. It is probably partly to avoid evoking this alienation that many non-Orthodox congregations substitute Leviticus 19 for Leviticus 18 on Yom Kippur afternoon. As a list of fundamental ethical (and cultic) precepts that define holy community, Leviticus 19 seems more in keeping with the themes of wide-ranging self-scrutiny and commitment to *teshuva* (repentance).

As someone who has long been disturbed by the content of Leviticus 18, I had always applauded the substitution of an alternative Torah reading—until a particular incident made me reconsider the link between sex and Yom Kippur. After a lecture I delivered in the spring of 1995 on rethinking Jewish attitudes toward sexuality, a woman approached me very distressed. She belonged to a Conservative synagogue that had abandoned the practice of reading Leviticus 18 on Yom Kippur, and as a victim of childhood sexual abuse by her grandfather, she felt betrayed by that decision. While she was not necessarily committed to the understanding of sexual holiness contained in Leviticus, she felt that in quietly changing the reading without communal discussion, her congregation had avoided issues of sexual responsibility altogether. She wanted to hear her community connect the theme of atonement with issues of behavior in intimate relationships, to have it publicly proclaim the parameters of legitimate sexual relations on a day when large numbers of Jews gather.

As a result of this conversation, I began to rethink the connection between *teshuva* and reading about sex on Yom Kippur. It struck me that the appeal of Leviticus 19 as an alternative Torah reading is not without its problems. Leviticus 19 makes a more comfortable reading because its injunctions are broader and more foundational. It reiterates a number of the Ten Commandments, links kindness to strangers with the experience of Egyptian slavery (verses 33–34), and enjoins the community to "love your neighbor as yourself" (verse 18). Yet injunctions that are broader are also more easily evaded, while the disturbing concreteness of Leviticus 18 reminds us that love of the neighbor begins at home. The family is the first sphere in which we learn about both love and domination, and it is also the closest and most frightening context in which we can begin to make changes in our relationships with others. As many voices in our society draw attention to the high incidence of incest and other forms of sexual abuse within the family and the ways in which patterns of family interaction are passed on through the generations, it becomes clear how important it is to connect the notion of atonement to the quest for holiness in intimate relations. Focusing on the issue of sexual boundaries may be a very important exercise for Yom Kippur because it makes *teshuva* concrete in ways that touch on a central area of both personal and communal life.

Problems with Leviticus

Yet if, in theory, it is entirely fitting to read about sexuality on Yom Kippur, the actual *content* of Leviticus 18 is deeply disturbing. Indeed, from a feminist perspective it seems that, far from fostering holiness in interpersonal relations, the chapter reflects and supports those structures of domination that undergird sexual and family violence. Thus, reading or not reading Leviticus 18 can be equally problematic. On the one hand, as my interlocutor made me realize, gliding silently away from the difficulties Leviticus 18 poses evades the responsibility of communal self-examination and *teshuva*. On the other hand, chanting it as sacred text colludes in promoting its values. In this situation, the question becomes not so much whether to read or not to read, but *how* to read, interpret, and appropriate the text in ways that are transformative.

The task of transforming Leviticus 18 begins with examining its problems, problems that start with its foreign context. Leviticus 18 is part of a larger Levitical "Holiness Code" (chapters 17–26) that lays out laws and ordinances incumbent on the entire people of Israel in order that they can attain holiness.[2] While, for the priestly authors of the code, holiness is not unconnected to morality, it is understood primarily through the categories of purity and pollution. Thus, while I just argued on moral grounds for reading Leviticus 18 on Yom Kippur, it is striking that the language of the chapter is the language not of right and wrong, but of abhorrence and defilement. "Do not defile yourselves in any of those ways, for it is by such that the nations that

I am casting out before you defiled themselves. Thus the land became defiled; and I called it to account for its iniquity, and the land spewed out its inhabitants" (verses 24–25).[3] The fact that the land itself can be contaminated suggests that holiness is at least partly identified with the avoidance of a quasi-physical contagion or pollution, a pollution that is dangerous to both individuals and the community.[4] Mary Douglas argues in her classic work *Purity and Danger* that the purpose of pollution beliefs is to impose order on the chaos of experience. Pollution arises from the violation of social boundaries and classifications, and from the failure to conform to one's class. Pollution rules can reinforce moral principles and moral indignation—as they do in Leviticus 18, where defilement is caused by individual behavior—but pollution is not identical with morality and involves a mystical surplus that cannot be reduced to it.[5]

Although these ideas are strange to the contemporary consciousness, it is not most centrally their remoteness that makes Leviticus 18 problematic, but the character of the social order that pollution laws protect. My interlocutor wanted to hear Leviticus read on Yom Kippur because, as a victim of sexual abuse by her grandfather, she wanted it proclaimed in the presence of the assembled community that the violation of granddaughters by men in power over them is morally unacceptable. But as I pointed out to her, it is not the purpose of the incest prohibitions of Leviticus 18 to protect the young and vulnerable. The laws address the situation of extended patriarchal families in which the honor and authority of male heads of household is the primary social value. Thus the first two incest rules in chapter 18 (verses 7 and 8) do not forbid the father/parent to sexually violate a child, but rather forbid *the son to violate the sexuality of his father* by committing incestuous adultery with the father's wife. The less powerful party is instructed not to dishonor the powerful, while the wife's sexuality is treated simply as her husband's possession. The other incest laws in verses 9–18, all of which are addressed to a male audience, serve several different functions: they protect the purity of the line of descent; they encourage exogamy; and they maintain order and reduce the likelihood of jealousy and conflict within the (polygynous) family group.[6] While this last purpose may work to the benefit of women, by outlawing marriage with two sisters, for example (verse 18), it is not women's concerns and interests that animate the text. Moreover, that it is not the intent of these rules to defend the weak is indicated by the striking absence of any mention of the most prevalent sexual violation, namely father/daughter incest. While both the Rabbis and many contemporary commentators take it for granted that such incest is subsumed under other categories, it is not clear that such an assumption is supported by the Biblical text.[7]

The marginalization of women within the social world presupposed by Leviticus 18 is underscored in a different way by the prohibition of sex with a menstruant in verse 19. On one level this prohibition fits quite seamlessly into the purity-related concerns of Leviticus and the associated concepts of pollution and defilement. Leviticus 15 defines a number of bodily emissions as defiling—semen and any other discharge from the penis, menstrual blood, and non-menstrual bloody discharge from the vagina—and sets out the proper procedures for purification. Since semen and menstrual blood are separately polluting, mixed together they represent a double danger to the community.[8] On another level, however, as Howard Eilberg-Schwartz points out in *The Savage in Judaism,* when menstrual blood is viewed not simply as a body fluid, but specifically as *blood,* it is negatively marked in a particular way. Unlike the blood of circumcision, which represents entry into the covenant and the end of the male infant's impurity caused by the mother's blood at birth, menstrual blood is contaminating. The prohibition of sex with a menstruant, repeated more forcefully in Leviticus 20:18, is part of a symbolic complex in which menstrual blood has many ugly associations.[9] The prophets link menstrual impurity with adultery, idolatry, and murder. Ezekiel, for example, compares God's revulsion at Israel's violence and idolatry with disgust at the "uncleanness of a menstruous woman" (36:17). The Book of Lamentations likens Jerusalem's degradation after the exile to a menstruating woman whose "uncleanness clings to her skirts" (1:9).[10] Thus, as Eilberg-Schwartz puts it, "menstrual prohibitions may be the sign par excellence of 'the difference of woman from man . . . her eternally inexplicable, mysterious and strange nature. . . .'"[11] Reading Leviticus 18, then, activates and reinforces a host of negative religious and cultural attitudes surrounding women's bodies.

The proscription of male/male intercourse in Leviticus 18:22 raises analogous purity-related and ethical issues. The original significance of this law is difficult to recover. Although the verse is most often read as a general condemnation of male "homosexuality," in fact, the prohibition against a man's lying down "the lying down of a woman" probably refers specifically to the insertive role in anal intercourse.[12] Because this law appears only in Leviticus (18:22 and 20:13) and not in other legal collections in the Bible that deal with sexual relations, it should probably be understood in connection with the distinctive concerns of the Holiness Code. Saul Olyan suggests that it be interpreted in the context of Leviticus 18's anxiety about mixing defiling fluids. Just as it is dangerous to mix semen with the blood of a menstruant, so, in this case, it is dangerous to mix semen with excrement, a substance that is also seen as defiling in other holiness contexts.[13]

Even if the original issue behind Leviticus 18 is quite limited, however, the history of its use and interpretation cannot be ignored. While in the Bible itself, male/male anal intercourse does not become a metaphor for other sorts of sin and defilement in the way that menstrual impurity does, the verse has long been understood as a judgment on all male homosexual relations and has provided a sanction for both Jewish and Christian homophobia. In contemporary debates about the status of gays and lesbians within Judaism, Leviticus 18:22 is often treated as divinely ordained and eternally binding by people who otherwise have little use for the directives of Leviticus. Thus to read this passage on Yom Kippur without discussion or comment is to lend support to a larger environment of social prejudice and discrimination against gays and lesbians.

A more general problem with Leviticus 18 that makes it alien to a contemporary perspective is the extent to which its rules are act centered. The chapter forbids a series of discrete behaviors that are linked by particular themes and purity-related concerns. Not only must the underlying principles at stake be deduced from the specific regulations, but also these principles have little to do with the emotional and psychological dimensions of sexual experience that today are considered so central to evaluations of sexual morality. Related to this, Leviticus 18 offers no *positive* vision of holy sexuality. Instead, holiness is defined as avoiding defilement—by *not* copying the practices of Egypt and Canaan and by *not* violating the categories and boundaries that order and preserve the social/religious world.

In terms of thinking about the Torah reading for Yom Kippur after-noon, then, Leviticus 18 poses a dilemma. On the one hand, the link made by the reading between *teshuva* and sexuality is very impor-tant. Ideally, reading Leviticus 18 should encourage us to focus on the quality of our family relationships as they affect the nature of com-munal life. In positing a connection between individual behavior and the viability of the whole land, the chapter draws attention to the ways in which the character of intimate relationships has ramifica-tions way beyond the interpersonal sphere. On the other hand, the moral, emotional, and psychological components of that link that are so central to us are not the concern of Leviticus, so that we can find meaning in the text only by using it as a starting point that is fairly quickly left behind. Thus it is not surprising that many synagogues have chosen to substitute a different Torah reading for Leviticus 18—or that many individuals have solved the problems it poses by com-ing to *mincha* (the afternoon service) a little late!

Transforming Leviticus

How, then, does one hold on to the value of connecting *teshuva* and sexuality without denying the very real difficulties of Leviticus 18? Or, put another way, how does one affirm the insights of Leviticus into the necessity for sexual boundaries and into the link between communal well-being and interpersonal behavior without abandon-ing the victims of its hierarchical and purity-centered worldview? It is easy enough to set out the contradictions of reading Leviticus in an article for a book, but bringing a critical consciousness to the Torah reading on Yom Kippur makes it difficult to focus on the tasks of self-examination and repentance. The synagogue on Yom Kippur is not a classroom in which to analyze the sociology of the liturgy. It is sup-posed to be a place to meditate on our relationship with God and to seek atonement. From this point of view, it may make sense to sub-stitute Leviticus 19 for 18, because, while the readings raise similar purity-related issues, Leviticus 19 also contains injunctions that fit with less distraction into the themes of the day.

To my mind, however, there is no easy way around the tension be-tween a critical consciousness and the ability to focus on worship and self-reflection. The fact that Leviticus 19 contains, alongside its profound moral injunctions, ritual commandments that seem utterly devoid of ethical content may serve only to highlight the gulf in worldviews between Leviticus and ourselves. To a large extent, this tension is inherent in the erosion of religious authority that was part of the emergence of modern science and historical criticism. There are many places in the Yom Kippur liturgy where an abyss may suddenly open between the text and ourselves. Rather than seeking a way around this dilemma by changing the Torah reading, we might better address it by placing the reading in a larger context of communal wrestling with and transformation of Torah.

In the aftermath of my conversation about these readings, I tried to envision a different way of dealing with Leviticus 18 other than simply substituting another portion without communal discussion. It occurred to me that small groups of Jews in many different contexts might grapple with issues of sexual responsibility and struggle to create statements of sexual values that engage both Leviticus and contemporary experience. Leviticus 18 enjoins Jews to holiness in the arena of sexual behavior. What constitutes holiness in 1997? What would it mean to begin to do *teshuva* in this area of our lives—both as a personal process, internal and behavioral, and as a Jewish community contending with the legacy of a hierarchical, patriarchal sexual ethic?

To ask such questions is to approach the Torah not as a static document that brings us a set of eternal truths, but—to use Rachel Adler's image—as one end of a bridge that might possibly carry us toward where we want to be. Borrowing Robert Cover's metaphor of law as a bridge between our present moral universe and those alternative universes a people might create through its concerted communal action, Adler suggests that Leviticus 18 is still usable, if we think of it as part of the Jewish historical teaching about sexuality that is holding down one end of the bridge.[14] As every lesbian and gay man listening to the *mincha* Torah reading on Yom Kippur knows, Leviticus 18 has shaped Jewish life and consciousness for good and for evil. Erasing it from the *machzor* (High Holy Day prayer book) will not in itself eradicate the homophobia it helps generate and justify any more than ceasing to read about menstrual taboos will generate a new set of positive attitudes toward women's bodies.[15] Leviticus 18 is read, however, in the context of congregations whose members, whether or not they are consciously critical, are generally living out very different sexual norms. Thus if Torah, like law, is a bridge between past and future, it is being reshaped on the ground by Jews whose attitudes and behaviors are necessarily affected by contemporary social movements and sexual values. This process of reshaping can become a more fully Jewish process—and a process of *teshuva*—if it involves conscious engagement with Leviticus 18 and other traditional sources with the intention of moving toward a new sexual ethic.

Grappling with Leviticus from a contemporary feminist perspective involves importing a set of assumptions radically different from those of the text. Any feminist reworking of Leviticus would have to address the ways in which many of its premises—for example, that the nakedness of the *fathers* is more in need of protection than the nakedness of daughters, or that menstrual blood is defiling—produce and support the sexual injustice that a sexual ethic should address and correct. While such a reworking would certainly attend to the social structures that undergird and make possible holy relationships, it would also be more person centered, focusing on qualities of human connection rather than on the supposedly intrinsic nature of particular sexual behaviors. It might be aware of the dangers of too easily equating certain feelings with holiness, yet it would at least attend to the place of feelings as a dimension of holy sexuality. Rather than understanding defilement as a quasi-mystical reality, the avoidance of which protects the privilege of the powerful, it would see it as the outcome of abuse of power and the violation of the vulnerable. Attempting to articulate both basic standards of sexual decency and a vision of possible holiness, it would attempt to connect sexual values with those ethical values that ought to guide all relationships. Rachel Adler points out that the exhortation in Leviticus 19:2, "You shall be holy, for I, the Lord your God, am holy," comes at the juncture of two sets of commandments. Leviticus 18 deals with sexual boundaries, while Leviticus 19 offers some basic principles for creating a just and loving community. Insofar as "you shall be holy" refers to both sets of laws, it is possible and necessary to rethink the laws of sexual relations, not as a discrete set of rules bearing on a unique capacity to sanctify or defile, but as a subset of the laws about justice toward the neighbor.[16]

Over the past few years I have participated in, or helped to facilitate, a couple of groups that have begun the process of rethinking Leviticus. In particular, Su Kasha, a lesbian and gay *chavura* in New York to which I belong, has been engaged in this project for over a year.[17] Each spring, as we have struggled with *Acharei Mot* and *Kedoshim* (the Torah portions that contain Leviticus 18 and 20), we have found ourselves questioning our relation to a tradition that sees male/male sex as an abomination. Writing our own Leviticus 18 has provided the opportunity to move beyond anger and a sense of victimization to explore our own assumptions, values, and differences. We began the process of rethinking Leviticus with a lengthy and serious discussion of the chapter, in which we laid out the text's interests and assumptions and examined what in it we rejected or affirmed. We also studied portions of *Shir Hashirim* (*Songs of Songs*) in order to place Leviticus in the context of a complex and multivocal tradition. We then entered into an open-ended and wide-ranging conversation about our own concerns, trying to delineate important lines of sexual responsibility and to explore our own values and "bottom lines" within them. We agreed that we would try to express our sexual ethic in positive terms, affirming our responsibilities to ourselves, to individual others, and to a larger community. We also agreed that, for the sake of coming up with an actual document, we would work toward consensus, although we were at the same time aware of many differences among us.

The process of trying to articulate our own sexual ethics has been challenging and exciting, eliciting insight along with playfulness. Engaging in the project has made us aware of the extent to which we normally dwell in the same zone of silence around sexuality that leads to the quiet substitution of Leviticus 19 for 18 on Yom Kippur. Although our culture is saturated with sexual images, there is an enormous gap between media fixation on sexuality and pressures toward sexual activity and the capacity of individuals to speak comfortably about and claim responsibility for their own sexuality. Rethinking Leviticus provides an opportunity to grapple with the painful contradictions between traditional sexual values and the realities of people's lives, and to think through the meaning of holiness in light of these conflicts. As Su Kasha has explored our agreements and talked through our differences, it has become clear to us that the point of the exercise is the process itself. Even though we have focused on creating a new text, we are aware that that task has provided a context for conversations that have been more important than the finished product—especially since any new document would function only as a basis for further discussion, either among ourselves or for others. In the spirit of providing a model for a process that any group can engage in, I have appended to this essay sections of a draft of the Su Kasha ethic, an ethic that is very much in process.

Conclusions

The task of rethinking Leviticus 18 seemingly takes us far away from the specific context of the Torah reading on Yom Kippur afternoon. Like criticizing Leviticus altogether, it is not so much a job for the holiday as for individual and group reflection during the rest of the year. Moreover, it is a rare congregation or *chavura* that would actually read a new statement of sexual ethics in lieu of the Torah reading, and, probably, the act of doing so would deflect attention from the task of self-reflection to arguments about specific content, or the status of Torah. On another level, however, rethinking Leviticus connects the theme of repentance to the ongoing life of the Jewish community. It is an act of communal *teshuva,* both in relation to those who are marginalized and anathematized by Leviticus 18 and those who are abandoned when it is abandoned without considered discussion. In this sense, continuing engagement with Leviticus provides a context that can enrich the experience of Yom Kippur. It allows us to move out from the Torah reading to thinking about *teshuva* in our personal relationships in a way that is both rooted in tradition and attentive to the realities of contemporary life. And it affirms a central insight of Leviticus 18: the relationship between holiness on the interpersonal and communal levels.

Appendix: The SuKasha Ethic (Selections)

I have selected those sections that, after laying out some basic assumptions, speak most directly to issues of interpersonal and communal sexual values and responsibility.[18]

You Shall Be Holy as I Am Holy

We believe that we honor the image of God by honoring the body. Through our bodies we can connect with each other, the world, and the sacred.

We affirm that each human being has sensual feelings from the beginning of life and that sensuality is the foundation of sexuality. Children have the right to grow up enjoying their bodies, to be nurtured by appropriate touch, and to have a positive physical self-image. These positive experiences are a foundation for a healthy adult sexuality.

We affirm that each human being must be taught that the awakening of sexual feeling and the desire for sexual activity are natural and good, and that an understanding of how to express sexuality must also be taught. It is good to talk about sexuality.

We affirm human sexuality in all its fluidity, complexity, and diversity. Many of the proscriptions on human sexuality that were established for the survival and differentiation of small tribes in earlier cultures have become tools of oppression and destruction in today's world and therefore unacceptable

We affirm that human sexual diversity is part of the richness and diversity of life. We envision a society in which sexual behavior, whether heterosexual, bisexual, homosexual, or celibate, is all considered healthy; and in which sexual ambiguity, including hermaphroditism, androgyny, and transgenderedness, is affirmed and neither feared nor despised. . . .

We affirm that we all have the right to make decisions about our own bodies. . . .

We affirm the goodness of sexual pleasure independent of the goal of procreation. . . .

Sexual Responsibilities to Others. No person twenty-one or older shall have intercourse with any child sixteen or younger.

All sexual activity between people must be consensual. No person shall touch another person without that person's permission.

No person shall abuse, exploit, control, humiliate, do violence to, or harm another human being physically, emotionally, or in any other way in the course of sexual expression.

If or whenever one person withdraws permission, the other must stop.

As our bodies are holy, we shall not do violence to others or put others in danger or at risk of disease through sexual behaviors.

No person shall have unprotected sex with any partner if s/he knowingly has any sexually transmitted disease.

Each person must take responsibility for the consequences of sexual activity, including pregnancy and children.

Sexuality shall not be used as an expression of status or power, and no person shall use status or power to gain consent for sexual activity.

Partners shall be forthright about sexual activities outside their primary relationship. . . .

The Communal Context of Sexuality. No person shall project sexual stereotypes on any person based on that person's perceived age, gender, sexual orientation, or membership in a racial or ethnic group.

It is the responsibility of the Jewish community to raise and discuss issues of sexuality and to help give parents the tools to discuss sexual issues with their children.

Communities have the responsibility to create spaces and contexts that allow for the discussion of and for the varieties of sexual expression and that acknowledge the variability and fluidity of sexual identities.

The Book of Jonah
Micah 7:18–20

1 Now the word of the LORD came unto Jonah the son of Amittai, saying: ²'Arise, go to Nineveh, that great city, and proclaim against it; for their wickedness is come up before Me.' ³But Jonah rose up to flee unto Tarshish from the presence of the LORD; and he went down to Joppa, and found a ship going to Tarshish; so he paid the fare thereof, and went down into it, to go with them unto Tarshish, from the presence of the LORD.

⁴But the LORD hurled a great wind into the sea, and there was a mighty tempest in the sea, so that the ship was like to be broken. ⁵And the mariners were afraid, and cried every man unto his god; and they cast forth the wares that were in the ship into the sea, to lighten it unto them. But Jonah was gone down into the innermost parts of the ship; and he lay, and was fast asleep. ⁶So the shipmaster came to him, and said unto him: 'What meanest thou that thou sleepest? arise, call upon thy God, if so be that God will think upon us, that we perish not.'

⁷And they said every one to his fellow: 'Come, and let us cast lots, that we may know for whose cause this evil is upon us.' So they cast lots, and the lot fell upon Jonah. ⁸Then said they unto him: 'Tell us, we pray thee, for whose cause this evil is upon us: what is thine occupation? and whence comest thou? what is thy country? and of what people art thou?' ⁹And he said unto them: 'I am a Hebrew; and I fear the LORD, the God of heaven, who hath made the sea and the dry land.' ¹⁰Then were the men exceedingly afraid, and said unto him: 'What is this that

א

1 וַיְהִי דְּבַר־יְהֹוָה אֶל־יוֹנָה בֶן־
2 אֲמִתַּי לֵאמֹר: קוּם לֵךְ אֶל־נִינְוֵה
הָעִיר הַגְּדוֹלָה וּקְרָא עָלֶיהָ כִּי־
3 עָלְתָה רָעָתָם לְפָנָי: וַיָּקָם יוֹנָה
לִבְרֹחַ תַּרְשִׁישָׁה מִלִּפְנֵי יְהֹוָה וַיֵּרֶד
יָפוֹ וַיִּמְצָא אֳנִיָּה | בָּאָה תַרְשִׁישׁ וַיִּתֵּן
שְׂכָרָהּ וַיֵּרֶד בָּהּ לָבוֹא עִמָּהֶם
4 תַּרְשִׁישָׁה מִלִּפְנֵי יְהֹוָה: וַיהֹוָה הֵטִיל
רוּחַ־גְּדוֹלָה אֶל־הַיָּם וַיְהִי סַעַר־
גָּדוֹל בַּיָּם וְהָאֳנִיָּה חִשְּׁבָה לְהִשָּׁבֵר:
5 וַיִּירְאוּ הַמַּלָּחִים וַיִּזְעֲקוּ אִישׁ אֶל־
אֱלֹהָיו וַיָּטִלוּ אֶת־הַכֵּלִים אֲשֶׁר
בָּאֳנִיָּה אֶל־הַיָּם לְהָקֵל מֵעֲלֵיהֶם
וְיוֹנָה יָרַד אֶל־יַרְכְּתֵי הַסְּפִינָה
6 וַיִּשְׁכַּב וַיֵּרָדַם: וַיִּקְרַב אֵלָיו רַב
הַחֹבֵל וַיֹּאמֶר לוֹ מַה־לְּךָ נִרְדָּם
קוּם קְרָא אֶל־אֱלֹהֶיךָ אוּלַי
יִתְעַשֵּׁת הָאֱלֹהִים לָנוּ וְלֹא נֹאבֵד:
7 וַיֹּאמְרוּ אִישׁ אֶל־רֵעֵהוּ לְכוּ וְנַפִּילָה
גוֹרָלוֹת וְנֵדְעָה בְּשֶׁלְּמִי הָרָעָה הַזֹּאת
לָנוּ וַיַּפִּלוּ גּוֹרָלוֹת וַיִּפֹּל הַגּוֹרָל
8 עַל־יוֹנָה: וַיֹּאמְרוּ אֵלָיו הַגִּידָה־
נָּא לָנוּ בַּאֲשֶׁר לְמִי־הָרָעָה הַזֹּאת
לָנוּ מַה־מְּלַאכְתְּךָ וּמֵאַיִן תָּבוֹא מָה
9 אַרְצֶךָ וְאֵי־מִזֶּה עַם אָתָּה: וַיֹּאמֶר

אֲלֵיהֶם עִבְרִי אָנֹכִי וְאֶת־יְהֹוָה אֱלֹהֵי
הַשָּׁמַיִם אֲנִי יָרֵא אֲשֶׁר־עָשָׂה אֶת־
10 הַיָּם וְאֶת־הַיַּבָּשָׁה: וַיִּירְאוּ הָאֲנָשִׁים

thou hast done?' For the men knew that he fled from the presence of the LORD, because he had told them.

¹¹Then said they unto him: 'What shall we do unto thee, that the sea may be calm unto us?' for the sea grew more and more tempestuous. ¹²And he said unto them: 'Take me up, and cast me forth into the sea; so shall the sea be calm unto you; for I know that for my sake this great tempest is upon you.' ¹³Nevertheless the men rowed hard to bring it to the land; but they could not; for the sea grew more and more tempestuous against them. ¹⁴Wherefore they cried unto the LORD, and said: 'We beseech Thee, O LORD, we beseech Thee, let us not perish for this man's life, and lay not upon us innocent blood; for Thou, O LORD, hast done as it pleased Thee.' ¹⁵So they took up Jonah, and cast him forth into the sea; and the sea ceased from its raging. ¹⁶Then the men feared the LORD exceedingly; and they offered a sacrifice unto the LORD, and made vows.

2. And the LORD prepared a great fish to swallow up Jonah; and Jonah was in the belly of the fish three days and three nights. ²Then Jonah prayed unto the LORD his God out of the fish's belly. ³And he said:

I called out of mine affliction
Unto the LORD, and He answered me;
Out of the belly of the netherworld cried I,
And Thou heardest my voice.
⁴For Thou didst cast me into the depth,
In the heart of the seas,
And the flood was round about me;
All Thy waves and Thy billows
Passed over me.
⁵And I said: 'I am cast out
From before Thine eyes';
Yet I will look again
Toward Thy holy temple.
⁶The waters compassed me about, even to the soul;
The deep was round about me;

יִרְאָה גְדוֹלָה וַיֹּאמְרוּ אֵלָיו מַה־זֹּאת
עָשִׂיתָ כִּי־יָדְעוּ הָאֲנָשִׁים כִּי־מִלִּפְנֵי
יְהוָה הוּא בֹרֵחַ כִּי הִגִּיד לָהֶם:
11 וַיֹּאמְרוּ אֵלָיו מַה־נַּעֲשֶׂה לָּךְ וְיִשְׁתֹּק
הַיָּם מֵעָלֵינוּ כִּי הַיָּם הוֹלֵךְ וְסֹעֵר:
12 וַיֹּאמֶר אֲלֵיהֶם שָׂאוּנִי וַהֲטִילֻנִי אֶל־
הַיָּם וְיִשְׁתֹּק הַיָּם מֵעֲלֵיכֶם כִּי יוֹדֵעַ
אָנִי כִּי בְשֶׁלִּי הַסַּעַר הַגָּדוֹל הַזֶּה
13 עֲלֵיכֶם: וַיַּחְתְּרוּ הָאֲנָשִׁים לְהָשִׁיב
אֶל־הַיַּבָּשָׁה וְלֹא יָכֹלוּ כִּי הַיָּם הוֹלֵךְ
14 וְסֹעֵר עֲלֵיהֶם: וַיִּקְרְאוּ אֶל־יְהוָה
וַיֹּאמְרוּ אָנָּה יְהוָה אַל־נָא נֹאבְדָה
בְּנֶפֶשׁ הָאִישׁ הַזֶּה וְאַל־תִּתֵּן עָלֵינוּ
דָּם נָקִיא כִּי־אַתָּה יְהוָה כַּאֲשֶׁר
15 חָפַצְתָּ עָשִׂיתָ: וַיִּשְׂאוּ אֶת־יוֹנָה
וַיְטִלֻהוּ אֶל־הַיָּם וַיַּעֲמֹד הַיָּם
16 מִזַּעְפּוֹ: וַיִּירְאוּ הָאֲנָשִׁים יִרְאָה
גְדוֹלָה אֶת־יְהוָה וַיִּזְבְּחוּ־זֶבַח
לַיהוָה וַיִּדְּרוּ נְדָרִים:

ב

1 וַיְמַן יְהוָה דָּג גָּדוֹל לִבְלֹעַ אֶת־יוֹנָה
וַיְהִי יוֹנָה בִּמְעֵי הַדָּג שְׁלֹשָׁה יָמִים
2 וּשְׁלֹשָׁה לֵילוֹת: וַיִּתְפַּלֵּל יוֹנָה אֶל־
יְהוָה אֱלֹהָיו מִמְּעֵי הַדָּגָה:
3 וַיֹּאמֶר קָרָאתִי מִצָּרָה לִי
אֶל־יְהוָה וַיַּעֲנֵנִי
מִבֶּטֶן שְׁאוֹל שִׁוַּעְתִּי שָׁמַעְתָּ קוֹלִי:
4 וַתַּשְׁלִיכֵנִי מְצוּלָה בִּלְבַב יַמִּים
וְנָהָר יְסֹבְבֵנִי
כָּל־מִשְׁבָּרֶיךָ וְגַלֶּיךָ עָלַי עָבָרוּ:
5 וַאֲנִי אָמַרְתִּי נִגְרַשְׁתִּי מִנֶּגֶד עֵינֶיךָ
אַךְ אוֹסִיף לְהַבִּיט
אֶל־הֵיכַל קָדְשֶׁךָ:
6 אֲפָפוּנִי מַיִם עַד־נֶפֶשׁ
תְּהוֹם יְסֹבְבֵנִי

The weeds were wrapped about my
  head.
⁷I went down to the bottoms of the
  mountains;
The earth with her bars closed
  upon me for ever;
Yet hast Thou brought up my **life**
  from the pit,
O LORD my God.
⁸When my soul fainted within me,
I remembered the LORD;
And my prayer came in unto Thee,
Into Thy holy temple.
⁹They that regard lying vanities
Forsake their own mercy.
¹⁰But I will sacrifice unto Thee
With the voice of thanksgiving;
That which I have vowed I will pay.
Salvation is of the LORD.
¹¹And the LORD spoke unto the fish,
and it vomited out Jonah upon the
dry land.

3 And the word of the LORD came
unto Jonah the second time, saying: ²'Arise, go unto Nineveh, that
great city, and make unto it the
proclamation that I bid thee.' ³So
Jonah arose, and went unto Nineveh,
according to the word of the LORD.
Now Nineveh was an exceeding
great city, of three days' journey.
⁴And Jonah began to enter into the
city a day's journey, and he proclaimed, and said: 'Yet forty days,
and Nineveh shall be overthrown.'
⁵And the people of Nineveh believed God; and they proclaimed **a**
fast, and put on sackcloth, from the
greatest of them even to the least of
them. ⁶And the tidings reached the
king of Nineveh, and he arose from
his throne, and laid his robe from him,
and covered him with sackcloth, and
sat in ashes. ⁷And he caused it to be
proclaimed and published through
Nineveh by the decree of the king and
his nobles, saying: 'Let neither man
nor beast, herd nor flock, taste any
thing; let them not feed, nor drink
water; ⁸but let them be covered with
sackcloth, both man and beast, and
let them cry mightily unto God; yea,
let them turn every one from his evil

סוּף חָבוּשׁ לְרֹאשִׁי׃

⁷ לְקִצְבֵי הָרִים יָרַדְתִּי
הָאָרֶץ בְּרִחֶיהָ בַעֲדִי לְעוֹלָם
וַתַּעַל מִשַּׁחַת חַיַּי יְהֹוָה אֱלֹהָי׃

⁸ בְּהִתְעַטֵּף עָלַי נַפְשִׁי
אֶת־יְהֹוָה זָכָרְתִּי
וַתָּבוֹא אֵלֶיךָ תְּפִלָּתִי
אֶל־הֵיכַל קָדְשֶׁךָ׃

⁹ מְשַׁמְּרִים הַבְלֵי־שָׁוְא חַסְדָּם יַעֲזֹבוּ׃

¹⁰ וַאֲנִי בְּקוֹל תּוֹדָה אֶזְבְּחָה־לָּךְ
אֲשֶׁר נָדַרְתִּי אֲשַׁלֵּמָה
יְשׁוּעָתָה לַיהֹוָה׃

¹¹ וַיֹּאמֶר יְהֹוָה לַדָּג וַיָּקֵא · אֶת־יוֹנָה
אֶל־הַיַּבָּשָׁה׃

ג

¹ וַיְהִי דְבַר־יְהֹוָה אֶל־יוֹנָה שֵׁנִית

² לֵאמֹר׃ קוּם לֵךְ אֶל־נִינְוֵה הָעִיר
הַגְּדוֹלָה וּקְרָא אֵלֶיהָ אֶת־הַקְּרִיאָה

³ אֲשֶׁר אָנֹכִי דֹּבֵר אֵלֶיךָ׃ וַיָּקָם יוֹנָה
וַיֵּלֶךְ אֶל־נִינְוֵה כִּדְבַר יְהֹוָה וְנִינְוֵה
הָיְתָה עִיר־גְּדוֹלָה לֵאלֹהִים מַהֲלַךְ

⁴ שְׁלֹשֶׁת יָמִים׃ וַיָּחֶל יוֹנָה לָבוֹא בָעִיר
מַהֲלַךְ יוֹם אֶחָד וַיִּקְרָא וַיֹּאמַר עוֹד

⁵ אַרְבָּעִים יוֹם וְנִינְוֵה נֶהְפָּכֶת׃ וַיַּאֲמִינוּ
אַנְשֵׁי נִינְוֵה בֵּאלֹהִים וַיִּקְרְאוּ־צוֹם
וַיִּלְבְּשׁוּ שַׂקִּים מִגְּדוֹלָם וְעַד־קְטַנָּם׃

⁶ וַיִּגַּע הַדָּבָר אֶל־מֶלֶךְ נִינְוֵה וַיָּקָם
מִכִּסְאוֹ וַיַּעֲבֵר אַדַּרְתּוֹ מֵעָלָיו וַיְכַס

⁷ שַׂק וַיֵּשֶׁב עַל־הָאֵפֶר׃ וַיַּזְעֵק וַיֹּאמֶר
בְּנִינְוֵה מִטַּעַם הַמֶּלֶךְ וּגְדֹלָיו לֵאמֹר
הָאָדָם וְהַבְּהֵמָה הַבָּקָר וְהַצֹּאן אַל־
יִטְעֲמוּ מְאוּמָה אַל־יִרְעוּ וּמַיִם אַל־

⁸ יִשְׁתּוּ׃ וְיִתְכַּסּוּ שַׂקִּים הָאָדָם
וְהַבְּהֵמָה וְיִקְרְאוּ אֶל־אֱלֹהִים
בְּחָזְקָה וְיָשֻׁבוּ אִישׁ מִדַּרְכּוֹ הָרָעָה

⁹ מִן־הֶחָמָס אֲשֶׁר בְּכַפֵּיהֶם׃ מִי־

305

way, and from the violence that is in
their hands. ⁹Who knoweth whether
God will not turn and repent, and
turn away from His fierce anger, that
we perish not?'

¹⁰And God saw their works, that
they turned from their evil way; and
God repented of the evil, which He
said He would do unto them; and He
4 did it not. ¹But it displeased
Jonah exceedingly, and he was
angry. ²And he prayed unto the
Lord, and said: 'I pray Thee, O
Lord, was not this my saying, when I
was yet in mine own country? Therefore I fled beforehand unto Tarshish;
for I knew that Thou art a gracious God, and compassionate, long-
suffering, and abundant in mercy,
and repentest Thee of the evil. ³There-
fore now, O Lord, take, I beseech
Thee, my life from me; for it is better
for me to die than to live.' ⁴And the
Lord said: 'Art thou greatly angry?'

⁵Then Jonah went out of the city,
and sat on the east side of the city,
and there made him a booth, and sat
under it in the shadow, till he might
see what would become of the city.
⁶And the Lord God prepared a
gourd, and made it to come up over
Jonah, that it might be a shadow over
his head, to deliver him from his
evil. So Jonah was exceeding glad
because of the gourd. ⁷But God
prepared a worm when the morning
rose the next day, and it smote the
gourd, that it withered. ⁸And it
came to pass, when the sun arose,
that God prepared a vehement east
wind; and the sun beat upon the head
of Jonah, that he fainted, and re-
quested for himself that he might
die, and said: 'It is better for me to
die than to live.' ⁹And God said to
Jonah: 'Art thou greatly angry for
the gourd?' And he said: 'I am greatly angry, even unto death.' ¹⁰And
the Lord said: 'Thou hast had pity
on the gourd, for which thou hast not
laboured, neither madest it grow,
which came up in a night, and perished in a night; ¹¹and should not I

יוֹדֵעַ יָשׁוּב וְנִחַם הָאֱלֹהִים וְשָׁב
10 מֵחֲרוֹן אַפּוֹ וְלֹא נֹאבֵד: וַיַּרְא
הָאֱלֹהִים אֶת־מַעֲשֵׂיהֶם כִּי־שָׁבוּ
מִדַּרְכָּם הָרָעָה וַיִּנָּחֶם הָאֱלֹהִים עַל־
הָרָעָה אֲשֶׁר־דִּבֶּר לַעֲשׂוֹת־לָהֶם
וְלֹא עָשָׂה: ד

1 וַיֵּרַע אֶל־יוֹנָה רָעָה גְדוֹלָה וַיִּחַר
2 לוֹ: וַיִּתְפַּלֵּל אֶל־יְהֹוָה וַיֹּאמַר
אָנָּה יְהֹוָה הֲלוֹא־זֶה דְבָרִי עַד־
הֱיוֹתִי עַל־אַדְמָתִי עַל־כֵּן קִדַּמְתִּי
לִבְרֹחַ תַּרְשִׁישָׁה כִּי יָדַעְתִּי כִּי אַתָּה
אֵל־חַנּוּן וְרַחוּם אֶרֶךְ אַפַּיִם וְרַב־
3 חֶסֶד וְנִחָם עַל־הָרָעָה: וְעַתָּה יְהֹוָה
קַח־נָא אֶת־נַפְשִׁי מִמֶּנִּי כִּי טוֹב מוֹתִי
4 מֵחַיָּי: וַיֹּאמֶר יְהֹוָה הַהֵיטֵב חָרָה
5 לָךְ: וַיֵּצֵא יוֹנָה מִן־הָעִיר וַיֵּשֶׁב
מִקֶּדֶם לָעִיר וַיַּעַשׂ לוֹ שָׁם סֻכָּה וַיֵּשֶׁב
תַּחְתֶּיהָ בַּצֵּל עַד אֲשֶׁר יִרְאֶה מַה־
6 יִּהְיֶה בָּעִיר: וַיְמַן יְהֹוָה־אֱלֹהִים
קִיקָיוֹן וַיַּעַל ׀ מֵעַל לְיוֹנָה לִהְיוֹת צֵל
עַל־רֹאשׁוֹ לְהַצִּיל לוֹ מֵרָעָתוֹ וַיִּשְׂמַח
יוֹנָה עַל־הַקִּיקָיוֹן שִׂמְחָה גְדוֹלָה:
7 וַיְמַן הָאֱלֹהִים תּוֹלַעַת בַּעֲלוֹת הַשַּׁחַר
לַמָּחֳרָת וַתַּךְ אֶת־הַקִּיקָיוֹן וַיִּיבָשׁ:
8 וַיְהִי ׀ כִּזְרֹחַ הַשֶּׁמֶשׁ וַיְמַן אֱלֹהִים רוּחַ
קָדִים חֲרִישִׁית וַתַּךְ הַשֶּׁמֶשׁ עַל־
רֹאשׁ יוֹנָה וַיִּתְעַלָּף וַיִּשְׁאַל אֶת־נַפְשׁוֹ
לָמוּת וַיֹּאמֶר טוֹב מוֹתִי מֵחַיָּי:
9 וַיֹּאמֶר אֱלֹהִים אֶל־יוֹנָה הַהֵיטֵב
חָרָה־לְךָ עַל־הַקִּיקָיוֹן וַיֹּאמֶר
10 הֵיטֵב חָרָה־לִי עַד־מָוֶת: וַיֹּאמֶר
יְהֹוָה אַתָּה חַסְתָּ עַל־הַקִּיקָיוֹן אֲשֶׁר
לֹא־עָמַלְתָּ בּוֹ וְלֹא גִדַּלְתּוֹ שֶׁבִּן־
11 לַיְלָה הָיָה וּבִן־לַיְלָה אָבָד: וַאֲנִי

have pity on Nineveh, that great
city, wherein are more than sixscore
thousand persons that cannot discern
between their right hand and their
left hand, and also much cattle?'

לֹא אָחוּס עַל־נִינְוֵה הָעִיר הַגְּדוֹלָה
אֲשֶׁר יֶשׁ־בָּהּ הַרְבֵּה מִשְׁתֵּים־
עֶשְׂרֵה רִבּוֹ אָדָם אֲשֶׁר לֹא־יָדַע
בֵּין־יְמִינוֹ לִשְׂמֹאלוֹ וּבְהֵמָה רַבָּה::

Micah 7

Who is a God like unto Thee, that
pardoneth the iniquity,
And passeth by the transgression
of the remnant of His heritage?
He retaineth not His anger for
ever,
Because He delighteth in mercy.
¹⁹He will again have compassion
upon us;
He will subdue our iniquities;
And Thou wilt cast all their sins
into the depths of the sea.
²⁰Thou wilt show faithfulness to
Jacob, mercy to Abraham,
As Thou hast sworn unto our
fathers from the days of old.

18 מִי־אֵל כָּמוֹךָ
נֹשֵׂא עָוֺן וְעֹבֵר עַל־פֶּשַׁע
לִשְׁאֵרִית נַחֲלָתוֹ
לֹא־הֶחֱזִיק לָעַד אַפּוֹ
כִּי־חָפֵץ חֶסֶד הוּא:

19 יָשׁוּב יְרַחֲמֵנוּ
יִכְבֹּשׁ עֲוֺנֹתֵינוּ
וְתַשְׁלִיךְ בִּמְצֻלוֹת יָם
כָּל־חַטֹּאתָם:

20 תִּתֵּן אֱמֶת לְיַעֲקֹב חֶסֶד לְאַבְרָהָם
אֲשֶׁר־נִשְׁבַּעְתָּ לַאֲבֹתֵינוּ מִימֵי קֶדֶם:

Jonah, Son of Truth

Devora Steinmetz

THE BOOK of Jonah is unique among the prophetic works included in the section of the Hebrew Bible that we call Latter Prophets. Though the book begins with the word of the Lord coming to Jonah, we soon find that the book contains very little prophecy. It is, rather, a narrative, a story *about* a prophet rather than the verbal message of God *through* a prophet.

In fact, we may even be justified in asking whether Jonah *is* a prophet, in the classical sense of that word. While Jonah is called a prophet in II Kings 14:25 and, as we have noted, his story is included in Latter Prophets, Jonah hardly acts like a prophet. The classical Biblical prophet is not only a receiver of God's word, as Jonah is, or even a relayer of God's word, as Jonah finally, reluctantly, becomes. The classical prophet seeks change. Most often he brings the divine word to individuals or to society in a plea for human change; frequently, too, he turns to God to plead for a change in divine decree.

Jonah, in contrast, does not call for change. Even when he finally speaks to the Ninevites, he simply and unequivocally proclaims their doom. It is the Ninevites who transform this proclamation into a call for *teshuva*—repentance, return, change. The Ninevites change their behavior, God changes his mind about their fate, and Jonah becomes exceedingly upset.

Change, it seems, has no place in Jonah's religious paradigm. Jonah is a man of truth. His full name, *Yona ben Amitai,* means Jonah son of truth, and it is truth, *emet,* that Jonah omits when he complains about God in the final chapter of the book. Jonah draws on the list of God's attributes in Exodus, a list that we recite over and over during the liturgy of the High Holy Days, but he leaves out the attribute of *emet*. Jonah, son of truth, criticizes the God who shows mercy—willingness to change the divine decree in response to human change—rather than *emet*.

Ironically, Jonah consistently brings about change: in people, from the unlikely sailors to the perhaps more unlikely Ninevites; in the natural world, the wind and the sea, the fish and the worm and the plant; and even in his own behavior. Chapter 3 finds him in precisely the predicament of chapter 1, yet this time Jonah follows God's directive, though in the most minimal way. Yet Jonah himself never really changes, and he never comes to terms with change. Indeed, the book ends with the prophet's silence. We are forced to conclude that the message of this book is not to be found in the prophet's words; it is to be found in the story. And the story, with its focus on human, natural, and divine change, is antithetical to the worldview of Jonah son of Amitai.

What I would like to suggest is that it is the very tension between the words of Jonah and the story of Jonah that gives the book its power, and it is this conflict that makes the book ring true to us as we read it each year on the afternoon of Yom Kippur.

In order better to understand the nature of Jonah as a prophet—his understanding of his role, his relationship to the people, and his understanding of God's ways and the ways of the world—we will need to look at two earlier prophets on whose stories the story of Jonah is modeled: Elijah and Moses. We will see later the literary parallels in the stories of Jonah and Elijah, of Elijah and Moses, and of Jonah and Moses. For now, though, let us first turn to the Elijah story and see how *this* prophet understands his mission.

Elijah appears in the narrative of the Book of Kings out of nowhere. He is called *hatishbi* (the Tishbite), and he is described as *mitoshavei* (one of the sojourners) Gilead (I Kings 17:1); a *toshav* is a sojourner, rather than a citizen, and Elijah's description as a *tishbi,* which echoes the word *toshav,* suggests that this is his fundamental quality. The narrative does not tell us where Elijah comes from or who his family is; instead of place of origin and patronym, we are told that Elijah is a sojourner—he has no place, and he has no family.[1] This quality of unrootedness is apparent in the contrast between Elijah and his disciple, Elisha. When Elijah finds Elisha, Elisha is plowing with twelve yoke of oxen; he is a man connected to the land, a farmer rooted in place, and the number of yoke of oxen represents the number of tribes of the people of which he is a member. When Elijah casts his cloak onto Elisha, Elisha recognizes that he has been called and leaves his oxen to run after Elijah: "I will kiss my father and my mother and go after you." Before he follows Elijah, Elisha slaughters the yoke of oxen, cooks the meat, and feeds the people, the first of many such acts of sustenance, that Elisha will do throughout his career.

Elisha has a place, a family, and a people, and his first words and actions demonstrate his concern for his family and people. While the rooted Elisha begins his career by feeding the people, the unrooted Elijah begins *his* career by imposing a famine: "As the Lord, God of Israel, before whom I stand, lives, there shall be no dew or rain these years, except according to my word" (I Kings 17:1).[2] Strikingly, Elijah's proclamation is not preceded by the word of God coming to the prophet; in fact, Elijah makes it clear that he himself is master of his word—he proclaims the forthcoming drought, and his word will herald the end of that drought. Elijah invokes God's name but does not bring God's word.

From the very first verse in which we encounter Elijah, we see a prophet who is not rooted in his people, who perceives himself to "stand before" God but speaks and acts independently of God, and who is willing to proclaim a terrible fate for the people. In the ensuing story, each of these qualities will be tempered, as Elijah is led through a series of experiences that form a sort of prophetic curriculum.

Immediately after Elijah's pronouncement, the "word of God" comes to him (I Kings 17:2), in sharp contrast with the prophet's own word to which Elijah has just referred. God tells Elijah to go eastward to a wadi where he will find water to drink and where ravens will be sent to bring him bread and meat twice daily (I Kings 17:3–6). Elijah, it seems, will be miraculously sustained, despite the drought that he has proclaimed on the land; he can leave the people, going eastward like others in the Torah who separate from their people[3]—he does not share the fate of the people against whom he has found it so easy to prophesy.

This apparent confirmation of Elijah's view of the prophet's relationship to the people, however, is short-lived; soon the wadi dries up, "because there was no rain in the land" (I Kings 17:7). Suddenly Elijah's fate has become intertwined with that of the people. So, now, Elijah has received God's word, though only concerning himself, and he has seen that he cannot avoid the people's fate. The next step will be for this *toshav* (sojourner) to settle among the people. God's word comes to Elijah again; this time he is told to dwell in a city, where God has arranged for a widow to sustain him (I Kings 17:8–9). Once again, God is assuring Elijah of sustenance despite the drought, but now it is among people and through a person, rather than away from people and through ravens.[4] Elijah finds the woman and asks for and receives a drink of water; when he asks for some bread, however, he finds out that the woman barely has enough for a single meal for herself and her son: "I have nothing baked but a handful of flour in the flask and a little oil in the cruse, and here I am gathering two sticks, and I shall go and make it for myself and for my son, and we will eat it and die" (I Kings 17:10–12).

Elijah needs this woman to sustain him, but his encounter makes him aware of her needs as well. He instructs her to feed him and then herself and her son, and then, for the first time, he speaks in God's name: "Thus says the Lord, God of Israel, the flask of flour shall not be spent and the cruse of oil shall not fail, until the day that God gives rain on the face of the earth" (I Kings 17:13–14). This is in striking contrast with Elijah's first speech; now Elijah promises sustenance, he speaks the word of God, he proclaims that rain *will* one day come, and that it is God who will bring it. While we have not heard that the word of God has come to Elijah proclaiming the sustenance of the widow, this passage ends by saying that the flask and cruse were not depleted "in accordance with the word of the Lord, which he spoke in the hand of Elijah" (I Kings 17:6). While Elijah still seems to author the word, or at least to reinterpret the word that God did speak to him concerning his own sustenance through the widow, the narrative here confirms that the promise is indeed the word of the Lord.

There is one final step in the education of this prophet that is a necessary prerequisite to Elijah's resumption of his role as prophet to the people. The widow's son becomes sick to the point of death, and the woman holds Elijah responsible for the boy's death. Elijah takes the boy, brings him to his room, lays him on his bed, and calls out to God: "Lord, have you done evil also to the widow with whom I lodge, by killing her son?" (I Kings 17:19–20). Elijah stretches out over the boy three times and again calls out to God to restore the boy's life. God listens to Elijah's voice, and the boy comes to life (I Kings 17:21–22). Elijah here has moved from speaking independently of God, to hearing God's word, to speaking in God's name, to challenging God. Elijah lives with this family and needs to care for them. God has acted to take away life; Elijah acts to restore life and challenges God to revive the boy; and God listens to his prophet.

The woman's response is a striking confirmation that Elijah has now completed his education as a prophet: "Now by this I know that you are a man of God, and the word of the Lord in your mouth is truth" (I Kings 17:24). The prophet is a man of God, not when he simply brings God's word, but when he challenges God; he speaks truth not when he foretells what will happen, but when he changes what *has* happened. The series of episodes that constitute Elijah's education comes to a close with a verse that parallels the verse in which Elijah first appears: "The word of the Lord came to Elijah in the third year, saying: 'Go, appear to Ahab, and I shall give rain on the face of the earth'" (I Kings 18:1). A comparison of these verses sums up the change in Elijah. Elijah's word is replaced by God's word, the message concerns sustenance rather than destruction, and human fate is changeable. The prophet who has learned to live with a family and care for its members can now bring God's word of salvation to the people; the man who restores life to a lifeless child can bring rain to a land plagued by drought.[5]

Like Elijah at the beginning of his career, Jonah seems to understand *emet* as justice, the idea that people ought to meet the fate that their behavior merits. The Ninevites have been evil and should be destroyed; the Israelites have been evil and should suffer a drought. Affinity for *emet* means a rejection of the possibility of change; human behavior sets in motion a process that must reach its fulfillment in appropriate consequences. Both Jonah and Elijah can be rigidly concerned with *emet* because they are separate from the people. Elijah, we have seen, gradually experiences the people's fate and learns to care for the people as he participates in the life of a small family. The widow's definition of *emet* stands in contrast with the one that Jonah and the early Elijah seem to hold: *emet* characterizes the prophet who brings change; mercifully and boldly challenging fate is what a prophet does who has God's word of truth in his mouth. These two contrasting definitions of *emet* sum up the contrast between Jonah, and the early Elijah, and the classical prophet, the contrast between proclaiming the people's fate and acting to change both the people's behavior and their fate.

In fact, Jonah initially resists even proclaiming the Ninevites' fate. He seems to recognize that crying out against the city might cause the Ninevites to change their ways and God to change their fate. This is the explanation Jonah later gives of his escape from his mission: "Was not this my word while I was on my land? Therefore I fled beforehand to Tarshish. Because I knew that you are a gracious and merciful God, slow to anger and great in lovingkindness and repenting of evil" (Jonah 4:2). Jonah's word is the antithesis of that which the widow recognizes as the true word of God, the call to change.

Like Elijah,[6] Jonah is presented as separate from the people; of course, Jonah is not one of the Ninevites, the people to whom he is sent, but he is also separate from everyone in this book. Each chapter shows Jonah in isolation from others; chapter 1, for example, has Jonah progressively isolating himself, moving down and away, until he finally falls asleep in the recesses of the ship on which he is escaping. Like Elijah, too, Jonah undergoes a series of experiences that seem designed to teach him about the human capacity for change and the human need for change. First, God appoints a fish to swallow Jonah, at once saving him from drowning and constituting the most extreme form of physical isolation. The experience prompts Jonah to pray to God and to recognize that God has chosen to respond to his need and to save him. While Jonah has, in the previous chapter, chosen death as the fate appropriate for the prophet who escapes from the creator of ocean and dry land, he now celebrates God's salvation and embraces life. For himself, then, Jonah is now willing to accept a change in fate. Second, Jonah demonstrates the capacity to change his own behavior. God commands the fish to vomit Jonah out onto dry land, and chapter 3 finds Jonah facing the same predicament as that with which the book opened. God's word comes to him, commanding him to go to Nineveh and proclaim to her God's message, and this time Jonah chooses to obey.

While Jonah experiences the need for change and even celebrates the change in fate that God brings about for him, and while Jonah shows himself capable of change, Jonah never seems to transfer this lesson to his role as prophet. He goes to Nineveh, as God commands, but can hardly wait to proclaim its doom—he speaks out after only a day's journey into this city of three days' journey in extent: "Another forty days, and Nineveh will be overthrown"[7] (Jonah 3:3–4). His proclamation includes no call to repent or hope for a change in fate, yet the Ninevites, great and small, human and beast, do penitential acts and return (*sh-u-v*) from their evil (*r-'-h*) ways, hoping that God will return (*sh-u-v*) from his plan of destruction as well (Jonah 3:5–9). God, indeed, sees their return (*sh-u-v*) from evil (*r-'-h*) and repents (*n-ch-m*) of the evil (*r-'-h*) that would have been their fate (3:10).

Once again, despite himself, Jonah has caused people to turn to God, just as the sailors did and just as he himself did. He is, perhaps, the most successful prophet in the entire Bible! Yet Jonah is displeased, and chapter 4 finds him isolating himself once more and condemning the potential for change in the way God governs the world.

After God returns (*sh-u-v*) and repents (*n-ch-m*) of the evil (*r-'-h*) that was in store for the Ninevites and returns (*sh-u-v*) from his anger (*charon af*) at their evil (*r-'-h*) ways, Jonah experiences a great evil (*r-'-h*) and becomes angry (*vayichar lo*) (Jonah 4:1). He prays to God about the divine attributes of mercy and slowness to anger, explaining that that was why he had initially escaped from his mission, and asks God to take his life. God responds obliquely: "Are you really angry?" Jonah leaves the city, settling eastward,[8] builds himself a shelter, and sits in its shade, waiting to see what will happen in the city (4:2–5).

This passage, too, parallels a passage in the Elijah story. Elijah has succeeded in dramatically and miraculously demonstrating to the people that the Lord of Abraham, Isaac, and Jacob is the only true God (I Kings 18). He now finds out that Jezebel plans to kill him, as she has previously killed most of God's prophets. Elijah rises and flees to Be'ersheva; leaving his lad there, he walks for a day's journey in the desert, sits down under a lone tree, and asks God to take his life (I Kings 19:2–4).

The Elijah and Jonah passages are not only similar thematically, they share a number of motifs as well: both Jonah and Elijah walk a day's journey (Jonah 3:4; I Kings 19:8); both stories include a mention of forty days (Jonah 3:4; I Kings 19:8); each prophet sits alone under a sheltering object (Jonah 4:5, 6; I Kings 19:5); each passage includes a choosing of life by the prophet who requests to die (Jonah 4:5–6; I Kings 19:6, 8); each includes a doubled conversation between the prophet and God (Jonah 4:3–4, 4:8–9; I Kings 19:9–10, 19:13–14);

each includes an elliptical response by God to the prophet's complaint (Jonah 4:10–11; I Kings 19:15–18).

Elijah now appears separated completely from the people. He believes that he is alone (19:10, 14), that, despite the people's affirmation of God in the previous chapter, Elijah alone remains loyal to God; since Jezebel plans to slay him, his mission will have failed, because there is no one to carry on. Elijah enacts his feeling of isolation by fleeing, leaving his lad, journeying through the desert, sitting under a lone tree, asking to die, lying down, and falling asleep (I Kings 19:3–5), acts that parallel both Jonah's initial escape from God's charge and Jonah's final response to the consequences of his message. Despite his depression and despair, Elijah chooses the shelter, and perhaps companionship, of a lone tree; when the angel offers him food, he accepts (I Kings 19:5–6). The despairing prophet who asks to die is, in some small way, embracing life. But Elijah immediately lies back down, and the angel speaks to him again, this time elaborating: "Get up and eat, because the way before you is great"[9] (I Kings 19:7). Eating, then, is not just sustaining life; Elijah's eating will fuel the next part of his mission. The choice to eat is a choice to go on. Indeed, the eating gives Elijah the strength to walk for forty days and forty nights until he reaches Horev, the mountain of God, the place of God's revelation to both nation and lone prophet[10] (I Kings 19:8).

Even at this place, Elijah secludes himself in a cave and rests there, but God's word comes to him: "What are you doing here, Elijah?" (I Kings 19:9). To Elijah's complaint of lone, isolated work for God in the face of a disloyal and hostile people, God responds with an invitation to experience a mysterious revelation: God appears not in the wind or earthquake or fire, but in a silent sound (I Kings 19:10–12). As Elijah stands at the entrance of the cave, his face wrapped in his cloak, he is again asked "What are you doing here, Elijah?" and he repeats the same complaint (I Kings 19:13–14). God responds with a series of instructions: Elijah is to return on his way, anoint a new king of Aram and a new king of Israel, and appoint a new prophet to carry on in his place. These people will bring about change, with the support of seven thousand Israelites who have remained loyal to God[11] (I Kings 19:15–18).

What is the meaning of this modest revelation and this practical message? God is in the silence. Elijah is right: true change will not come about through the miraculous, powerful revelation of Mount Carmel. But change can come about through the acts of a small, loyal community led by committed leaders. Elijah, God notes, is not truly alone; in fact, Elijah himself previously has found this out through his encounter with the loyal Ovadia, who has saved a group of God's prophets (I Kings 18:3). But if Elijah still feels that he is alone, repeating his complaint after experiencing the revelation of silence, then he is not the man who can go on to lead the community to change. He will hand over the cloak of leadership to Elisha, a man who, as we have seen, is one of the people and who will be able to work with the people in small ways to achieve gradual and subtle change.

Elijah's aloneness is both his strength and his weakness. It is what allows him to emerge as a prophet at a time when almost the entire nation has turned from God. Yet it limits his ability to work for the people and with the people. Ultimately Elijah's vision of a renewed covenant with God stands, but Elijah is not the one who can continue to work with the people in realizing the vision. Elijah is a harsh man with an extreme commitment to what is right; while his harshness becomes tempered with concern for people, his extreme standards cause him always to be alone and his vision to remain unrealized.[12]

Jonah shares some of Elijah's traits, though we never see him joining with others and empathizing with their suffering. Like Elijah, Jonah is suspicious of the change brought about by the prophet. Like Elijah, Jonah retreats into depressed isolation after causing the people to return to God, although, unlike Elijah, Jonah has no objective reason to doubt the success of his mission. Like Elijah, too, Jonah chooses life despite his request to die: he builds a hut to enjoy its shade, and he rejoices in the plant that God causes to grow for him (4:5–6). Both prophets act in ways that belie their words. While they ask to die, they embrace life. Elijah's choosing to live, though, is bound up with continuing his work and transmitting his mission. Jonah's is not; he chooses life and comfort for himself but does not go on to work on behalf of the people. The book ends with God's oblique response to Jonah's request to die; Jonah, however, neither responds nor takes action.

Before returning to examine God's response and Jonah's silence, I want to turn briefly to the prophet on whom both the Elijah and Jonah stories are based—Moses.

Elijah clearly is modeled on Moses.[13] The people's acceptance of God at Mount Carmel parallels the Israelites' commitment to God at Sinai, and the episode of Elijah's despair and lone encounter with God at Horev parallels Moses' encounter with God after the people so suddenly stray from God and worship the Golden Calf. But Moses, though always different from and separate from the people, sees himself as one of them, and he links his fate to theirs. God offers Moses an opportunity to survive and achieve greatness without this sinning people: "And now, let me be, and my anger will burn against them, and I will consume them, and I will make you into a great nation" (Exodus 32:10). Moses pleads on behalf of the people, perhaps understanding from God's request to be left alone that it is the leader's job *not* to leave God alone. Using the same words that will describe God's response to the Ninevites' repentance, Moses asks God to "repent (*n-ch-m*) of the evil" that God plans for the Israelites, and God does so (Exodus 32:12, 14). Moses refuses God's offer to save Moses alone and to make him into a great nation; despite the people's great sin, Moses demands that God forgive them, "and if not, please wipe me out of your book which you have written" (Exodus 32:31–32). Instead of despairing when the people fall from the height to which Moses had led them at Sinai, Moses achieves his true greatness as a leader and prophet in this episode. He insists on linking his fate to the fate of his people, he demands that God forgive the people and reverse the evil decree against them, and he goes on to work with the people on recognizing their sin, cleansing their community, and turning back to God.

As in the Elijah story, the grand revelation to the people is followed by a quiet, private revelation to the prophet. Moses asks to see God's glory, and God allows Moses to experience his presence from the cleft of the rock, as Elijah does from the entrance of the cave. But, among many differences between these two stories, one stands out in the context of our study: for Moses, this private experience of God's presence is intertwined with the leader's concern for his people. Moses has just asked for God's presence to accompany the people on their journey, despite their sinfulness; it is in this context that Moses asks God to reveal himself to him.

Moses, then, experiences much the same failure and frustration with the people that Elijah later does, with the people shifting swiftly between exalted moments of commitment to God and behavior that reflects rebellious rejection of God. But Moses, in this episode, refuses to give up on the people, refuses to see himself as separate from them; he pleads with God to change the evil decree, and he achieves his own personal communion with God in the context of his prayer that God allow the divine presence to accompany the people. It is in this episode that God reveals to Moses the divine attributes, attributes to which Jonah refers in his complaint to God after the Ninevites repent and God forgives them.

A fascinating midrash on this episode highlights the tension in Moses between his strict sense of justice and his growing awareness that he must care for the people despite their unreliable and frequently disheartening behavior. After God reveals the divine attributes to Moses, "Moses hurried and bowed his head toward the earth and worshipped" (Exodus 34:8). On this verse, the midrash asks:

> What did Moses see? Rabbi Hanina ben Gamala said: "He saw 'slow to anger,'" and the rabbis said: "He saw 'truth'" (Exodus 34:6). It has been taught in accordance with the one who said, "He saw 'slow to anger,'" for it has been taught: When Moses went up to heaven, he found God sitting and writing "slow to anger." He said before him: "Master of the world, 'slow to anger' for the righteous!" He said to him: "Even for the wicked." He said to him: "The wicked shall be destroyed." He said to him: "Now you see what you need." When Israel sinned [in the episode of the scouts], he [God] said to him: "Did you not say to me thus: '"Slow to anger" for the righteous?'" He said to him: "Master of the world, and did you not say to me thus: 'Even for the wicked?'" And thus it is written: "Please let the power of the Lord be great, as you have spoken, saying . . ." (Numbers 14:17).

> (SANHEDRIN IIIA)

According to this midrash, Moses, early in his career, cannot understand why God should show merciful slowness to anger to the wicked; those who do evil should be punished as befits their deeds. God does not answer Moses' question but hints at a future time when Moses will need to take advantage of the very divine quality that he has challenged. God, according to the midrash, is alluding to the second great sin that the newly delivered children of Israel commit—the sin of the scouts. In this episode, as in the episode of the Golden Calf, God threatens to destroy the people and to make Moses into a great nation (Numbers 14:12). Moses again pleads with God to spare the people, but this time he has an additional tool: the very attributes that God has revealed to him in the aftermath of the sin of the Golden Calf. Presenting himself as reiterating God's own self-description—"as you have spoken (*d-b-r*), saying"—Moses says: "Lord, slow to anger and great in lovingkindness . . . Forgive the iniquity of this people according to the greatness of your lovingkindness" (Numbers 14:17–19). What the midrash has picked up on is crucial to our study: Moses, though claiming to quote God's own words, has in fact amended them to fit his current need to defend the people. Moses has stressed the qualities of slowness to anger, of lovingkindness and forgiveness, and he has omitted that quality so dear to him, and to Elijah, and to Jonah: *emet*, truth. God, according to this midrash, has encouraged this audacious behavior on the part of his prophet: "Now you see what you need." In the Biblical text, God affirms Moses' plea and agrees to his request: "I have forgiven, according to your word (*d-b-r*)" (Numbers 14:20). As in the Elijah story, when the widow affirms the truth of Elijah's word and his status as a man of God, the prophet is seen to be most true when he pleads with God, on behalf of others, to change the divine decree and to grant life and salvation.

Moses' revision of the divine attributes is particularly germane to our study, because Jonah, too, lists these attributes and revises them. Like Moses, Jonah focuses on the attributes of slowness to anger and forgiveness, and he omits the attribute of truth. But Jonah's behavior, here, is antithetical to Moses': Moses is appealing for forgiveness, asking God, in effect, to lay truth or justice aside for the moment; Jonah, in contrast, complains about God's forgiveness, lamenting God's laying aside of the attribute of truth.

What is God's response to Jonah? I would like to suggest three possible understandings of God's response.

First, God may be seen as pointing out the irony in Jonah's behavior. The first time Jonah complains and asks to die, it is in reaction to the change in the Ninevites' behavior and the change in God's decree. "Are you really angry?" asks God[14] (Jonah 4:4). Jonah then leaves the city, settles to the east, builds himself a hut, and sits in the shade. God appoints a *kikayon* (gourd) plant "to be shade over his head and to save him from his evil," and Jonah rejoices greatly (Jonah 4:5–6). But, at dawn the next day, God appoints a worm that attacks the plant so that it dries up; he then appoints a strong east wind that beats on Jonah's head. Jonah once again asks to die, and God once again responds: "Are you really angry about the *kikayon* plant?" (Jonah 4:7–9). God's repeated query creates a sense of irony: first we see Jonah as a man of principle, who asks to die rather than live in a world that so violates his sense of justice; but then we see Jonah as a small man, rejoicing easily in a comforting plant and once again asking to die when his plant is taken away from him. A man who so easily shifts from feeling "great evil" (Jonah 4:1) to feeling "great joy" (Jonah 4:6) and who experiences the same frustration at the death of a plant as at a change in world events becomes almost a figure of humor here; the great moral philosopher/prophet acts like a spoiled child, and his behavior undercuts the strength of his moral claim.

A second reading has God take Jonah more seriously: God's response may be read as pointing out, not the triviality of Jonah's concerns but the inconsistency in Jonah's positions. While Jonah laments the *chesed* (lovingkindness) that God has shown the Ninevites, he embraces the *chesed* that God shows him; his second request to die comes as a response to the withdrawal of an act of kindness, the death of the *kikayon,* while his first request to die was in response to an act of God's *chesed*. The *kikayon* must surely be seen as an act of *chesed* on God's part: God causes it to grow not only to provide needed, lifesaving shelter—after all, Jonah has already built himself a hut for that purpose—but "to save him from his evil"[15] (Jonah 4:6), the evil that afflicts Jonah in the aftermath of his mission (Jonah 4:1). God has saved the Ninevites, too, from evil; when they turn from their evil path, God repents of the evil that would have been their fate (Jonah 3:10). The parallel between God's forgiveness of the Ninevites and God's granting Jonah the comfort of the *kikayon* points out Jonah's inconsistency: both are acts of *chesed,* yet Jonah rejects one but embraces the other. In fact, the odd name of this plant may highlight its nature as an undeserved act of *chesed*. *Kikayon* may be a play on Jonah's earlier deliverance from the depths of the ocean: the great fish, like the plant, is "appointed" by God (Jonah 2:1; 4:6), and after Jonah beseeches God and celebrates divine salvation, God tells the fish to vomit Jonah up: *vayakei et Yona* (Jonah 2:11). Jonah has cele-brated God's salvation from death (*vayakei et Yona*), and he rejoices over God's comfort from evil (*kikayon*) yet he persists in complaining about the *chesed* that God exhibits in his governance of the world.

A third reading of God's response focuses on God's final words, in which God emphasizes his concern for the world on which he has la-bored. Human and animal, plant and fish, wind and worm—all are part of the world that God cares about and that he desires to sustain.[16] Perhaps, too, the perspective of the Creator can be seen to obliterate the sharp distinction between the truth that Jonah affirms and the change that he scorns. Jonah accepts the *kikayon*'s existence and mourns its loss, but, as God points out, a day ago the plant had not yet come into being. The state of affairs that human beings accept as a given may be a new phenomenon, while occurrences that human beings see as changes or departures from the way things ought to be may be, in reality, simply a return to the way things were. Who is to say that the Ninevites are really wicked and that their repentance and God's forgiveness are changes in the way things ought to be? Perhaps their repentance should be seen not as "turning around," but as "turning back"—return, *teshuva*—to the way things originally were and ought to be. While this little book is full of sudden changes in na-ture—winds and fish and plants and worms suddenly appearing and taking center stage—all are presented as called by God to do the di-vine will. Do these represent miraculous changes in nature, or are these simply instances of God's world functioning as it should, sus-taining itself and all of its creatures in accordance with the will of the creator? Perhaps God's diverse attributes are only ways in which hu-mans, imbedded in the here and now, understand the divine will. God, though, governs the world according to a single principle, the love and concern of a creator for his helpless creation.

Strikingly, Jonah does not respond to God's final words. The book ends with the prophet's silence. It is Jonah's very silence, though, that I think speaks most eloquently, for we must look, finally, not to what Jonah says, but to what he does. Jonah asks to die, but he em-braces life; Jonah complains about change, but he himself changes and brings about change and welcomes change. The message of this book is conveyed not through the prophet's words, but through the prophet's silent behavior.[17]

Jonah is a troubled prophet, and his trouble, I think, is that which plagues us when we examine our own lives, as we do, especially, on Yom Kippur. Yom Kippur is a celebration both of the human capacity for change and of the divine power to forgive. The book Jonah is concerned explicitly with the latter, with the divine attributes of truth and mercy. For many of us, it is the human side of this issue that seems more problematic; as the time comes round each year for us to examine our lives and commit ourselves to changing our lives for the better, we may justifiably question our ability to do so. As a child, I puzzled over the image, in the *Avoda* (service of the high priest) section of the Yom Kippur service, of the scarlet thread tied to the horn of the scapegoat. Each year the thread would be found to have turned white, and the people would rejoice that their sins had been forgiven. Instead of the whitened thread, though, I found myself focusing on the next year's scarlet thread. Doesn't the fact that we will once again tie a scarlet thread on the scapegoat's horn undermine our faith in repentance and atonement? Do we truly have the power to transform our lives?

Throughout the Yom Kippur service, we celebrate change, affirming *teshuva* (repentance/return) and *selicha* (forgiveness). We do this, most noticeably, through our frequent repetition of the *Selichot* prayers, which center on the recitation of the divine attributes that God teaches Moses. We begin to recite *Selichot* daily as Rosh Hashana approaches; on Yom Kippur we recite them in each prayer. Actually, our recitation of the attributes constitutes our own revision of the Biblical passage in Exodus. In fact, in reciting the *Selichot* service, we are following Moses' lead, using the attributes to urge God to exercise his power of forgiveness. Instead of reciting the entire list of attributes, which ends with "and clear he will not, punishing the iniquity of the fathers on the children and on the children's children, to the third and fourth generation" (Exodus 34:7), we end our recitation of the list of attributes with the word "and clear." We have not only omitted the end of the list; we have transformed an attribute of judgment into an attribute of forgiveness! Our audacity in changing God's words, modeled as it is on Moses' revision of God's words when he pleads for forgiveness in the episode of the scouts, is further reflected in our recitation of the words with which God accedes to Moses' request: "And God said, I have forgiven in accordance with your word"

(Numbers 14:20). We have changed God's word into our word and have linked to this revised word God's acquiescence. Through the power of the word, we have changed punishment into forgiveness, at once radically affirming the human capacity for transformation and the divine willingness to forgive.

Yet, as the Day of Atonement draws to a close, we allow ourselves, just once, to give voice to our doubts. We do so by reading the words of Jonah, which include Jonah's own revision of the divine attributes as a challenge to the process of *teshuva* and *selicha* that we have spent the day so staunchly affirming. Jonah's critique of the attributes of mercy and forgiveness, Jonah's doubts about the process of transformation, subtly articulate our own doubts about the very process in which we are engaged and which we are celebrating.

Our reading of Jonah, then, offers a liturgical counterpoint to the *Selichot* service. It does so, moreover, at the time of day that, on other fast days, is reserved for an affirmation of *teshuva* and *selicha,* for the Torah reading for the *Mincha* (afternoon) service of fast days is none other than the passage from Exodus in which God teaches Moses the divine attributes and agrees to forgive the people's sin. At the service during which we would expect to celebrate God's paradigmatic promise to forgive, we read instead Jonah's critique of this very process.

We allow ourselves to give expression to our doubts through the words of Jonah, yet we are left with the message of the book of Jonah. Like Jonah, despite our doubts, despite our knowledge that next year the thread will once again be scarlet, despite the fact that, like the children of Israel, we have been forgiven before but have sinned again, we choose to go on, embracing life and accepting the challenge to transform and shape our lives.

And why was he called Jonah (yona)? Because he was like Noah's dove (yona). Noah sent out the dove three times, and Jonah went out three times. The first time Noah sends forth the dove, she returns to the place from which she started out, bearing no message (Genesis 8:8–9). So, too, when God first sends Jonah forth, Jonah returns to the place from which he started out, without having brought a message. The second time Noah sends forth the dove, she returns with a message—she brings an olive leaf, and Noah understands that the flood waters have abated (Genesis 8:10–11). So, too, when God sends Jonah forth again, Jonah delivers a message to the people. The third time Noah sends forth the dove, she does not return to him (Genesis 8:12)— and this is the strongest message of all. For it is not enough for the dove to announce that the world is habitable once more; it is her silent choice to begin life anew in the world which allows Noah to hear God's command to leave the ark and build a new world (Genesis 8:15–19). So, too, Jonah goes out a third time and does not return. Just as the dove's silence is the loudest message for Noah, Jonah's silence is the loudest message for us. It is Jonah's choice to continue, despite his doubts, which urges us to begin again.

A Carnival at the Gates:
Jonah and Laughter on Yom Kippur

RACHEL ADLER

A CHASIDIC saying declares in a paradoxical pun: *Yom kippurim yom kepurim.*[1] Yom Kippur is a day like Purim. A powerful paradox! Here are two holidays that seem to be each other's antithesis. Yom Kippur is a fast, a day of tears and introspection. Purim is a feast, a day of laughter and carousing. Yom Kippur demands bodily deprivation. Purim mandates bodily pleasure. Whereas Yom Kippur reinforces traditional laws and values, Purim stands them on their heads. Boundaries are eroded. Roles are reversed. For men to dress as women is in some communities a traditional Purim masquerade. Even the daily services lack their usual solemnity; they are punctuated by jokes, interruptions, and, in some communities, irreverent parodies of other liturgies. "Purim Torah" caricatures the study of sacred texts. Satires mock teachers and communal leaders. The rules require unruliness: "Raba said, on Purim, one is obligated to drink until one does not know [*ad shelo yada*] the difference between 'cursed be Haman and blessed be Mordecai.'" (Megilla 7a)[2]

Viewing Purim as the inverse of Yom Kippur brings us closer to understanding their likeness, for an inversion is merely a likeness reversed. Yom Kippur is a fast preceded by a feast, while Purim is a feast preceded by a fast. Purim is a celebration tinged with somberness, whereas Yom Kippur is a solemn occasion pervaded by celebration. Hence, Yom Kippur's liturgical structure closely resembles festival liturgies. Sanctuary and Torah scrolls are decked in white. Worshipers wear their best clothes. Only their feet, in nonleather shoes, bespeak fasting and mourning. This amalgam of joy and mourning is also expressed by the *kittel,* a white garment worn by the service leader and by traditional worshipers, a white garment that also serves as both wedding robe and shroud.

The central liturgical performance of Purim is the reading of the

Book of Esther, whose laughter is frequently undercut by mourning, dread, and violence. Traditionally, at certain points in the narration, its lively cantillation slides into the haunting melody in which the Book of Lamentations is chanted, suggesting the tenuousness of all escapes. Texts, as Paul Ricoeur says, "explode the worlds of their authors."[3] Our judgment and our laughter are dynamic responses altered by changes in the world, the community, and the self we bring to every reading or ritual enactment. Layered upon the text of Esther are memories of the Holocaust, the story in which Haman won; of the terrible Purim celebration of 1994, at the Cave of Machpelah in Hebron, where Baruch Goldstein reenacted upon the bodies of praying Muslims the revenge of the Jews of Persia upon their enemies; and the 1996 terrorist retaliation against Israeli teenagers. These shadows upon an already shadowed text are manifestations of Yom Kippur amid the uproar of the carnival. We are forced to recall the reality and finality of death, the sins of vengeance, and the terrible repetition compulsion to which they shackle both victor and vanquished.[4]

Death and justice are central themes for both Purim and Yom Kippur. On both we acknowledge that existence, individual and communal, is precarious, and human power and knowledge are limited. We have responsibility but little control. We figure in patterns that are beyond our discernment and can be hurt by forces and currents that are beyond us as well as by the repercussions of our own acts.

Purim commemorates a narrowly averted holocaust decreed through a perversion of justice. Falsely accused, the Jewish people are abandoned by a king who hands over his authority to a biased and greedy official. Justice reinstated expresses itself as another kind of favoritism: salvation for the Jews but pitiless retribution for their enemies. Life and death, justice and injustice, are arbitrarily dealt out to winners and losers in the great game of power. A palace bureaucracy riddled with cabals is checkmated by an even more mysterious opponent: the divine strategist whose name is never mentioned in the Book of Esther.

On Yom Kippur, life and death and the administration of justice are equally central concerns, but there are tensions and ambivalences in their definitions. One set of liturgical themes derived from the Book of Kohelet (Ecclesiastes) radically and reductively articulates human impermanence and ultimate insignificance: "What are we? What is our life? What is our piety? What is our righteousness? What is our attainment, our power, our might?[5] Human beings are no different from animals, for all are fleeting and futile [*ki hakol hevel*]."[6] There is no favoritism in Kohelet's account of divine justice. An imperfect humanity must account for itself before an impersonal, impartial, and omniscient deity. In a second set of themes, however, justice is personal, flexible, and leavened with compassion. The cornerstone text for this theology of justice is the declaration of God's mercy as proclaimed by God to Moses after the sin of the Golden Calf (Exodus 34:7) and by Moses back to God after the spies return with their false report and the people lose faith in God's promise of the land (Numbers 14:18): "YHWH YHWH God, showing-mercy, showing-favor, long suffering in anger, abundant in loyalty and faithfulness, keeping loyalty to the thousandth [generation], bearing iniquity, rebellion and sin."[7] The Rabbis heighten this theology of justice-as-compassion by an audacious undermining of the text. They repunctuate the final clause of the verse, so that instead of the literal reading "and clearing, he surely does not clear [the guilty], but visits the iniquity of the parents upon children and children's children to the third and fourth generations," they obtain the reading we use liturgically: "and clearing even the guilty."[8] This formula, which we recite over and over, expresses the tacit subversion of retributive justice at the heart of Yom Kippur.

Purim belongs to those festivals that invert or subvert rules and norms overtly rather than covertly. Many cultures have such festivals. The ancient Romans called them saturnalia. Medieval Europeans called them feasts of fools and carnivals. Such festivals glorify bodily pleasure and celebrate the comic, the grotesque, and the excessive. These characteristics of the carnivalesque have in recent years attracted the attention of literary scholars and anthropologists.[9]

It is late in the day of Yom Kippur that the carnivalesque bursts into our liturgy.[10] At the afternoon service, with blood sugar at low ebb and self-congratulation for our asceticism on the rise, we read what may be the funniest book of the Bible, Jonah.

The custom of reading Jonah on Yom Kippur is very old. Its first written source, interestingly, is in Megilla 31b, the tractate of the Babylonian Talmud whose major topic is the laws of Purim.[11] These ancient liturgical associations with Purim can serve as a portal into a

book that is rather off-putting for women. The fictional world of
Jonah is devoid of feminine presences. God and prophet, Jew and
non-Jew, land and sea, animals and plants, represent difference in
Jonah, but the difference of women is absent. Understandably it is
easier for women to read themselves into the Book of Esther, where
sexuality and the difference of Jew and non-Jew are the tensions that
move the plot, and heroes and villains are both male and female. Yet
some primary tenets of feminist spiritualities inform the womanless
world of Jonah: a profound tenderness for others, even others wholly
different from ourselves, and a moral universe brimming with forgiv-
ing laughter. Laughter, provoked by burlesque and by the carnivalesque, is the bridge that connects Jonah with Purim.

Jonah is a parody, burlesquing other Biblical stories and punning
outrageously.[12] It is also the most carnivalesque of Biblical books, rich
in monstrosities, curiosities, spectacles, and monkeyshines. The star
of this freak show is the world's most recalcitrant prophet. Ordered to
Nineveh, he hops a ship to the other end of the known world. In the
violent storm that ensues, everyone else is on deck, praying. Jonah
has to be dragged to his devotions by the captain. After the lot falls
on Jonah, and he acknowledges that he is the cause of the storm, it is
Jonah who suggests that he be heaved overboard; the sailors are
shocked. First they attempt to get back to land, then they pray not to
be condemned for shedding Jonah's "innocent blood." Reluctantly
they toss in the prophet, and when the sea miraculously calms, they
hold a regular revival meeting, complete with sacrifices, testimonials,
and vows to YHWH. This demonstration of faith presages Jonah's inexplicable conversion of Nineveh. Although he lacks any discernible
gifts either of evangelism or of charm, wherever this curmudgeon of
a prophet goes, he leaves a trail of people beating their breasts and
shouting hallelujah.

After the reluctant evangelist's own purifying immersion, we encounter the most impressive beast in the carnival's menagerie: a giant
fish that can swallow prophets but just can't digest them. Our sympa-
thies are with the fish; Jonah, as the audience has begun to discover,
is pretty hard to stomach. After three days and nights, Jonah capitu-
lates. In a stunning and lyrical psalm of repentance, he both apolo-
gizes and recounts his excellent adventure as the world's deepest
diver. This travelogue features such exotic locales as the belly of

Sheol, the heart of the seas, the primal abyss, the roots of the mountains, and the barred gates that hold the sea back from the earth.

God's response to Jonah's effusion is brief and businesslike; He speaks to the fish and it throws up, a literal demonstration of "return" to a prophet unclear on the concept. Spat out onto dry land, to receive his prophetic mission a second time, Jonah does turn himself around and make tracks for the gigantic metropolis to which he has been ordered, a city it takes three days to cross. Ambling a mere third of the way into the city, Jonah begins racking up more world records. First he gives the world's most laconic prophecy, a mere five words in Hebrew: "Forty days more and Nineveh will be overthrown" (3:4).

To Jonah's intense distaste, this curt and uninviting oracle is monumentally and unprecedentedly effective. Isaiah, Ezekiel, Jeremiah, pour floods of eloquence, indignation, passion, and pleading upon God's chosen people to no effect whatever. Jonah dumps the naked facts of doomsday on an unpromising bunch of *goyim,* and they fall all over themselves rushing to do *teshuva.* To add insult to injury, the second marvel in the carnival menagerie reveals itself: in this burg, even the dumb animals fast in sackcloth and ashes, a sly hint, perhaps, that even they are better at *teshuva* than the folks on Jonah's home turf.

Inadvertently Jonah has produced a howling success, and, characteristically he immediately begins howling. He flings in God's face a blasphemous version of the very litany the Yom Kippur liturgy has been repeating all day: "This is why I hurried to run away to Tarshish!" he complains. "Because I knew that you are a God showing-mercy, showing-favor [*El chanun verachum*], long-suffering in anger and abundant in loyalty [*erekh apayim verav chesed*], and indulgent of evil [*venicham al hara'a*]."[13] Jonah's unorthodox ending to the verse traduces God for the very quality we have been imploring God to exercise: clearing the guilty. Jonah is also at cross-purposes with the Yom Kippur worshiper in his surly rejection of life. "Remember us for life," we plead repeatedly in High Holy Day prayers. We reiterate such passages as Deuteronomy's "Choose life so that you may live" (30:19) and Isaiah's "Turn from your evil ways; why should you die, house of Israel?" (55:6). Jonah tells God, "Go ahead, kill me. I'd rather be dead than alive." To which God, like the perfect therapist, replies, "Should you really be this angry?"

Still hoping for a replay of Sodom and Gomorra, Jonah builds a *sukka* outside the city so he can anticipate Nineveh's downfall in comfort. God roofs the structure with a shade plant that shoots up like Jack's magic beanstalk but also equips it with an equally speedy worm to chomp it down, the last beast in the marvelous menagerie. When Jonah, seared by sun and scorched by wind, again begs for death, God responds therapeutically once again: "So you're really angry about losing the plant?" That sets God up for the punch line: "You cared about the plant though you did not cultivate it or grow it. Shouldn't I care about a city where there are hordes of people who don't know their right from their left [and hence, unlike the People of the Book, may just not know any better], and besides [a final dig in the ribs] there are all those terrific animals!" The liturgy appends its own gentle joke to the ending, two verses from Micah (7:18–20) praising God, the forgoer of retribution and acceptor of *teshuva*. God "hurls our sins into the depths of the sea"; unlike the recalcitrant prophet, we do not have to be hurled in bodily along with them.

The afternoon Yom Kippur prophetic reading of Jonah, like the morning prophetic reading from Isaiah 57–58, balances the religious teaching offered by the Torah portion it follows. After a Torah portion detailing the priestly ritual for Yom Kippur, the Isaiah reading attacks the sanctimonious for commodifying religious ritual and consuming it at the expense of those they exploit and oppress. In the afternoon, a Torah portion enumerating a variety of sins of the flesh is followed by Jonah, in which the sins of the spirit are exposed, a narrative in which the official representative of godliness is rigid, pitiless, and oblivious of the wonders and oddities popping up all around him.

Probably the most religious response to the reading of Jonah would be a hearty guffaw. That guffaw would distance us enough to see in comic perspective the bodies we are so righteously afflicting and the spirits we are so assiduously burnishing. It would indicate that we understand the Book of Jonah's answer to the question posed by Isaiah's nettled audience: "Why do you not notice when we fast? Why do you not heed when we afflict ourselves?" (Isaiah 58:3). God's answer in Jonah is: "Because when you posture and preen yourselves on your temporary bodily deprivations without attaining an iota of concern for the needs and sufferings of other living beings, I find you shocking and ridiculous. This time, my gambit is to laugh you and tease you into compassion." By mocking the sins of the spirit, Jonah sends us back into our afflicted bodies to be made whole, to know ourselves as bodies flooded with spirit. If we have understood, we will be able to extrapolate from our own growling bellies, aching heads, boredom, and weariness to the infinitely precious and vulnerable spirit-flooded bodies of other living creatures. Leaving behind us both self-abasement and self-congratulation frees us to see ourselves as God sees us, with amused tenderness and persistent hope.

This brief moment of illumination is the carnival prize waiting to be won. Snatch it up quickly, before the curtain falls and the tents are struck and the monsters bedded down. The lights of the carnival are dimming fast. At the far end of the field loom a pair of great gates, and those gates, ladies and gentlemen, are closing.

Afterword: Meeting God's Gaze

ARLENE AGUS

Shuva eilai ve'ashuva aleichem.
Return to me and I will return to you.

MALACHI 3:7

Who is It to whom human beings cling in passionate,
all-consuming love and from whom they flee in mortal fear and dread?

RABBI JOSEPH B. SOLOVEITCHIK
Lonely Man of Faith

With the poignancy of a plea but the peremptoriness of a command, the prophet Malachi beckons the people Israel to resume its relationship with the waiting God through an act of return.

Personal turning or returning is interpreted by tradition to mean repentance, in Hebrew *teshuva*. Reaching toward repentance, though an act of great psychological and spiritual intimacy, is nonetheless enacted in the context of community. It was through the Brooklyn streets at dawn that the *shofar* (ram's horn) would sound in the days before Rosh Hashana, echoing the summons of Malachi, shaking into consciousness the community in which I grew up. It was there that I came to know the mysterious vortex of High Holy Day forces, a vast corpus of rituals and texts and liturgies that had—and have—the capacity to increase one's closeness to God, if not to transfigure utterly the behavior and destiny of a Jew.

It was there that I learned to speak my heart to a personal God. And there that God first answered.

The psychospiritual power of this sacred season, welcomed and dreaded, is described here in the form of personal testimony. Inevitably a religious portrait of this kind will contain elements that strike readers as local, unfamiliar, or particularistic. I trust to the reader's understanding . . . and seasonal forgiveness.

No less than our mortal lives are at stake during these fateful days; no less than a radical remodeling of our human clay will suffice to meet the standards of the divine potter.

The solitary odyssey toward self-transformation demands of each of us the very humility and inner strength we lacked when committing our sins; the prospect of facing the inscrutable judge with self-incriminating truths is spiritually daunting as well as psychologically risky, the dread untempered by previous pardons.

So, on the one hand, mindful of the urgency of *teshuva* (return, repentance), we seek out God and struggle earnestly against our natural complacency, laziness, and cynicism. On the other hand, we shrink back from the demands of the Infinite, hide *our* faces from God, and try, like Jonah, to flee from the divine eye under whose blinding scrutiny we fear we will shrink to our actual size.

We are not left alone to reconcile our conflicting intentions, as the Almighty extends not just the summons, but the means by which to respond to it. Ingeniously designed to address both our recoiling fears and our self-protective inertia, the High Holy Day ritual deploys an intricate strategy for alternately arming and disarming us.

The ritual arms us by deftly reassuring us, by emboldening us, and by encouraging the expression of our existential fears. It disarms by jolting us, prodding us out of denial, self-satisfaction, and skepticism and into a *teshuva* state of mind.

How does the liturgy embolden us?

First, through repetitive speech. "For the sin, for the sin, for the sin." *Avinu Malkeinu, Avinu Malkeinu* (Our Father, Our Sovereign). The same prayers, the same melodies, repeated over and over with comforting familiarity. Such repetition evokes the visceral security of a rocking cradle and, on a deeper level, transmits to the penitent the welcome illusion of immortality by continually promising one more refrain.

Then, the liturgy reassures us through soothing stories, especially accounts of the efficacy of the prayers of mothers—Sarah, Hagar, Rachel, Hannah; reminiscences of the youthful romance between God and Israel with glorious fantasies of the sovereign's future coronation;[1] and moral cliff-hangers culminating in miraculous rescues, like the *Akeda* (the binding of Isaac) and Jonah.

Finally, we engage in cathartic, mystical behavior to dramatize and calm our primal fears: some communities dress in white, shroudlike clothes, fearing the answer to, "Who shall live and who shall die";[2] others fling sin-contaminated bread crumbs into rivers; worshipers elaborately reenact the Temple service of the high priest through liturgical readings; magical incantations are invoked by those circling their heads with coins, if not live chickens, in a Kabbalistic atoning rite; and our collective nerves hang on the bellows issuing from the horns of an animal.

But that *shofar* blast explodes our equanimity, reverberating through our bodies like the wailing howl of grief, the hollow desolation of solitude, and the urgent cries of the newborn. It is one of many cathartic rituals jarringly interpolated into the liturgy as disarming assaults on our complacency.

The *machzor* (High Holy Day prayer book) erupts with tales of spiritual and physical dislocation: Abraham searching for God, Jonah fleeing from before God, scapegoats banished with our sins into the wilderness, little boys—Isaac, Ishmael, Samuel—forced from their homes for premature encounters with destiny.

Meanwhile, the similes of the supplicant erode our dignity: we are called wayward children, inconsequential as dust. Menacing metaphors warn of gates closing out our prayers, books shutting out our names. Guilty as charged, we feel utterly vulnerable before the heavenly court, needing God's help even to pray.

The atmosphere is ominously charged as even the angelic hosts tremble in foreboding. We plead for the cleansing of our self-inflicted stains, only to be reminded by the story of the ten martyred sages[3] that reward cannot be guaranteed, even by righteousness.

Suspense grows into dread as pride yields to shame. We fall prostrate—literally, in some congregations—in awe and anguish: "Before You we pour out our souls," "When our strength fails us, Do not abandon us."[4]

In unrelenting counterpoint, for the ten awe-filled days linking Rosh Hashana with Yom Kippur, the combined impact of arming and disarming thus equips us to face God and face down death in the name of renewing our lives.

⊂∷⊃

But having been thus equipped, how do we begin to face God?

Kechu imakhem devarim veshuvu el Adonai.
Take words with you and return to the Lord.

HOSEA 14:2–3
PROPHETIC READING, *Shabbat Shuva* (Sabbath between
Rosh Hashana and Yom Kippur)

Ma nomar lefanekha [yosheiv marom] . . . Uma nesaper
lefanekha [shokhein shechakim], halo kol hanistarot ve-
haniglot ata yodei'a.
*What can we say to You . . . and what claims can we make be-
fore You? For You already know all things, secret and revealed.*
MUSAF (ADDITIONAL) SERVICE, YOM KIPPUR

Most of the Biblical characters moving through the High Holy Day
texts model a very specific approach to personal or collective change:
direct interaction with God. God speaks and they respond. They call
out and God reacts. Direct communication with God seems a natural,
almost casual phenomenon; God's guiding hand readily apparent, as
though expected.

But rather than emulate these personal confrontations, we typi-
cally only recount them, timidly hoping that scripted manuals and
group confessionals will secure for us a listing in the Book of Life.
And though tradition urges us to "seek out God when God can be
found"[5] during this *eit ratzon,* this propitious period of divine acces-
sibility, we treat revelation as a distant hope, rather than surge toward the immediacy of God's presence.

How, then, does one find the courage and the language to address
God in one's own voice? And where does one begin?

⊂∷⊃

When I have sought the presence of God, it has often been late on
Yom Kippur day, when the onset of *Ne'ila* (closing service of Yom Kip-

pur) reminds me that true inner reckoning has not yet taken place. The gates of heaven have started to close and my heart begins to sink with the sun.

My confessions thus far have revealed nothing new to me, and certainly nothing new to my Maker. Having recoiled from stretching to my spiritual limits, I feel as yet unworthy of forgiveness, in itself a punishment for a religious person.

With growing self-awareness and personal admissions my final journey begins. I have hidden—huddled—in the safe harbor of community, craving familiarity in the face of the unknown. Though tomorrow this community will tempt me toward recidivism through its indelible memory of my former stains, radical detachment remains difficult today.

But avoiding the moment of truth is riskier than facing it. I isolate myself, cover my head with a *tallis* (prayer shawl), and prepare to encounter God. To borrow an image from Plato, I begin to turn from the shadows dancing before me to the fire burning behind.

For me, encountering God has meant addressing God directly in my own words and seeking a direct reply in any form describable as divine revelation—God becoming manifest to humans. However, establishing such a connection is almost impossibly difficult, not necessarily because God is inaccessible—quite the contrary—but because I am. I hesitate to make the approach, feeling unworthy, daunted by the prospect of absolute vulnerability, unprepared no matter when it is, fearful of raw, unmediated truth, and, absurdly, embarrassed by the lack of parity between me and the One I am about to address.

Haltingly, I abandon the prescribed prayers and begin to speak aloud. Self-conscious of every syllable, I find that my words choke on the obvious: what can I say to the One who knows everything? By the time thoughts form into words they feel like worn, rusty phrases, even to me. Speech has been robbed of its instrumental purpose and I fall silent, censoring too much. I start again.

This time I force myself to keep on talking, to use speech to penetrate the dense layers of internal sediment. Eventually the barrage of even meaningless words succeeds in bypassing conscious thought, and I begin to free-associate, to empty my mind of every available thought, until, finally, the rust runs clear and what begin to emerge are ideas that haven't been packaged, images that are completely new to me.

The protective crust encasing my innermost feelings begins to crack, releasing with great force a torrent of emotions of every kind: ferocious fury and consuming love, insatiable longing and boundless gratitude, utter despair and extravagant hopes, laughter—*laughter!*—and unbearable grief, genuine humility as well as brazen accusations against both God and self.

With increasing intensity I perceive shadowy inklings from beyond: a formless, vibrant presence conveying patient receptivity and focused interest, intimacy and immediacy, a looming Being that is somehow molten yet fragile and, most ironically, unseasonally unjudgmental.

My internal barriers begin to dissolve, piercing the invisible film that seems always to separate Creator from created. I know now that I am in the presence of God.

The experience is one of great buoyancy, like being inflated with helium. I swell amid a rich sense of completeness, of wholeness unlike anything I have ever known. It is a total experience: a sublime blend of the physical, the emotional, the psychological, and the spiritual . . . the ultimate human experience. Awareness of the divine is a palpable, nonsensory sensation. There is a certitude about what is being experienced and a clarity so absolute that it renders obsolete all doubt and leaps of faith.

The sensation is so exotic, so intoxicating, that it leaves me very nearly unaware, and certainly uninterested in any experience beyond itself, reluctant to let go and resume normal life. Spontaneously my thoughts fix on a phrase we recite every day during this season: "I have only one request of you, O God, to spend the rest of my life in Your presence."[6]

If this description recalls feelings observed in other contexts—the secular epiphany found in art, literature, and poetry—there the analogy ends.

For what happens during a religious epiphany is unmistakably not of my own invention, be it an insight, an unaccountable act of nature, perhaps a solution or sudden awareness that enters my mind, that has been transmitted into my mind as though by spiritual modem. It is not simply a set of sensations, but a reaction, a response, if not quite a dialogue. Something has been communicated from a transcendent source—from *the* transcendent source—and it is exactly what I needed, whether I knew it or not, whether I sought it or not.

Certain crucial characteristics of the experience become clear to me only when it is over.

I become aware of having been oblivious to the life around me. The experience of the All, of *everything,* has evidently demanded the temporary suspension or negation of the rest of life. A heightened life of the self has necessitated a kind of death of the self. As Dov Baer of Mezhirech describes it, "When one sows a single seed, it cannot sprout and produce many seeds until its existence is nullified."

Thus the metamorphic contact with the source of life presupposes contact with death. Life and death. Everything and nothing. Simultaneous characteristics of God.

In choosing to return to God for transformational renewal, a person enters a liminal state connecting life and death.

The paradoxical powers of this state are perhaps most clearly manifest in the face of actual death—that is, in a house of mourning. Grief, like repentance, is an intensely solitary experience that is intended to be undergone in the presence of others. Traditional Jewish families will spend seven days—*shiva*—in the same household, observing such customs as wearing the same clothes every day and sitting on low stools. Mourners, having accompanied loved ones to the very borders of this world, and who still cling to them by sitting close to the ground, spend a week suspended between the living and the dead. But while their bodies are entirely circumscribed and static, their experience is far from stagnant; rather, they frequently undergo meaningful change and growth during this period, as though death itself were organically germinating life.

Similarly, without knowing "who shall live and who shall die," we move through Yom Kippur in suspended animation, making deathbed confessions and pledges of charity to avert the severe decrees. Relinquishing loved ones through death, and relinquishing our present selves through penitential change, forces the crucial confrontation with our own mortality, thereby eliciting restorative intervention by the Immortal. "They reached the gates of death. In their distress they cried to the Lord and the Lord saved them. . . ."[7]

⟨⋯⟩

Not only in God does a fearsome, fertile void exist; each of us bears within us a dark internal place, foreign and forbidding, sealed and concealed. Locked in this place are skeletons of shame: primal fears, paralytic insecurities, haunted memories of pain inflicted irretrievably on loved ones, unredeemable violations of our own standards, inconsolable regrets. Entering such a realm is surely akin to the high priest's entry into *kodesh hakodashim,* the Holy of Holies: we aren't sure we will emerge alive, whether it be womb or tomb.

It is precisely to this psychological inner sanctum that the process of repentance beckons us. For there lie the words that are waiting to be revealed; the poisoned words already spoken, the spiteful words thrust at a silent God, the withered words of hope that has died. These are the words to be bundled and brought, a word offering to the One who created with words.

These are the words of *teshuva,* spoken to God in the first-person singular. With them we declare our willingness to endure the harshness of judgment, but, with the dignity of the created, also to impose our own measure of judgment on the Creator. With this offering we declare our eagerness to receive the softness of majestic mercy, but also to extend a measure of human kindness, even forgiveness, to God.

Worn down by unrelenting ritual, exhaustion, and hunger, the ultimate tools of the Ultimate, we rededicate ourselves to the One who binds the shards of our broken hearts and clears a path for our journey of return.

And, indeed, I have returned. As I recede reluctantly from this privileged, humbling state, stunned, flooded with emotion, I cover my eyes and take three steps back.

"Then when you call the Lord will answer and when you cry out the Lord will respond: Here I am."[8]

The reciprocity of *teshuva* ensures that neither divine nor human disappointment will ever dissolve the immutable bond that joins God and Israel. Like the honey with which we envelop our festival food, and whose stickiness never quite disappears, we cling to God, literally for dear life, mirroring the pattern of mutuality set forth in the covenant long ago. A pattern of eternal commitment, eternal trust, always turning and returning to one another. God to us, and we to God.

Now, having reached the pinnacle of purity, how shall we live the rest of the year?

Notes

Hagar and Sarah, Sarah and Hagar

Note: The author used *The Pentateuch and Haftorahs,* ed. J. H. Hertz (London: Soncino, 1937).

Sarah and Hagar: The Heelprints upon Their Faces

Note: The author used *The Pentateuch and Haftorahs,* ed. J. H. Hertz (London: Soncino, 1937).

1. See, for example, Lila Abu-Lughod, "A Tale of Two Pregnancies" and Ellen Lewin, "Writing Lesbian Ethnography," in Ruth Behar and Deborah A. Gordon, eds., *Women Writing Culture* (Berkeley: University of California Press, 1995); Helena Ragoné, "Chasing the Blood Tie: Surrogate Mothers, Adoptive Mothers and Fathers," *American Ethnologist* (1996) 23 (2): 352–365.
2. Ariella Zeller, a graduate student at the University of Michigan, is currently writing a dissertation on the history of abortion among Jewish women and the specifically Jewish pressure placed on Jewish women to bear children.
3. Irena Klepfisz, "Women without Children, Women without Families, Women Alone," in her *Dreams of an Insomniac: Jewish Feminist Essays, Speeches, and Diatribes* (Portland, Ore.: Eighth Mountain Press, 1990): 11.
4. Phyllis Trible, "Hagar: The Desolation of Rejection," in her *Texts of Terror: Literary-Feminist Readings of Biblical Narratives* (Philadelphia: Fortress Press, 1984): 13.
5. F. E. Peters, *Children of Abraham: Judaism/Christianity/Islam* (Princeton: Princeton University Press, 1982): 197.
6. Katheryn Pfisterer Darr, "More Than a Possession: Critical, Rabbinical, and Feminist Perspectives on Hagar," in her *Far More Precious than Jewels: Perspectives on Biblical Women* (Louisville, KY: Westminster/John Knox Press, 1991): 147–48.

7. Delores S. Williams, *Sisters in the Wilderness: The Challenge of Womanist God-Talk* (New York: Orbis Books, 1993): 2.

8. John Gwaltney, *Drylongso: A Self-Portrait of Black America* (New York: New Press, 1993): xv.

9. Williams, *Sisters in the Wilderness:* 2–3.

10. Barbara Christian, *Black Feminist Criticism: Perspectives on Black Women Writers* (New York: Pergamon Press, 1985): 219–220.

11. Williams, *Sisters in the Wilderness,* 108–109.

12. Alice Walker, "In the Closet of the Soul," in her *Living by the Word: Essays* (New York: Harcourt Brace, 1988): 80.

13. Renita Weems, *Battered Love: Marriage, Sex, and Violence in the Hebrew Prophets* (Minneapolis: Fortress Press, 1995): 115.

14. Martha Nussbaum, *Poetic Justice: The Literary Imagination and Public Life* (Boston: Beacon Press, 1995): 65, 119.

The Trials of Sarah

Note: Biblical quotations are from *The Five Books of Moses,* translated by Everett Fox (Schocken Books, 1995).

1. Everett Fox, *In the Beginning* (Schocken Books, 1983), 63.

2. Avivah Gottlieb Zornberg, *Genesis: The Beginning of Desire* (Jewish Publication Society, 1995), 113.

3. Ilana Pardes, *Countertraditions in the Bible: A Feminist Approach* (Harvard University Press, 1992), 163, n. 2.

4. See Barry W. Holtz, "Midrash," in *Back to the Sources,* ed. Barry W. Holtz (Summit Books, 1984), who discusses "overliteralism" creating "an opportunity for Midrash to operate" (p. 200), and James L. Kugel, "Two Introductions to Midrash," in *Midrash and Literature,* ed. Geoffrey H. Hartman and Sanford Budick (Yale University Press, 1986), 77–103.

5. Jo Ann Hackett, "Rehabilitating Hagar: Fragments of an Epic Pattern," in *Gender and Difference in Ancient Israel,* ed. Peggy L. Day (Fortress Press, 1989), 21.

Hearken to Her Voice: Empathy as Teshuva

1. The translation for this chapter is taken from *The Jerusalem Bible* (Jerusalem: Koren Publishers, 1992). I would like to thank Penina Adelman, Mitch Mirkin, Cantor Jodi Sufrin, Dr. Janet Surrey, Marion Weinberg, and Rabbi Ronald Weiss for their advice and suggestions.

2. Leila Leah Bronner argues that childless women had the most tenuous status in Biblical society. For an elaboration, see her text *From Eve to Esther: Rabbinic Reconstructions of Biblical Women* (Louisville, Ky.: Westminster John Knox Press, 1994).

3. I would like to thank my colleagues at the Stone Center, and in particular Judith Jordan, Jean Baker Miller, Irene Stiver, and Janet Surrey, for their teachings about empathy and empathic listening. Their writings on this topic may be obtained through Work in Progress, Stone Center at Wellesley College, Wellesley, MA 02181.

4. Michael Lerner presents the *Akeda* as a consequence of Abraham's difficulty in distinguishing between the true voice of God and the voice of false gods. Lerner connects this problem to Abraham's midrashic early childhood experiences in *Jewish Renewal: The Path to Healing and Transformation* (New York: HarperCollins Publishers, 1995).

Brothers and Others

Note: I am using Robert Alter's translation. *Genesis: Translation and Commentary* (New York: W. W. Norton & Co., 1996).

1. Robert Alter's discussion of the "type scene" in Biblical narrative, which changes in significance as it is repeated for different characters in different contexts, includes the "life-threatening trial in the wilderness" of each of Abraham's sons in Genesis 21 and 22, respectively. *The Art of Biblical Narrative* (New York: Basic Books, 1981), 181–82. Phyllis Trible shows the parallels in form and the contrast in meaning between the banishment of the Egyptian bondswoman from Abraham's tent to the wilderness and the exodus of the Hebrew slaves from Egypt to the wilderness. *Texts of Terror: Literary-Feminist Readings of Biblical Narratives* (Philadelphia: Fortress Press, 1984), 9–36.

2. Marc Shell, *Children of the Earth: Literature, Politics and Nationhood* (New York: Oxford University Press, 1993), 36. "Jewish particularism heeds tribal difference in such a way that it can become precisely the basis for realistic tolerance." Ibid. I have borrowed Shell's rubric "brothers and others," while giving it a somewhat different twist.

3. I am trying to use the names Sarai/Sarah and Abram/Abraham as they appear in the text, before and after they are aggrandized.

4. Y. H. Brenner, "Nerves," trans. Hillel Halkin, *Eight Great Hebrew Short Novels,* eds. Alan Lelchuk and Gershon Shaked (New York: New American Library, 1983), 36.

5. In Uri Eisenzweig's critique of Zionism, "la dénégation de l'Autre" is the counterpart to "l'affirmation du Même," specifically among the Jews who came from the Pale of Settlement. *Territoires Occupés de l'imaginaire juif: essai sur l'espace sioniste* (Paris: Christian Bourgois Editeur, 1980), 34.
6. Edward Said, *Orientalism* (New York: Vintage Books, 1979), 307.

Sarah and Hagar: The Laughter and the Prayer

Note: The translation of the Bible used was *The Jewish Publication Society editions of The Torah* (Philadelphia: Jewish Publication Society, 1962) and *The Prophets* (Philadelphia: Jewish Publication Society, 1978).

1. My translation of Rashi.
2. *Ramban (Nachmanides) Commentary on the Torah: Genesis,* trans. and ann. by Charles B. Chavel (New York: Shilo Publishing House, 1971), 239.
3. See Mary Calloway, *Sing, O Barren One: A Study in Comparative Midrash* (Atlanta: Scholars Press, 1986), chap. 2.
4. For a variety of *midrashim* about Satan's role in the *Akeda,* see Louis Ginzberg, *The Legends of the Jews,* vol. 1 (Philadelphia: Jewish Publication Society, 1968), 276–87.
5. My translation.

The Power of Prayer: Hannah's Tale

1. A version of this essay that focuses on other aspects of this tale will appear in a chapter titled "Hannah Wills a Son," in Nehama Aschkenasy, *Women at the Window* (Detroit: Wayne State University Press, 1997).
2. Abraham J. Heschel has described prayer as an "act of self-purification" and a "quarantine for the soul." See *Man's Quest for Freedom* (New York, 1954), 8.
3. The author has consulted the Hebrew Bible as her primary source and used her own translation of I Samuel 1–2.
4. I first studied Hannah and Elkanah as countercultural figures when we were only beginning to tune in to the hidden voices and attitudes underlying the Bible's predominantly patriarchal cadence; see N. Aschkenasy, "A Non-Sexist Reading of the Bible," *Midstream* 27, 6 (1981), 51–55.
5. See Erik H. Erikson, "Womanhood and the Inner Space," In *Identity: Youth and Crisis* (New York: Norton, 1968), 261–294.
6. Nina Auerbach, *Communities of Women* (Cambridge, Mass: Harvard University Press, 1978), 13 *et passim.*
7. Phyllis Bird, "Images of Women in the Old Testament," in Rosemary Ruether, ed. *Religion and Sexism* (New York: Simon & Schuster, 1974), 51.

8. Erich Fromm, *The Art of Loving* (New York: Harper & Row, 1974), 18.

9. Fromm, 17.

10. Wordless crying has been always regarded by tradition as an integral part of praying. The Kabbalist work the Zohar maintains that crying is sometimes even more effective than actual verbal entreaty to God. See Robert Gordis, *A Faith for Moderns* (New York: Bloch, 1971), 271.

11. In *The Kuzari*, Hirschfeld trans. (New York, 1978), 386.

12. *Man's Quest for God* (New York: Crossroads, 1984), 18.

13. As suggested by R. Hamnuna in Babylonian Talmud Brakhot (31a), in a discussion that starts with "How many important rulings may be derived from the verses about Hannah at prayer."

14. On the Hebraic understanding of time as potentially open, and of humanity as possessing the freedom of and capacity for choice, see Tom F. Driver, *The Sense of History in Greek and Shakespearean Drama* (New York: Columbia University Press, 1967), 44, 49, *et passim*.

15. P. Kyle McCarter contends that the concluding benediction of the psalm suggests that the psalm's original context is that of the birth of a royal heir and therefore is anachronistic in the mouth of the premonarchic Hannah (I Samuel, the Anchor edition, 73). Our view of Hannah as a female protagonist in a tale that manifests literary consistency and integrity, however, allows us to study the psalm as Hannah's composition and thus an expression of the woman's particular state of mind.

16. *The Insecurity of Freedom* (Philadelphia, 1966), 20.

17. George Eliot's definition of motherhood as "the common yearning of womanhood," which is the compromise of a woman of "spiritual grandeur" who meets with a "meanness of opportunity," applies perfectly to Hannah's situation. See the "Prelude" to *Middlemarch* (Cambridge, Mass.: Riverside, 1956; first published in 1871–72), 3.

Akeda: The View from the Bible

1. The term is Erich Auerbach's, in his classic study in *Mimesis* (Princeton, N.J.: Princeton University Press, 1968), chapter 1.

2. Another example of this use of "withhold" may be Psalm 19:14, where God's servant prays for God to hold him back from evildoers so that they do not rule over him. The translations all add "deeds" or "sins" to *zeidim*, "evil ones." In context this makes excellent sense since the psalmist has just prayed for God to cleanse him of accidental wrongs; however, the phrase "that they rule not over me" doesn't fit as well with deeds, and the idea may be "make me pure and keep me safe."

3. In another example of the meaning of allegiance to God the widow of one of

Elisha's disciples asks for help, declaring, "you know that my husband was a God-fearer" (*hayah yarei et YHWH*) (II Kings 4:1).

4. God honors them (Psalm 15:4), keeps an eye on them (33:18), pours grace on them (103:12), and fulfills their wishes (145:19). They suffer no want (34:10) and are blessed with children and grandchildren (128:1–6).

5. "answer," "defend," "send (help)," "support," "remember," "accept (offering)" "give (heart's desire)," "fulfill (your desires)," "fulfill (your wishes)."

6. "rejoice" and "be arrayed with banners."

7. For the Iphigenia stories, see Peggy Day, "From the Child Is Born the Woman: The Story of Jephthah's Daughter," in Peggy Day, ed. *Gender and Difference* (Minneapolis: Fortress Press, 1989), 58–74, esp. 60–62.

8. Quoted in Eusebius, Praparatio Evangelica 1.10.45, who relates that the god Chronos (whom the Greeks equated with the Canaanite-Phoenecian "El") resorted to this custom in time of great danger of war. He took Iedoud, his only son by a nymph, arrayed him in royal garments, and slaughtered him. The best assemblages of these ancient sources on Child Sacrifice are in David Marcus, *Jephthah and his Vow* (Lubbock, Texas: Texas Tech Press, 1986), and John Day, *Molech: A God of Human Sacrifice in the Old Testament* (Cambridge: Cambridge University Press, 1989).

9. Book IV, paragraph III 23.

10. Diodorus Siculus XIII, 86.3.

11. For a description of Puzo Moro and a study of the Biblical passages, see Jon Levenson, *The Death and Resurrection of the Beloved Son: The Transformation of Child Sacrifice in Judaism and Christianity* (New Haven, Conn.: Yale University Press, 1989).

12. II Kings 16:3; 21:6; II Chronicles 33:6.

13. Isaiah 57:5; Ezekiel 16:20, 36; Psalm 106:38.

14. Leviticus 18:21.

15. II Kings 23:10.

16. "your only son," which appears twice, does not use the word *ben*.

17. Even the "third day" is significant; not only is it the walking distance from Beersheba, but three days' journey was also the zone from which individuals were required to come to the Temple in order to offer a nonpenitential *zevach* (the type of sacrifice that individuals would offer); from farther away, one could simply slaughter an animal and spill its blood on the ground.

18. For a discussion of verses 15–18 as a commentary, see R. Walter Moberly, "The Earliest Commentary on the Akedah," *Vetus Testamentum* 38 (1988), 302–323.

Child Endangerment, Parental Sacrifice:
A Reading of the Binding of Isaac

Note: Thanks to Jamie Wacks for imaginative research assistance and to Joe Singer and Avi Soifer for comments.

1. Martin Buber, *Tales of the Hasidim: Later Masters* 92 (Schocken Books: New York 1948).
2. Tom Coakley, "Christian Science Couple's Conviction in Death Overruled," *Boston Globe,* Aug 12, 1993, p. 1; *Commonwealth* v. *Twitchell,* 617 N.E.2d 609 (Mass. 1993).
3. Judicial action may follow petitions of neglect brought by a state agency when parental refusals of medical treatment expose the child to serious harm even if those refusals are sincerely motivated by religious beliefs. See In the Interest of D.L.E., 645 P.2d 271 (Colo. 1982) (approving dependencing determination after parent failed to assure child with epilepsy followed prescribed medical treatment).
4. In the Matter of Elisha McCauley, 409 Mass. 134, 565 N.E.2d 411 (Mass. 1991); *Sampson* v. *Taylor,* 29 N.Y.2d 900, 278 N.E.2d 918, 328 N.Y.S.ed 686 (NY 1972); In re Pogue (No. M-18-74 Super. Ct. D.C. Nov. 11, 1974).
5. Custody of a Minor, 375 Mass. 733, 751, 379 N.E.2d 1053, 1064 (quoting mother).
6. *Nicholson* v. *Honda,* 600 So.2d 1101 (Fla. 1992) (mother convicted of felony-murder and aggravated child abuse after child died of starvation; mother had followed religious prophesies against gluttony).
7. Jetta Bernie, quoted in Bella English, "No Excuses for Child Abuse," *Boston Globe,* Nov. 30, 1992, p. 13.
8. See Avivah Gottlieb Zornberg, *Genesis: The Beginning of Desire* 106 (The Jewish Publication Society: Philadelphia, 1995).
9. See, e.g., *People* v. *Pierson,* 176 N.Y. 201, 211-212, 68 N.E. 243, 247-8 (NY Ct. Ap. 1903) ("We are aware that there are people who believe that the Divine power may be invoked to heal the sick and that faith is all that is required. There are others who believe that the Creator has supplied the earth, nature's storehouse, with everything that man may want for his support and maintenance, including the restoration and preservation of his health, and that he is left to work out his own salvation, under fixed natural laws. . . . But sitting as a court of law for the purpose of construing and determining the meaning of statutes, we have nothing to do with these variances in religious beliefs, and have no power to determine which is correct. We place no limitations upon the power of the mind over the body, the power of faith to

dispel disease, or the power of the Supreme Being to heal the sick. We merely declare the law as given to us by the Legislature").

10. See, e.g., In re Willmann, 24 Ohio App.3d 191, 199, 493 N.E.2d 1380, 1390 (Ohio Ct. App. 1986) (Keefe, J. concurring) ("This matter has been for me an extremely difficult case mainly because of the troublesome conflicting authorities between loving parents on the one hand, and the juvenile court on the other.") Despite the difficulties, Judge Keefe concurred in the decision to substitute state judgment for parental judgment.

11. For a novelist's observation, see Louise Erdrich, *Love Medicine* (Harper-Perennial: New York, 1993, 1984): "Here God used to raineth bread from clouds, smite the Phillipines, sling fire down on red-light districts where people got stabbed. He even appeared in person every once in a while. God used to pay attention, is what I'm saying."

12. See Nehama Leibowitz, *New Studies in Bereshit (Genesis)* 189 (trans. Aryeh Newman, Eliner Library, Hemed Press, Jerusalem) (discussing Maimonides' commentary on the binding of Isaac).

13. See Søren Kierkegaard, *Fear and Trembling* 89–91 (trans. Alastair Hannay, Penguin Books: London, 1985); see Jerome I. Gellmann, *The Fear, the Trembling, and the Fire: Kierkegaard and Hasidic Masters on the Binding of Isaac* 18 (University Press of America, Inc.: Lanham, Mary., 1994).

14. Mishael Maswari Caspi and Sascha Benjamin Cohen, *The Binding [AQEDAH] and Its Transformations in Judaism and Islam: The Lamps of God* 28 (Mellen Biblical Press: Lewiston, 1995). If Isaac stoically accepted the role of the sacrificed, he prefigured the passion of Jesus. Id, at 50.

15. See Ellen Frankel, *The Classic Tales: 4,000 Years of Jewish Lore* 69 (Jason Aronson Inc.: Northvale, N.J., 1993).

16. Caspi and Cohen, at 23; Leibowitz, at 189.

17. Lillian Smith, *The Journey* (World Publishing Co.: Cleveland, 1954), 256; Women's Quotes 30.

18. See Virginia Woolf, *The Letters of Virginia Woolf,* vol. II 1912–1922, 585 (Harcourt Brace Jovanovich: New York, 1975) ("I read the book of Job last night—I don't think God comes well out of it").

19. Shalom Spiegel, *The Last Trial: On the Legends and Lore of the Command to Abraham to Offer Isaac as a Sacrifice: The Akedah,* 46–47 (trans. Judah Goldin, Jewish Lights: Woodstock, Vt., 1969); Jon D. Levenson, *The Death and Resurrection of the Beloved Son: The Transformation of Child Sacrifice in Judaism and Christianity* 198 (Yale University Press: New Haven, 1993).

20. Louis Ginzberg, *Legends of the Jews* 274–5 (Henrietta Szold, trans. The Jewish Publication Society of America: Philadelphia, 1938).

21. Caspi and Cohen, *supra,* at 31 (citing Midrash Bereshit Rabbati 955\90).

22. Caspi and Cohen, *supra* at 35 (citing ninth-cent. Midrash Tanhuma, Vayera 81); id at 41 (citing Ginzberg, at 286).

23. Ellen Frankel, *supra* at 74–75.

24. Zornberg, *supra*, at 126–7 (discussing midrash).

25. See Caspi and Cohen, *supra*, at 125–6 (describing Sarah's silent cry of anguish).

26. Ignaz Maybaym, "The Sacrifice of Isaac: A Jewish Commentary," Leo Baeck College Publication No. 1, London (1959).

27. Ellen Frankel, *supra*, at 72 (Abraham tells Isaac that Abraham and Sarah will survive but a few days before following Isaac to the grave).

28. Carol Pearson, *The Hero Within,* 105–6 (Harper & Row: San Francisco, 1989) (women's quotes. 279).

29. Toni Morrison, *Beloved* (Knopf: New York, 1987).

30. William Styron, *Sophie's Choice* (Random House: New York, 1979); Doris Lessing, *The Fifth Child* (Knopf: New York, 1988); Amy Tan, *The Joy Luck Club* (Putnam's: New York, 1989).

The Ashes of the Akeda, the Ashes of Sodom: A Mother-Daughter Dialogue

Note: All quotes from the Bible are from *The Five Books of Moses, The Schocken Bible,* translation Everett Fox, Schocken Press. Translations of Rashi and other commentaries are our own.

1. Descartes, *Meditation on First Philosophy: Meditation 2, The Philosophical Works,* vol. 4, trans. Elizabeth Haldane, GRT Roth (Cambridge University Press, 1970), 149.

2. Erich Auerbach, *Mimesis: The Representation of Reality in Western Literature,* trans. Willard R. Trask (Princeton University Press, 1991), 15.

Our Mother of Sorrows

1. See commentary in *The Chumash,* Artscroll Series, Stone Edition (Brooklyn, N.Y.: Mesorah Publications, 1993), to Genesis 29:1–12, 147. Future references to this commentary will be cited as Stone Chumash with the verse numbers. In this essay I have used easily accessible commentators and editions so that readers can pursue on their own the direction of thought suggested here.

2. Ibid.

3. Stone Chumash, notes on *Haftaras* Rosh Hashana—Second Day, 1236–37.

4. The *Meam Loez* commentary notes that it was a custom in some parts of the ancient Near East to marry two wives but sterilize one to preserve her beauty, while the other would bear children. Rachel may have feared that Jacob was using some secret technique to prevent her becoming pregnant.

5. For a traditional chronology of the sons and their birth dates, see the *Meam Loez* commentary to Genesis 30.

6. Most commentators view them as some kind of idols; the speculation that they may have been oracles comes from R' Samson Raphael Hirsch, Commentary to Genesis 31:19, in *T'rumath Tzvi: The Pentateuch,* multivolume edition (New York, 1980). The popular one-volume edition of Hirsch's commentary does not, unfortunately, include his analysis of the word *terafim*.

7. The *Meam Loez* commentary on Genesis 35:19 explains that a woman who died in childbirth was covered with blood and therefore should be buried in contact with the earth immediately.

8. The Stone Chumash summarizes the various major commentators succinctly; see on 35:16–20 and on v. 19.

9. *Meam Loez* on 35:21.

10. Hirsch Pentateuch, multivolume edition, on Genesis 35:18.

11. For a related but slightly different reading, see Avivah Zornberg, *Genesis: The Beginning of Desire* (Philadelphia: Jewish Publication Society, 1995), 215.

Firstborn to You: Remembering the God of Mercy

I am indebted to Naama Kelman for the references to the daughters of Tzelofchad, which she cited in her ordination address in Jerusalem, July 1992.

In the midst of writing, I read two books that amplified my thinking and enabled me to juxtapose a range of sources against these Rosh Hashana narratives. They are: *When Brothers Dwell Together: The Preeminence of Younger Siblings in the Hebrew Bible,* by Frederick E. Greenspahn (New York, Oxford: Oxford University Press, 1994) and *The Death and Resurrection of the Beloved Son: The Transformation of Child Sacrifice in Judaism and Christianity,* by Jon D. Levenson (New Haven and London: Yale University Press, 1993).

Aspects of this essay are a response to the influence of two essays by Rachel Adler, "Tum'ah and Taharah: Ends and Beginnings" (in *The First Jewish Catalogue* [Philadelphia: JPS, 1973]) and "In Your Blood, Live: Re-visions of a Theology of Purity" (*Tikkun,* Jan./Feb. 1993).

I am grateful for the readings suggested by friends, and particularly to Dr. Edward Greenstein. The applications are my own.

Journey into the Wilderness

1. *The Torah: A Modern Commentary,* commentary by W. Gunther Plaut (New York: Union of American Hebrew Congregations, 1981), 858.
2. *The JPS Torah Commentary: Leviticus,* commentary by Baruch A. Levine (Philadelphia: Jewish Publication Society, 1989), 99.

The Yom Kippur Avoda within the Female Enclosure

1. Ba'al Shem Tov, *Nachalei Bina on Yom Kippur.* Chaim Yehuda Katz, Brooklyn, N.Y., 1978, 237.
2. The Ashkenazi *piyyut* was composed by Meshullam b. Kalonymus. There are various versions and combinations of introductory and closing acrostics depending on the *machzor,* holiday prayer book. The main *piyyutim* in current usage were composed during the Middle Ages by Yose ben Yose, Solomon ibn Gabirol, Judah Halevi, and Moses ibn Ezra. I shall not divert attention by analyzing the differences among the versions here. In terms of content, they are sufficiently comparable to allow us to proceed to the unadorned account of the *Avoda* proper, the acts performed by the *kohen gadol,* which was compiled prior to the fourth century B.C.E. This description, drawn from Mishna *Yoma,* 1–6, is consistent in the *machzorim* (prayer books) for the holy days, except in the Reform *machzor,* where a confession by the high priest is substituted for the complete *Avoda.*
3. This is the singular occasion in the entire cycle of Jewish prayer that complete prostration is instituted.
4. Isaiah 1:18.
5. I refer to the prayer leader with the feminine pronoun here.
6. I elaborate this analogy more fully in my paper "Ritual impurity and the Temple Mount in Mishnaic Tractate *Kelim:* A Feminist Textual Analysis," delivered at the American Academy of Religion Annual Meeting, Philadelphia, 1996, to be published in a forthcoming book on purity in Judaism and Hinduism, Barbara Holdrege (ed.), with Mary Douglas.

   Mircea Eliade has described a "house-body-cosmos" homology. *The Sacred and the Profane* (trans. Willard R. Trask, New York: Harper & Row, 1961), 172.
7. Numbers 1–4.
8. Here I interpret the utterance of the Name to be an accompaniment to the ecstatic loving encounter.
9. In his preface to *Yom Kippur Service* (1982), xii.
10. I credit Adin Steinsaltz for this conceptualization at a teaching in Jerusalem in 1978.

11. The Zohar only once mentions the metaphor of sexual intercourse between human, in this case Moses, and God, the *Shekhina:* Zohar I 21b–22a. The imagery of God and the *Shekhina* in holy sexual union is ubiquitous in mystical literature. Yesod, the ninth *Sefira,* emanation, is the procreative life force that activates the universe. The idea that a person at prayer is engaged in sexual intercourse is articulated by Chasidic masters but has its roots in the Kabbala. Isaac Luria describes the return of the exiled *Shekhina* as a divine union and a goal of prayer, *Etz Chayim,* ch. XXXVI.

12. Recorded in *Pirke de'Rebbe Eliezer* 28.

13. I am grateful to Jessica Bonn for suggesting a textual proximity of blood ritual with sacred space. The circumcision by Zipporah of hers and Moses' child following the revelation at the burning bush is one case to which she points (Exodus 3:2–5; Exodus 4:25–26).

14. See Baruch Levine, *In the Presence of the Lord,* (E. J. Brill, Leiden, Netherlands: 1974), 55–79. The second use of expiation blood, according to Levine, is for the protection of God from demonic forces that threaten God's "life" on account of the sins committed by the people, 78–79.

15. Here I distinguish my interpretation from Baruch Levine's view of chetonic deities and God's forceful anger that demand the blood ransom. *In the Presence,* 69–77.

16. Nehemia Polen clarified this allusion in a conversation about the passage.

17. The consummation of the union will find a full and intoxicated public celebration at the nuptial canopy of Simchat Torah.

Repentance, Responsibility, and Regeneration: Reflections on Isaiah

Note: Quotations are from *The Prophets* (Jewish Publication Society, Philadelphia).

1. For description and discussion of the *techina* as a form of woman's prayer, see Chava Weissler. "Traditional Piety of Ashkenazi Women" in *Jewish Spirituality,* ed. Arthur Green (New York, 1987), vol. 2, 245–275. Weissler has written extensively and illuminatingly on this topic.

Sexuality and Teshuva: Leviticus 18

1. I first raised this issue in my short article "Sex and Yom Kippur," *Tikkun* 10/5 (September/October 1995): 71–72, parts of which I repeat here.

2. Baruch A. Levine, *The JPS Torah Commentary: Leviticus* (Philadelphia: Jewish Publication Society, 1989), xiv, 110–111.

3. Biblical references are to the new JPS translation.

4. Stephen F. Bigger, "The Family Laws of Leviticus 18 in Their Setting," *Journal of Biblical Literature* 98/2 (June 1979): 195–96.

5. Mary Douglas, *Purity and Danger: An Analysis of the Concepts of Pollution and Taboo* (London and New York: Routledge, 1966), 3,36,133.

6. Bigger, 196–202.

7. Bigger, 188.

8. Bigger, 202.

9. Howard Eilberg-Schwartz, *The Savage in Judaism: An Anthropology of Israelite Religion and Ancient Judaism* (Bloomington and Indianapolis: Indiana University Press, 1990), 179–80.

10. Eilberg-Schwartz, 180–181; Rachel Adler, "In Your Blood, Live: Re-visions of a Theology of Purity," *Tikkun* 8/1 (January/February 1993): 40.

11. Eilberg-Schwartz, 180. He is quoting Freud.

12. The translation is Saul Olyan's, "'And with a Male You Shall Not Lie Down the Lying Down of a Woman': On the Meaning and Significance of Leviticus 18:22 and 20:13," *Journal of the History of Sexuality* 5/2 (1994).

13. Olyan, 200–203.

14. Rachel Adler, "Feminist Folktales of Justice: Robert Cover as a Resource for the Renewal of Halakhah," *Conservative Judaism* 45 (Spring 1993):42; *Engendering Judaism* (Philadelphia: Jewish Publication Society), forthcoming.

15. Cf. Rebecca Alpert, "In God's Image: Coming to Terms with Leviticus," *Twice Blessed: On Being Lesbian or Gay and Jewish*, ed. Christie Balka and Andy Rose (Boston: Beacon Press, 1989), 68–70.

16. Adler, *Engendering Judaism*.

17. The members of Su Kasha are Sandy Abramson, Martha Ackelsberg, Joseph-Chaim Alpert, Victor Appell, David Bank, Ora Chaiken, Bob Christensen, Terry DeFiore, Marla Gayle, Colin Hogan, Larry Kay, Rosanne Leipzig, Betsy Leonard-Wright, Gail Leonard-Wright, Judith Plaskow, Irma Ross, Melanie Schneider, and Jason Stone. For the first year, the process was ably facilitated by Jason Stone.

18. What I have left out is the large area of sexual responsibilities to oneself.

Jonah, Son of Truth

Translations of Biblical texts: Jerusalem Bible and author's own.
Translation of rabbinic texts are author's own.

1. Note Ovadia's comment about Elijah's tendency to move around: "the spirit of the Lord will carry you whither I know not. . . ." (I Kings 18:12). In later traditions about Elijah, the prophet's quality of unrootedness in place be-

comes Elijah's distinctive way of being *with* the people, or at least with individuals who need him; Elijah suddenly can appear anywhere and everywhere.

2. Perhaps an even more striking contrast is presented by Elisha's first act after his master dies and he receives Elijah's spirit and mission—he cures bad water for the inhabitants of Jericho (II Kings 2:19–22). The contrast between the two prophets may be seen in Elijah's response to Elisha's comment about kissing his father and mother: the response seems to reflect a disdain for this impulse and possibly doubtfulness whether a man connected in this way to his family and people can serve as a true prophet (I Kings 19:20). Note that Elijah is described as "a hairy man with a girdle of leather around his loins" (II Kings 1:8), a kind of unsettled wild man. Compare the insult cast at Elisha after his master's death: "Go up, bald head; go up, bald head" (II Kings 2:23–24); perhaps Elisha is so disturbed by this because of the implicit contrast with the man whom he seeks to emulate.

It is interesting and instructive to note the ways in which the figures of John the Baptist and Jesus are modeled on Elijah and Elisha, especially in Matthew, and on the references to Moses and to Jonah in that book.

3. For a discussion of the occurrences and significance of going eastward, see the author's *From Father to Son: Kinship, Conflict, and Continuity in Genesis* (Westminster/John Knox, 1991).

4. Elijah's sustenance through ravens in particular seems to be negative; in addition to the negative connotations of ravens in general, we should consider the connotation of the raven in the story of the Flood and, interesting for our context, the contrast between the raven and the dove, *yona*. For possible connections between Noah's dove and Jonah, see following.

5. Resurrection of the dead is often associated with rain in the rabbinic tradition. See, for example, the statement at the beginning of Masekhet Ta'anit about the three "keys" reserved for God: the key of childbirth, the key of resurrection of the dead, and the key of rain. The second blessing of the *Amida* also includes these two themes: "You are eternally powerful, Lord, it is you who are resurrector of the dead, great in salvation, who causes the wind to blow and the rain to fall. . . ."

Note the fascinating midrash in Sanhedrin 113a that describes Elijah as requesting and receiving the key of rain but eventually having to give it back to God. God takes pity on the people when Elijah has withheld rain from the land, so God arranges to get the key of rain back by setting in motion the events that lead to Elijah's requesting the key of resurrection in order to revive the widow's son. God tells Elijah that it would not be right for him to have more keys than God; he will have to return the key of rain in order to receive the key of resurrection. Hence, God says: *"I will give rain"* (I

Kings 18:1), because God has taken the key of rain back from Elijah, who has been unmerciful in its use.

6. Jonah is identified as the child whom Elijah brought back to life, hence as Elijah's spiritual son, in a number of rabbinic sources; see Talmud Yerushalmi, Sukka 5:1 (55a) and Midrash Tehillim 26, and parallels. The latter source also comments that Jonah entered the Garden of Eden alive, a further connection to Elijah.

7. Contrast Jonah's declaration that Nineveh will be destroyed with what God tells Jonah in chapter 1: "Call out against her, for her evil has come up before me" (1:2). God's instructions certainly leave room for something more than a declaration of destruction. In chapter 3 God tells Jonah ". . . and call to her the calling which I tell [d-b-r] you" (3:2). Has God already told Jonah the content of the message, or does God plan to do that when Jonah reaches Nineveh and is about to utter his message? If the latter, might we see Jonah's haste to deliver the message before he reaches the center of town as a way of delivering his own interpretation of an appropriate prophetic message before God instructs him as to what he ought to say? If so, Jonah is behaving much like Elijah here; he is a prophet who insists on delivering the message that *he* believes is appropriate, not necessarily the message God commands. Perhaps Jonah's delivery of his message after only a day's journey into the city should be seen as another instance of the prophet not entering among the people and hence finding it easier to declare their doom.

8. Note the parallel to Elijah's going eastward after proclaiming the people's doom. A play on words links Jonah's behavior here to his initial response to God's call: Jonah isolates himself *mikedem*—"to the east" (Jonah 4:5); he describes his initial escape with the word *kidamti*—"beforehand" (Jonah 4:2).

9. Note that the word for "great," *rav,* is the same word that Elijah uses in his complaint: "It is *rav* [enough/too much]; now, Lord, take my life" (I Kings 19:4). It is as if the angel is saying: "It is not yet too much for you; you still have a great way to go." Others, though, translate the angel's words as "the way is too great for you," which could be read as setting the stage for the information and instructions that God will give Elijah later in this episode.

10. The phrase "the mountain of God, Horev" recalls especially the story of the burning bush, Moses' lone encounter with God that prefigures both the revelation of Sinai and Moses' later solitary encounter with God, to be discussed below. (See Exodus 3:1.)

11. Seven, of course, is the number of covenant. Elijah has complained that the people have abandoned God's covenant (I Kings 19:10, 14), and God reassures him that there is a covenantal community left that has remained loyal to God.

12. Note Elijah's characterization as a *kapdan,* a person who is strict and prone

to anger, in Sanhedrin 113a–b; Elijah's anger at this characterization is seen to prove the point.

Later traditions about Elijah have him continually participating in acts of covenant, communal continuity, and redemption, as well as in simple acts of assistance to those in need, especially needy Torah scholars. This participation is sometimes seen as a kind chastening of Elijah, similar to the angel's reminding the despairing Elijah that he has a long way in front of him; his experiences serve as both a lesson and a gift. For example, Elijah's presence at circumcisions is seen as a way of showing Elijah that he was wrong—the people have *not* abandoned God's covenant; at the same time, of course, it is a way of acknowledging that Elijah continues to participate in the building of the people's covenantal relationship with God. Interestingly, Elijah does so in small ways, working within families, the smallest unit of community, and with its smallest, newest members. It is this very sort of loyal presence among the people that Elijah fails to recognize when he despairs in chapter 19. Elijah also functions in the circumcision ceremony as a sort of godfather, much as he functions for the widow's son; all little boys, then, are spiritual sons of Elijah. Elijah's visit to the family *seder* table is similar in many ways to his presence at circumcisions.

Elijah of the Book of Kings does not fulfill his mission, but he works to create mechanisms for ongoing movement toward fulfillment. Already in Malachi, Elijah is seen as paving the way for "the great and awesome day of the Lord," by an act of returning: "he shall return, *veheishiv,* the heart of the fathers to the children and the heart of the children to their fathers" (Malachi 3:23–24). Pirkei Rabbi Eliezer sees Elijah as the only person who will ultimately bring about great and lasting repentance, *teshuva,* strikingly seeing in Elijah's description as *hatishbi,* not a reference to his transience, but a reference to his ability to cause a return to God (PRE 47).

13. The parallel between the episode of I Kings 19 and the episode of Moses' encounter with God after the Golden Calf was first introduced to me by David Silber, who also has pointed out that the name of Elisha, Elijah's disciple, is a variation of the name of Joshua (Yehoshua), Moses' disciple. One indication that Elijah is a new Moses is the information we are given just before Elijah appears: in Ahab's day, Jericho was rebuilt and the curse attendant on that project came true, as God had spoken through Joshua (I Kings 16:34; see Joshua 6:26). The conquest and destruction of Jericho represents the beginning of Joshua's mission of establishing the children of Israel in their land. The violation of Joshua's instructions regarding Jericho suggests that we have moved backward, that everything accomplished since Moses has been corrupted, and that a new Moses is needed to set things right.

14. An alternative translation might be: "Are you right in being angry?" The

first interpretation of God's response to Jonah fits better with the first translation, while the second interpretation fits better with the alternative. Note that the word in question here, *haheiteiv,* is related to the word *tov,* "good," and thus stands in contrast with the *ra'a,* "evil," which afflicts Jonah. This contrast underscores the challenge implicit in God's question and perhaps the irony that God is pointing out.

15. Note the play on words here: the word for "shade" is *tzel,* and the word for "to save" is *lehatzil.* The physical comfort of this object provides a sort of existential comfort as well.

16. Note, in this context, the surprising juxtaposition of animals and humans in the last verse of the book and also the odd mention of the animals of Nineveh participating in penitential acts (Jonah 3:7–8).

17. A midrashic comment on the book's final verse is interesting in the context of this reading and of the midrash quoted earlier about Moses: "And should I not have compassion for Nineveh, that great city. . . . At that moment, he [Jonah] fell on his face and said: 'Conduct your world through the attribute of mercy, as it is written, "to the Lord our God belong mercy and forgiveness"' (Daniel 9:9)." (Yalkut Shimoni II, 551).

A Carnival at the Gates: Jonah and Laughter on Yom Kippur

1. Avraham Finkel, *The Essence of the Holy Days* (New York: Jason Aronson, 1993). Finkel attributes this saying to Rabbi Isaac Luria, the great sixteenth-century Kabbalist, also citing Rabbi Simcha Bunim, who explains that the affliction of Purim is greater than that demanded of us on Yom Kippur, since the commandment to drink *ad shelo yada* afflicts our reason and judgment, the loss of which is the greatest possible catastrophe (130–31). I am indebted to Chaim Seidler-Feller for calling this citation to my attention.

2. My translation.

3. Paul Ricoeur, "The Hermeneutical Function of Distanciation," *Hermeneutics and the Human Sciences* (Cambridge: 1981), 139.

4. Michael Lerner, *Jewish Renewal* (New York: G. P. Putnam Sons, 1994). Lerner sees liberation from the repetition compulsion to abuse as the central ethical theme of Judaism.

5. *Mahzor for Rosh Hashanah and Yom Kippur,* 2nd ed. Edited by Rabbi Jules Harlow (New York: Rabbinical Assembly, 1978), many locations, but see p. 715. These words are based on Kohelet (Ecclesiastes) 2:15–23.

6. My more literal translation of this sentence in the prayer referenced above, in note 5. This verse is taken from Kohelet (Ecclesiastes) 3:19.

7 Although I will generally use the JPS Tanakh for Biblical quotes in this es-

say, this passage has been quoted from *The Schocken Bible v. 1: The Five Books of Moses,* trans., commentary, and notes by Everett Fox (New York: Schocken, 1995). I have quoted Fox's translation because I wanted to convey the features of the Hebrew upon which later interpretation would rest.

8. Both "clearing" and "he will surely not clear" are accounted for by the rabbinic exegesis in Yoma 86a: God will clear the guilty who do *teshuva,* but not the unrepentant sinner. This provides a liturgical justification for ending the verse with "clearing" (the guilty), since prayer is part of the penitential process. Rosh HaShana 17b refers to the liturgical use of this passage.

9. The foundational work on this theme is Mikhail Bakhtin, *Rabelais and His World,* trans. Helene Iswolsky (Bloomington: Indiana University Press, 1984).

10. Some of the material in the following paragraphs has been adapted and expanded from Rachel Adler, *Engendering Judaism: Inclusive Theology and Egalitarian Ethics for the Twenty-first Century* (Philadelphia: Jewish Publication Society, 1997).

11. Ismar Elbogen, *Jewish Liturgy: A Comprehensive History,* trans. Raymond Scheindlin (Philadelphia and Jerusalem: Jewish Publication Society and Jewish Theological Seminary, 1993). Elbogen notes that this is the only prophetic reading for an afternoon service that can be proven to exist from the time of the Talmud (148).

12. Arnold Band, "Swallowing Jonah: The Eclipse of Parody," *Prooftexts* 10 (May 1990), 177–195.

13. I am echoing Fox's translation of Exodus 34:7 in the Schocken Bible. The final phrase is my translation.

Afterword: Meeting God's Gaze

I am grateful to Joan Cohen, Norma Joseph, Arthur Melzer, Anita Norich, and Debbie Weissman, whose wisdom, insights, sensitivities, and suggestions contributed significantly to this piece.

1. *Malkhuyot* (Sovereignty) and *Zichronot* (Remembrance) sections of the additional service on Rosh Hashana.

2. *Unetane tokef* prayer, additional service on Yom Kippur.

3. First- to second-century C.E.

4. *Shema koleinu* prayer, Yom Kippur liturgy.

5. Isaiah 55:6.

6. Psalm 27.

7. *Seder Kaparot,* atoning ritual before Yom Kippur; Psalm 107:18–20.

8. Isaiah 57–58/*Haftara* Yom Kippur.

Acknowledgments

We first had the opportunity to explore the concept of this book at Hebrew College. Bernice Lerner, the director of continuing education, invited us to design the first program of a continuing series called "Jewish Women Discovering Ourselves." Our program on the readings for the first day of Rosh Hashana drew an audience whose size and enthusiasm encouraged us to move forward with this book. We are grateful to Bernice for the invitation and to Ahuva Halberstam, who joined the two of us in presenting a range of perspectives on the texts.

Charlotte Sheedy responded to our idea with her characteristic energy and thoughtful support. She's been a constant source of wise counsel and practical advice. We also thank our editor, Penny Kaganoff, for immediately recognizing the value of our proposal and moving the book to completion. Many able hands furthered the move to completion, especially those of Diana Newman, Rachel O. Alexander, and Michelle Kwitkin.

We are delighted to have a photograph by Joan Roth on the cover of this book. Her excitement with this project and graciousness in providing us with a range of possibilities were much appreciated.

The contributors to this book responded with extraordinary creativity and devotion to our invitations to explore particular texts. Thanks to them, an interesting concept grew into the rich texture of this book. The encouragement of other friends and colleagues has sustained us as well. We must especially single out Joyce Antler, Merle Feld, Marianne Hirsch, Shelly Tenenbaum, Evelyn Fox-Keller, Nessa Rapoport, Rachel Jacoff, Frances Malino, Margery Sabin. We have also had the good fortune to draw from two wellsprings of Jewish knowledge and commitment to women's learning—Ma'yan: The Jewish Women's Project in New York and Ma'ayan: The Torah Initiative for Women in Boston.

We could not have started, let alone completed, this volume without the continuing support of our families, most especially our husbands, William Kates and Joseph Reimer. Partners in our efforts at a fully engaged relationship with the Torah, they value and nurture the partnership we began with our work on *Reading Ruth*.

Contributors' Biographies

RACHEL ADLER is a feminist theologian with a doctorate in Religion and Social Ethics. She is the author of *Engendering Judaism*.

ARLENE AGUS is Senior Associate and Jewish Continuity Project Director at Ukeles Associates Inc. in New York City. As one of the founders of the Jewish feminist movement in the United States, she founded the first woman's *kolel* (community-supported Torah study), later the Drisha Institute, in 1973, and co-founded Ezrat Nashim, the first Jewish feminist organization in America. Her publications on such issues as Jewish thought and ritual, bioethics, pluralism, Jewish women, Soviet Jewry, and the Jewish communal agenda have appeared in *Celebrating the New Moon, Jewish Women: New Perspectives, What Happens After I Die?, Lifecycles, The Jewish Women's Encyclopedia,* and *The Jewish Almanac,* as well as in numerous periodicals.

NEHAMA ASCHKENASY is Professor and Director of Judaic Studies and Middle Eastern Affairs at the University of Connecticut at Stamford. Among her publications are *Eve's Journey: Feminine Images in Hebraic Literary Traditions,* winner of the Present Tense Literary Award; *Biblical Patterns in Modern Literature;* and the forthcoming *Woman at the Window: Paradigms of Female Existence in Biblical Civilization,* as well as numerous essays.

RUTH BEHAR was born in Havana, Cuba, in 1956 and came to live in New York with her parents in 1962. She currently lives in Ann Arbor, Michigan. A poet, essayist, and anthropologist, Behar is the author of *Translated Woman: Crossing the Border with Esperanza's Story* (Beacon, 1993), the editor of *Bridges to Cuba/Puentes a Cuba* (Michigan, 1995), and coeditor, with Deborah Gordon, of *Women Writing Culture* (California, 1995). Her poems have appeared in *Tikkun, Witness, Michigan Quarterly Review,* and *Prairie Schooner.* Her newest book is a collection of essays entitled *The Vulnerable Observer: Anthropology That Breaks Your Heart.*

ROSELLEN BROWN has published nine books, the most recent of which are the novels *Before and After* and *Cora Fry's Pillow Book,* a sequel to her 1977 *Cora Fry,* which she calls "a novel in poems."

TAMARA R. COHEN is the Program Director of Ma'yan: The Jewish Women's Project, a Program of the Jewish Community Center, on the Upper West Side of Manhattan. She writes, teaches, and leads workshops on Jewish feminism and Jewish gay and lesbian issues.

RACHEL B. COWAN, born in 1941, received her B.A. in Sociology from Bryn Mawr College, and her M.S.S. from the University of Chicago, School of Social Services Administration. A graduate of Hebrew Union College–Jewish Institute of Religion, she and her late husband, Paul, wrote *Mixed Blessings: Untangling the Knots in an Interfaith Marriage* and *A Torah is Written,* a children's book on the making of a *sefer* Torah. She is currently Director of the Jewish Life Program at the Nathan Cummings Foundation. Her ethnic roots are New England American, back to the *Mayflower.* As a convert to Judaism after sixteen years of marriage, Rabbi Cowan speaks out on the ways Jewish communities can be more open to non-Jewish spouses and leads workshops for interfaith couples.

SIDRA DEKOVEN EZRAHI was born in the United States and has lived most of her adult life in Israel. She is Associate Professor of Comparative Jewish Literature at the Hebrew University of Jerusalem. Since her first book, *By Words Alone: The Holocaust in Literature,* she has written widely on literary representations of the Holocaust and displacement. She is completing a book on exile and homecoming in the modern Jewish imagination. She has been very active in the peace movement in Israel and was one of the founders of the longest-lasting dialogue between Israelis and Palestinians.

TAMAR FRANKIEL, a scholar of comparative religion, is author of *The Voice of Sarah: Feminine Spirituality and Traditional Judaism* and coauthor with Judy Greenfeld of *Minding the Temple of the Soul: Balancing Body, Mind, and Spirit with Traditional Prayer, Movement and Meditation.*

TIKVA FRYMER-KENSKY is Professor of Hebrew Bible at the University of Chicago and was formerly Director of Biblical Studies at the Reconstructionist Rabbinical College. She is the author of *In the Wake of the Goddesses: Women, Culture and Biblical Transformation of Pagan Myth* and *Motherprayer: The Pregnant Woman's Spiritual Companion.* She is also one of the authors of *Feminist Approaches to the Bible* (Hershel Shanks, ed.) and is the English translator of *From Jerusalem to the Edge of Heaven: Meditations on the Soul of Israel* by Ari Elon. She is currently working on *Victims, Victors and Virgins: Reading the Women of the Bible,* to be published by Schocken, and *The Judicial Ordeal in the Ancient Near East,* forthcoming from Styx.

LAURA GELLER is the Senior Rabbi of Temple Emanuel in Beverly Hills, California. She was the first woman to be selected to lead a major metropolitan synagogue.

Ordained by Hebrew Union College in 1976, Rabbi Geller was the third woman in the Reform movement to become a rabbi. Her articles on Jewish feminism have appeared in *Tikkun, Sh'ma, Reform Judaism,* and other journals, and she has written chapters in several books, including *Four Centuries of Jewish Women's Spirituality, On Being a Jewish Feminist, The Jewish Woman, Spinning a Sacred Yarn,* and *Gender and Judaism.* She has also written Torah commentaries for *Torah Aura* and for *Torat Hayim.*

REBECCA GOLDSTEIN graduated from Barnard College, and received her Ph.D. in Philosophy from Princeton University. She then returned to Barnard College, where she taught philosophy for ten years. She is the author of the novels *The Mind-Body Problem, The Late-Summer Passion of a Woman of Mind, The Dark Sister,* and *Mazel,* which received the National Jewish Book Award. She has also published a book of short stories, *Strange Attractors.* In 1996 she became a MacArthur Foundation Fellow.

YAEL GOLDSTEIN is presently a student at Harvard College, where she is majoring in philosophy. She was a senior in high school at the time of the dialogue published here and has since read Kierkegaard's *Fear and Trembling.*

BONNA DEVORA HABERMAN, an academic and social activist, is currently Visiting Lecturer and Research Associate at Harvard Divinity School. While in Israel, she initiated Women of the Wall, an eight-year spiritual, political, educational and legal effort to secure the prayers of Jewish women at the Western Wall. Born in Canada, she has studied and taught in the United States, London, and Israel.

CAROLIVIA HERRON is a novelist, a multimedia developer, and a scholar in the field of epic literature. She is author of the novel *Thereafter Johnnie* and the children's book *Nappy Hair.* She is a founding member of the Alliance of Black Jews and is currently a Visiting Scholar at Harvard's Graduate School of Education.

JUDITH A. KATES received her Ph.D. in Comparative Literature from Harvard University, where she taught for eleven years. She now studies and teaches Bible and Rabbinics in many programs of adult education in the Jewish community and is Visiting Associate Professor of Jewish Women's Studies at Hebrew College, Brookline, Massachusetts. She has published in the areas of Renaissance Studies, Women's Studies, and Jewish Studies and coedited (with Gail Twersky Reimer) *Reading Ruth: Contemporary Women Reclaim a Sacred Story.*

NAAMA KELMAN was born (1955) and raised in New York. Descendant of rabbis from both sides and of various denominations, she was ordained as the first woman rabbi in Jerusalem in 1992 at the Hebrew Union College–Jewish Institute of Religion. Since making *aliyah* in 1976 she has lived in Jerusalem, where she is in charge of Jewish Education for Progressive Judaism in Israel. In addition, she is very active in promoting feminism and interfaith dialogue.

FRANCINE KLAGSBRUN is the author of more than a dozen books, most recently *Jewish Days: A Book of Jewish Life and Culture Around the Year.* Her other works include *Voices of Wisdom: Jewish Ideals and Ethics for Everyday Living* and *Mixed Feelings: Love, Hate, Rivalry, and Reconciliation Among Brothers and Sisters.* She edited *Free to Be . . . You and Me.* A columnist for *Moment* magazine and the *Jewish Week,* she lectures widely on social, religious, and family issues.

MARTHA MINOW received her J.D. from Yale University and her Ed.M. from Harvard. A faculty member at Harvard Law School, her scholarship includes articles on discrimination law affecting women, children, disabled persons, and members of ethnic, racial, and religious minorities. She is the author of *Making All the Difference: Inclusion, Exclusion, and American Law,* and the forthcoming book, *Not Only for Myself: Identity Politics and Law.* She joined Gary Bellow to edit *Law Stories,* essays on legal advocacy.

MARSHA PRAVDER MIRKIN is a clinical psychologist in private practice in Newton, Massachusetts, and is on the faculty of the Jean Baker Miller Institute, Stone Center, Wellesley College. She is the editor of *The Handbook of Adolescence and Family Therapy* (with Stuart Koman), *The Social and Political Contexts of Family Therapy,* and *Women in Context: Toward a Feminist Reconstruction of Psychotherapy.* She is currently leading workshops that integrate contemporary psychological issues with Torah stories.

JUDITH PLASKOW is Professor of Religious Studies at Manhattan College. Author of *Standing Again at Sinai: Judaism from a Feminist Perspective,* she writes and lectures widely on issues related to feminism and religion. She is currently at work on *Theology of Sexuality.*

NESSA RAPOPORT is the author of a novel, *Preparing for Sabbath,* and of *A Woman's Book of Grieving.* She is coeditor, with Ted Solotaroff, of *The Schocken Book of Contemporary Jewish Fiction.* Her short stories and essays have been widely published. She speaks frequently about Jewish culture and imagination.

GAIL TWERSKY REIMER is founder and director of the Jewish Women's Archive, the nation's first major archive and center for research and public programs dedicated to documenting the lives and achievements of Jewish women. She holds a Ph.D. in English and American Literature from Rutgers University, has published in the areas of Victorian studies, Women's studies, and Jewish studies, and coedited (with Judith A. Kates) *Reading Ruth: Contemporary Women Reclaim a Sacred Story.*

ALICE SHALVI was born in Germany and educated in England and has lived in Jerusalem since 1949. She was a Professor of English Literature at the Hebrew University, where she taught from 1950 to 1990, established the English Department at Ben Gurion University of the Negev (1969–1973), and served as head of the Institute of Languages and Literature at the Hebrew University (1973–1976). From 1975 to 1990 she served in a voluntary capacity as Principal of Pelech Experimental High School for Religious Girls in Jerusalem. Since 1984 she has been the founding chairwoman of the Israel Women's Network, the country's major advocacy organization on women's rights and status.

DEVORA STEINMETZ is founder of the Beit Rabban Day School and Director of the Beit Rabban Center for Research in Jewish Education. She teaches Biblical and Rabbinic Literature at Drisha Institute and the Jewish Theological Seminary. She is the author of *From Father to Son: Kinship, Conflict, and Continuity in Genesis.*

AVIVAH GOTTLIEB ZORNBERG was educated in England at Gateshead Seminary and Cambridge University, where she earned a Ph.D. in English Literature. She has been a lecturer in English at Hebrew University and, since 1981, has taught Torah and Midrash to thousands of students in Israel at MaTaN, Jerusalem College for Adults, Midreshet Lindenbaum, and Pardes Institute. She also lectures widely in North America. She is the author of *Genesis: The Beginning of Desire.*